Politics of Play

Politics of Play

Wargaming with the US Military

AGGIE HIRST

OXFORD
UNIVERSITY PRESS

OXFORD
UNIVERSITY PRESS

Oxford University Press is a department of the University of Oxford. It furthers
the University's objective of excellence in research, scholarship, and education
by publishing worldwide. Oxford is a registered trade mark of Oxford University
Press in the UK and certain other countries.

Published in the United States of America by Oxford University Press
198 Madison Avenue, New York, NY 10016, United States of America.

Library of Congress Cataloging-in-Publication Data
Names: Hirst, Aggie, author.
Title: Politics of play : wargaming with the U.S. Military / Aggie Hirst.
Other titles: Wargaming with the U.S. Military
Description: New York, NY : Oxford University Press, [2024] |
Includes bibliographical references and index.
Identifiers: LCCN 2024009080 (print) | LCCN 2024009081 (ebook) |
ISBN 9780197629208 (paperback) | ISBN 9780197629192 (hardback) |
ISBN 9780197629222 (epub)
Subjects: LCSH: War games—United States. | Military education—United States. |
Soldiers—Training of—United States. | Simulation games—United States. |
War video games—United States. | War—Computer simulation.
Classification: LCC U310 .H538 2024 (print) | LCC U310 (ebook) |
DDC 355.4/80973—dc23/eng/20240323
LC record available at https://lccn.loc.gov/2024009080
LC ebook record available at https://lccn.loc.gov/2024009081

DOI: 10.1093/oso/9780197629192.001.0001

Paperback printed by Marquis Book Printing, Canada
Hardback printed by Bridgeport National Bindery, Inc., United States of America

From Bosnia to Kosovo, from Afghanistan to Iraq, virtuous war had taken on the properties of a game, with high production values, easy victories, and few bodies.

—James Der Derian, *Virtuous War*

[I]t is reality itself that disappears utterly in the game of reality.

—Jean Baudrillard, *Simulations*

Contents

Acknowledgments

This book would not have been possible without the time and hospitality so generously given by the US military wargaming community. My sincere thanks are extended to all who hosted me at schoolhouses, wargaming events, and conferences and conventions, and to those who agreed to be interviewed. I thank the current and former service members who talked with me about their experience of wargaming in recruitment, training, and rehabilitation, in particular Stack Up founder Steve Machuga and his excellent co-workers. For his kind invitations to the Yudh Abhyas 2017 and Viking 2018 command post exercises, and his most generous hosting, I am grateful to Scott Moreland.

My colleagues at the King's Wargaming Network have worked tirelessly to create the leading academic hub for the study of wargaming. For their support and hard work in promotion of wargames and my research, I sincerely thank Ivanka Barzashka, David Banks, Anna Nettleship, James W. E. Smith, and Philip Sabin. I am grateful also to three research assistants who transcribed the mountain of interview recordings generated for this project: James Bridgman, Thomas Hooper, and Marion Messmer.

For their engagement with the text, I am especially grateful to Ellie Bartels, Dan Öberg, Jenna Allen, Meera Sabaratnam, Claudia Aradau, and Antoine Bousquet and for the conversations that initiated this research project, I thank Chris Rossdale and Tom Houseman.

For their support from the earliest days of my career, I will forever be grateful to Michael Dillon, Larry George, and Mustapha Pasha. Their belief in what I might accomplish has made possible what I have accomplished. The title of this book takes its inspiration from Mick's *Politics of Security*. I am grateful to Kimberly Hutchings and Elizabeth Frazer for their support in the early stages of this project. Their encouragement was decisive in my getting it off the ground. For their more recent guidance, I thank Claudia Aradau, Mervyn Frost, and Vivienne Jabri.

I am grateful to the KCL War Studies writing sprint group for motivation, accountability, and warmth. The Anarcho-Creativity Mob also furnished solidarity and encouragement during the long writing process.

The research for this book was conducted using a Leverhulme Research Fellowship (RF-2018-573\7) and a British Academy/Leverhulme Small Grant (SRG\171460), for which I thank both funding bodies.

Substantive parts of Chapter 2 are also published in "States of Play: Evaluating the Renaissance in US Military Wargaming," *Critical Military Studies* 8, no. 1 (2002): 1–21.

I sincerely thank David McBride and Sarah Ebel at Oxford University Press for their excellent guidance on this book from proposal to publication. And I am grateful to Neil Bousfield for granting permission to use his beautiful artwork "My Dream Still (The Sentry)" on the cover.

At the very last moment before publication, I have been informed of the death of wargames godfather Peter Perla. My sincere condolences go to his family and colleagues, and I count myself extremely lucky to have benefited from his wisdom and generous spirit. I am grateful to him, to Ed McGrady, and to James Der Derian for their most generous endorsements of the book. Finally, I am indebted to Paul Kirby in more ways than I can count.

Abbreviations

3OS	Third Offset Strategy
A2AD	anti-access/area denial
ACDP	Advanced Capability and Deterrent Panel
AI	artificial intelligence
CAPE	cost assessment and program evaluation
CASL	Center for Applied Strategic Learning (at NDU)
CoP	community of practice
CISA	College for International Security Affairs (at NDU)
CNA	Center for Naval Analysis
DARPA	Defense Advanced Research Projects Agency
DIB	Defense Innovation Board
DII	Defense Innovation Initiative
DIUx	Defense Innovation Unit—Experimental
DoD	Department of Defense
DWAG	Defense Wargaming Alignment Group
FYDP	Future Years Defense Program
IR	international relations
JWGA	Joint War Games Agency
LAC	Line of Actual Control
LRRDP	Long-Range Research and Development Plan
MIME-NET	military-industrial-media-entertainment network
MORS	Military Operations Research Society
MMORPGs	massively multiplayer online role-playing games
NDU	National Defense University
ONA	Office of Net Assessment
OR	operations research
OSD	Office of the Secretary of Defense
R&D	research and development
RMA	revolution in military affairs
SCO	Strategic Capabilities Office
TRADOC	Training and Doctrine Command
YA	Yudh Abhyas

Introduction

Wargames Resurgent

[T]here is a distinctive American way of *peace*, and that it is the best
way of peace for all sides. To implement such a peace, the good guys
first have to win the war. We have established that wargaming is one
way to gain an edge to help win wars.
—Colonel Matthew B. Caffrey Jr., Air Force Reserve (ret.)[1]

Wargaming saves lives. From board games to virtual reality platforms, US
military wargamers claim that their craft can at once improve chances of victory and keep warfighters from harm. In a crisis such as nuclear escalation,
for example, by poring over a map, counters, and dice, wargames can enable
commanders to play out and refine possible strategies so as to avoid disaster
in the real world. Similarly, as militaries scramble to adapt to the changing
character of war in the twenty-first century, digital training games can allow
warfighters to gain synthetic experience and cultivate mental and physical
muscle memory to increase their chances of survival in, for instance, an
urban combat operation. As the global security environment has become increasingly destabilized—from the Russian invasions of Crimea and Ukraine
to the rise of cyber warfare—the United States and its allies have turned
to wargaming as a key method of identifying, managing, and countering
threats. In an era of ludic capitalism (Soderman 2021), in which gaming
has become the world's most lucrative popular cultural medium,[2] it is vital
to critically evaluate wargaming as an emergent pillar of the US military's
warmaking apparatus.

---

[1] See Caffrey 2019, 370.
[2] Since 2010, the games industry has generated higher profits than the Hollywood movie and popular music sectors combined. In 2022, the games market was projected to total $184.4 billion, with
the Asian market accounting for 48 percent ($87.9 billion), North America 26 percent ($48.4 billion),
Europe 18 percent ($32.9), Latin America 5 percent ($8.4 billion), and the Middle East and Africa
4 percent ($6.8 billion) of the global share (Mitic 2022; Newzoo 2022).

Politics of Play. Aggie Hirst, Oxford University Press. © Oxford University Press 2024.
DOI: 10.1093/oso/9780197629192.003.0001

With the meteoric rise of the commercial videogames industry in the late twentieth and early twenty-first centuries, much has been written, and many hands have been wrung, about the relationship between simulated and real-world violence. From school shootings to bullying, racism, and gender violence, videogames have long been under fire in both the media[3] and academic debates.[4] And yet, with some exceptions in the realm of science fiction,[5] the use of games by military institutions and actors—which raises the stakes of blurring the boundaries between real and simulated violence still further—has generated comparatively little attention.[6] Since the 1990s, the US military has developed a symbiotic relationship with the commercial games industry, investing heavily in applied games technologies research (Kaempf 2019; Hammond and Pötzsch 2020). In the same period, with the rise of remotely piloted and artificial intelligence (AI) technologies, the conduct of war itself has become increasingly gamelike, intersecting and overlapping with commercial games that feature recreationalized combat as a central component. Authors interested in this relationship have variously traced a "military-industrial-communications complex," the phenomenon of "militainment," a "military-entertainment complex," and a "military-industrial-media-entertainment network" (MIME-NET) (Hammond and Pötzsch 2020, 3). What these analytics share is a concern with the ways in which games, and related popular cultural products, have coalesced in the production of ludic militarism[7] and are put to work in the service of warmaking.

In the US military, a professional wargaming community of practice (hereafter, CoP) has pioneered the use of games throughout the life cycle of warfighters and across the spectrum of rank. Comprising games designers, facilitators, and instructors, this community of military wargamers has long espoused the power of games as tools of military recruitment, education, training, and research. In the current ludic century (Zimmerman 2013), their campaign has met with considerable success. Indeed, since 2014 a renaissance in military wargaming has been under way. On PlayStations, PCs, and smartphones, free-to-download wargames function as strategic

---

[3] See, for example, Jacobs 2014; Kaufman 2019; Patel 2019.

[4] Important texts include Ferguson 2008; Leonard 2009; Markey et al. 2020.

[5] For example, the 1983 movie *WarGames*.

[6] In recent years, however, this has started to change. In the arts world, for instance, in 2022–2023 an exhibition titled "War Games" was shown at the Imperial War Museums in London, England and Ottowa, Canada, and another, "World of War Games: A History of Wargaming," was curated at the Strong Museum in Rochester, New York, USA.

[7] I am grateful to Dr. Meera Sabaratnam for this framing.

communication devices designed to attract young potential recruits by giving them a taste of soldierly life.[8] Digital and virtual reality games are used to train warfighters in such spheres as weapons proficiency, vehicle and aircraft handling, and language and cultural sensitivity skills. Tabletop and seminar wargames are utilized in professional military education to experiment with past, present, and future combat and crisis scenarios, and to generate synthetic experience in leaders and policymakers. Wargames are deployed in the military's research and analysis projects to trace patterns in human decision-making. They are played in mess halls and barracks—at home and on deployment—to manage downtime and boost unit cohesion, and with interagency and international partners to promote interoperability and diplomacy. Wargames are also employed as tools of healing and rehabilitation following physical and psychological injury, both in the military's formal recuperation programs[9] and at the grassroots level in veterans' gaming groups like Stack Up.[10]

I have spent seven years researching US military wargaming, generating more than one hundred hours of interviews with the CoP, conducting fieldwork at their on-base wargames and exercises, participating in their conferences and conventions, and examining their publications, reports, and online commentaries. This book is the result. It is the first of its kind in the

---

[8] The prime example is *America's Army*, created at the Naval Postgraduate School's Modeling Virtual Environments and Simulation Institute (MOVES) under program manager Col. Casey Wardynski and development director Michael Zyda.

[9] Since the 1990s, the US military has been exploring the use of games and virtual reality as tools for managing and treating PTSD and other mental health problems experienced by (ex)service members. At the center of these developments is the Institute for Creative Technologies (ICT), founded at the University of Southern California. Under the leadership of Albert "Skip" Rizzo, the ICT team developed *Virtual Vietnam* in the late 1990s, and more recently *Virtual Iraq* (later renamed *Bravemind*), both gamified exposure therapy systems for treating combat-related PTSD (Rizzo et al. 2010). Used at over sixty treatment and research sites, *Virtual Iraq* is the manifestation of how "technological advances in the areas of computation speed and power, graphics and image rendering, display systems, tracking, interface technology, authoring software, and artificial intelligence have supported the creation of low-cost and usable PC-based VR systems." This has led, its creators explain, to a new discipline, "clinical virtual reality," which promises to transform the future of veterans' mental health provision (Rizzo et al. 2010, 155).

[10] Stack Up was founded in 2015 by Stephen Machuga, a former Army captain who claims that videogames saved his life (Hirst 2021). Experiencing debilitating mental health issues that left him unable to leave his house after his return from Iraq, Steve argues that gaming helped him manage his symptoms and create communities of mutual assistance. Stack Up's mission covers four primary programs: "Supply Crates," which involves providing care packages of games and consoles to deployed and discharged service members; "Air Assaults," which focuses on funding veterans' trips to conventions and gaming events; "The Stacks," dedicated to online and in-person community-building during transition/reintegration periods; and the "Overwatch Program" (StOP), a 24/7 crisis support network dedicated to suicide prevention. To date, Stack Up has run 346 community events in its twenty-nine chapters across the contiguous United States, in addition to those in Canada, Australia, New Zealand, Japan, South Korea, and Scotland, and provided support to 35,944 veterans.

discipline of international relations (IR). While a literature on videogames has emerged in recent years as part of the turn to the study of popular culture, military gaming has been broadly ignored in the field since the publication of the 2009 edition of James Der Derian's pathbreaking book *Virtuous War: Mapping the Military-Industrial-Media-Entertainment Network*.

Rooted in the twentieth-century revolution in military affairs (RMA), Der Derian shows how, through the rise of network-centric warfare and heteropolar matrices of power grounded in interconnectivity, virtuality had become the "fifth dimension" of the US's virtuous war-making capabilities (Der Derian 2009). Most importantly for the current study, Der Derian draws into focus the reality-producing properties of virtual technologies.[11] Insofar as they function as "the continuation of war by means of verisimilitude," he explains, simulations have "demonstrated the power to displace the 'reality' of international relations they purport to represent," creating a new space in which "actors act, things happen, and the consequences have no origins except the artificial cyberspace of the simulations themselves" (1990b, 301). In other words, simulations have come to produce a new reality—hyperreality—which has fundamentally altered the character of both global politics and war.

Der Derian's work builds upon Jean Baudrillard's prescient diagnosis of the perils of the era of simulation. Baudrillard shows how the play of the real and the imaginary, of thing (signified) and word (signifier), that once generated reality has been obliterated in an age dominated by models that operate as closed systems. In this process, he argues, the dialectical play of meaning-making is supplanted by a hyperreality generated by systems devoid of contradiction, tension, and difference. We have thus moved from the era of representation—understood as a relational mode involving interaction between reality and construct—to an age of ontologically unitary systems. As a result, in his words, "the contradictory process of true and false, of real and imaginary, is abolished in this hyperreal logic of montage" (Baudrillard 1983, 122). While advocates in both the military and commercial sectors espouse the freedom and agency of their medium, this book shows that wargames conform to this logic of the hyperreal model, in which the dialectical play of meaning is replaced by a totalized system. Wargames, it argues, are a "utopia of rules" (Graeber 2015) that contribute to producing and maintaining the

---

[11] While Der Derian explores the hyperrealities of models, simulations, exercises, and games together in a combined analysis (1990b, 300–301), this book focuses solely on military wargaming, making it the first book to do so in IR.

world around us. In the era of simulation, we are caught in a forever game that produces a contradictionless reality with no outside; "it is reality itself that disappears utterly in the game of reality" (Baudrillard 1983, 148).

Picking up where Der Derian left off, this book argues that wargames— disaggregated from simulations and exercises—produce not just realities but also people. Wargames engage and influence players' thoughts, feelings, and identities in ways that endure long after a specific game has ended. In other words, wargaming subjectifies its players. It does so by intervening both in players' cognitive realms, which are responsible for thinking, evaluating, and analyzing, and in their affective realms, which deal with values, motivations, and emotions. As Paul A. Roman and Doug Brown explain, wargames are proliferating in the military precisely because they provide "a cost-effective means to provide experience-based learning with emphasis on cognitive and increasingly affective training domains" (2008, 1). Because they engage both the thinking and feeling aspects of the player, wargames are a powerful pedagogical tool. As Kurt Squire elaborates, "[g]ame-based learning can be understood as a particular kind of designed experience, where players participate in ideological worlds, worlds designed to support a particular kind of reaction, feelings, emotions, and at times thoughts and identities, which game-based learning designers are leveraging for education and training." Consequently, he continues, the military "is hiring game designers for their knowledge of how to create compelling user experiences that can be the basis for changing understandings, behavior, beliefs, and even identities" (Squire 2008, 9).

Accordingly, in order to grasp the reality- and people-producing capacities of wargames, the closed systems of those games need to be prised open. My wager in this book is that play is a powerful means by which to do this. Grounded in the thought of Jacques Derrida, I propose a mode of critical analysis called "deconstructive play," which can be operationalized to critically examine the power relations at work in wargaming. Distinct from conventional forms of gameplay, which involve following the rules and incentives in order to win, I show that deconstructive play can introduce cracks in the closed system of the game that expose the assumptions, hierarchies, and ordering principles contained within it. Accordingly, I argue that Derrida's thought offers a mode of resistance to the enclosures diagnosed by Baudrillard in his account of the era of simulation. While there is no escape from the hyperreal productions that constitute our reality—as there is no "real" reality hidden behind them—I argue that deconstructive play can occupy and subvert the smooth running of the models that produce and maintain them, allowing us to glimpse and contest the power relations smuggled into their design and operation.

Aimed at scholars interested in games and popular culture, military wargamers in the US and internationally, and global communities of hobby gamers, the book seeks to accomplish three tasks. First, it endeavors to shift the parameters of academic debates about gaming in two ways. On the one hand, it redirects scholarly focus from commercial gaming to the uses to which games are put in the military. In IR, as interest in popular culture has increased,[12] an important corpus on the politics and possibilities of videogames has developed. Variously tracing the violence, militarism, and emancipatory potential of recreational gaming, this literature has convincingly demonstrated how and why games matter in global politics.[13] In addition, scholars in the field have explored how games might be used in the classroom to engage students of the gamer generation.[14] However, with the exception of a few articles (Mackay 2015; Pauly 2018; Robinson 2019; Öberg 2020; Emery 2021; Lin-Greenberg, Pauly, and Schneider 2022), military gaming remains seriously underresearched in the discipline. Moreover, in associated fields such as games studies and media and communications, with some notable exceptions (Lenoir 2000; Stahl 2010), military gaming has similarly garnered far less attention than the commercial gaming sector. However, in the context of the digital, virtual reality, and AI revolutions, it is vital to examine how games—usually considered unserious, apolitical, and outside the realm of real-world effects—are being used in the creation and deployment of the world's most powerful fighting forces. This book provides the most substantive contribution to the production of knowledge about this topic in IR to date.

On the other hand, the book seeks to introduce the study of play to IR. In spite of growing scholarly interest in recreational gaming, play has been almost entirely sidelined throughout the discipline's one-hundred-year history. Seen as the preserve of children, animals, and leisure time, play is assumed to be singularly unserious, situated beyond the boundaries of IR's focus on the

---

[12] Key texts include Weldes 1999, 2003; Grayson, Davies, and Philpott 2009; Dittmer 2010; Shepherd 2013a; Caso and Hamilton 2015; Shepherd and Hamilton 2016; Daniel and Musgrave 2017; Aistrope 2019.

[13] See Salter 2011b; Robinson 2015, 2016; Ciută 2016; Hayden 2016; Brown 2017; Schulzke 2017; Berents and Keogh 2018; Jarvis and Robinson 2021.

[14] Key studies include Asal 2005; Asal and Kratoville 2013; Arnold 2015; Horn, Rubin, and Schouenborg 2016; de Zamaróczy 2017.

grave business of war, security, and politics. Where it does appear in scholarly debates about games, it is usually treated as synonymous with gameplay. Against these elisions and conflations, I argue that far from being one and the same, games sit in tension with play. This is because games are systems or structures, often imposed from outside, that arrest and direct play, while play involves the making and breaking of such rules by players themselves. As David Graeber has noted, while often treated as indissociable, play and games "seem to be opposites, as one suggests free-form creativity; the other, rules" (Graeber 2015, 190). To make this case, the book draws on scholarly fields as broad as philosophy, psychology, social and political theory, history, and sociology, revivifying debates that have been overshadowed by a focus on games in the past several decades to demonstrate the power of play as a mode of critical analysis. Grounded in the thought of Derrida, the concept of "deconstructive play" is offered as a practical means by which the totalizing reality-productions of models in the era of simulations might be challenged. By introducing tension, contradiction, and difference into the closed systems of games, thereby disrupting their contributions to the production of hyperreality, I show how play can be a powerful tool of resistance.

Second, the book seeks to engage with wargaming professionals, both within the US military and in militaries across the globe. Having spent the better part of a decade conducting research with this community, the book offers the first detailed examination of the politics and power relations at work in military gaming. It does so by presenting, and critically examining, the CoP's activities as set out in its members' own words in the extensive interviews conducted. The CoP's advocacy of gaming is grounded in the axiomatic claim that, if done correctly, it can save lives (Longley-Brown 2019; Schechter 2020). This narrative is supplemented by claims of efficacy; the CoP argues that wargaming is cost-effective, replicable, and generates valuable synthetic experience by allowing players to experiment and learn in safe to fail environments. However, these accounts leave unposed the question of how wargaming works and the effects on those who use them. It also skirts the broader question of what it means to operationalize games—which we ordinarily assume to be frivolous and harmless—as tools to impart military doctrine and skills intended for lethal use in the real world. By addressing questions of player agency including the power dynamics at work between designers, facilitators, and players, the cultivation of a desire to win, and the generation of a non-reflexive state of immersion, the book seeks to open new critical debates among wargaming professionals. It thus moves beyond advocacy and efficacy to pose fundamental questions about how wargaming produces people in the age of simulation.

Third, the book addresses the global hobby gaming communities (and their discontents). As I was told time and again by members of the CoP, there are almost no professional military wargamers who are not also hobbyists. Indeed, many flagged childhood wargaming as key to why they joined the military, and claimed it made them better strategic and tactical thinkers relative to their non-gamer peers. Many also noted that their early gaming carried a stigma, placing them in an unfavorable position in the hierarchy of "jocks" versus "geeks." In the past twenty years, however, the social capital of gamers and gaming has radically transformed. While gaming was once considered niche or nerdy, as one report put it, "[i]n the last decade alone, the years-long stigma against gamers has all but disappeared. What's more, the past year has seen many brands—including the biggest companies in apparel, automotive, and even financial services—connect with gaming in bigger and better ways than ever before" (Newzoo 2019, 2). This shift has been mirrored in the military; with the rise of remotely piloted and AI assets, technical expertise is turning out to be of greater value in some areas than physical prowess (Coker 2013).

In 2023, 70 percent of adults in the US, and 3.24 billion people globally, played videogames (Jovanovic 2023; Statista 2023), making it the world's most popular hobby. In addition to providing escapism and relief from the pressures of day-to-day life, gaming has become a site of parenting, education, and conducting business. In both its online and analog formats, it has become a locus of political and social interaction. Games have become popular movies and television series,[15] and games companies and gamer practices have become themes of others.[16] Consequently, as part of this ludic revolution, gaming has become an important site—and microcosm—of global politics. Harassment and persecution have been widespread in controversies like #gamergate, with social media coming under fire for facilitating cyber bullying, misinformation, and far-right recruitment (Chess and Shaw 2015; Massanari 2017; Mortensen 2018), and discriminatory tropes associated with imperialism and racism continue to permeate gamespace (Dyer-Witheford and De Peuter 2009; Mukherjee 2017). Equally, gaming communities have generated spaces of solidarity and emancipation for queer, racialized, and

---

[15] Key titles include *The Last of Us*, *Sonic the Hedgehog*, and *Resident Evil*.
[16] For example, *Mythic Quest* and *Dead Pixels*.

countercultural communities (Barbrook 2014; Boluk and LeMieux 2017; Ruberg 2019), and as official transition and rehabilitation programs offered by the military are experienced as inadequate by many (ex)-service members (MacLeish 2013, 2020), games are being repurposed as sources of community and recovery (Colder Carras et al. 2018b, 2018a; Hirst 2021). This book seeks to contribute to these sites of contestation by proposing that deconstructive play can promote critical engagement with the politics and power relations of gamespace by, and to the benefit of, all of its members.

Politics of Play

Unlike existing treatments of wargaming, this book develops its analysis by means of a detailed exploration of theories and philosophies of play. While the study of games and gaming has increased in IR in recent years, a corresponding exploration of play has yet to be developed in the discipline. Play features implicitly in a number of key areas in the field—for example, in game theory, videogames, and pedagogical role-plays and simulations—but little work has been done to explore its potentials for global politics or theory. Calls to take play seriously have issued from scholars such as Maria Mälksoo, who argues for "the return of play in the scholarship and practice of IR" (Mälksoo 2012, 492). Mark Salter has also raised the question of play, claiming that when

> IR theorists invoke the "rules of the game" or game theory as a frame for systematically separating agents from structures, and the conditions of possibility for politics, they are limiting the bounds of play—ascribing a set of primarily social conventions (rules) to an abstract structure of world politics (the game). Play and these ludological tropes are as vital to our political imagination as a self-styled "serious" reading of politics. (Salter 2011a, 453)

In addition, play appears in IR debates as a metaphor for the movements of poststructural language games and deconstruction, as noted by Michael Dillon (2003, 25), Nick Vaughan-Williams (2005), and Mark Hoffman (1991). Play has thus featured both concretely and allegorically in the discipline, at least in passing, but there remains a need for a focused exploration distinct from the study of gaming at both conceptual and practical levels.

In addition to reviving the study of military gaming, this book seeks to introduce the study of play to IR by demonstrating its centrality to understanding how wargaming produces people. This is important because play and games are often conflated in both popular and scholarly discussion. Consequently, as Graeber has argued, we need to examine the relationship between play and games. He reflects, "We play games. So does that mean play and games are really the same thing? It's certainly true that the English language is somewhat unusual for even making the distinction between the two—in most languages, the same word covers both. (This is true even of most European languages, as with the French *jeu* or German *spiele*)" (2015, 190). While from Huizinga's *Homo Ludens* to the "Great Game" of empire, games might be assumed to have left the greater mark on the cultivation and conquest of human civilization, I argue that play contains within it yet more significant possibilities. Play is the force that brings games to life. We experience games through play (Bogost 2016, 92); indeed, games can be understood as an artistic form that derives from the impulse to play (Costikyan 2013, 7). As their animating force, however, play far exceeds the games that direct and delimit it. As Stuart Brown explains, "[l]ife without play is a grinding, mechanical existence organized around doing things necessary for survival. Play is the stick that stirs the drink. It is the basis of all art, games, books, sports, movies, fashion, fun, and wonder—in short, the basis of what we think of as civilization. Play is the vital essence of life. It is what makes life lifey" (quoted in Feezell 2014, 14).

Contrary to common assumptions that play is frivolous and apolitical, then, play animates and energizes human existence. It can also be illuminating: "[p]lay and playful technologies might help us rethink artificial realities of culture and communication—and the reality of the artifice" (Giddings 2016, 155). Play can be political, displaying our defiance at the world's limitations and helping us understand our capacities and potentialities (Henricks 2015, 13, 82). Far from a distraction from the world, play is one way to take part in it (Bogost 2016, 223). It might, for this very reason, be understood as more challenging and unpredictable than games. As Graeber puts it, "there is also something potentially terrifying about play . . . [b]ecause this open-ended creativity is also what allows it to be randomly destructive. Cats play with mice. Pulling the wings off flies is also a form of play. Playful gods are rarely ones any sane person would desire to encounter.... What ultimately lies behind the appeal of bureaucracy is fear of play" (Graeber 2015, 192–193).

Under conditions of ludic capitalism, it is often supposed that play will save the day by offering a solution to relentless alienation and exhaustion (Soderman 2021). In such accounts, Braxton Soderman explains, the "flowing subject" of gameplay is subsumed within, rather than escaping, logics of consumption and commodification. While it may be tempting to seek in play emancipatory alternatives and revolutionary possibilities, in this reading play has been enclosed and put to work in the service of profit and governance. This means that—rather than valorizing play, and especially avoiding the tendency to reduce play to gameplay—a reconceptualization of play is necessary (Soderman 2021). Tracing a genealogy of play in Western philosophy from ancient Greece to the postmodern period, this book takes up this challenge by developing a new theorization of play: "deconstructive play."

Beginning from the claim that *what* we play is less important than *how* we play, deconstructive play calls for the cultivation of an autodeconstructive player who self-consciously and consistently punctuates the dreamlike immersion of gamespace with questions and reflections. Such a player moves from being a consumer to being an interpreter of game artifacts (Sicart 2016, 316). They query the incentives and constraints that direct play in games, asking, "Why am I playing this game the way I am playing it?" (Murray 2016, 323). They problematize the hero-warrior player construct, which often obscures rather than cultivates this critical disposition (Murray 2016, 321). And they take seriously the ways in which games are productive of realities and people, including their own identities, values, and subjectivities. This deconstructive ethos is used throughout this book to interrogate and critically analyze how wargaming works to produce people, and with what effects. To that extent, I side in this book with play over games, because through its movements and remakings the former can draw into focus and challenge the rigidities and hierarchies at work in the latter. Insofar as wargames constitute part of the era of simulation—in which "the order of ends yields to the play of molecules, and the order of signifieds to the play of infinitesimal signifiers" (Baudrillard 1983, 109)—I argue for the return of play to push against the enclosures of hyperreality by reintroducing contradiction, tension, and difference into seemingly closed models.

Wargaming with the US Military

This book is grounded in extensive fieldwork carried out with members of the US military wargaming CoP between 2017 and 2019. I was first introduced to this community through Connections UK, a professional wargamers' conference held at King's College London in September 2016. There I met many of those I would later interview, and the presentations, conversations, and gameplay drew into focus the importance of military wargaming for IR. Having acquired research funding from the Leverhulme Trust and British Academy, I embarked on a series of fieldwork trips lasting between one and four weeks to conduct interviews with the CoP.

Beginning in North Carolina and making my way through Virginia to Washington, DC, and finally to Boston, on my first research trip I interviewed members of the CoP and veteran gamers at the National Defense University (NDU), the Center for Naval Anaylses (CNA), and the PAX East gaming convention. In September 2017 I attended the Yudh Abhyas command post exercise (CPX) at Joint Base Lewis-McChord in Washington State, an event run annually between the US and Indian armies, at which I interviewed organizers and trainees. In April 2018 I took part in the Viking 18 CPX held in Enköping, Sweden, and simultaneously in Brazil, Bulgaria, Finland, Ireland, and Serbia, interviewing participants and facilitators. In November and December 2018 I took a final research trip to the US attending the Interservice/Industry Training, Simulation and Education Conference (I/ITSEC) in Orlando, Florida, and visiting Austin, Texas, to conduct further interviews. In addition, in August 2019 I took part in Connections US at the Army War College in Philadelphia, interviewing members of the CoP.

I conducted a total of seventy-three interviews with designers, instructors, trainees, and veterans across the US Army, Marine Corps, Air Force, and Navy, each lasting between thirty and ninety minutes.[17] Individuals were interviewed at the National Defense University, Naval War College, Army War College, Naval Postgraduate School, TRADOC, Joint Staff J7, Center for Naval Analyses, US Army Pacific, US Army Command and General Staff College, US Army Simulation and Training

---

[17] Ethical approval was granted by the research ethics offices at King's College London and City, University of London. Written consent was secured from each participant to audio-record and utilize data from interviews. Interviewees specified whether they preferred to be named in publications resulting from the interviewees or for material to be quoted anonymously. The interviews undertaken represent the views of participants, not the institutions for which they work.

Technology Center, DoD Modeling and Simulation Coordination Office, NATO Modeling and Simulation Research Department, Defense Forensic Science Center, Marine Corps Systems Command, National Guard Bureau, Military Operations Research Centre (MORS), School of Advanced Military Studies, RAND, Naval Air Warfare Center, Marine Corps Warfighting Laboratory, Air Force Research Laboratory, Joint Multinational Simulation Center, Joint Interagency Task Force, and Stack Up. Thirty-eight interviews were conducted remotely (by Skype or phone) and thirty-five in person.

These interviews have made the book what it is, and I sincerely thank all who gave their time and insights. The experience of conducting interviews on military bases, in formal training sites as well as in mess halls and kitchens, at gaming conventions, and in cafés and restaurants have left a lasting impression. From my inexpert attempts to flip taco shells with Latina service members cooking on-base for their peers to the driving tours and tech demonstrations given by wargaming professionals, these interpersonal encounters brought the project to life and turned on their head many of my assumptions about the place and function of games in the military. In quoting extensively from the interviews, I hope to infuse the text with something of the richness of these conversations and experiences. I expect too that the many ambivalences generated by conducting research in this sphere as a civilian researcher[18] with long-standing anti-war commitments will be in evidence throughout the book. Among other conundrums, I remain confounded by the tension between the warmth and welcome offered to me by people who comprise(d) the US military and the horrors of the post-9/11 invasions in Iraq and Afghanistan prosecuted by the same forces that drove me to become a scholar of global politics.

Importantly, while they feature centrally in what follows, I have not used these interviews to attempt to establish definitive truths about the nature of wargaming. While the professionals interviewed are indeed experts at the top of their field, that in itself does not mean that their testimony can resolve the many questions that military wargaming poses. Rather, I use the interviews in two ways. First, I use them to paint a picture of what wargaming professionals think of themselves as doing with their craft. Rather than

---

[18] The fact of my being a woman academic conducting research with a community consisting in the vast majority of men clearly plays a role here too. It remains to be seen whether gender will play a role in the reception of this book among various gaming communities.

seeking to fill gaps in the historical record, the aim here is "to learn about individual beliefs, perceptions, and preferences" in order to fashion an account of the CoP's perspectives on the role, effects, and possibilities of wargaming today. In other words, following Damien Van Puyvelde, I seek to "examine how reality is constructed and represented during interviews" (Van Puyvelde 2018, 378).

Second, having constructed as detailed a picture as possible of the CoP's understanding of its activities, I use the interviews as a foil for the critical deconstruction of the implications, possibilities, and silences contained in their account. In other words, following a Derridean logic, I treat the interviews as texts to be deconstructed. As Penny Griffin explains, "[r]efusing the separation of text and exterior application of method," Derrida argues that "deconstruction [must] be always internal to the text." The point, she continues, "is that the text always carries within itself its own undoing." Accordingly, a deconstructive researcher endeavors to highlight the incoherences, inconsistencies, and assumptions hidden in the text. Thus, she concludes, "it might be more in keeping with Derrida's own thinking to see deconstruction as a form of critical sharpness rather than a method in and of itself" (Griffin 2013, 209).

Structure of the Book

The book is organized into four sections. The first two chapters conceptualize and contextualize US military wargaming. Chapter 1 charts a course through the conceptual quagmire surrounding what a wargame is and can do. It situates wargames in relation to simulations and exercises, showing that while these terms are often used interchangeably, important practical, methodological, and epistemological differences are at work. From there, it examines the CoP's diverging viewpoints on the respective benefits and limitations of manual and digital gaming and the generational divides that obtain in these debates. Thereafter, it turns to the key applications of wargames as research, teaching, and training tools, and the open-ended versus deterministic styles of gaming conventionally associated with these spheres. The chapter interrogates the types of pedagogy at work in research, education, and training games, respectively, emphasizing that they sit on a continuum between "processual" and "product" learning objectives. It concludes that there is considerably less daylight between games used for research, education, and training than is often supposed, because *all* games teach their participants something.

With this conceptual background established, Chapter 2 sets out the current state of play of wargaming in the field of IR and the US military. It begins by tracing the role and function of games in the field of IR from the mid-twentieth century to the early twenty-first, reconstructing a hitherto neglected history. It then locates the recent resurgence of interest in gaming in IR to developments in the defense establishment since 2014, inaugurated by DoD-wide memos from then Defense Secretary Chuck Hagel and Deputy Secretary Bob Work. It details how these memos called for a reinvigorated wargaming effort across the services via two major reform programs: the Defense Innovation Initiative (DII) and the Third Offset Strategy (3OS). The chapter then explores the key role given to wargaming as a vital element of this program of reform—namely, the generation of new operational and strategic concepts necessary to make good use of the leap-ahead technologies. Central to these developments, the chapter shows, was a demand for a better grasp of the "human dimension,"[19] encompassing critical thinking, the ability to navigate complexity, and improved decision-making skills. It concludes by setting out the methodological dissensus surrounding whether wargaming should be understood as an art or a science, and showing how the wargaming renaissance reflects the beginning of a paradigm shift from quantitative approaches, which seek to reduce complexity in favour of parsimony, to qualitative explorations of complexity that seek to map and interpret patterns of human decision-making. These chapters should be of interest to all readers; for the uninitiated they introduce key concepts and contexts, while for seasoned wargamers they weigh in on enduring debates to offer some clarifications.

From there, the second section of the book focuses on theories and philosophies of play. Chapter 3 traces a genealogy of play in Western philosophy from the Presocratics to modern phenomenologists. The chapter opens by establishing two discursive modes of play, Apollonian and Dionysian[20]—setting out the former's focus on reason, order, being, and presence, and the

---

[19] The "human dimension" here refers to individuals within the US military. Human dimension gaming impacts upon those who are taught or trained, as opposed to an external target population. This is not to be confused with the "human domain," which relates to individuals and groups outside the US military, such as the local population in a conflict zone, which may alternatively, or also, be the target of military wargaming.

[20] I borrow this framework from Mihai Spariosu (1989), though I use it to trace discursive modes rather than to posit historical periods.

latter's tendency toward unreason, disorder, becoming, and the disruption of presence. It then explores key ancient framings of play, beginning with the insights of Heraclitus and turning to the challenges posed by Plato and Aristotle. From there, the chapter explores play in the modern philosophical era, focusing on the German Idealist tradition. Having done so, the chapter turns to Nietzsche's challenge to the Western philosophical tradition and the accompanying return of the Dionysian in and beyond play, and thereafter to the phenomenological ideas of Heidegger and Gadamer.

Building upon this theoretical groundwork, Chapter 4 explores play in the era of poststructuralism and offers a new conceptualization that I term "deconstructive play," grounded in the thought of Jacques Derrida. It begins by tracing the role of play—understood not as directed but rather as free play—in Derrida's thought and his conceptualization of deconstruction. Having done so, it sets out deconstructive play as a third type that differs from both the Apollonian and Dionysian modes. This reconceptualization echoes the Dionysian embrace of festival, unreason, and groundlessness but challenges its tendency to reify and romanticize a warrior-hero play subject. The chapter finally shows how deconstructive play can help expose the politics of gaming by disentangling play from game, cultivating a deconstructive player-subject, and operationalizing deconstructive play in gameworlds. In doing so, the chapter shows how deconstructive play can be used to critically interrogate the capacity of wargames to produce people by introducing fractures in their hyperreal productions in the era of simulation. These chapters perhaps will be of most use for games and play scholars, as well as for readers engaged with theory and philosophy. Those who are primarily interested in empirical wargaming matters may prefer to jump ahead to the final four chapters of the book.

The third section of the book seeks to operationalize this deconstructive mode of thinking by critically analyzing how wargaming works and with what effects on those who use them. Chapter 5 examines the ways in which wargaming intervenes in players' cognitive realms through a series of learning processes. It begins by setting out the benefits proponents of wargaming claim for their craft, specifically that wargaming saves lives by reducing conflict, mitigating risk, building cohesion, and providing safe-to-fail learning and experimentation environments that can hone a range of skills including abductive reasoning, procedural literacy, psychomotor skills, systems thinking, and cultivating reflexes. From there, the chapter turns to the question of how the CoP seeks to demonstrate these benefits, noting the difficulty of proving the efficacy of wargaming. Having established these fundamentals, the chapter sets about showing how wargaming produces people by intervening in the cognitive dimension through: (1) generation of buy-in and engagement, (2) consolidation through iteration, (3) consolidation through critical thinking, and (4) retention. It draws a broad distinction between research and education games, which include all four of these steps, and training games, which often though not always skip the third of these processes. Having demonstrated this, Chapter 5 returns to the work of Der Derian and Baudrillard to explore precisely how wargames produce hyperrealities. It concludes by showing that despite its ostensibly "unreal" status, wargaming produces people by intervening in the cognitive realm.

From there, Chapter 6 shows that, in addition to impacting upon this cognitive realm, wargames intervene in the affective register. The chapter begins with an examination of the politics of game design, exploring the power relations at work between the designer, sponsor, facilitator, and player. It then turns to the ways in which games mobilize affect and emotion in order to impact powerfully upon players in both their conscious and unconscious registers. The chapter explores the ways in which, by promoting Apollonian play, forcing player decisions, and generating synthetic experience, gaming impacts upon players in ways that circumvent their reflexive capacities. As this suggests, the question of player agency sits at the heart of this chapter. The core aim is to show that while many designers and practitioners emphasize the importance of player agency—and note in particular manual wargames' capacity to encourage critical thinking, reflexive decision-making, path selection, and post-game analysis—it is also clear that players' choices, beliefs, and even identities are deliberately targeted as part of military wargaming. To that extent, wargaming produces people by intervening in their affective realms.

The final section of the book identifies and critically explores two key drivers of wargaming. Chapter 7 demonstrates that the imperative to win— that is, the pursuit of victory conditions—is crucial. The chapter opens by examining what is fun about wargaming. From there, it turns to the place of winning and competition in US military culture in general and its wargaming regimes in particular, tracing the ways in which competition and agonism are used in and by the CoP. Having established prevailing naturalist assumptions in the CoP that view the winning imperative as a spontaneously occurring feature of human nature, the chapter demonstrates that wargames work by producing and harnessing precisely these tendencies in players as part of their subjectifying capacity. It does this by elucidating how wargames use systems of reward and punishment, orchestrate profusive forms of loss and failure, and instantiate systematic iterative irresolution which at once incentivizes, precludes, and devalues winning. While the attainment of a win state is broadly immaterial to a wargame's success or failure, players are kept in the dark about this and are strongly encouraged to strive to achieve victory—a sleight of hand that ultimately makes wargames perpetual-motion learning machines.

Having established and problematized the central role of the winning imperative in US military wargaming, Chapter 8 examines a second driver of wargaming: the state(s) of flow and immersion. It argues that the different states of immersion generated in different game types—across manual, digital, research, teaching, and training games—serve to apprehend players in a state of unreflexive engagement. The chapter begins by conceptualizing immersion and its accompanying "flow state," drawing in detail on the work of psychologist Mihaly Csikszentmihalyi, who coined the latter term in the 1970s. It then turns to the wargaming CoP's accounts of the power of immersion in their activities. It shows that many in the CoP argue that immersion is vital for efficacious wargaming because it generates and prolongs player focus, confers game validity, and improves the extent to which the game's lessons are internalized and experienced as "real." The chapter then turns to the question of how, and with what effects, immersion functions as a tool of player subjectification. It sets out how a state of immersion can be cultivated—namely, through the use of narrative, via the (apparent) exercise of choice, and by means of encouraging the player to refer to their in-game persona in the first person. Finally, it argues that immersive play desubjectifies players by circumventing their self-conscious and self-reflective capacities. At the same moment, it argues, immersive gaming resubjectifies players by instilling in them reflex actions. In light of these critiques, the chapter concludes by deconstructing immersion.

Having worked through these topics, the conclusion to this book makes the case for an academic (sub)field of wargaming and turns the deconstructive lens on its own arguments in order to expose the assumptions at work and lay the groundwork for future research.

1

Conceptualizing Wargaming

Introduction

A defining feature of the US military wargaming community of practice (CoP) is an enduring lack of consensus surrounding what a wargame is and does. The purpose of Chapter 1 is to chart a course through this conceptual quagmire with a view to establishing the key features and applications of wargames for the purposes of this book. In doing so, it seeks to show that, against prevailing accounts that posit a clear distinction between games used for research and games designed to teach or train their players, all wargames have pedagogical effects. As games designer and theorist Raph Koster argues, "[A]ll games are edutainment" (Koster 2013, 47).

The chapter begins by situating wargames in relation to simulations and exercises, showing that while some in the CoP use these terms interchangeably, others insist they are strictly distinguished along practical, methodological, and epistemological lines. From there, it examines the CoP's diverging viewpoints on the respective benefits and limitations of manual and digital gaming and the generational divides that obtain in these debates. Thereafter, it turns to the key applications of wargaming as research, teaching, and training tools, and the open-ended versus deterministic styles of gaming conventionally associated with these spheres. The chapter interrogates the types of pedagogy at work in research, education, and training games, respectively, emphasizing that they sit on a continuum between "processual" and "product" learning objectives. The conclusion drawn at the close of the chapter is that there is considerably less daylight between games used for research, education, and training than is often supposed because all wargames teach their participants—players, facilitators, designers, and/or sponsors—things that endure long after the game has come to an end.

Politics of Play. Aggie Hirst, Oxford University Press. © Oxford University Press 2024.
DOI: 10.1093/oso/9780197629192.003.0002

What Is a Wargame?

The US military utilizes wargames across its recruitment, research, teaching, training, and rehabilitation apparatuses. These include manual games such as those played on boards or hex grids, using cards and counters; digital games played on computers, consoles, and handheld devices; virtual and augmented reality games involving dismounted technologies including full-immersion headsets, artificial weapons, vehicles, and electronic body armor; and seminar and matrix games that involve no material artifacts and rely on role-play and group discussion. Games can vary in size from a handful to many hundreds of participants and can involve intra-service, inter-service, and international players. The US military currently uses, and historically has employed, wargames for strategic planning, tactical training, and operational preparedness across areas as diverse as futures experimentation, conventional and asymmetric combat operations, acquisitions, vehicles/weapons training, crisis response, negotiation and peacekeeping, language, and cultural sensitivity training. This has led some commentators to argue that the "war" in wargaming is misleading and should potentially be replaced with a term that better incorporates the medium's non-kinetic applications.

The games used by the military may be developed in-house, produced using contractors, or adapted (or in some cases not adapted) from commercial off-the-shelf games. Military wargames can be set in the past, present, or future, allowing for the revisiting of specific conflicts and an exploration of the factors that led to historical outcomes; the examination of current courses of action and their implications; and a mapping of possible future events in order to explore the consequences of particular decisions and pathways. These various temporalities can be coupled with real historical or contemporary events or framed in an imaginary context in order to explore particular issues or themes. To conceptualize wargaming and substantiate this chapter's claim that across all its forms and applications it functions as a pedagogical medium, the following sections explore the relationship between games, simulations, and exercises; manual and digital gaming; commercial and military gaming; and open-ended versus deterministic gaming.

Games, Simulations, Exercises

A key point of contention within, and indeed beyond, the CoP is the relationship between games and simulations. On the one hand, as Der Derian notes, wargames are often treated as synonymous with simulations. In an article introducing the topic of military wargaming to the field of IR more than three decades ago, he explained: "It may grate on the ears of some of the players to hear 'gaming,' 'modeling' and 'simulation' used interchangeably. Yet in the literature and during interviews I found users using all three terms to describe practices that could be broadly defined as *the continuation of war by means of verisimilitude* (Der Derian 1990a, 300–301). On the other hand, many professional wargamers blanch at the notion that wargames and simulations are one and the same, insisting that they are practically, methodologically, and epistemologically distinct.

To begin unraveling this dissensus, one can usefully start with the question of terminology. As one wargames designer explained, because they were seen "as a hobby and something that children play . . . in the past the word 'game' was disallowed from the Army's lexicon . . . The old saying is '[W]e don't play games. We do simulations to achieve training objectives'" (interview 2017). As this suggests, some ambivalence appears to remain in the military surrounding the use of the term "game" because of its association with childhood, leisure, and unserious pursuits. James Markley, deputy director of Wargaming at the Center for Strategic Leadership at the Army War College, reflected on this point: "I don't think that the general force is prepared to look at games, as opposed to combat simulations, as useful tools. We have combat simulations in pretty much each of our major army bases [but] they don't really do games" (interview 2017).

However, others in the wargaming CoP suggest that in recent years it has become more permissible in the military to refer to games as such. As Scott Moreland, formerly program manager at the Center for Civil-Military Relations at the Naval Postgraduate School, noted:

> [A]mong older generations, the term "games" has a certain connotation that doesn't fit into their view of what the military should be doing. But I think that is almost a non-issue with the up-and-coming generation of officers and soldiers and sailors. They've lived in a world that's saturated

with games of one sort or another, and some of the games are very serious. For them gaming doesn't carry that sort of negative connotation, and they can talk about gaming a bit more forthrightly. They understand that there are games for play, that there are games for work, there are games for learning. So there's not that cultural aversion to the word "gaming." (interview 2017)

In light of these changing cultural attitudes, precipitated by the recent integration of games into all manner of professional, commercial, educational, and recreational pursuits, the days of euphemizing games as simulations for pragmatic purposes may be over.

Beyond preferred terminologies and cultural predilections, many in the CoP argue that games and simulations are substantively different. Some in the CoP claim that the key distinction is the degree of fidelity to real-world constraints like the laws of physics or operational specificities of weapons. As one wargames designer commented: "[S]imulations require physics. Games do not.... [When] playing the game *Call of Duty*, no one has gone in and made absolutely sure that the chance of hitting somebody at 1,000 meters with this particular anti-tank weapon is accurate. [Whereas in a] simulation we have to use data that is as real as we know it to be. When you're in a game, you may have outcomes that don't have any real relationship with reality. . . . So you could be learning bad lessons" (interview 2017). Similarly emphasizing this distinction between simulations' realism and games' license to deviate from reality, wargames designer and instructor Brant Guillory insisted:

> [G]ames and simulations are not the same thing even though there is an overlap. A simulation is on a continuum that is based on a relative level of realism and how much fidelity to the real world you are trying to include in the system. Whereas a game is an inherently competitive exercise that needs a winner and a loser . . . Take tic-tac-toe as an example. It's a realistic game—it's got a winner and a loser—[but] it's not a realistic simulation. [On the other hand,] the flight simulator is a simulation, not a game. There is no inherent win condition unless you impose one on it. (interview 2017)

In line with this framing, many in the CoP suggest that simulation has more in common with modeling than with wargaming. This is because, as Phillip Pournelle, senior operations analyst and wargame designer at Group W, explained, "modeling and simulation are about how things are to the degree that we understand them. Wargaming tries to understand what we can aspire to. . . . They really are vastly different. They can be complimentary, but they are not the same" (interview 2017).

To complicate this distinction, however, many in the wargaming CoP contest the claimed capacity of modeling and simulations to accurately apprehend reality. As Chapter 2 will explore in more detail, since the 1960s the US military's operations research (OR) community has utilized a quantitative approach to defense analysis that claims to accurately model reality as it is, free from subjective or value-laden influences. Their ability to deliver on these promises has, however, been limited. As Pournelle put it:

> [T]he problem is that the modeling and simulation are only as good as your understanding of the phenomenology which the opposing sides are competing on. If you don't fully understand it, then the model is not going to do you any good. . . . On top of that, in modeling and simulation you've prescribed the behavior. . . . So if you have not explored the decision space of the competing sides before you implement them into a model, I question the validity of the model. (interview 2017)

Such a view is shared by many in the wargaming CoP. One designer echoed Pournelle's critique, noting that in a simulation "you have to assume that the variables we've built in are actually accurate in the first place. We tend to make the assumption that . . . each piece we inject is accurate in and of itself. Of course, logically, if any one of those pieces is inaccurate then the entire model will be off" (interview 2017).

One way around this—a move that draws simulations closer to wargaming—is to include a "human-in-the-loop." As Moreland reflected, "There are practical limitations to what simulations can do and what they can stimulate at present. Where the simulations lack, you've got be able to backfill that with a knowledgeable and well-educated human coach-trainer" (interview 2017). The integration of at least one human decision-maker is, many in the CoP suggest, the crucial difference between a simulation and a wargame. In Perla's influential definition, "[A] wargame is an exercise in human interaction, and the interplay of human decisions and the simulated outcome of those decisions makes it impossible for two games to be the same." Other tools, he continues, among them simulations, "are better suited to the investigation of other more technical aspects of reality" (Perla 1990, 164). Indeed, "[w]ithout human players there may be a model, but there is no game" (Perla

1990, 274). In short, simulations may or may not include human decision-makers, but to count as a game one or more must feature.

A further, and related, distinction between games and simulations is that games involve the pursuit of victory conditions, while simulations do not. As Guillory commented, "[I]f there's no potential for a winner or loser, then it's no game. It's a simulation" (interview 2017). Another wargames designer concurred, noting that, unlike a simulation, "a game has an objective, an outcome, and a scoreboard to give feedback to the person as they are progressing through it. They're working through the steps to achieve those objectives" (interview 2017). In this framing, then, a simulation is process-oriented, while a game is directed toward a set of victory conditions, which players must seek to attain. As Chapter 7 will explore, this compulsion to win—rather than actually achieving victory—is a key driver of wargaming.

The presence or absence of victory conditions may appear, then, to establish daylight between games and simulations. However, many in the CoP argue that this division is overly simplistic. This is because, while simulations may not be explicitly designed with winning and losing in mind, people can and do play simulations competitively. Guillory acknowledged, "[O]ne certainly can play a simulation. I think a lot of people do. I think the fact that flight simulators have taken off to a huge degree on the commercial market . . . says a lot about that" (interview 2017). Notwithstanding their intended purpose, then, simulations can be played to win. Another designer similarly explained, "[T]he simulations that we do use are a game to a degree. They have a live competitive opposing force that enables them, the training audience, to learn those lessons" (interview 2017). Blurring the lines between simulations and games still further, Jerry Hall, deputy director of strategic exercises at US Army Pacific, provided a helpful elaboration:

> [T]he technical definition of a simulation is a model over time. The model models a discrete thing, like a tank—how fast does it go, what's its armor, how far can it shoot? . . . And then, when you put a bunch of models in a simulation and run it over time, all of those interactions are the simulation . . . A board game does the same things, but manually. It takes models, because a board game, typically, will use cardboard counters that have perhaps a combat value and a movement value, and that's the model of that infantry unit or that armory unit or whatever. And then the rules provide how those models or units or counters interact in the game over time. (interview 2017)

Thus, simulations leave space for playing to win, whether in terms of competing with the system, other users, or oneself, in ways that are not readily distinguishable from gaming's explicit emphasis on the pursuit of victory conditions. In the framing of Perla and fellow wargame designer and CNA analyst Ed McGrady, "[Y]ou can play a game inside a simulation and, at the same time, [a] simulation is kind of what you do in the real world. So what's the relationship between play and simulations? Well, you play in the simulation and the simulation itself is not played" (interview 2017).

As this suggests, many in the CoP assert that the difference between games and simulations is not well defined. Indeed, some suggest that designing wargames and simulations is broadly similar. Perla and McGrady noted, "[H]aving designed simulations, it's the same process. It may be different objectives, but the process is the same" (interview 2017). Others question whether games and simulations are meaningfully separable at all. In the words of one wargames trainer, "I don't see any difference between gaming and simulation" (interview 2017). Moreland reflected further on the matter:

> All of it is simulation, right? I mean, a game is a simulation, just by definition. *World of Warcraft*—that's a simulated world with simulated conditions and simulated characters. All of that is simulation. So it's, again, how is that simulation being applied? In this case it's being applied in the form of a game, whereas you can use that simulation in a different way—if it's more rigid and more structured—to be applied as a training aid. So they're all simulations. It's a matter of what's your focus. Do you want to focus on experiential learning—you know, learning through experimentation, through trying new things? Or do you want to learn by rote? (interview 2017)

One particularly helpful suggestion has been proffered by Elizabeth Bartels, coordinator of the RAND Center for Gaming, who proposes that we can "treat the game as an instantiation of a particular model describing an aspect of conflict" (2016, 503).

Confusion is often generated by the application of the term "wargame" (or, frequently, "war game") to events that are more properly described as military exercises. This occurs with considerable regularity in the media; indeed, as Bartels mentioned at the 2023 ISA Annual Convention when one reads about military wargames in the news, more often than not the activity referred to is an exercise. For example, in 2022 the *Financial Times* reported the return of wargames between the US and South Korea, only to describe a series of field exercises that features joint aircraft carrier strike drills and amphibious landings (Davies 2022). Similarly, the same year the *Telegraph* relayed that Britain would be joining France in Operation Orion, the largest wargame since the Cold War, in response to Russian aggression in the Donbas; it went on to report upon a series of exercises involving the deployment of 20,000 Allied forces, including 7,000 troops undertaking air and sea landings and the French aircraft carrier *Charles de Gaulle* (Samuel 2022).

As this suggests, the key distinction between a wargame and an exercise is that the former usually happens indoors, uses digital software or analog game pieces, involves role-play, and generally has a smaller number of participants. In contrast, the latter occurs in the field, whether on base or abroad, usually with larger-scale deployment, and making use of real weapons, vehicles, and maneuvers. Exercises are consequently often more visible than wargames, and can generate corresponding real-world diplomatic effects. For example, in 2023 the US expressed concerns about South Africa hosting joint naval exercises called Mosi II with Russia and China on the anniversary of the invasion of Ukraine, raising a "diplomatic challenge" by taking the opportunity to "strengthen the strong bonds" between these states (Carter 2023). To the extent that they are often played behind closed doors, the real-world effects of wargames tend, in contrast, towards their participants and policy-formulation rather than diplomacy (though there are of course exceptions to this rule). While it is certainly possible that exercises include gamified elements, there remain important differences.

In the course of the research for this project, I attended two such exercises—the computer-assisted command post exercises Yudh Abhyas 2017 (YA) and Viking 2018.[1] Viking is the largest exercise of its kind, run out of Sweden and including participants from fifty countries and thirty-five organizations. Established in 1999 at NATO's fiftieth-anniversary summit, Viking has run every two years with the aim of training and educating civilian, military, and police participants to meet the challenges of current and future multidimensional crisis response and peace operations. As one senior Swedish officer explained to me at the 2018 exercise, "[T]he first [Viking] exercise was in 1998–99 and it was a result of the war at the Balkans. . . . Sweden and the US had a discussion about having a common agreement about how to cooperate concerning education and training and one area that I think

---

[1] For the invitations to these events, and the most generous hosting and facilitation of interviews with organizers and participants, I am grateful to Scott Moreland.

both [were] interested [in is] . . . to teach military, civilian, and police to work together, and to achieve a higher level of competence in all these three organizations. The other reason was that to deal with the old post-Soviet countries like Kazakhstan, Uzbekistan" (interview 2018). As tensions with Russia continue to rise and NATO expands into Scandinavia, it will be of increasing importance to take note of actions and reactions to upcoming Viking events.

Beginning in 2002, YA is a bilateral joint exercise run annually by the US and Indian armies to promote defense cooperation, run on an alternating basis at various locations within the two countries. The key purpose of YA is the promotion of interoperability. As one YA staff member described it to me:

[T]he purpose, in my opinion, is bilateral partnership with the country of India, through shared experiences and shared scenarios where the Indian Army and US Army work together to—I don't want to say come up with a solution; it's more execute the operation. . . . I think the interoperability of the two nations is really the main thing. Interoperability isn't just soldiers on the ground doing squad and platoon tactics that the FTX [field training exercises] are doing, but it's also how do staffs plan and execute orders. And then, the third part is the social interaction and the relationship-building that we're building with our counterparts from India. So, really, it all boils down to one thing and that's interoperability. (interview 2017)

In addition, however, YA has had significant political effects. The 2022 iteration, for example, was held in Uttarakhand close to the border with China. According to one article, China officially objected to both India and the US that the exercise threatened the Line of Actual Control (LAC), a mutually agreed demilitarized zone located around 100 kilometers away (Kumar 2022).

The degree to which exercises are experienced as "unreal" in a way similar to games is, however, important to note. As one YA organizer explained, "[Y]ou know you're in an exercise and you know you're playing a game. . . . But then, there's this meta level of understanding that takes place where you're playing the game and you're part of the game, or the exercise. That meta level makes you reflect on yourself and makes you, kind of, see more critically the other people involved. . . . It helps build this understanding of the whole picture, even if you have just the minor part or major part, you're still connecting across with this macro or meta understanding of what's going on" (interview

2017). While different from games in terms of the concrete practices and artifacts used to conduct them, then, exercises contain gamified elements.

Of course, like wargames, the insights generated from exercises have not always been embraced, sometimes leading to devastating outcomes. For example, as the neoconservative push for regime change in Iraq began in the days following 9/11 (Hirst 2013), they became a source of foreign policy contention. On the basis of a series of games and exercises, General Eric Shinseki, chief of staff of the Army between 1999 and 2003, challenged the claims of then Defense Secretary Donald Rumsfeld and Deputy Secretary Paul Wolfowitz about minimal post-occupation troop numbers, telling the Senate Armed Serves Committee that a force of several hundred thousand soldiers would be required. Based on the now declassified Desert Crossing exercises (Strother 2006) conducted in 1999 under the leadership of General Anthony Zinni of the Marine Corps, it was clear that the invasion would likely generate a substantive insurgency that any occupation would need to counter with a substantial ground force (Augier and Barrett 2021). Such was the reaction to this conclusion that not only was Shinseki managed into early retirement, but other skeptics of neoconservative estimates were silenced also (Diamond 2004; Fallows 2004). His claims were later vindicated (Shanker 2007).

One lesson learned from early twenty-first-century exercises that is particularly pertinent for wargaming was demonstrated in the Millennium Challenge 2002, a $235 million exercise run over three weeks to test readiness shortly before the invasion of Iraq. Playing a Saddam Hussein–like role, retired Marine Lieutenant General Paul K. Van Riper deployed tactics that presaged those used by opposing forces in Iraq. While it was later claimed that the enemy turned out to be different from the one the military had wargamed, Van Riper did in fact employ militia tactics, only to have them disallowed by game facilitators. With elements of the game being reset to accord with prevailing assumptions, including the resurrection of several sunk Blue ships, Van Riper quit the exercise, writing later: "Instead of a free-play, two-sided game . . . it simply became a scripted exercise." The conduct of the game did not allow "for the concepts of rapid decisive operations, effects-based operations, or operational net assessment to be properly assessed . . . It was in actuality an exercise that was almost entirely scripted to ensure a Blue 'win'" (quoted in Kaplan 2003; see also Koerner 2002). While the lessons learned from these two examples are pertinent not just to exercises but also to wargames proper, the two should not be conflated.

Having examined the distinctions between wargames, simulations, and exercises, the following section turns to the equally contentious question of the potentials and pitfalls of manual and digital military wargames.

Manual Versus Digital Wargames

Famously referred to as "paper time machines," manual wargames constitute the majority of the historical record (Harrigan and Kirschenbaum 2016, xix). However, the US military is increasingly interested in transitioning to computer-based gaming, and the CoP is acutely aware of this pressure to adapt. Guillory lamented that in the current digital age "you say the word 'wargame' and [one] immediately thinks *Call of Duty*. We have to get beyond that. The idea that a wargame can be a lot of things that don't involve a power cord is a very tough hill to climb for a lot of folks" (interview 2017). This transition to digital gaming began in the 1980s. As Henry Lowood writes, at that time a period of "conversion" ensued which involved "a general shift of energy and ideas from 'manual' to computer games" (2016, 100). By the 1990s, as James Dunnigan explains, the development of powerful PC hardware and the first-person-shooter format were recognized by the military as potentially valuable resources (2016, xxxvii). The last two decades have, Sabin argues, witnessed a revolution in military wargaming "with growing crossover in the field of real time 3D computer simulations" (2014, 35).

Across the US military, it is assumed that computer platforms and digital programs are of great appeal to younger service members. As Susi, Johannesson, and Backlund point out, digital game-based learning is a key new trend because, first, "the thinking patterns of learners today have changed, that is, today's students are 'native speakers' in the language of digital media" (2007, 2). Second, this generation has experienced a radically new form of computer and video game play; they quote Marc Prensky's claim that, "[T]his new form of entertainment has shaped their preferences and abilities and offers an enormous potential for their learning both as children and as adults" (Susi, Johannesson, and Backlund 2007, 2). A wargames designer echoed this claim: "I think the increase we are seeing is because we're seeing a generation of officers who grew up with videogames, and especially military videogames, and so they are a lot less resistant to using games as part of the training and educational regime" (interview 2017).

These broader societal trends have compelled the military in general, and the wargaming CoP in particular, to embrace digital gaming. As Kirklin Bateman, then chair of the College for International Security Affairs (CISA) at the National Defense University, reflected:

> As education institutions we have to think about making changes to our pedagogical approaches as we get in students that are more and more native digitally. . . . As the service members . . . [become] more and more sophisticated—digital natives versus digital immigrants—they're going to be much faster at being able to pick [things] up. If you have a thirty-eight-year-old and you're putting them in a tank for the first time ever, their learning curve is vastly different from the eighteen-year-old that's being put in the tank with them. Their ability to manage and master digital systems . . . is completely different. (interview 2017)

Such a generational distinction is noted by many others in the CoP. Said a wargaming instructor, "We have people coming up who have recreationally played these types of games or systems. They are able to interact directly with it. . . . There is going to be some trepidation [among] older participants regarding . . . how digital works. [That's] the thing that usually trips people up . . . because older generations haven't grown up necessarily with videogames or the interfaces or the controllers" (interview 2017). Howard Lee, of the Operational Environment Training Support Centre at TRADOC, noted something similar: "I think that the other reason that we see a growth in gaming, is the nature of the generation that is coming into the military now—the eighteen- to twenty-five-year-old—that has such a level of experience with the videogaming industry. It's something they're familiar with. It's something they can connect to and, as a result, I think it helps them to more rapidly embrace their understanding of a particular series of activities or actions" (interview 2017).

As this suggests, many in the CoP are convinced that the younger generation learns in fundamentally different ways to previous generations. "[O]ur students are of a generation now that do not learn the same way that we did. And we have to revisit that and update our methods as well as some of the technologies that we use to teach. A lot of that goes back to gaming—learning by doing— . . . because these are people who did not get where they are by sitting quietly in chairs. These are action-oriented people . . . [so we must] create opportunities for them to get reengaged and experiment and debate. And, at the same time, get feedback on their decisions. I think [this] is much more appealing to the students," said Steven Goodwin, director of the Strategy and Operations Division at NDU's Center for Applied Strategic Learning (CASL) (interview 2017). Kenneth Kligge, deputy director of CASL, agreed: "[T]hose that are coming up through the ranks now have a different way of processing information" (interview 2017). What is centrally important, the CoP frequently claims, is that games appeal to this generation and keep them engaged. As Goodwin argued, "[K]ey to videogame success is the inability to always win. In fact, the challenge is to beat the game, and so you continue to fail but [with] each failure you learn and that's what keeps them coming back" (interview 2017).

Accordingly, as the younger generation rises to greater prominence, the embrace of digital gaming looks set to expand. Moreland observed, "[I]t's an era where the young are the experts. For an institution that's used to seniority and rank, and years of experience being your stock and trade, somebody coming in with a skillset that's completely disruptive and completely unfamiliar and hasn't been trained in all your twenty years of military experience, but that is absolutely mission essential . . . it's very uncomfortable but very necessary. Young people are empowered in a way that they have never been in the military right now" (interview 2017). Appealing to this generation is, then, a key driver of digitization. Noted Guillory: "[I]f you go to some senior leader and say, 'I'm going to put this tabletop game on the table,' they're going to say, '[W]ait a minute, why can't we put this on the computer?' Well, you don't have to put it on a computer. . . . It's almost sort of digital determinism" (interview 2017).

Some argue that the shift to digital games is broadly unproblematic. Troy Goodfellow, for example, suggests that computer wargames have been, for the most part,

roughly identical to their board-and-counter cousins. The distinguishing factor in how they have been played is usually not design, setting, or audience, but speed. A computer can calculate the results of combat, track weather effects, and referee the rules with consistence and accuracy . . . at a pace a hundred times faster than a similar board-and-counter game. . . . Since the game can now be completed more quickly and more often, players can more easily detect flaws or way to exploit a game's AI or core rule set. (2016, 149)

Bill Lademan, director of the Wargaming Division at the Marine Corps Warfighting Laboratory, viewed things similarly: "[Y]ou can take almost any methodology and make it appropriate to your audience based upon the objective you have. I can develop a training game or an education game that happens to be a board game just as I could develop a digital game that might have applicability at a four-star level" (interview 2017).

Others counter that digital gaming offers some noteworthy advantages as compared to manual gaming. As James Casey and Scott Martin of the Virginia Serious Games Institute at George Mason University explained, "[T]he nice thing about the digital format is you can replicate anything you can do and supplement anything that you can do in the physical world with tools and additional engagement features . . . including a lot more assessment and data collection and analysis that you rely entirely on human interaction to do" (interview 2017). Rex Brynen similarly notes the educational advantages of gaming software, including standardization, geographic reach, less reliance upon skilled facilitators, and built-in feedback mechanisms (2016, 490). And Jon Peterson summarizes: "With the capacity to guard secret information from players, compute combat results without error, supply an opponent in the absence of a human, and even regulate a fair game without turns, how could computers not replace the boards and table-tops of traditional wargames?" (2016, 28).

However, many in the CoP point to a series of limitations specific to digital gaming. First, because of the coding skills required to program digital games, their rules and assumptions are less accessible to players. This is a problem because, as one wargames designer reflected, "the wargaming experience can be so powerful, and this is especially true with computer games because we don't get to see the algorithms and variables under the hood nine times out of ten. We tend to accept results and our perception of cause and effect as fact" (interview 2017). Pournelle voiced a similar concern, noting that the younger generation is "much more open to doing gaming but I am uncertain as to the value of videogames . . . I see as a potential downside that they may be too dependent upon the videogames and not open to using more matrix style games or other argument-based games of hex boards and miniatures, which I find very engaging" (interview 2017). One major pitfall of digital gaming, as Brynen explains, is that they create "expectations of immediate gratification, and encourage players in serious games to enter a sort of 'win at all costs' gamer mode that can interfere with the learning process" (2016, 497).

Consequently, a preference for manual gaming persists among many of the CoP field leaders. John Foley puts it succinctly: "If wargaming is to 'reflection' as video gaming is to 'reaction,' it stands to reason that the typical, effective medium for reflection has continued to be a paper vehicle, not a computer vehicle" (2016, 121). Harrigan and Kirschenbaum seem to agree: "Manual games are accessible, teachable, and customizable in ways that most computer games are not, especially to a novice audience of nonprogrammers. Board wargames thus teach what we now call procedural literacy" (2016, xix, citing Philip Sabin). As this suggests, a key differential between manual and digital games is the degree to which players can access, evaluate, and alter the mechanics and rules. One wargames designer reflected: "[T]he advantage manual games have is how automatically transparent they are with regards to the model itself. As soon as I have a computer code involved in delivering the simulation, I've imposed a barrier between the player and the model. And while I'm immersed—perhaps because when I run around the scenery changes and it reminds me of actually running around in a field—I don't necessarily know why what just happened happen[ed] . . . How do I know the code is any good? How do I know it's realistic? However, if I learn the rules to a manual game, to operate the model, I know exactly why I just lost" (interview 2017). Matthew K. Green, assistant professor at the United States Command General Staff College, echoed this point, observing that manual gaming "requires the player to know more about the rules and so they spend more time thinking about why it works or how it's working. Whereas oftentimes the player who shows up to an interface on a computer game, the mechanics of it is all lost on them. So they're putting in input, they're moving a joystick, their interface may get a result, and they're measuring the result. They don't necessarily understand what the variables or the theory behind how it went from A to B" (interview 2017).

Interestingly, the difference between such accessible and inaccessible styles of gaming does not rest on content. Indeed, the very same game played on manual or digital formats will be experienced very differently by players. Bateman described a game he runs at NDU:

[W]e play the game first in a board game format, with actual tactile pieces, because [in] the computerized version of it . . . it's very easy to get sucked into just pushing buttons. . . . I think the board version forces [players] to slow down as they're having to do things themselves. Without doing the board game they will immediately get into that mode of playing the game to win. . . . I think it helps force them to slow down a bit and concentrate less on winning the game and more on drawing out the concepts and the principles. (interview 2017)

Such decision-making is important because, as Pournelle observed, "you don't want to alienate the players from their decisions. . . . In a matrix-style game there's a debate—[One Blue player] says, 'I'm doing this and this is why it's going to work'; [another says,] '[N]ot so fast, this is why it's not going to work' . . . With a computer simulation, it's a black box. So their actions and the results are being alienated from each other" (interview 2017).

In manual wargaming, then, a game's rules, assumptions, and mechanics are more accessible to, and contestable by, players. This is important, Sabin explains, because wargame design should not "become the sole preserve of those rare individuals or teams who combine advanced computer programming skills with an interest in military simulation." Digital games, he continues, function without the player knowing what is going on "under the hood," while manual games are more open and explicit about their rule sets and, crucially, give users the "scope to add their own interpretations and improvisations" (2014, 26–27). As he puts it elsewhere, manual games "expose their rules systems as a necessary component of learning to play them, and if one disagrees with their assumptions, it is fairly simple to tweak the rules or scenarios to accord better with one's own judgment" (2016, 426). Perla also notes that computer games can deprive players "of much of the data they need to make informed decisions . . . In a very real sense, board games provide their players with the pertinent preprocessed data, and computer games typically do not" (1990, 213).

Accordingly, many in the CoP question the desirability of further digitizing wargaming. While some argue that greater player buy-in and adjudication reliability accompany digitization, others argue that the transparency of rulesets and the interpersonal aspect of manual gaming should be preserved against the proliferation of digital gaming. As Perla and McGrady explained, "[D]igital has a limited toolbox based on development processes, frankly, and the platform limitations, language limitations and all that stuff. But with manual you have an almost infinite number of tools and so that's why we feel like manual is far better for these large-scale decision-making games as opposed to digital. Everybody wants to go to digital, but they don't realize some of the limitations" (interview 2017). Such a push is as often as not precipitated by a cultural predilection rather than a concrete advantage of digital media. Casey and Martin observed, "[T]here is a trend towards '[L] et's try to make it as realistic as possible' and then, of course, people say, '[W]ell, why don't we do virtual reality or do augmented reality?' That might help [but it might be] just extra weight. A simple simulation, if it's done with the right type of mechanisms behind it, can teach just as well" (interview 2017).

A general—though not absolute—trend is that manual games allow for the more exploratory and agential learning associated with strategic applications, while digital games tend to be more deterministic and oriented toward rote learning, and are consequently of more use for training activities. Bateman suggested: "I would see at the tactical level much more emphasis on virtual reality and immersive experiences for the gamer to try to replicate stressful environments that they might be in in an actual deployment or combat scenario, and much more realism. . . . [While] at the strategic and the operational [levels] it's going to be much more the boardgame scenarios" (interview 2017). Such a distinction tends to follow the formal rank hierarchies that structure military life. As Lee explained: "[Y]ou move from gaming, which is in my mind generally oriented more on the tactical level, [which uses] videogame muscle memory to develop the soldiers' understanding of the battlefield environment, up through and into more the constructive simulations, where you're beginning to develop leaders to have those critical thinking skills so that they can understand maneuver options. Sort of like really good chess players that have seen and remember different situations in the past and call on those memories to help frame their way ahead" (interview 2017).

Despite these concerns, what does seem clear is that an increasing emphasis is being placed on integrating advanced technology into military gaming. Two military instructors commented: "[T]he military is, as a whole, more interested in technology and cyberspace and is treating that as an increasingly significant element of warfare" (interview 2017). The adoption of such advanced technologies has already begun in earnest, pointed out one wargames designer: "[A]ll of our soldiers . . . have an Android phone on their chest now. It's something we're working toward and that's going on in the field. Even now, they've got digital terrain at their fingertips instead of a map in your pocket. Most things have gone digital and gaming and simulations can [show that] those devices are of benefit" (interview 2017). Accordingly, the wargaming CoP has begun to adapt, said one designer:

[O]ne of the things I'm working on is developing some of the board games that I've got into games for iPad or things like that, that can then be used for distance education. Because, at the moment, for the distance education pieces there's very little interaction between people. They occasionally have a seminar they tie into, digitally, virtually, and they post messages backwards and forward, but that's often about it. The advantage of games, particularly for the term-based digital, where you have an exchange, [is that] they can actually take those classes they're doing and then have games that then support the learning outcomes. . . . Particularly with the millennials coming through, there's a great deal of potential in terms of really assisting students to think, cooperate . . . or play games against each other. (interview 2017)

Emphasizing the importance of integrating the advantages of manual gaming into new digital formats, Lademan asserted: "[T]he future wargame is going to use [advanced] technology, there's no doubt about that, but the key is to use technology that does not intrude upon the ability of the human to think, the ability of the human to maneuver knowledge. Instead, it facilitates and collaborates and it's transparent while it does it" (interview 2017). With perhaps a tinge of the reluctance common to many established military gamers, Moreland similarly reflected: "We can't ignore the reality of virtual reality. Without, you know, twisting the words around too much. So the military has to embrace it to some extent" (interview 2017).

If the military is to effectively embrace digital gaming, the CoP argues, it is vital that it be sophisticated in a way that's comparable to the commercial games played widely by service members. Casey and Martin noted that "a lot of . . . recruits now are used to *Call of Duty* and then they are given PowerPoints or these stick-figure games, and they are really disappointed and frustrated. . . . They don't learn the same. Their morale is low. . . . They recruited some gamers into the military to fly drones and I asked them if it's like playing games and they were like '[N]o, the graphics are horrible. The controls are horrible. It's just not good'" (interview 2017). Bartels also addressed this point, commenting: "[T]he minute that you put something on a computer screen people are comparing it to the commercial games they play. Try to explain to someone that 'yes, I know *Call of Duty* looks great, but that's because they have a massively huge budget that we can't possibly afford' . . . [The Army has] a lot of money to compared to other branches of the government [but] it's still nothing compared to what commercial developers are putting into the games" (interview 2017). Michael Rupert, professor at CISA, said something similar: "[I]f you're going to go down the digital route, you better be as good in your digital creations as what they've been growing up on. You can't have a 32-bit soldier running down the thing when everyone is used to all that. And it still has to be in line with what you're trying to train. When I make a video game simulation for whatever, Xbox, I'm trying to make it as fun as possible. When I'm doing it for the military, I'm trying to make sure that you understand a particular lesson as well as possible" (interview 2017). Accordingly, the following section explores the CoP's rationales for, and reservations about, the use of commercial games in the military.

Commercial Versus Military Wargames

The games used by the US military are variously designed and produced in-house, created by contractors, or acquired "off the shelf" from the recreational sector. Off-the-shelf games are sometimes used as purchased and at other times are modified to better suit specific training or learning objectives. Two military wargaming instructors explained that military games "have a fair amount of commonalities in terms of usability, user interface, control schematics" with commercial games. In fact, military games today "have more in common with commercial products or with actual recreational computer games than past tools might have had" (interview 2017). The CoP is broadly in agreement regarding the increasing interconnectedness of the commercial and military gaming sectors. Noted a wargames designer: "[A]bout five years ago there was a big uptake in innovation and the idea that the kind of work that was going on in Silicon Valley [would be useful for] the military" (interview 2017). Hall elaborated: "[W]e recognized the value of gaming, which is primarily commercial videogames, and we adapt those and use those for individual training. . . . So we bought a lot of commercial off-the-shelf [games], and we developed some other systems, and so now we have dismounted soldiers interacting with vehicles in the gaming environment. And they get training in that environment" (interview 2017). In the intervening period, the military has experimented with the possible uses to which commercial games might be put. "[W]e have learned a lot of lessons over recent years about integrating commercial off-the-shelf by buying off-the-shelf products across the board," said one designer. "I know I have been party to engagements with commercial enterprises about their methodologies [about] how can we speed up getting what you have" (interview 2017).

However, the relationship between these sectors is by no means new. As one designer and instructor explained: "[A] lot of the technology comes out of places like Disney World and the movie industry. Modeling and simulation technology for the military came out of Orlando, Florida, which was where a lot of the visualization occurred" (interview 2017). However, in a reversal of the conventional relationship between the military and commercial sectors (, in which the former drives innovation and the latter repurposes products for civilian use, in recent years recreational developers have been driving progress. As Moreland explained, "[I]n the very early days [it was the] military-funded projects that then they found a commercial application for. . . . I think that's been turned on its head now and there's often a commercial incentive to do something well before there's a defense research incentive to do something, or the commercial incentive outpaces the defense investment. . . . You see it in cybersecurity in particular" (interview 2017). He continued: "[W]ho we have to thank for that really is the private sector [which developed] MMORPGs. . . . They have driven an environment that can be delightfully messy and the best simulators I've seen on the defense side are those that try to replicate those conditions" (interview 2017). Contemplating the future of this inverted relationship, he cautioned:

> [W]hat's a little scary about AI is that it's not necessarily the defense sector that's driving all the research. . . . It could emerge completely in the private sector well in advance of the defense sector, and that's true of network-enabled technologies in general. . . . The military's going to have to navigate public-private partnerships in ways they haven't in the past because a lot of times the private sector's outpacing us. . . . The private sector's so much more sophisticated in realistic and useful gaming and sims, and we tend to model our games and sims off things that already exist in the private sector. (interview 2017)

Lee noted the same issue: "[T]he commercial vendors are the ones who have the brilliant young software engineers who are thinking outside of the box and can really move the state of the art forward. We need in the military to take advantage of that capability to really push things forward" (interview 2017).

Because of the greater resources available to the videogames sector, many in the CoP argue that it makes sense for the military to license and adapt commercial games, particularly when it comes to digital games. In the words of one wargames instructor, "[I]f you include the technologies that are being developed right now for commercial gaming—Xbox and

PlayStation, and all the various Nintendo devices, and that type of thing—if you include gaming systems and then translate that to the human-machine interfaces that the soldiers or others would be using in the field, then I think you have a real benefit. If kids grow up using an Xbox controller and then they use that same type of controller for whatever system they're using in the military, then you have a definite advantage for using those gaming devices" (interview 2017). A designer and instructor elaborated: "[I]n general we're probably going to use contractors to do the heavy lifting, but you need to have sufficient experts. We have a specialty for our officers for simulation and wargaming, so we have people who are devoted to that, but most of the technical development work is done by contractors. . . . They have a pretty mature iterative design process for all the ones I've worked with" (interview 2017).

As this indicates, the programmers who make the military's games are often not members of the military. One wargames designer explained that they employ "government programmers to build our simulations. Then we bring in contractors. Thinking about it right now, I don't have any programmers with military experience. We give them experience here, we get them up into some of the schools and trainings, and then we work with commercial organizations. . . . Nobody really had military experience there. So we had to show them—we had to provide video of what an explosion really looks like, we're talking about the different calibers, there's differences in the looks and sounds of an explosion" (interview 2017).

When it comes to manual games, however, the relationship between the commercial and military gaming sectors is still closer. Indeed, the two are often composed of the very same people. As Rupert described, "[I]t's really a small community. . . . Some of the people who are in the gaming community for the military . . . are the same guys who are in the wargaming society, and the same guys in the role-playing societies. [Those in the military] just found a job that allows them to do it and pays better" (interview 2017). Reaffirming this interconnectedness, the vast majority of CoP members assert that recreational wargaming preceded their professional career and in most cases was the catalyst for it. A wargame designer noted: "[M]y getting into the military had a lot to do with my board-gaming hobby. I became a person who loved the military through wargames, and ultimately enlisted and got a commission. . . . The gaming side of it was a big deal for me" (interview 2017). Goodwin made a similar point: "I've been a hardcore gamer since a child. So I understand what they can do and what they can't do. I wouldn't have had the success in government that I had were it not for my gaming experience" (interview 2017).

As these comments suggest, recreational gaming overlaps significantly with the military careers of many in the CoP. Hall reflected: "I played all kinds of different wargames as a child, and through my teenage years, and then since I've been in the military. My gaming interests were across the spectrum, but they were, kind of, focused to my rank. So when I was an enlisted soldier or a junior officer, I was more interested in tactical war games—miniatures or computer simulations that were at the individual tank or squad, individual soldier level. Then, as I've increased in rank and responsibility, I've branched out" (interview 2017). A wargames designer similarly emphasized the importance of hobby gaming in his career progression: "I attribute my success in the military realm of modeling and simulation to my commercial wargaming times. . . . There definitely is some liquidity between having an experience with hobby gaming and trying to do these kinds of scenarios for education purposes" (interview 2017). Guillory went further still:

> I don't personally know of anybody who is a strong proponent of wargaming for legitimate military training purposes who is not also on the side a hobby wargamer. There may be some that exist—I haven't met any. . . . The idea that you would have guys in the military interested in the value of wargames for training but are not playing them on the side almost seems laughable. Conversely, what you'll almost never find is someone who is a hobby war gamer and a military officer who doesn't believe in war games' value for training—those guys don't exist either. They kind of go hand in hand. If you're looking at games for military training value, they're hobbyists and vice versa. (interview 2017)

Interestingly, as one wargames instructor and analyst commented, games purchased from commercial vendors for training purposes can find themselves again repurposed back to recreation: "[B]esides simulations created specifically for the military we've employed at least one time down here a commercial off-the-shelf game which was created for the gaming community to use, but that requires also someone who has the ability to run it. We happen to have some guys around here that actually play the game in their off time" (interview 2017).

As with digital games, however, many in the CoP voice concern about integrating commercial games into military applications. One key problem identified is that the production of games in these realms is differently incentivized. While commercial games are designed for enjoyment, military games have a specific research, teaching, or training objective in mind. Observed one designer and instructor: "[P]art of the problem is . . . [the games we need are] all about logistics and command and control. That's not sexy. The commercial vendors don't build games [for that]. . . . They're either ground strategic, or tactical, or very low operational, but to get at the level that we operate at there isn't anything" (interview 2017). As this indicates, the military's use of commercial games is limited by the disincentive for the latter to produce games for tasks that are not fun.

A second, related issue is that commercial games are made to create profit, while, again, military gaming is focused on a particular learning objective. Hall reflected: "[W]e have trouble staying abreast of the civilian sector, mainly because of our acquisition process. . . . They're interested in profit margin, and we're interested in realistic, relevant training" (interview 2017). As former Army communications officer Joseph Nieves elaborated, these two imperatives sit in tension:

[I]f you were to make a videogame to use it as a recruiting tool or training tool for the military, you'd have to make it from a company that makes games for money, but the game couldn't be made for money. That's the complicated part. You wouldn't be able to get it made. It wouldn't be useful if you had it made by some technical people who aren't used to making entertaining, interesting stuff. It's that strange gray area that doesn't exist. There's nothing wrong with entertainment being the purpose. The problem is you can't make a commercially successful game that's informative. But if your audience is the military, that would make perfect sense. To build a game that's both intuitive but also entertaining. (interview 2017)

In this framing, the as-yet-unrealized ideal from a military perspective would combine the fun of commercial gaming with the pedagogical efficacy of military gaming.

Third, military games need to more accurately reflect reality than do commercial games. One designer noted that if a game "is designed to entertain and [to] make it fun to play but if it doesn't work the way it does in real life, the soldiers are going to learn the wrong lesson" (interview 2017). As David de la Vega, knowledge manager at the Army's 4th Infantry Division, explained, "[C]ivilian gaming could look great, but if it's not accurate to

[how] the machine or the equipment works, you're going to lose their sus-pension of disbelief. In military gaming, if it doesn't look that great and shiny and high-resolution but the equipment acts like it's supposed to, you're going to get the buy-in there" (interview 2017). Lee offered an example, noting that commercial games have

> a certain gee-whiz level. People are leaping and flying and shooting while they do it. That is unrealistic. So there's a bit of detraction that occurs there, but it may be that people get weaned off of that, when they actually have to go out into the field and kick in doors or climb through wood, and they re-alize, "I am not going to be jumping over a ten-foot wall; I've got to figure out how to climb the darn thing." . . . The constant tension you have there is between the civilian sector's interest in fun and winning, and the military's desire for an accurate representation of the environment. (interview 2017)

Thus, many in the CoP emphasize the need to exercise caution about the military use of commercial games. As one wargames designer stated: "[W]e need to go through the verification, validation, and accreditation tools be-fore we implement [commercial games] in training. . . . Just saying '[T]his is a popular thing and it looks about right' [isn't enough]. Some more rigorous standards need to apply to the evaluation of that before we put our soldiers through this, just because the outcomes are catastrophic if it is wrong." He continued: "[T]he companies who are doing games commercially—*Call of Duty* and some of that—they spend a lot of money to provide high-quality pictures, and if we don't do the same thing, then the soldiers will disregard it. Meaning if we are not on par with some of the gaming we develop, then the soldiers won't play it. That could be a problem. When you think about it, a lot of folks get their idea of what we do operationally from *Call of Duty* and that's not necessarily accurate" (interview 2017).

Having explored the roles and limitations of commercial gaming, the fol-lowing section examines the CoP's varying views on the use of deterministic verses open-ended gaming in the military's research, teaching, and training regimes.

Deterministic Versus Open-Ended Wargames

As noted above, a general—but not absolute—trend is that manual games allow for a more exploratory and agential player experience, while digital games tend to be more deterministic and oriented toward rote training. In other words, some games present and incentivize a specific series of actions because there is a specific end state coded in, while others have no such end state and therefore leave more room for players to decide upon courses of action.

Deterministic gaming is variously promoted and critiqued among members of the CoP. Its proponents claim it has important benefits from a training perspective. As Lademan argued, "[I]n a training education game, things [are] deterministic. The results [are] sort of predetermined based upon the actions that you take. [This isn't] necessarily a bad thing. Because what we're trying to do is basically give the young officer, give the trainee, a substrate off of which he can then act in the future" (interview 2017). Another wargames designer made a similar case: "If you were teaching cadets, absolutely, a more deterministic game would work. . . . [We have used] a computer-based game to teach them how to communicate well together and how to work well within a team. We had to give them a strict lane—you stay in this lane and if you move out of this lane, we are going to push you back—because at the end of this lane, something is going to happen and you have to be able to react to it. And that's how we taught it" (interview 2017).

Learning in this type of gaming occurs through rote practice. Stephen Downes-Martin and Peter Pellegrino of the Naval War College explained that when it comes to training, "there is a desired outcome that is 'the preferred outcome.' Remember training is designed through exposure and repetition [for] you learn to 'do the right thing.' [Say] we want you to learn to turn left, not right. Every time you turn right the game punishes you, but if you turn to the left it rewards you. Okay, that's pretty straightforward because you've learned through whatever experience that turning to the right is the right thing to do" (interview 2017). As Guillory similarly reflected, such games are a "very easy way to put a competitive twist on new students learning a new skill that gets them engaged and competitively wanting to beat each other, particularly if you get some kind of award at the end of it all. But that's only appropriate for very discrete individualized skills" (interview 2017).

Deterministic games are also used for less explicitly doctrinal purposes. One designer explained: "[Y]ou'll often find games—and this is where there is a problem with gaming—designed essentially to give us a very specific outcome to a solution, to support a budget action or something. That can be problematic for two reasons that I think should probably be self-evident: one, because obviously that's just intellectually dishonest in the first place, and [two,] because if the players are aware it can turn them off gaming, which means they won't use it even if it's of utility" (interview 2017). Bateman expanded on this: "[I]f you get to the point where, 'Well, if I make this move, then I always know that this countermove is going to occur, the system is always going to do this, just because that's the way the code was written,' then it sort of becomes, 'Well, we know how to beat this, right.' And so the students get sucked into playing the game, as opposed to using it as a tool to explore some of the concepts and the principles that we've talked about in class" (interview 2017).

And yet many in the CoP argue that deterministic gaming has an important part to play in service members' career progression. Noted one designer:

> [T]heir job up until they reach the middle ranks has required them, for safety's sake if nothing else, to be incredibly detail-oriented. As they come through, what they're then transitioning to is that they're not meant to focus on the detail—that, actually, it's often bad if they focus on the detail. This is counterintuitive to their own social conditioning within the services so then [they] have to take a step up and look at the broader picture. The gaming needs to reflect that. . . . It's often a huge leap for people to make that transition in the real world. . . . That's where the gaming can actually help that transition. (interview 2017)

This suggests that while deterministic gaming can facilitate the rote training necessary to instill specific skill sets and doctrinal principles in junior service members, open-ended gaming can play a key role in their transition into critical and reflexive decision-making once they have reached a particular rank or position of authority.

In contrast to rote-training games aimed at junior service members, open-ended games, as Moreland explained, can involve "pretty high-level military staffs, brigade level and above, where there's very complex problem sets, very cluttered mission spaces with lots of variables impacting on military operations. What I use simulators for more than anything is to replicate that complexity, that multifaceted environment they work in, so they can make informed decisions. It's not predetermined what the outcomes are going be" (interview 2017). In such games, one instructor suggested, "we want the students to appreciate that [the] outcome is not deterministic. It is a plausible result. It's not a definitive result" (interview 2017). Instead, as Guillory noted, such games "are more process-focused, where you are not necessarily looking for the right answer to come out of the other end of the exercise.

What you are looking for is, how has the staff gone through their process? Are they asking the right questions? Are each of the staff members doing the right things within their lanes of responsibility?" (interview 2017).

Many in the wargaming CoP emphasize the importance of open-ended gaming at higher military levels. Brynen explains: "Games built on the asserted certainty of doctrine may be less effective—even counterproductive—in encouraging military personnel to question prior assumptions and treat each individual case in its own social and political merits. Yet, inculcating a critical and questioning attitude may be essential" (2016, 492). And as Moreland observed, when it comes to teaching or training members of higher ranks, "if you were looking at a modern simulator that couldn't be responsive to decisions or actions that weren't predetermined, then it's probably not a very good simulator. It's approaching obsolescence" (interview 2017). Another designer pointed out: "[Y]ou have got to be open-minded in your thinking and your strategy. . . . If you start to dictate where you're going to go during the game, you are always going to get to the same place and the student is not going to learn any consequences. It is the consequences that are some of the best learning tools that I have seen" (interview 2017).

Open-ended gaming does not have fixed end states coded in. Mark Herman says that such games "should not have any doctrine. The players themselves are the ones putting in doctrine. If the game models reality in some way that you're comfortable with, then how you employ the forces is the doctrine" (quoted in Allen 1989, 97). Lademan made a similar point, noting that "when you get to the higher games—the games that are more exploratory, discovery, are more concerned with concepts and issues as opposed to doctrine and standard operating procedures—that's where you want free will to have its way" (interview 2017). Reemphasizing the importance of rank, one wargames designer commented that "as you grow in your career, the wider the lane should become. So if you were to build a triangle . . . for gaming within education it would be an inverted triangle with the narrower path at the bottom with . . . the freshmen, and as you get to the graduate level you are opening new apertures so that you are really letting them make the decisions based on what they want to do and they have to suffer their consequences" (interview 2017). Markley elaborated that these types of games are

not necessarily intended to teach anybody anything specific, so those games are all open-ended, we don't know where they're going. And it would be wrong to say that people walk away having learned nothing. The point is you don't know what they're going to learn, you're not sure what they're going to take away . . . Now, you postulate some ideas or some thoughts or some questions about where the game might go, but the game goes where it goes. And so you've got to be prepared to capture the information about where that game is going, what the decisions were that were being made, what were the participants thinking at the time they were making their decisions. (interview 2017)

As this implies, gaming can teach participants to acknowledge and offset the limitations of doctrinal rigidity. Hall explained, "[O]bviously, we teach our junior leaders the battle drills and the doctrinal way to respond. But sometimes that's the wrong answer, you know, sometimes you have to do something that goes against your training, but in whatever unique situation you're in that's the right answer. When we talk about developing agile and adaptive leaders who thrive in uncertainty, we want them grounded in the doctrine and the tactics, but we want them to be able to think on their own, so that's really the challenge" (interview 2017).

A tension thus sits at the heart of wargaming, and the CoP, when it comes to the use of deterministic versus open-ended games. Most use both, though for different purposes. Guillory summarized it thus: "[T]here are times where I am conducting wargaming as a decision-focused thing so that I am teaching people how to make a good decision. There are times where I'm exercising a staff process on using wargaming as a training aid to make sure that the people doing stuff in the real world, in the interpersonal dialogues, are doing the right kinds of things. . . . What you are looking at along those two different tracks is, what are we doing for decision-focused gaming and what are we doing for staff-focused gaming and process-focused gaming?" (interview 2017). Hall said something similar:

[I]n general, at the tactical level we want the instantaneous right answer response according to our doctrine and our tactics, techniques, and procedures. It gets a little more nebulous at the strategic level, where they have to apply a lot more critical thinking and reasoning. [At the lower levels] we really want the soldiers to be getting that, call it muscle memory, mentally, so that they know what to do in a given situation, and it's more deterministic in that respect. At the higher level, when you're beginning to be the junior officer, you need to have the flexibility to see a situation unfolding, assess what's going on, and then be able to apply any number of options in terms of, you know, maneuvering your forces around to address the situation. (interview 2017)

Rupert expressed it this way: "[M]ilitary personnel are taught to think within their particular lanes. Even officer training to a certain extent is a process from sectional training which is to teach you a way of doing and a way of thinking. When they get to our point they're taught doctrine and how to think about things and we always tell them, you know, 'At the strategic level now you're trying to think outside doctrine, to question it'" (interview 2017). In sum, the deterministic or open character of a game should be determined, as Moreland noted, by its objectives:

> If your learning outcome is "I want these folks to get to an answer that we collectively believe is right" then you design the game to encourage certain behaviors and certain decisions and certain actions to be taken. What you're talking about in the second case, with more senior leaders and more indeterminate answers, [is] there is no right answer that you can prescribe, no prescription. . . . So if you design it as an experiment, leaders and staff can play with lots of different options. If you design it more as a training event with predetermined doctrinally approved outcomes, then you can train more junior staff, to learn what right looks like, you know, for less complex problems. (interview 2017)

In this reading, a game designer is faced with options to be decided between on the basis of the game's audience and purpose.

This distinction is troubled, however, by the adjudication procedures that accompany particular games. On the one hand are games with rigid adjudication, "which controls the experience of players through a rigid set of objectively applied rules and procedures that restrict player options and, within some small range of random numbers, strictly determines results" (Perla 1990, 219). Rubel elaborates:

> We describe as "rigidly assessed" those games that proceed strictly according to rules governing movement, detection, and combat. . . . The game goes where the rules take it; if the rules and the combat-resolution tables are good representations of reality, the outcome constitutes artificial military history, and one can usefully work backward from outcomes and look for reasons. This would be so whether the game is played by hand around a

board or at computer workstations. . . . The game goes where it goes. (Rubel 2006, 118)

In marked contrast, in "free" adjudication, "although the assessors use rules, models, and charts as aids, they rely on their own knowledge, beliefs, and experience to determine outcomes of the engagements, and this to control and direct the experience of the game's players" (Perla 1990, 219). While this approach has more flexibility, and makes possible responses to unforeseen game events, because it relies on human judgment it is difficult to validate, as it "contains that critical subjective element of assessor expertise, experience, and instinct" (Perla 1990, 219). In free adjudication,

> the flow of the game is governed by umpires and game directors. Instead of following game rules, players make plans and decisions as they would in real life, more or less, and umpires, collecting the interacting moves of all the players, translate them into force movements, detections, and combat results. The umpires may be aided by computers. The key difference is that the game's progress, including move results, are governed by the objectives of the game's sponsors, the time available, and sometimes the conflicting interests of stakeholders. Control may determine that a certain set of conditions must occur at a specific point if the game's objectives are to be met. . . . That is, the umpires deduce tactical outcomes, the necessary inputs, by working backward from a set of desired results. (Rubel 2006, 118)

The choice of adjudication style relates to the problem and objectives explored in the game. Pournelle posited: "[I]f you have an unstructured problem, you don't even know what the adjudication mechanics are going to be, so you're going to use a matrix-style argumentative structure. Whereas some areas of games may be extremely structured . . . So that's if you try to create knowledge" (interview 2017).

The key point here—which will be explored in more detail in Chapters 5 and 6—is that, even in ostensibly open-ended games, play and players' decisions are mediated and directed by facilitators and/or adjudicators whose primary directive is to impart the game's objectives. As de la Vega explained:

> [Y]ou need observer controllers, who are experts as well, observing the training audience and saying, "Okay, are they having this aha moment where they're seeing how the dots connect and seeing where the process is

failing and where they have to identify a gap between the process and reality and how they are bridging it? Are they exercising critical thinking?" That's where the vigilance of a good teacher comes in, to see if they are making decisions. . . . The facilitator, teacher, has to be there at every step to be able to poke the training audience, poke the students, to get into that higher critical thinking mode. (interview 2017)

And one instructor noted: "[Y]ou just can't let [students] at the simulation and figure it out for themselves. They need someone there to act as a guide and to help facilitate the discussion and the decisions that they're making. There needs to be an investment and a staff development process to get the facilitators up to speed. You're not just born that way" (interview 2017).

This approach is not condoned by some in the CoP. One designer reflected: "Often in service games you will have somebody who has a very specific idea of what something should look like, and if the students aren't doing what they think something should look like, they will often intervene to force the students to do that. . . . I tend to avoid that, and the reason for that is, I think, that if you're going to do that, unless you're incredibly self-aware about all your prejudices, you tend to be pushing them into the solution that you think is correct, rather than the one that they come up with" (interview 2017). And yet the game controllers wield significant power in directing players' behavior. As Perla and McGrady joked, "I like to say it's to manipulate the players, but I'm being mean. It's to keep the players in the universe on a useful storyline without having them go off into never-never land or get tangled up in things that are unimportant" (interview 2017). David Maher, a contractor with the National Guard Bureau Joint Staff, pointed out that even in ostensibly open-ended games, "an analogy [is] the Jim Carrey movie *The Truman Show*. When you're in exercise control and managing a game, you make it look like a realistic world. There's free play but then there are people behind the scenes that are conducting a big production" (interview 2017).

The foregoing examined a series of key contentions surrounding how wargames should be conceptualized. The remainder of this chapter problematizes the prevailing assumption that education and training games have a pedagogical function while research games do not, and it demonstrates that *all* wargames—whether process- or product-oriented—teach their participants something, and that these lessons endure long after the game ends.

What Are Military Wargames For?

Among the wargaming CoP, distinctions of various kinds are drawn between games used for research, for education, and for training. Some treat education and training as synonymous, while others argue they are vastly different. Indeed, some claim that education gaming has more in common with open-ended research gaming than with deterministic training gaming. It is thus important to interrogate these tension-ridden framings in order to establish the common pedagogical imperative underpinning wargaming of all kinds. As a more deterministic form of gaming, training games "presume that the questions and correct answers are known. They are used to rehearse actions and determine the extent to which the players know the answers to contingencies that have accepted solutions" (Hanley 2018, 54). Perla and McGrady similarly explained that training is defined by "fundamental coding of a series of processes [which stipulate] 'do this, don't do that, do that, it's wrong, do this, it's right.' There is a right and wrong" (interview 2017). As this suggests, training games are highly directed, and players' actions within them are strictly delimited. One wargames designer commented: "You don't want the players thinking outside the box. You want them to practice the muscle movements of what they're supposed to do" (interview 2017). Pournelle provided an example of such training: "[W]hen I was the executive officer of the ship and we needed to train the crew to fight a main space fire in our engineering plant we wanted muscle memory. We wanted something so that they could be woken up in the middle of the night so that they would fall into specific—so that they would know 'I go here, I put this equipment on, and I use this in this manner.' You want that muscle memory for that specific task. That's training. On the other hand, if you're trying to get people to be strategists, that's education" (interview 2017).

These comments highlight that many in the CoP believe education gaming is fundamentally different from the deterministic types used in training. Pournelle put it this way: "[I]f you're trying to convey knowledge, then the question is, is this for training or for education? If you have a structured problem and you're trying to convey knowledge, that's training. . . . If you're trying to educate people on the larger context and you have an unstructured problem, then you don't necessarily know what the different sides are going to do" (interview 2017). Two wargaming instructors elucidated further: "if your goal in that exercise is to follow the book and just practice, that is training. On the other hand, if you are given a novel new capability or given a situation and told, 'Okay, don't just follow the book, how would you approach this?' then that becomes education" (interview 2017). In this sense, strategic seminar games are educational but not training-related. Conversely, a game that imparts key skills such as piloting a helicopter should be considered a training game but not an educational game. These forms of learning can sometimes sit in tension with each other. Kligge noted that service members "go through a lot of this pure training where it becomes muscle memory. Then they come to the university and there's trying to get them to find an answer as opposed to working to the answer, and so again sometimes we struggle with the difference between training and education. How I break it down: training, I can pull a trigger all day every day in a first-person shooter. It's muscle memory. . . . In education we're trying to get them to think through a process. Put another way . . . do we care about product or process, product being more training based?" (interview 2017).

In comments that reflect this distinction, Bartels posits that educational games can be broken down into three key categories: "providing an active learning experience of their own, reinforcing lessons taught in a more traditional academic setting, or evaluating the extent to which students have assimilated such lessons." The core aim of such games is "for participants to interrogate and absorb the model by demonstrating first, how a world described by a model would work, and second, how that artificial world parallels reality in ways that make what is learned in the game helpful in real life." She provides the example of the game *Connected Shadows*, used at CISA, which depicts "a current irregular conflict according to some of the theories taught." This game, she argues, "was designed to closely mirror the environment, roles, and rules highlighted in the CISA model of irregular warfare," with the aim of "more fully embedd[ing] the players in the model to increase their understanding of the rules it proposed" (Bartels 2016, 504–507).

Another wargames designer noted that in educational gaming "you want a bunch of people to learn something about some region of the world or some conflict and so you immerse them in a gaming environment and then the players come out of the game better educated" (interview 2017). This suggests that educational gaming allows for more interrogation and exploration of subject matter than does a training game, which aims to impart a specific skill set or doctrinal principle. Some in the CoP suggest that training happens at the start of the service member's career, and only later do they progress to education. As Kligge put it, in the military "you start with

training, go through education, and then they move on into the real world"
(interview 2017).

If training and education wargaming seek—albeit in more or less rote
ways—to impart specific skill sets or consolidate theoretical knowledge, research wargaming is often more exploratory in character. Perla makes clear
that research games focus on "developing or testing strategies and plans,
identifying issues, or building a consensus among participants" (1990, 194).
Pournelle elaborates that research games aim at "creating ideas, options,
concepts of operations, and strategies; testing and tightening tentative
plans, whether operations plans or program plans, seeking to make them
more robust; sensitizing policymakers to known serious problems that, because of their abstraction, have not proved gripping enough to cause action;
and creating shared understanding of issues . . . and the general nature of
options and adversaries through communication and professional socialization" (2017, 7). They increase understanding of "adversaries, including
their mindsets, objectives, strategies, and perceptions; potentially 'irrational'
behaviors (in our eyes)" (2017, 17) and manage the excessive amounts of information now channeled to decision-makers.

Describing the game *Scattered Lights*, also used at CISA, Bartels notes
that it "allowed for established experts to challenge both the school's framework . . . and their own understanding of current topics of interest to the
policy community." In doing so, it "effectively reverses the process of the education model: Instead of the game designer teaching a model by instantiating
it in a game, the participants effectively teach the game designer their mental
models through their discussion." She concludes: "Over the course of the
game, players instantiated a new model . . . [and] created an alternative vision
of how irregular warfare occurs and how the state counters it" (2016, 508–
509). To frame it more broadly, the aim here is that by "exercising, testing, and
modifying that model, analysts and wargamers can explore the implications,
not of some unknowable future reality, but of our current, restricted, and uncertain view of what that reality might be like" (Perla 1990, 241). In gaming
of this kind, rather than being the receivers of a game's objectives, players
are the instruments through whom data is generated. As one wargames designer explained, in analytic gaming "what I want from the players is the information that I'll then turn into analysis and the output product that I need,
whether that happens to be a ConOps [Concept of Operations] to be put into
a computer simulation or insights that are fed back to a sponsor who has
asked for the wargame to be conducted" (interview 2017).

As a subset of research games, analytic games seek to "establish traceability in a very concrete sense from what was the end state of the game and what was the path each other players used or the path of activity that got them to the end state," said a wargames designer. "The Naval War College has spent a lot of time creating a computer system that captures what the players do. . . . It's focused on the traceability of an outcome back to the players' decisions that led to the outcome" (interview 2017). Bartles elaborates: "If the purpose of the game is analytical, the designer helps participants instantiate their own (often mental and unarticulated) models in the game to improve and disseminate understanding of a phenomenon. While the structure of game elements may be similar to those of an educational game, the purpose of an analytic game is to open space for critique so that the model instantiated in the game can be refined based on participants' experience" (Bartels 2016, 507). Rather than reinforcing a specific theory or element of doctrine, said a wargames designer, analytic games are "meant to produce a product that can be used somewhere else" (interview, 2017).

These comments reveal that some in the CoP think the distinction between training, education, and research games is less clear than is often claimed. Two wargaming instructors commented the "tension that gets portrayed between training and education is often artificial. . . . A lot of that tension comes from a need to classify and distinguish between activities. Whether it is the [Joint Staff] J-7 or whoever that says, '[We need to distinguish between what are training activities and what are educational activities right now' . . . Then you can backfill, creating a framework that makes sense. In reality, I think there is quite a bit of blur" (interview 2017). Markley echoed this point: "[G]aming is useful to learning, and learning includes the aspects that we traditionally think of as being both education and training" (interview 2017). Indeed, as two wargames instructors pointed out, the critical thinking associated with research gaming often applies more to training than is commonly acknowledged:

Even in training you are still applying some critical thinking, even if all the training you are doing is training on how to do dumb weights. There is still some critical thinking about "[W]ell, when are my arms going to give out, when do I need to stop doing this because I can't do anymore?" There is still an expectation to do some critical thinking and certainly, in tactical training, there is a lot of critical thinking going. How do you maneuver that squad of infantry against the target? "I have the incomplete information, how do I process it, how do I think when I tell my section leader to my left what to do, how do I word [it] so that he understands my intent and that provides the right information for him or her to make their decision?" That is still a lot of critical thinking going on in what is an absolutely doctrinal peer military, big-T training event. (interview 2017)

The ultimate consequence of this, as one wargames designer explained, is that "if you substitute the objectives and issues of the sponsor for a game with learning objectives or training objectives then I think you can build an educational or a training game exactly the way you build an analytic game" (interview 2017). While training games alone are thought to emphasize repetition, "there is an iterative training process to decision-making as well," another designer proffered. "If you look at the service education historically—if you go back to the nineteenth century—what the Germans do is they do an enormous amount of education of their officers. And then the key bit that they emphasize is, they iteratively practice decision-making and make it more and more and more rapid. So it's not just actually accumulating knowledge and using education, it's then the practice of the decision making utilizing the information from their education" (interview 2017).

What all military gaming has in common is the delivery of particular objectives. As Goodwin summarized, "In the gaming world, we always will challenge the educators who are requesting it: 'What are the objectives?' In the training world, it's always 'These are the objectives of what we're trying to do,' and therefore we create scenarios that will help us achieve those. So, in that respect, the structures are very similar" (interview 2017). As this suggests, the form chosen for a particular game will depend on its objectives. Indeed, the success or failure of a game depends upon clarity of objectives. He continued: "The most critical thing is: what are your objectives? What are your educational objectives and your training objectives? You will always have to identify those, otherwise you're just wandering around blind" (interview 2017). De la Vega observed, "Your objectives have to be clear, they have to be nested in what you want your learners to take out of it" (interview 2017). Another designer echoed this point, explaining: "If we want to teach or train, we want to give people a better capacity. It's knowledge, skills, and attitudes, and you can get at all of them with gaming. It just depends on what kind of combination and that calls for different types of gaming. . . . But you can teach that with so many different games, you can teach knowledge in so many different ways as you know. You're practicing knowledge" (interview 2017).

Just as with the distinction between gaming and simulation, the line between teaching and training is by no means definitive. Perla and McGrady reflected:

> The reason that that difference comes up is because the words mean different things to different people. So, in their minds, training essentially meant everything that had to do with imparting knowledge to someone that they were supposed to use. So that's much broader than training muscle memory or training procedural steps. So, that anything that is trying to give you practical knowledge about how to do things, it seems like a reasonable definition of training. But teaching you how to think by giving you examples of situations in which you are forced to think and then telling you what someone observed, how you thought and where you did well and where you did poorly, in giving you practical examples of why you made the decisions that you did and where you may have been wrong on facts, wrong on predictions, wrong on simple cognition, that's where games and simulations played as games can help. (interview 2017)

This suggests that, insofar as the purpose of a game is necessarily the delivery of a set of objectives—whether procedural or product—*all* wargames teach their participants something. "A war game teaches both intellectually and emotionally—it is an experience one lives through" (Robert Specht, quoted in Ghamari-Tabrizi 2000, 192). While the type of knowledge imparted varies widely, playing games is a pedagogical activity. This function—which I refer to as "play as pedagogy"—will be elucidated in Chapters 5 and 6, which trace how wargaming works in production of people.

Conclusion

This chapter has charted a course through the enduring dissensus among the wargaming CoP surrounding what a wargame is and does. The key conclusion emerging from the chapter's examination of these key debates is that there is less daylight between games used for research, education, and training than is often posited. The chapter has thus established the premise that all games have a pedagogical purpose. As Koster affirms: "Games teach you how aspects of reality work, how to understand yourself, how to understand the actions of others, and how to imagine. . . . Basically, all games are edutainment" (2013, 47). Another designer echoed this point, commenting: "Learning is almost synonymous with training. . . . When we are talking about learning outcomes, a lot of the times we are talking about training outcomes for a particular unit, but it all depends upon whether it is in the schoolhouse or in your training or educating leaders or you are training soldiers. They're almost synonymous but this is a slightly different language." In both training and education, he continued,

> what we are collectively trying to do is take either the learning audience or the training audience through a problem set. As they apply the tools that they have, whether they are going through a planning process in more of a cerebral way or whether they're actually going through a physical lane or a physical training event where they are part of a force-on-force competitive exercise in a training environment, [what matters] is their application of our doctrine and our techniques and procedures in order to go through that event. The outcome is not focused on what the end state is, it is focused on the lessons that can be learned by doing. (interview 2017)

Many in the CoP have disagreed over the years about how and whether to draw lines between these gaming types. As Perla and McGrady joked, "We won't get into the distinction between those because some of our colleagues, or former colleagues now, smacked me around vociferously when I said 'Training or education, it's all the same.' . . . The objective of the game is to allow the designer's point of view to come across" (interview 2017). Lademan had a similar point of view: because "wargaming has tremendous power in both training and education, and in these more arcane development, discovery exploration games, you can [use] your design methodologies to bring about the kind of outcome that you're looking for, based upon the audience that you're trying to serve, and obviously the issues and the objectives that they've established" (interview 2017). In light of this, the position taken in this book is that while research games and training games may appear as polar opposites, the constraints, directives, and processes they bring to bear are productive of people in comparable ways.

2

The State of Play

Introduction: Worlds of Wargames

Having established what a wargame is and can do in Chapter 1, this chapter sets out the origins and context of the twenty-first-century wargaming renaissance. It begins by tracing the role and function of games in the field of international relations from the mid-twentieth century to the early twenty-first, reconstructing a hitherto neglected history. It then locates the recent resurgence of interest in gaming among IR scholars in developments in the defense establishment since 2014, inaugurated by DoD-wide memos from then Defense Secretary Chuck Hagel and Deputy Defense Secretary Bob Work that called for a reinvigorated wargaming effort across the services. Integrated into two major reform programs—the Defense Innovation Initiative (DII) and Third Offset Strategy (3OS)—the chapter shows how wargaming has proliferated to offset the closing gap between the US' advanced capabilities and those of competitors by generating new operational and strategic concepts necessary to make good use of leap-ahead technologies.

Key to these developments, the chapter shows, has been a rise in demand for a better grasp of the "human dimension,"[1] encompassing critical thinking, the ability to navigate complexity, and improved decision-making skills in the new security environment. As the character of war changes and global power hierarchies continue to become destabilized, wargaming's ubiquity and relative status in the DoD analysis community has increased significantly, resulting in a decade-long renaissance at the time of writing. The chapter shows that this resurgence reflects a challenge to the operations research (OR) approach associated with conventional defense analysis. By leveraging advanced civilian technology and drawing upon the appeal of

---

[1] The "human dimension" here refers to individuals within the US military. Human dimension gaming impacts upon those who are taught or trained, as opposed to an external target population. This is not to be confused with the "human domain," which relates to individuals and groups outside the US military, such as the local population in a conflict zone, which may alternatively, or also, be the target of military wargaming.

Politics of Play. Aggie Hirst, Oxford University Press. © Oxford University Press 2024.
DOI: 10.1093/oso/9780197629192.003.0003

gameplay, the chapter concludes, the wargaming renaissance reflects the beginning of a paradigm shift from quantitative approaches, which seek to reduce complexity, to qualitative explorations of complexity, which seek to map and interpret patterns of human decision-making.

Gaming International Relations

A form of black magic is at work in games. . . . We know they have power over people, but we can't quite characterize that power, which makes it all the more tempting to find a way to control it. (Bogost 2016, 61)

While currently enjoying a peak in what Perla has called a "sine wave of popularity"—in which wargaming experiences a "roller-coaster ride of favor and disfavor among the [defense] department's leadership" (2017, 87)—wargames precede the ludic century. In their earliest iterations in ancient civilizations, they were practiced by political elites and used to develop strategic thinking and confer citizenship rites.[2] Wargames that simulated movement and combat emerged in Europe in the seventeenth century as part of new modes of imperial and military mapping and modeling, culminating in Prussia in the nineteenth century with Georg von Reisswitz's *Kriegsspiel,* the first modern tabletop war simulation (Caffrey 2019, 14–16).[3] This new method was first taken up in the US Army and Naval War College in the 1870s and 1880s, and regular wargaming was in effect at the Army Command and General Staff College and Army War College by the 1930s (Bessner 2014, 96).

By the early twentieth century, recreational wargaming was widespread, even among pacifists like H. G. Wells, who, in an attempt to show the folly of all-out war in Europe, published *Little Wars* in 1913.[4] Wargames were used by both the Allied and Axis powers in World War II. In an oft-repeated tale, Fleet Admiral Chester Nimitz wrote to the president of the Naval War College

[2] The earliest estimate puts the first abstract strategy wargame at 2300 BCE in China, versions of which spread to Korea in AD 400 and Japan in AD 600, where it was given the name *Go.* Warlike games were practiced in ancient Greece and Rome as part of gladiatorial training, and at least one example of such a game has been found depicted in an Egyptian tomb dating to 2000 BCE. An intact game discovered in Iraq was dated to 600 BCE, and what we know as chess today originated in India in approximately AD 550 (Caffrey 2019, 12–13).

[3] *Kriegsspiel* quickly proliferated across the Prussian army and from there internationally in the 1870s, in part due to Prussia's successes in its war with France.

[4] Wells is credited with publishing the first coherent rule set for hobby wargaming. He claimed that one need only play *Little Wars* a handful of times to see how futile a Great War would be (Timpson 2013).

claiming that, with the exception of kamikaze tactics, there was nothing the Japanese did in the Pacific theater that had not been envisaged by the US Navy through wargaming (Morgan 1991; Perla 2022, 201).[5] Following the uprisings of May 1968, situationist strategist Guy Debord, along with partner Alice Becker-Ho, developed *Game of War* as a tool of subversion and struggle against Fordist capitalism.[6] Dubbed "paper time machines" by influential designer James Dunnigan (2016, xxxiii), wargames had by this stage become not only tools of military strategy, operations, and tactics, but also artifacts of intrigue and leisure among cultural elites and civilians.

Despite this long-standing role in political and military affairs, the study of play and games has been treated as singularly unserious in the discipline of IR since its founding. Framed as frivolous, childish, apolitical, and even, in more philosophical terms, the "other" of Western metaphysics (Hirst 2019; Nagel 2002), play and games are often ranked below other popular cultural media—such as film, television, and music—as of import for global politics. Among other consequences, this elision has obscured the place of wargames in the field's history. With the explosion of games in the digital age, however, a reconstruction of the roles of games in the theory and practice of IR has become necessary.

Wargaming became interwoven with IR only a few decades after the field's first chair was established at the University of Wales, Aberystwyth. Beginning in the 1950s, with the heightening of tension between the Eastern and Western blocs, the revolution in military affairs (RMA), and the dawning of the nuclear age, novel forms of experimentation and forecasting were developed to make sense of the new security environment (Bessner 2014; Pauly 2018; Emery 2021). Overseen by strategic thinkers including Andrew Marshall, Herman Kahn, and Thomas Schelling, games and simulations elicited "fascination, ardour and scepticism," becoming the "vogue of the moment" (Ghamari-Tabrizi 2000, 203).[7] Combining insights from *Kriegsspiel* and social psychology (Banks Groom, and Oppenheim 1968, 2), as the Cold War heated up, games and simulations provided a "less explosive arena than

---

[5] In addition, a reengagement with the British WRNS (better known as Wrens), young women who ran wargames on how to combat German U-boats in the Western Approaches Tactical Unit (WATU), is currently under way (Lee and Strong 2016).

[6] Grounded in Clauzewitzian strategic thinking, Debord's *Game of War* has inspired the contemporary left-wing gaming project Class Wargames: https://www.classwargames.net/.

[7] Eminent scholars at University College London and the London School of Economics observed with some consternation this "new American attitude to foreign policy making" in which "problems are reduced to scenarios" and "antagonists are pitted again each other in a confrontation" in a "showdown" (Banks, Groom, and Oppenheim 1968, 1).

the real world for playing our their more risky hunches" (1968, 15). In 1961, the Joint Chiefs of Staff set up the Joint War Games Agency (JWGA) (Pauly 2018, 155), and by the mid-1960s, "[d]espite the newness of simulation of international behavior, there ha[d] been considerable utilization of the technique at several research sites" (Guetzkow and Jensen 1966, 262—263).[8]

Also elided in conventional disciplinary histories is the extent to which games and simulations were interwoven with the development and testing of IR theory (Verba 1964). As William D. Coplin of Wayne State University put it, "[S]imulators themselves are theorists" and "simulation is a way of theorizing about international relations" (Coplin 1966, 562). Harold Guetzkow and Lloyd Jensen, two leading simulators at Northwestern University in the 1960s, took a similar view:

> Having recognized that there are many ways of building theory in international relations, we have been interested in ascertaining the relationship between the more familiar verbal efforts in theorizing and the use of simulation for theory-building. To do this, simulation models have been juxtaposed to the more traditional modes of verbal theory-building of such writers as Morgenthau, Wolfers, Claude, and Kaplan. (Guetzkow and Jensen 1966, 266)

This gave these games and simulations a distinctly realist flavor. As George Modelski of the University of Washington noted, Guetzkow's simulation "constitutes a model of the pure nation-state system which, in turn, is the dominant theoretical construction of international relations" (1970, 117). Guetzkow and Jensen acknowledged the "tremendous aid" provided by realist theorists, and conceded that their simulations "rely heavily upon verbal hypotheses in programming their constructions, even though most of these hypotheses are derived intuitively and have not been validated through systematic, empirical work" (1966, 266).

Anticipating critiques of (neo)realism developed in IR beginning in the 1980s, some scholars of the day saw in simulations and games the opportunity to move beyond this state-centrism. As Banks, Groom, and Oppenheim

---

[8] For example, Oliver Benson's *Simple Diplomatic Game*; Raytheon's *Technological, Economic, Military, Political Evaluation Routine* (TEMPER); the Simulatics Corporation's *Grisiscom*; Lincoln P. Bloomfield's RAND-sponsored political-military games at MIT (in partnership with Thomas Schelling, then at Harvard); and Guetzkow's *Inter-Nation Simulation* (INS). On the last of these, see Pauly 2018.

observed, "[F]or historical reasons traditional international relations theory tends to be state-orientated and not systems-orientated." Understood as sites of theory production, they continued, games and simulations could help redress the balance (1968, 11–12). Other commentators offered further-reaching critiques. Again foreshadowing later debates in the discipline, Modelski asked: "[I]s the international relations literature of the mid-1960s a satisfactory representation of the realities of international relations? . . . . The 'realities' we perceive in international relations depend in part on the theories we use. . . . [I]s the international relations theory of the mid-1960s good enough for our purpose? . . . [A]t this point doubts arise" (1970, 114–115).

Alongside these research applications, IR scholars also affirmed the benefits of simulations and games for education and training. By 1966, simulations were being used in IR teaching at the Universities of Michigan, Ohio State, Oregon, San Francisco State, Northwestern, Wisconsin, Columbia, Stanford, Princeton, and MIT, in addition to armed services academies (Guetzkow and Jensen 1966, 264). Such was the interest on the military side that from 1955 all defense force crews in the Air Force were trained with simulations developed at RAND (Ghamari-Tabrizi 2000, 187–188). As Banks, Groom, and Oppenheim argued, "[T]here is now general assent to the view that gaming-simulation techniques are a useful teaching aid, especially in international relations," for honing such skills as "perception, communication, consensus formation, timing, interpretation of documents, environment, escalation, [and] tension spirals" as well as improving student interest, motivation, and emotional investment (1968, 15–16). Simulations thus generated a "mood of enthusiasm and commitment to the lessons derived from the particulars of play" (Ghamari-Tabrizi 2000, 199).

In addition to key IR departments, the RAND Corporation played a central role in the development of this new analytical tool. Indeed, it was at RAND that simulations and games began to split into two methodologically distinct forms of analysis (Bessner 2014; Emery 2021). On the one hand, the Mathematical Analytics Division (MAD)[9] applied economic modeling, game theory, and quantitative methods to their Cold War simulations. Often involving no human participants, such simulations were "highly controlled and deductive" and played out automatically on computers (Verba 1964, 429). These developments constituted part of the rise of behavioralist and

---

[9] The acronym for this, MAD, is not to be confused with the that used to stand for "mutually assured destruction."

social scientific approaches to IR from the 1950s. As Stanford's Robert C. North explained, "[U]ntil recently political science—particularly in its concern for international relations—has been imprecise and generally vulnerable to value preferences" (1963, 119). Seeking to make IR more scientific (Guetzkow and Jensen 1966, 261), scholars turned to positivist methods and advanced computers capable of "handling of multiple variables and vast quantities of raw data which scholars would not have dreamed of touching, except impressionistically, as recently as five years back" (North 1963, 120).[10]

On the other hand, exploring the very same Cold War conundrums, the Social Sciences Division (SSD) treated wargaming as an art, emphasizing the cultivation of intuition, judgment, and human decision-making (Emery 2021, 2). Following a historically focused social science approach that corresponded with the work of leading IR theorists including E. H. Carr, Willian T. R. Fox, Hans Morgenthau, and Reinhold Niebuhr (Bessner 2014, 94), the SSD focused on political-military gaming that included not just battles but also "the domestic negotiations and diplomatic exchanges that preceded and continued during a military engagement" (Bessner 2014, 91). The virtue of this approach was the examination of the subjective aspects of decision-making, including "the emotions and the ethical intuitions of the players" (Emery 2021, 5). Such an approach enabled analysis to "study the behavior of the participants in a way which other techniques do not easily afford" (Banks, Groom, and Oppenheim 1968, 11). The advantages of this were that the outcomes were meaningfully affected by players' decisions and that a deep emotional engagement was cultivated among players, alerting the defense analysis community to "the value of disinhibited play as a vehicle for creative research" and the capacity of games to generate "synthetic experience" (Ghamari-Tabrizi 2000, 179–180).

Notwithstanding these benefits, wargaming quickly lost favor because its results did not pass the validation and verification tests of quantitative modeling and simulation (Ghamari-Tabrizi 2000; Emery 2021). As Perla elaborates, simulations created by civilian academics—collectively termed "whiz kids" or, more pejoratively, "egg-heads"—came to dominate US defense analysis under the leadership of Robert McNamara during the Kennedy administration (Perla 1990, 105–109). The ultimate result was a significant

---

[10] Much to the distress of many senior figures in the military, the accession of this positivist orientation would privilege methodology and scientific authority over combat experience and veteran intuition (Ghamari-Tabrizi 2000, 163–165).

reduction in wargaming during the Vietnam War and a concomitant lack of interest among IR scholars. Nevertheless, a small but committed wargaming community of practice remained devoted to their craft, and as the Cold War drew to a close a handful of pathbreaking books were published making the case for wargaming over modeling and simulations (Allen 1989; Perla 1990; Dunnigan 2000).

While wargaming had fallen out of favor, modeling and simulation generated increasing interest across the defense establishment and among IR scholars. Reflecting broader meta-theoretical debates and the rise of post-positivist IR theory, modeling and simulations were critically examined as a key technique of power capable not of anticipating political and economic realities but rather of producing them in line with their designers' coded-in assumptions. As Richard K. Ashley argued, echoing critiques made in the 1960s and 1970s (Banks, Groom, and Oppenheim 1968, 13; Modelski 1970), simulations produce realities at least as much as they apprehend or represent them. Ashley's pathbreaking critique called attention to the unacknowledged politics and biases of these celebrated techniques of world-modeling. Challenging positivism's search for fixed laws and unifying theory, and modeling and simulations' erasure of normative and critical questions, Ashley likened the practice to Bentham's panopticon and indicted its advocates for failing to justify its "utilitarian metaphysics, positivist methodology, and techno-rational interests in knowledge as an instrument of control" (Ashley 1983, 532).

While the field at large neglected wargames, James Der Derian pioneered the study of military gaming and simulations in IR over a period of thirty years (1990a, 1990b, 1997, 2000, 2003, 2009). Der Derian diagnosed a "hybridization of warring and gaming," in which, "[f]rom the early spatial movement of toy soldiers and cardboard ships on contoured sand tables to the live, virtual and constructive simulations of fully immersive environments, a quantum leap in verisimilitude has been made in war gaming. Improvement produced an ironic outcome: the better the simulation, the higher the risk of confusing war as game" (2003, 39). The ultimate consequence of this was, he concluded, that "from the decision to deploy troops to the daily order of battle, from the highest reaches of policy-making to the lowest levels of field tactics and logistics, war games, computer simulations, and command post exercises make war into a game" (2003, 41). As discussed in the Introduction, the most significant of Der Derian's conclusions for this book is that virtual technologies are hyperreal—that is, they are productive of realities. This book builds on this insight to show how—disaggregated from simulations and exercises—wargaming is productive of people.

While the study of military gaming has broadly lain dormant since the publication of the 2009 edition of Der Derian's *Virtuous War*, in recent years IR scholars have examined the violence, militarism, exceptionalism, and emancipatory potential of recreational videogames.[11] These themes have also been explored at some length outside the field, notably in defense studies,[12] media studies,[13] English,[14] philosophy,[15] and games studies.[16] In addition, debates in IR on pedagogy increasingly emphasize the utility of the "active learning" made possible by games and simulations for teaching IR theory and core concepts. Echoing claims made in the 1960s (Banks, Groom, and Oppenheim 1968, 15–16), many contemporary scholars argue that pedagogical gaming can increase student motivation, engagement, knowledge retention, teamwork, and analytical skills, as well as introducing an element of fun.[17] Despite these rich contributions, the study of military gaming stalled well into the second decade of the twenty-first century.

A new generation of scholars interested in military wargaming is, however, currently on the way to securing a foothold in IR. Discussions about military gaming have featured in the work of Antoine Bousquet (2015), Dan Öberg (2020) and Nick Robinson (2019). Reid Pauly has explored the role of wargames in nuclear deliberations among US elites in *International Security* (Pauly 2018), while Reddie and coauthors have examined the uses of advanced technologies in next-generation wargames in a policy forum in *Science* (Reddie et al. 2018). John Emery has traced the place of moral considerations and language in mid-twentieth-century wargaming at RAND in the *Texas National Security Review* (Emery 2021), and Erik Lin-Greenberg, Reid Pauly, and Jacquelyn Schneider have evaluated how political scientists can use wargaming as a method of study in the *European Journal of International Relations* (Lin-Greenberg, Pauly, and Schneider 2022).

[11] See Salter 2011; Robinson 2015; Barbrook 2014; Ciută 2016; Hayden 2016; Brown 2017; Schulzke 2017; Berents and Keogh 2018; Jarvis and Robinson 2021.

[12] See Smith 2010.

[13] Including Dyer-Witheford and De Peuter 2009; Huntemann and Payne 2010; Stahl 2010; Lammes and de Smale 2018.

[14] See Mead 2013.

[15] See Galloway 2006; Wark 2007.

[16] Notably, Bogost 2010; Mukherjee 2017; Hammond and Pötzsch 2020.

[17] See Asal 2005; Asal and Kratoville 2013; Arnold 2015; Horn, Rubin, and Schouenborg 2016; de Zamaróczy 2017.

In addition, David Banks, academic director of the King's Wargaming Network, has developed a typology of the methodological machineries of wargaming (Banks 2022), and a number of outstanding PhD theses exploring various aspects and applications of wargaming have been completed in recent years, notably by Elizabeth Bartels (Bartels 2020). Straddling the line between IR scholarship and the military practitioner audience, a series of recent publications has made the case for the utility of gaming across a series of strategic, operational, and tactical remits, in particular in *War on the Rocks*.[18] Research on wargames in the field will be boosted by a new wargames archive at the Hoover Institution, curated by Jaquelyn Schneider, and a steady increase in panels and works at major conventions is in evidence. There has been an upsurge in new wargames practitioner handbooks and guides (Caffrey 2019; Longley-Brown 2019; Wojtowicz 2022, 2023), and the presence of wargames-related panels at leading conferences and conventions is also increasing.[19]

The catalyst for these developments was an ambitious project of reform known as the Defense Innovation Initiative (DII), which was launched in 2014 by then Secretary of Defense Chuck Hagel. The DII's mandate was to pursue innovative ways to sustain and advance US military preeminence by overhauling key elements of the defense establishment's culture and practice to mitigate the complexities and uncertainties of the twenty-first-century security environment. Key to the DII's program of innovation was the Third Offset Strategy (3OS), overseen by then Deputy Defense Secretary Bob Work. The 3OS focused on leveraging advanced commercial technology to counter—offset—declining US advantage associated with the potential or actual acquisition of comparable capabilities by competitors. As the following section demonstrates, key to this initiative was a reinvigorated wargaming effort across the Department of Defense (DoD).

[18] See Work and Selva 2015; Jones 2016; Lacey 2016, 2019; Pettyjohn and Shlapak 2016; Bartels 2017, 2018; Bae 2018; Jensen, Cuomo and Whyte 2018; Pauly 2018; Schuety and Will 2018; Barzashka 2019b; Lin-Greenberg 2019; McArdle, Kehr, and Colabatistto 2020; Schechter 2020; Wong and Heath 2021; Burke and Cameron 2022.

[19] The 2023 International Studies Association annual convention featured five panels examining wargaming, as well as a preconference workshop titled "Wargaming in International Relations: Toward an Interdisciplinary Community," which brought together over twenty scholars working on wargames as either a method or object of study in IR.

The Defense Innovation Initiative and
the Third Offset Strategy

On November 15, 2014, Defense Secretary Chuck Hagel launched the Defense Innovation Initiative. Its mission, he stated in a widely circulated memorandum, was to "pursue innovative ways to sustain and advance our military superiority for the 21st Century and improve business operations throughout the [Defense] Department" (Hagel 2014a, 1). Speaking at the Reagan National Defense Forum in Simi Valley, California, he elaborated:

> The Department of Defense is undergoing a defining time of transition. After 13 years of war fought by an all-volunteer force, we're facing a reshaping of our enterprise by a fiscal environment plagued by constant budget uncertainty and a large, continuing decline in resources, and by a historic realignment of interests and influences around the world.... DoD's responsibilities are to be prepared to address a broad range of contingencies and unpredictable crises well into the future. That means we must prepare our defense enterprise for the challenges of that uncertain future. We face the rise of new technologies, national powers, and non-state actors; sophisticated, deadly and often asymmetric emerging threats, ranging from cyberattacks to transnational criminal networks; as well as persistent, volatile threats we have faced for years. [Therefore,] [t]oday I'm announcing a new Defense Innovation Initiative—an initiative that we expect to develop into a game-changing third "offset" strategy. (Hagel 2014b)

The DII was expansive in scope, aiming to overhaul key elements of DoD culture and promote fresh thinking in spheres as diverse as concepts of operations, research and development, capabilities, leader development, and business practices (White 2017b, xi). Hagel's vision was of an ambitious, department-wide project of reform that would improve procurement and business through a process of "acquisition transformation" (Christiansson 2018) as well as develop leaders of the future (Hagel 2014b). This would prepare the US for the new security environment and facilitate the "new American way of war," grounded in "speed, maneuver, flexibility ... precision firepower, special forces, and psychological operations" (Max Boot, quoted in Caldwell and Lenoir 2016, 257). In short, "the initiative would maintain U.S. military dominance by sustaining its competitive edge in power projection capabilities, balancing technological innovation with fiscal reality" (Boyd and Kimball 2017, 7).

Key to the DII was the development and adaptation of advanced technology for DoD use. It was intended to build on the activities of the Defense Advanced Research Projects Agency (DARPA) and the Office of Net Assessment (ONA), which had long been focused on developing and repurposing technology for military applications (Christiansson 2018, 268). Its remit complemented the activities of the Strategic Capabilities Office (SCO), founded by then Deputy Defense Secretary Ash Carter in 2012; while the SCO focused on ensuring US advantage by exploring the potential military applications of existing technologies, DII was dedicated to the development of next-generation capabilities (Ellman et al. 2017, 12–13). The aim was to ensure continued US advantage through the creative use of technology. As Hagel bluntly commented, "America does not believe in sending our troops into a fair fight. Bob Gates, Leon Panetta, all of our predecessors believe that—and were responsible for ensuring that didn't happen. But that is a credo we will not be able to honor if we do not take the initiative and address these mounting challenges now. DoD must continue to modernize our nation's capabilities and sustain its operational and technological edge" (Hagel 2014b). This focus on technology lay at the heart of the DII's Third Offset Strategy.

The 3OS was described by Hagel as "game-changing" (Hagel 2014b). Based on the classical economic principle of comparative advantage, the 3OS sought to establish how the US could tip the balance in its favor through the creative use of technology by maximizing strengths and efficiencies while offsetting those of an opponent (Norwood and Jensen 2016, 35). The US was entering an era, Hagel claimed, in which its dominance in a number of key areas was being gradually eroded; it was estimated that its technological advantage would persist for no longer than five years without significant innovation (Ellman, Samp, and Coll 2017, 1). The DoD faced a situation in which budgets were reduced and debts had accumulated (Martinage 2014, iii) at the same moment as adversaries were modernizing and expanding their disruptive capabilities across the spectrum of conflict (Hagel 2014a). Of particular concern was the maturation of anti-access/area denial (A2AD) capabilities, such as ballistic and cruise missiles, integrated surface-to-air defenses, fourth-generation aircraft, sophisticated surveillance systems, and electronic and cyber weapons, which would impede US forces' capacity to access key areas in Eurasia and elsewhere (Ochmanek 2014, 1–2). The aim was to counter these dual problems of a closing technology gap and fiscal austerity through a "capabilities race" (White 2017b, xix) that would offset the weaknesses evidenced in the US's interventions in Iraq and Afghanistan. As Work summarized:

> While the United States and our closest allies fought two lengthy wars over the past 13 years, the rest of the world and our potential adversaries were seeing how we operated. They looked at our advantages. They studied them. They analyzed them. They looked for weaknesses. And then they set about devising ways to counter our technological over-match. So across the board, we see rapid developments in nuclear weapons, modernization of nuclear weapons; new anti-ship, anti-air missiles; long-range strike missiles; counter-space capabilities; cyber capabilities; electronic warfare capabilities; special operations capabilities that are operated at the lower end. All are designed to counter our traditional military strengths and our preferred way of operating (Work 2015a).

Differently put, these wars and occupations "gave potential near-peer competitors a blueprint for how to counter the core capabilities that underpin U.S. military superiority. This, then, is the world to which the Third Offset Strategy is responding" (David Kilcullen, cited in Ellman, Samp and Coll 2017, 5). In response to this, the core purpose of the 3OS, as Luis Simón has argued, was "to articulate a conceptual and discursive framework that integrates existing initiatives and channels the financial and intellectual resources of America's strategic and technological epistemic communities around a coherent vision" (2016, 422).

Hagel was replaced by Ash Carter in February 2015, who had established the SCO in 2012 (Pellerin 2016). Under Carter's direction approximately $3.6 billion in research and development funding was dedicated to Third Offset Strategy pursuits in the fiscal year 2017 budget, amounting to the "first major public manifestation of the strategy" (Walton 2016, 7). Funding for the 3OS was allocated from the Future Years Defense Program (FYDP). In February 2016, the President's budget was released, which included $18 billion over the course of the FYDP for 3OS-related activities. In fiscal year 2017, $3.8 billion was allocated to the 3OS (Ellman et al. 2017, 11).

The 3OS was implemented by Work, whose vision for innovation was no less grand than that of Hagel and Carter. As Perla notes, Work saw "the similarity of our strategic and technical environment today to that of the interwar period; but the stakes are even higher and so too is the requirement for even more innovation" (2017, 85). Work argued that it was important to identify "leap-ahead" technologies (Lovelace 2017, ix) and to explore and develop new "operational and organizational constructs that give you an advantage and an offset against your adversaries who might outnumber you" (Work 2015b). He claimed that the US's global position was being challenged on an increasing number of fronts. In 2013, he stated, the government had to worry about three contingencies: North Korea, Iran, and China. By 2015, he continued, Russia and ISIL had been added to the list (Work 2015b). He echoed Hagel's claims that the emergent "great powers" had "been heavily investing in military modernization programs to blunt our military's technological edge, fielding advanced aircraft, submarines, and both longer range and more accurate missiles. They're also developing new anti-ship and air-to-air missiles, counter-space, cyber, electronic warfare, undersea, and air attack capabilities" (Hagel 2014b). As Work noted in 2016, this condition meant that these adversaries "can throw as much and as deep as we can," and "have a theater battle network as good as we currently have" (quoted in Perla 2017, 85).

The solution to this problem, then, was not to attempt to compete directly with adversaries tank for tank or ship for ship. Such an approach was unfeasible in a "fiscal environment of austerity. Budget pressure makes it impossible to increase size of forces or viably 'outspend' any potential adversary" (Christiansson 2018, 268). Instead, the aim was to concentrate funding on exploring creative offset solutions to deter aggression and cement the US's position by means of "a more innovative and agile defense enterprise" (Hagel 2014a, 1). This would be done across a number of key domains, including A2AD, guided munitions, undersea warfare, cyber and electronic warfare, human-machine teaming, and wargaming and concepts development (White 2017b, xi).

Particular note was made of autonomous learning systems, human-machine collaborative decision-making, assisted human operations, advanced manned-unmanned systems operations, and network-enabled autonomous weapons and high-speed projectiles. The idea was that advancement in these areas would "boost current conventional capabilities past the ability of near-peer competitors to counter them, as well as allow for development of new conventional capabilities that are beyond the current and projected ability of competitors to counter" (Ellman, Samp, and Coll 2017,

3). As this suggests, Work envisioned a future "in which autonomous deep learning systems (artificial intelligence), human-machine collaboration, human-assisted operations, combat teaming (robotics), and autonomous weapons will give U.S. forces a competitive advantage" (Norwood and Jensen 2016, 34).

Interestingly, the delivery of the 3OS deviated significantly from conventional defense development and procurement practices. Rather than relying on in-house agencies or familiar DoD contractors, Hagel and Work placed á strong emphasis on drawing upon the commercial sector for the required technological innovation. As Work noted, in the twentieth century these advances were generally "military capabilities that were brought along by military labs. But now with robotics, autonomous operating guidance and control systems, visualization, biotechnology, miniaturization, advanced computing and big data, and additive manufacturing like 3D printing, all those are being driven by the commercial sector" (Work 2015b). This commercial turn, as Magnus Christiansson notes, reflects a shift from state to private dominance in technological innovation over the last half century. He explains that while in the 1960s the US government's investment in research and development (R&D) was roughly twice the size of the private sector's, in 2016 the global private sector invested $1.9 trillion while the US government budget was $71.8 billion (Christiansson 2018, 268).

While in the past the commercial sector found civilian applications for military-developed technologies such as microchips, GPS, and the internet, today the commercial sector leads the way in the development of cutting-edge technologies like robotics, advanced computing, minimization, and 3D printing. As Carter noted in 2016, "When I began my career, most technology of consequence originated in America, and much of that was sponsored by the government, especially DoD. Today, not only is much more technology commercial, but the competition is global" (quoted in Christiansson 2018, 268). Somewhat paradoxically, then, this proliferation of civilian technology is both the cause of and solution to declining US dominance. As one report explained, "[T]he current erosion of the U.S. technological advantage derives not from adversaries' numerical superiority or superior volumes of investment, but from the increasing global and commercial nature of the innovation environment and the increasing applicability of commercial technologies to military operations" (Ellman, Samp and Coll 2017, 2). Key to solving this problem is, as Work stated, recognizing that "the vibrancy in the [Silicon] Valley is a national asset that if we don't tap into, we're going to fail" (Work 2015b).

It should not be forgotten, however, that the interweaving of commercial and military advanced and televisual technologies sectors began long before this. In addition to long-standing collaborations with the production of Hollywood movies and TV shows through the twentieth and twenty-first centuries, the military sought to leverage the immersive power of videogames from the 1990s. The establishment of the Institute of Creative Technologies (ICT) at the University of Southern California in 1999 was intended to do precisely this (Der Derian 2009; Stahl 2010; Kaempf 2019). As Roger Stahl explained in an interview with Sebastian Kaempf, "ICT brought together Hollywood filmmakers and scriptwriters along with military personnel and military theorists, toymakers, video game makers and brought them all to this common clearinghouse where they could exchange the ideas. You might say it is a kind of 'Rosetta stone' of the military-entertainment complex" (Kaempf 2019, 552). As ICT's director, Dr. Randall Hill, elaborated in another of Kaempf's interviews:

> When the DoD established this place and really the sponsorship came from the US Army, they were very interested in how they can improve training and education opportunities. What they saw from the entertainment industry was, number one, with video games they saw these very inexpensive, very interactive platforms that they'd like to be able to take advantage of. They said there's something there. People want to play these games, they get addicted to these games, they can't seem to stop playing them, and what is it about that interaction in that environment that draws them in and gets them so focused. (quoted in Kaempf 2019, 552–553)

Active for more than twenty years, at the time of writing the ICT runs a number of virtual reality training and rehabilitation programs, including BraveMind for the treatment of trauma and PTSD.

Perhaps the most successful military-commercial hybrid game, *America's Army*, was developed not at the ICT but rather at the Naval Postgraduate School. Launched in 2002 and active for a twenty-year period, the free-to-download first-person shooter aimed to recruit young gamers into the Army. As its development director, Michael Zyda, explains, "[T]he Army needed people who could actually play and operate video game consoles and the controllers that came with consoles as future weapons systems were being designed with such interfaces." He continues: "The Army was looking for young Americans between the ages of 11 and 14 to play this game. The Army knew that if a young American between those ages played this game, when they turned 18 they would be twice as likely to consider a career in the Army as young Americans who knew nothing about the Army" (Zyda 2022, 113–114). *America's Army* represents "a monumental step into twenty-first century military consumer culture" (Kaempf 2019) and is thought to be the most successful recruitment tool ever developed by the US military. One study concluded that 30 percent of Americans between the ages of sixteen and twenty-four had a more positive view of the Army from playing the game (Edery and Mollick 2009, 141). As this suggests, as part of the "relationship of mutual exploitation" characteristic of the commercial and military televisual industries, software and game developers can release military simulators and training tools for commercial sale while game environments and mechanics provide new insights into how warfighters might be recruited, trained, and managed (Kaempf 2019, 553)

Building on these developments, the 3OS was underpinned by a policy of "interactive networking between government representatives and commercial actors without traditional connections to defense industry" (Christiansson 2018, 263). As Hagel put it in 2014, the idea was to "reach out to hear from everyone—industry, trade groups, think tanks, and Congress— and finding ways to work together." DoD should, he continued, "seek proposals from the private sector . . . and from those firms and academic institutions outside DoD's traditional orbit" (quoted in Christiansson 2018, 269). Accordingly, four organizations were established to "tunnel through" the impenetrable barriers built around DoD (Work 2015b) and build links with the commercial sector.

The Advanced Capability and Deterrent Panel (ACDP), chaired by Work, meets quarterly and functions as an oversight panel dedicated to considering the long-term development of the future battlefield (Christiansson 2018, 269). The Long-Range Research and Development Plan (LRRDP) was initially chaired by Undersecretary of Defense for Acquisition, Technology, and Logistics Frank Kendall, best known for his Better Buying Power initiative, focusing on procurement reform. LRRDP was divided into five working groups composed of experts from DoD, industry, and academia. Its remit is the identification of breakthrough technologies that could be turned into DoD development projects in a five- to ten-year period (Christiansson 2018, 270).

The Defense Innovation Unit-Experimental (DIUx), which was established in Silicon Valley, functions as a liaison body between DoD and industry. Work explains: "DIUx is supposed to be a place where DOD could identify the pieces of potential future capabilities that are of interest. Moreover, DIUx can ask industry if there are any commercial products that it might bring to the table for consideration. DIUx is also a means by which a commercial entity could come to DOD and present a new technology it thinks might be useful, but needs the Department to help them think it through. The whole idea of DIUx . . . is designed to allow that connection to the commercial industry" (quoted in Eliason 2017, 9). It functions to recruit firms and personnel for short-term projects for the military (Christiansson 2018, 270).

Finally, the Defense Innovation Board (DIB), as the name suggests, is an advisory forum designed to bring commercial leaders into direct conversation with the secretary of defense. It has been chaired by former Google CEO Eric Schmidt, and includes members such as Amazon founder Jeff Bezos and LinkedIn chairman Reid Hoffman (Christiansson 2018, 270). According to one report, Carter identified three DIB recommendations he intended to implement: "First, making computer science a 'core competency' of DoD. Second, creating a DoD Chief Innovation Officer who will sponsor, promote, and identify innovation. Third, utilizing prize challenges, competitions, and tournaments to create investment incentives" (Ellman, Samp, and Coll 2017, 3).

As this suggests, some in the military claimed that this technological partnership would be easily realized because there is a "natural symbiosis between military and civilian innovation" (White 2017b, xiii). They argued that financial incentives would suffice to cement this cooperation; as one report claimed, "[T]he potential for enormous profits will drive industry to push the envelope" (Lovelace 2017, ix). Others, including Work, argued that DoD needed to "capture the commercial sector" (Work 2015a) by creating other incentives to show that working with DoD is good for business (Ellman, Samp, and Coll 2017, 7). These included competitions and prizes such as those piloted by DIUx on computer vision and machine learning (Ellman, Samp, and Coll 2017, 3–4). As Carter noted in 2016, "We have to build a relationship, we have to build a familiarity, we have to build trust" (quoted in Christiansson 2018, 271). Key firms involved in these activities in addition to those mentioned above include Booz Allen Hamilton, In-Q-Tel, Boeing, and Roboteam Inc. In 2015, Work stated that DoD projects had been established with 75 laboratories, 10 federally funded R&D centers, 13 university-affiliated research centers, and 319 multi-university research centers (Work 2015b).

As the above shows, the 3OS placed a strong emphasis on the development of advanced technology. Its architects also made clear, however, that technology alone would not resolve the decline in US advantage. Simón explains: "[W]hat matters is not so much technology itself, but rather its ability to generate concrete operational and strategic effects. New strategic and operational challenges call for innovative concepts of operations, which in turn require new capabilities as well as doctrinal and organizational reforms within the armed forces" (2016, 418). Douglas Lovelace similarly emphasizes the limitations of relying on technology in isolation: "[T]he acquisition of technology alone will not achieve the Third Offset Strategy. It must include enabling operational and organizational concepts that enable US forces to realize the offset advantage" (2016, 6). What is required in addition to technology, then, are new ways of thinking and operating and a fresh approach to decision-making. The architects of the 3OS identified wargaming as a key element of this endeavor.

The Wargaming Renaissance: Gaming the Human Dimension

In a widely circulated memorandum dated February 9, 2015, Work set out the place of wargaming in the 3OS and DII. It began:

> I am concerned that the [Defense] Department's ability to test concepts, capabilities, and plans using simulations and other techniques—otherwise known as wargaming—has atrophied. To most effectively pursue an innovative third offset strategy, avoid operational and technological surprise, and make the best use of our limited resources, we need to reinvigorate, institutionalize, and systematize wargaming across the Department. Reinvigorated wargaming across the defense enterprise fits with the Defense Innovation Initiative, which aims to bolster the credibility of US security guarantees at home and abroad through innovative and agile thinking and actions. (2015c, 1)

Here and in a number of articles, speeches, and interviews in 2015, Work expanded upon Hagel's statement the previous year that a "reinvigorated wargaming effort will develop and test alternative ways of achieving our strategic objectives and help us think more clearly about the future security environment" (Hagel 2014a, 2). A total of $500 million was allocated for expanding wargaming and operational concept tests and demonstrations from the FYDP budget (Mehta 2016).

Wargaming's role as a source of doctrinal innovation, Work argued, should be restored in the new security environment (2015c, 2). Specifically, as one article suggested, the DoD "should pursue a joint wargaming initiative designed to generate new concepts around the proposed offset technologies. Wargames serve as a time-tested mechanism for generating new ideas about warfare" (Norwood and Jensen 2016, 35). In keeping with the 3OS's agenda of innovation, the role of wargames was to devise and experiment with novel applications for emergent technologies and the US's broader operational approaches. In a security environment characterized by widespread ambiguity and complexity, wargaming would be a key driver of conceptual innovation. In a coauthored article with Paul Selva, then vice chairman of the Joint Chiefs of Staff, Work laid out the central applications of DoD wargaming:

> Wargames provide opportunities to test new ideas and explore the art of the possible. They help us imagine alternative ways of operating and envision new capabilities that might make a difference on future battlefields. When creatively and rigorously applied, wargames help us to think through and begin to resolve complex military challenges, foster the testing of new strategic and operational concepts, stimulate debate, and inform investments in new capabilities. Wargames help strip down a strategic, operational, or tactical problem and reduce its complexity in order to identify the few, important factors that constrain us or an opponent. They provide structured, measured, rigorous—but intellectually liberating—environments to help us explore what works (winning) and what doesn't (losing) across all dimensions of warfighting. They permit hypotheses to be challenged and theories to be tested during either adjudicated moves or free play settings, thereby allowing current and future leaders to expand the boundaries of warfare theory. And they provide players with the opportunity to make critical mistakes and learn from them—and to perhaps reveal breakthrough strategies and tactics when doing so. (Work and Selva 2015)

With this restored faith in the innovative capacities of wargaming, its resurgence began.

In his February memo, Work set out his vision for three time horizons for the new DoD-wide wargaming initiative. Led by the Combatant Commands and Services, near-term wargaming (up to five years into the future) would focus on the execution and improvement of current operational plans, using workshops, red-teaming, tabletop exercises, and modeling and simulation for planning, experiments, and prototype development. Midterm wargaming (five to fifteen years), led by the Joint Staff, would be dedicated to the development of new capabilities and operational/organizational concepts by incorporating innovative approaches and technologies into force planning. Using workshops, seminar-style wargames, exercises, and modeling and simulation, future scenarios would be gamed to explore future US and adversary orders of battle and promote operational innovation. Long-term gaming (beyond fifteen years) was to assess the operational impacts of technology, explore future challenges, and craft long-term competitive strategies. The Office of Net Assessment would oversee this future-focused initiative (Work 2015c, 1–2).

Having been periodically embraced and rejected over the course of the twentieth century, wargaming has been enjoying renewed interest since the launch of the 3OS and DII in 2014 (Appleget et al. 2016, 18; Curry 2016, 33; Norwood and Jensen 2016, 35–36), and the committed wargaming CoP has been well placed to capitalize on this attention over the past decade. Speaking at the first of three Military Operations Research Society (MORS) Special Meetings on Wargaming, Work called upon the CoP to seize the opportunity afforded by the 3OS and demonstrate the value of the wargaming process for the DoD and the nation (Pournelle ed. 2017, 7). The experience of the CoP could be used to "revolutionize" DoD's approach to gaming (Davis 2017, 16) and avoid a return to disfavor resulting from incorrect uses of wargaming by those bandwagoning on its resurgence (Perla 2017, 87–88). The core tasks of the CoP were to demonstrate that wargaming is a "key cylinder of the Department of Defense's innovative engine" (Gorak 2016, 4) and to integrate it into larger analytic processes (Pournelle ed. 2017, 5).

To that end, several organizations and working groups were established. The Defense Wargaming Alignment Group (DWAG) was set up to drive innovation. Dubbed a "group of the willing" (Deaton and Stetson 2018, 14), the DWAG initially met fortnightly. Its members include representatives from "COCOMs, Services, NGB, JS-J7, JS-J4, OSD-AT&L, OSD-CAPE, OSD-Policy, Office of Net Assessment, and the Under Secretary of Defense for Intelligence" (Gorak 2016, 6), and it produced a monthly report on wargaming activities and development in and around DoD. It was furnished with a $10 million incentive fund to support wargaming activities; by 2017 it had funded fifty-eight games (Gorak 2016, 6; Deaton and Stetson 2018, 14). In addition, a wargaming repository was established in the Cost Assessment and Program Evaluation (CAPE) group housed in the Office of the Secretary of Defense (OSD) to oversee and catalogue the proliferation of wargaming activities. The repository is "a centralized hub for sharing of information as well as identifying number of wargames conducted (including upcoming games), capabilities, capacity, cost, and insights gained." It is updated monthly, and by 2016 it had accumulated over 550 wargames, 260 organizations, and 212 support tools (Gorak 2016, 5).

At the same time, handbooks and doctrinal documents focusing on wargaming proliferated. In 2015 the Army War College published the *Strategic Wargaming Series Handbook* detailing its activities and best practice guidance, and the *Applied Critical Thinking Handbook* was released by TRADOC in association with the University of Foreign Military and Cultural Studies. In 2017, Joint Publication 5.0, *Joint Planning*, situated course-of-action wargaming as the fourth of seven steps of its Joint Planning Process (JPP). As this suggests, wargaming activities have become more widespread and more visible in recent years in military schoolhouses and research institutions, including the Naval Postgraduate School (Appleget et al. 2016), the Marine Corps University (Norwood and Jensen 2016, 36), the Air Force Research Laboratory (Bestard 2016), and the Center for Army Analysis (Pournelle ed. 2017, 21). In parallel, civilian research centers were developing wargaming activities, often sponsored by DoD, such as RAND's Center for Wargaming. As these developments suggest, wargaming has been identified as a key means by which challenges faced by DoD could be mitigated. The remainder of this chapter explores the wargaming CoP's core missions in offsetting uncertainty and complexity using critical thinking with a view to improving decision-making skills under pressure.

Uncertainty and Complexity

Underpinning the 3OS and DII was a concern with the complexities and uncertainties that characterize the twenty-first-century security environment. As Hagel commented in 2014, "[U]ncertainty is the only certainly in an interconnected world of seven billion people" (Hagel 2014b). Other commentators have noted that DoD faces a context beset by "yawning unpredictability" (Sabin 2014, 55) and "complexity and structural uncertainty"

(Wong 2016, 532). In Christiansson's view, the "'runaway world' of reflexive modernity is one way of contextualizing this tendency for rationality to break down. . . . It emphasizes the pace, scope, and profoundness of change compared with previous historical periods. Not only is society becoming increasingly complex, the speed of increased complexity increases" (Christiansson 2018, 274). The result, as one report puts it, is a strategic environment that is volatile, uncertain, complex, and ambiguous. Increased interconnectedness, it continues, will cause news and events to propagate faster, and the resultant excess of information will likely compromise decision-making and prediction capabilities (Boyd and Kimball 2017, 3). As Der Derian summarizes, when concrete adversaries are wanting, uncertainty has come to function as a virtual enemy: "'We don't do countries' . . . In short, they now 'do' uncertainty" (2009, 211–216).

Wargames, it is argued, can be used to mitigate this complexity and uncertainty. Work explains:

> Military-relevant systems and technologies are changing quickly and new tactical and operational challenges are intensifying and proliferating, all during a period of fiscal pressure. During similar periods of technological and geostrategic flux, wargaming proved to be a useful tool both for improving our understanding of complex, uncertain environments and the changing character of warfare. When done right, wargames spur innovation and provide a mechanism for addressing emerging challenges, exploiting new technologies, and shaping the future security environment. They can potentially make the difference between wise and unwise investment trajectories and make our forces more successful in future conflicts. (2015c, 1)

When practitioners are faced with an incomprehensibly complicated series of issues, pathways, and variables, wargames, it is argued, allow them to manage the complexity and chaos of lived experience by transposing them into ludic systems and procedures so as to experiment with possible courses of action (Harrigan and Kirschenbaum 2016, xvii). Differently put, at its best wargaming reflects the "almost infinite complexities of warfare within a model that is simple enough to be played" (Sabin 2014, 68). It has the capacity, its proponents claim, to "apprehend" complexities (Train and Ruhnke 2016, 528). Importantly, in contrast to conventional analytical methods that seek to reduce complexity to its constitutive elements, wargaming explores complexity in all its complexity. It does this by constructing models into which the player can climb in order to explore and experiment to see what the effects of various courses might be (Train and Ruhnke 2016, 526). Thus, the CoP argues, the novel contribution wargaming can make in an era of seemingly limitless complexity is to build ludic environments in which analysts can play with as many possible scenarios as desired. As Hanley puts it, "[G]aming historically has been useful in exposing infeasible, inadequate, unacceptable, or incomplete courses of action when faced with an intel- ligent adversary; in exposing factors that will govern successful strategies; in enriching an appreciation of logical adversary courses of action; and in exposing knowledge required for better planning and analysis" (2018, 59).

As this process of "climbing inside" complex systems suggests, the key in- tervention made by wargaming is in the human dimension. This is because, as one report claims, wargames "provide a unique space for exploring the human element in complex scenarios" (Deaton and Stetson 2018, 13). Unlike quantitative methods such as operational research and systems analysis, wargaming addresses the messy business of human thinking and decision- making. This is vital, as Levis and Elder note, because "[c]urrent military operations need, and future operations will demand, the capability to un- derstand the human terrain and the various dimensions of human behavior within it" (2016, 475). During and since the invasions and occupations of the post-9/11 period, military strategists and planners have been increasingly focused on non-kinetic areas such as the political, economic, cultural, and human domains as key elements of operational success. These conflicts made it clear that "[a]ctions taken by all agents, together with beliefs, perceptions, intentions, and actions of all the people involved in an area of operations in- teract to affect the outcome" (Levis and Elder 2016, 475).

No less than the contemporary security environment, the human domain is "infinitely complex" because it "pushes back, evolves, and changes rapidly and unpredictably. We currently lack sufficient analytical power to reliably understand functions in the human domain in the same way we can in the biological or engineering domains" (TRADOC 2015, 35). While the human domain is irredeemably unruly, the promise of wargames in this context is to teach personnel to cope with and manage complexity in order to (re)gain an advantage. As Perla explains, wargaming enables decision-makers to "learn about how to deal with an uncertain and unpredictable future; to learn about how to understand its complexities; and to learn about how to make good decisions today and tomorrow in spite of those complexities, uncertainties, and unpredictability" (2016, 159). Some wargame advocates have described this learning process as developing a "capacity for intuition" or a "feel" for how to respond in a particular situation (Losh 2016, 359). The ultimate goal is to use wargaming to "deepen our understanding of patterns in organizational decision-making" (Deaton and Stetson 2018, 19). In order to address these questions of human decision-making, the military has turned to the idea of "critical thinking."

Critical Thinking

Since the launch of the 3OS and DII, the concept of critical thinking has become increasingly visible across the DoD. Work drew attention to this issue from the outset, emphasizing the need for "innovative and agile thinking" (Work 2015c, 1), while TRADOC published a 250-page *Applied Critical Thinking Handbook*, produced on the basis of a program taught at the University of Foreign and Cultural Studies. Focusing on "red-teaming," the *Handbook* states as its goal the development of a "disposition of curiosity" and "self-awareness" in the service of avoiding the predictable failures that people and organizations unwittingly court as a result of their "mindsets, biases and experiences, which are formed in large part by their own culture and context" (TRADOC 2015, 1). It recommends learning to think "meta-cognitively" and promises to teach personnel how humans think and how culture shapes thought in order to "facilitate strategic and operational decision making which is informed by cultural empathy" (TRADOC 2015, 6). In so doing, students will break away from "cognitive auto-pilot" and "unreflective dependence upon our intuition" (TRADOC 2015, 48).

By promoting critical thinking, then, wargames can bring biases and errors to light. Cultural wargames, for example, work "by deliberately placing participants in the position of an unfamiliar culture, with rules and procedures and objectives that reflect that culture specifically[,] and then expos[ing] them to a scenario that places strain on their assumptions and challenges them to respond *culturally* to the crisis" (Wallman 2016, 545). This, in turn, allows them to develop "an enhanced enemy mindset" (Pournelle and Deaton eds. 2018, 9). Importantly, and unlike forms of critical thinking and reflexivity promoted in (some) civilian scholarly and pedagogical practice, this exploration of bias and assumption is explicitly tied to military ends; the program aims to improve "cultural understanding with

the goal of enhancing the chances of successful outcomes in military planning . . . It is only meaningful when regarded as part of a larger body of
thought (e.g., strategy, design, campaign planning)" (TRADOC 2015, 38). In
a context characterized by diversity and ambiguity, then, the critical thinking
provided by wargaming can help "safeguard against individual and organizational tendencies toward biases, errors in cognition, and groupthink. . . . Our
goal is to be better prepared and less surprised in dealing with complexity"
(TRADOC 2015, 1).[20] As will be explored in detail in Chapter 4 and beyond,
however, the understanding of critical thinking used here is very different
to—indeed in some ways sits in opposition to—the critical reflexivity I advocate in this book.

Futurity

From the outset, Work noted that the 3OS had a focus on the future. His
memo stipulated that wargaming across different time horizons would
bring together "teams of defense professionals to think critically about potential future challenges" (Work 2015c, 2). Identifying a key difference with
the first and second offsets, he elaborated elsewhere: "[I]t's going to have a
much more trying temporal component. . . . So, we'll be looking for promising technologies that we can do in what we call the FYDP, the future
years defense program, generally about five years out. We'll identify long-
range advances that we can pull up and hopefully field in the '20s, and then
we'll plant the seeds for R&D, which will give us an advantage for the '30s"
(2015a). Wargames' capacity to model the future has long been a topic of debate in both the civilian and professional CoPs; perhaps the most well-known
statement on the topic is Dunnigan's claim that a wargame is a "paper time

[20] This framing of "critical thinking" is different in its stated aims from that used in critical civilian
academia. While TRADOC emphasizes that these reflexive explorations are in the service of greater
operational effectiveness, civilian academia aims to encourage such critical engagement with issues
and theories in order to expose and problematize latent hegemonic power relations. Of concern for
the latter group here is that the terms used to frame these activities are disquietingly similar to their
own approaches to research and pedagogy. TRADOC's *Handbook* advocates the deconstruction of
arguments and "challenge[s] students to examine things they hold sacrosanct. We expose them to
the ethnocentrism of their own thinking, their overreliance on method, their tendency to default to
Western/Aristotelian logic, their lack of appreciation for the frames that subconsciously capture their
thinking" (TRADOC 2015, 5). One would not be surprised to see these words in the opening pages
of a critically oriented module guide or research grant application. This perhaps signals an important instance of the appropriation and enclosure of critical methods and practices in the service of
state power.

machine" (cited in Sabin 2014, 3). Sabin explains that while hobby games have tended to be focused on the past, modeling and reconstructing historical battles, the professional community is more interested in current and future conflicts in order to anticipate and prepare for challenges to come (Sabin 2014, 36). This interest has been crucial to the wargaming renaissance.

Many key figures in the wargaming community are adamant that wargaming cannot predict the future. Perla, for example, has stated that "[i]t is quite impossible, in the hobby world or the professional world, to build a wargame or a combat model that is *certain* to reflect accurately the reality of future combat for the simple reason that we do not *know* what that reality will be" (1990, 241; emphasis in original). Ewell similarly notes that "[g]ames are really good with showing possible outcomes and really bad at predicting outcomes" (quoted in Deaton and Stetson 2018, 16), while John Hanley observes that "one play of a game can no more predict a specific outcome any more than one play of a baseball game can predict the score and player injuries of a following game" (2018, 60). Games cannot be predictive because they apprehend and model elements not of an "objective" present or future reality but rather of the designer's subjective perception of it. In Perla's words, "The only realizable goal for a model of future warfare is to reflect, in the most complete and coherent way possible, the analysts' (or the analytical community's) beliefs and understanding of the key elements of that combat" (Perla 1990, 241). Treating these as predictive can, and has, led to significant errors in the past and contributed to wargaming's previous falls from grace in the DoD.

In spite of this, however, there remains an interest in the possibility of using wargames to anticipate events to come. Thomas Allen has described this as the "quest for the simulation that will predict the future." He explains: "Military modelers know, as an article of faith, that the future cannot be predicted. And yet, without saying it aloud, many do want to discover come way to simulate the future," an aim that is sometimes implicitly encouraged by superiors (Allen 1989, 96). Many designers and practitioners have begun to claim for gaming a specific type of predictive potential. Some point to the prophetic character of games played about twentieth-century conflicts. Hanley, for example, notes the "predictive value" of gaming at the Naval War College that anticipated tactics and predicted the outcome of the Russo-Japanese War, and the successful operational gaming of Russia and Germany in World Wars I and II. These gaming activities, he explains, are "legendary for anticipating the character of future campaigns, developing operational schemes, and promoting the development of technology and systems of conduct campaigns" (Hanley 2018, 61). Allen similarly describes the "prophetic" character of US gaming during the Vietnam War in his comparison of game and real-world events (Allen 1989). These "chilling glances into future realities" (Allen 1989, 5) are of significant appeal to the DoD in the 3OS era.

Wargaming, it is claimed, is useful for exploring why future conflicts might turn out in particular ways and for mapping these possible paths in more detail than could be accomplished simply by thinking about or discussing them. Its predictive capability lies not in determining which outcome or course of action will come to pass but rather in exploring a range of alternatives so as to prepare for a series of possibilities. Members of the wargaming CoP emphasize that it is potential, possible, or probable futures that wargaming can illuminate, rather than definitive trajectories or outcomes. As Perla explains:

> By exercising, testing, and modifying [a] model, analysts and wargamers can explore the implications, not of some unknowable future reality, but of our current, restricted, and uncertain view of what that reality might be like. We can do no better than to try to identify the hidden interconnections and consistencies of our current thinking as objectively as possible. But such a goal, as limited as it may appear to those who seek crystal balls in computer code, is not only a worthy one but essential as well. (Perla 1990, 241)

In other words, wargaming is useful in exploring contingent rather than concrete futures. It is this that explains its apparently prophetic legacy in twentieth-century conflicts. Wargames are helpful, it is argued, in spite of their limitations, biases, and oversights. As Yuna Huh Wong argues, it is not a matter of *if* a game is wrong, in the sense of being subjective, selective, and an imperfect representation of reality, but rather *how* wrong it is. Games can still be useful despite their inaccuracies and flaws (Wong 2016, 535–536). Wargaming can thus be used as a "supplement to simple intuition as a means of deciding what forces to develop and what strategies to adopt should war come" (Sabin 2014, 57). As Caffrey summarizes: "Wargames do not predict the future—wargames don't even forecast a *potential* future—but they do produce outcomes that may (or may not) suggest plausible futures," and have a record of corresponding with future events, "occasionally with 'eerie' precision" (Caffrey 2019, 279–280).

With these caveats in mind, then, the wargaming CoP has made significant headway within DoD through the future-oriented potential of their enterprise. By exploring a range of possible trajectories, wargames have reestablished their place in the analysis community because they "are good for exploring situations that are too complicated to predict" (Ewell quoted in Deaton and Stetson 2018, 16). They can be used as a crystal ball to the extent that they offer "advance insights into how future engagements might develop given a certain set of initial conditions," functioning like weather forecasts (Sabin 2014, 63). While concrete predictions tend to be wrong, gaming can tell you "what your problems are going to be" (Allen 1989, 154). As this suggests, the more DoD focuses on the future as a key terrain of the 3OS, the greater the role for wargaming. As Joint Publication 5.0 notes, "Anticipation is key to effective planning. . . . JFC [joint force commanders] may avoid surprise . . . by thoroughly and continuously wargaming to identify probable adversary reactions to joint force actions" (Joint Publication 5.0 2017, IV-34). White points out that as structural complexity and uncertainty progresses, "[p]redicting will be more important than understanding" (2017a, 24). The experience generated by these games can, then, help acclimate personnel to operating in conditions of ambiguity because they "prepare decision makers to cope with the unexpected" (Sabin 2014, 56). To that extent, "games can get closer to predicting how people will act and react to circumstances far better than other techniques" (Perla 2018, 76). This interest in mapping actions and reactions is key to wargaming's focus on human decision-making.

Decision-making

The central means by which wargaming intervenes in the human dimension is through mapping and cultivating particular kinds of decision-making practices. Indeed, a focus on decision-making is the central distinguishing feature of wargaming, setting it apart from other kinds of models and simulations that do not have a "human in the loop." In Perla's words, "[A] wargame is an exercise in human interaction, and the interplay of human decisions and the simulated outcomes of those decisions" (1990, 164). Wargames "are about people making decisions and communicating them in the context of competition or conflict, usually with other people—all the while plagued by uncertainty and complexity. Through these processes, the players live a shared experience and learn from it" (Perla 2016, 173). The

Naval War College's *War Gamers' Handbook* similarly defines wargaming as "a tool for exploring decision-making possibilities in an environment with incomplete and imperfect information" (Naval War College 2015, 3).

According to its advocates, wargaming works by placing players in a situation in which they are compelled to make decisions (Perla 1990, 203). By slotting participants into a scenario that calls for urgent action, they argue, gaming provides a safe-to-fail space within which to gain decision-making experience. As Perla has noted, games work "not by asking people to predict how they would react, but by forcing them actually to react, even if that action is within the context of the simulacrum of reality that is the game" (2018, 77). Ghamari-Tabrizi describes games that employ a "model of learning under stress," in which people "learn only with pain and travail." In this framework, she continues, pressure and tension were identified as key drivers of learning (Ghamari-Tabrizi 2000, 186).

A wargame is, in effect, "a conflict simulation run on the human brain rather than a computer" (Perla 2018, 76–77). The decisions taken in-game are thus a proxy for establishing what steps may need to be taken in a real conflict. As the Army War College's *Strategic Wargaming Series Handbook* explains, "[P]layers often discover the need to make unanticipated decisions in order for the game to progress. The rationale associated with decisions reached in the 'game-world' may illuminate the need for 'real-world' decisions while also informing the decision itself" (Army War College 2015, 2).

The aim, then, is to generate real experience in a synthetic environment, to become more proficient in making decisions under pressure and managing the consequences of those decisions. This involves an "active and absorbing involvement in the challenge of making 'life and death' decisions" (Perla 1990, 8), providing a "dress rehearsal" for the crises in which "participants feel time and events tightening on them," which is important because in a game, "as in a crisis, snap judgments—even hunches—drive decisions" (Allen 1989, 238). What wargaming accomplishes, then, is the development of an intuition on the basis of which decisions can be made. This is necessary because in the foreseeable future,

> [d]ecision events will increase in frequency and speed. The "observe, orient, decide, and act" (OODA) loop decision cycle—must be compressed in the short-term to "recognize, decide, act" (RDA). Observation and orientation as discrete actions will be a luxury that the future battlefield will not allow. Superiority will be predicated on further evolving the decision cycle to

"predict, decide, and act" (PDA)—with the goal of reducing (or ultimately eliminating) the time to decide—or "predict and act" (PA)—through automation, AI, and IA. (White 2017a, 23–24).

As this suggests, the aim of wargaming is to develop specific cognitive and affective reactions. As such, it intervenes squarely in the human dimension. As one report put it, "Beyond fielding a force that simply competes in the physical domains, the Army of 2035 and beyond must be designed to dominate and achieve overmatch in the cognitive domain; for the greatest potential for superiority or supremacy lies here" (White 2017a, 25). What is necessary to make progress in this dimension, it is claimed, is to understand the conscious and unconscious elements of decision-making processes rehearsed and developed through wargaming. The ultimate goal of these explorations of decision-making seems to be to use individual players in-game as nodes that collectively shed light on organizational or institutional decision-making. While it is not possible to determine from the actions of a single player in a game what the decisions taken in a real-world conflict would be, it is, it seems, possible to aggregate decision-making data collected in a game to gain a viable picture of real-world group decision-making. As noted above, the aim is to "use game results to build models that deepen our understanding of patterns in organizational decision-making" (Deaton and Steson 2018, 19). These people-producing properties will be explored in detail in Chapters 5 and 6.

Methodological Divergences: Art Versus Science

These discussions raise central questions about the epistemological basis and proper applications of wargaming. Those who reject the notion that wargaming is predictive subscribe broadly to the idea that it is an art, or more properly a craft, more akin to history or even visual and written art forms than to science. As Ghamari-Tabrizi notes, in this framework, designing a game "can be understood as equivalent to drafting a concrete world-picture . . . Likewise, apprehending the tangle of influence and disruption wrought by a host of incompatible variables, tendencies and interest could approximate an aesthetic appreciation of the particular intelligibility of a novel, a painting, a drama" (Ghamari-Tabrizi 2000, 189). Those who are keen to claim for wargaming a predictive capacity, in contrast, tend to view it as a science in the harder sense, and espouse a commitment to the promises of quantitative research methods to yield objective results. This account is complicated, as noted above, by the fact that several members of the wargaming CoP who subscribe to the idea that it is an art rather than a science nevertheless claim for it a predictive capacity. By reframing what it means to predict under conditions of uncertainty and complexity, wargamers have claimed for their enterprise a contingent form of anticipation that allows the exploration of a range of possible courses of action while remaining clear that it cannot predict which will come about.

This debate is further complicated by the issue that the quantitative methods associated with OR and other elements of conventional military analysis have never themselves been convincing in their claims to predict the future. Over the last several decades, post-positivist challenges—poststructural, feminist, Marxian, de/postcolonial—across the social sciences have convincingly demonstrated the extent to which positivist research methods are rarely successful in their predictive endeavors. Perhaps counterintuitively, many in the wargaming community have mounted a similar challenge to positivistic operations research, the dominant approach in DoD analysis. Davis, for example, notes that "even quantitative models are often loaded with subjective guestimates" (Davis 2017, 15). Similarly, Perla argues:

> [T]here is hidden subjectivity even in physical science. That subjectivity manifests itself in the assumptions underlying the model (usually mathematical) the scientist constructs to represent the phenomenon, as well as in the means the scientist uses to define, collect and interpret physical data. This subjectivity tends to be swept under the rug when analysts present their results by emphasizing the mathematical rigor of the calculations themselves rather than the assumptions that lay behind them. (2018, 75)

Paradoxically, then, it is precisely in wargaming's rejection of the quantitative methods that frequently but erroneously claim to have predictive capacities that its novel potential for DoD analysis lies. The architects of the 3OS recognized that models that contain rather than reduce structural uncertainties are the most promising for forecasting uncertain but possible futures.

As this suggests, a division or "schism" (Davis 2017, 13) exists within the DoD analysis community regarding whether or not wargaming should be considered a subset of modeling. This debate cuts to the heart of the epistemological and methodological issues raised by the recent renaissance in wargaming. The conventional account is that the quantitative approaches associated with OR, modeling, and simulation are objective, while wargaming's qualitative status limits it to subjective claims By bringing wargaming closer to the quantitative-objective side of the epistemological continuum, it has been suggested, wargaming can be improved: "[T]he integration of S&T [science and technology] skillsets to facilitate data exploitation (e.g., operations research, science and engineering) . . . will not only increase the quality of wargames and their products, but will facilitate data-driven exploration of military utility for new and integrated S&T concepts" (Bestard 2016, 13). Many in the wargaming CoP are, however, less convinced about such an integration,[21] and argue, in ways that perhaps surprisingly chime with post-positivist critiques of positivist social science in the civilian academy, that quantitative methods do not yield objective results.

Speaking at the 2016 MORS Special Meeting on Wargaming, Davis claimed that Work's call to reinvigorate wargaming was "the result of senior officials not being satisfied with what was coming from the 'analysis community' or, more specifically, the 'modeling community.'" Work's memo, he continued, "was directed specifically toward the goal of innovation" and was driven by "dissatisfaction with what was being delivered" (Davis 2017, 13). The dissatisfaction in question was directed at the limitations of the results produced by quantitative analysis, which had dominated the DoD since the mid-twentieth century. Just as in civilian academia, the 1950s saw a methodological shift toward quantitative methods that prized mathematical, statistical, and "scientific" approaches. The result of this in the defense analysis community was the rise of operations research, a method that claimed to be a science rather than an art (Allen 1989, 124). As Davis explains, in this period defense modeling and systems analysis "emphasized being scientific, rigorous, quantitative, and tied to mathematics. This was to be an antidote for hand-waving subjective assertions. That desire translated into an emphasis on 'closed' models with no human interactions, which allowed reproducibility." Accompanying this shift, he continues, came a devaluation of methods perceived as less scientific and objective. Quantitative analysts became "disdainful of such other forms of modeling as the history-based formula models

---

[21] Indeed, even those who believe the methods to be compatible in the course of a particular research project still maintain they function according to different epistemological and methodological assumptions (Davis and Bracken 2022).

of Trevor Dupuy and the commercial board games of Jim Dunnigan and Mark Herman. These alternative approaches [were] seen as somehow 'lesser,' because they were allegedly less rigorous and scientific" (Davis 2017, 14). "Attacks" of this kind have persisted to the present day (Perla 2018, 78).

The OR approach advocated a rationalist framework in which "the most rational possible decisions" would be programmed into computers, "which would quickly calculate the outcomes of many such decisions" (Perla 1990, 109). Humans, with their unruly and unpredictable tendencies, were to be kept "out of the loop" so as to ensure these maximally rational inputs and outputs. This led to a situation in which there was more math than common sense (Dunnigan 2016, xxxiv). As Hanley explains, in the late 1960s and early 1970s "military modelers concentrated on modeling combat and logistical processes as though they were physics problems. As computer speeds increased exponentially with Moore's Law, these models were aggregated into ever more complicated campaign simulations, losing sight of the Operation Research Group's cautions and methods for estimating confidence factors" (Hanley 2018, 65). Models thus took humans entirely out of the equation, rejecting a focus on actual decision-making processes in favor of ideal ones.

As this suggests, this approach is limited in a series of significant ways and has been challenged by the wargaming CoP in ways that mirror post-positivist challenges issued to positivist orthodoxies by critical traditions in the social sciences and humanities. The wargaming CoP argues that the results produced by various models created by different analysts lead to a wide range of conclusions that themselves were not verifiable or refutable (Allen 1989, 245). Quantitative methods, many in the wargaming CoP argue, are not effective in conditions of uncertainty; some aspects of conflict are not amenable to rationalization because, as Jon Peterson puts it, "they reflect the unfathomable depths of interpersonal relationships" (2016, 15). Thus, Tetsuya Nakaruma concludes, despite the hubris of quantitative social science, its fruits prove limited and the gap between simulation and "truth" persists (2016, 43).

Conclusion

This chapter has set out the origins and context of the twenty-first-century wargaming renaissance, beginning by reconstructing a hitherto neglected history of the role and function of games in the field of international relations beginning in the mid-twentieth century. It showed that the recent resurgence of interest in gaming in IR corresponds to a wargaming resurgence in the defense establishment since 2014, inaugurated by DoD-wide memos from Chuck Hagel and Bob Work that called for a reinvigorated wargaming effort in collaboration with the commercial sector across the services. Setting out their claims that wargames offer benefits across managing uncertainty and complexity, promoting critical thinking, and offering insights into the future. The chapter argued that the wargaming renaissance has precipitated a profound challenge to the prevailing methods used in DoD analysis. As one report states, "DoD modeling has been too dominated by a narrow approach. The analytic community should take this seriously and reform, as suggested here. This will include incorporating human gaming in the larger activity of modeling, simulation, and analysis, and also using modeling to inform the design and execution of human gaming" (Davis 2017, 16).

In an era of complexity, models that rely on mathematics and try to make predictions are limited by their inability to cope with uncertainties in inputs and the effects of such uncertainties on outputs (Perla 1990, 238). As Perla more recently explained, wargaming does not advocate

> the reductionist disassembling of problems into their component and quantitative parts. Instead, it is about the holistic integration of problems and the human beings who have to confront and act to overcome them. . . . Here is where most of the classic forms of modeling and simulation fall down. They cannot forecast outcomes that are already embedded in the underlying mathematical constructs of the model or simulation. . . . They do not, in fact, generate new knowledge. . . . Wargaming is a far better tool for going beyond old knowledge and exploring unforeseen consequences and . . . illuminat[ing] dark corners of future possibilities. (Perla 2016, 178)

What is required, then, according to the wargaming CoP, is a fresh approach that explores, rather than avoids or ignores, the complexity, uncertainty, and unpredictability of the contemporary security environment. The key area of study in the new security environment is, they claim, that of human decision-making. What matters is not the results of games framed quantitively in terms of wins/losses/hits and so forth, but rather the mapping of decisions taken and paths not taken. The player, then, is the object of study, standing in for whoever else might be making equivalent decisions in a "real-world" conflict. Importantly, wargaming works as a process of teaching players how to make decisions and, in some cases, what decisions to make: "Wargaming across different time horizons will also serve a crucial educational function by bringing together teams of defense professionals to think critically about potential future challenges" (Work 2015c, 2).

With Chapters 1 and 2 having established the conceptual and historical fundamentals of the wargaming renaissance, the following two chapters develop a theorization of play aimed at understanding how military wargaming works and how their seemingly closed internal systems might be cracked open.

3

A Genealogy of Play

The Presocratics to the Moderns

Introduction: Theorizing Play

Having laid the empirical foundations of the US military wargaming renaissance in Chapters 1 and 2, the following two chapters turn to the topic of play. Far from a curiosity or simple downtime activity, I argue that if we are to understand how wargames work, and how their closed systems might be pried open, we need to explore the politics and possibilities of play. While the study of games has proliferated in the digital era, accompanying explorations of play remain rare. As Seth Giddings explains: "Play as an aspect of culture, popular media or mode of everyday lived experience is undertheorized in media studies, cultural studies in particular[,] and the humanities and social sciences in general" (2016, 8). This neglect is not accidental. Rather, it reflects—and perpetuates—what Mechthild Nagel calls a "malediction of play" in Western philosophy (2002).

Play has been marginalized across our scholarly traditions because it is viewed as singularly unserious. It is assumed to belong to the realms of childhood and the animal kingdom; to become an adult is, it is frequently assumed, to cease the silly business of play. While in our formative years, so the story goes, we indulge in play, make-believe, and fantasy, it is a mark of maturity to put away childish things and get real. In this reading, play is frivolous and purposeless. Sometimes, in a romantic vein, we lament our loss of play, idealizing the purity and freedom of the child at play. But, for better or worse, to be taken seriously a grown person must keep their distance from the silliness of play. Indeed, as noted in the Introduction, some experience play as "terrifying" and "randomly destructive," as when cats play with mice or ancient gods with humans, and consequently prefer the security and order of games (Graeber 2015, 192–193). For these combined reasons, play has been both banished and domesticated across our scholarly traditions.

Politics of Play. Aggie Hirst, Oxford University Press. © Oxford University Press 2024.
DOI: 10.1093/oso/9780197629192.003.0004

It is, however, crucial to explore the politics of play if the power rela-tions and people-producing properties at work in gaming are to be properly interrogated. Indeed, as James S. Hans suggests, as compared to games, "play is by far the broader and more important concept" (1981, vi). This is because "play precedes game" (Wark 2007, 181). Roger Caillois elaborates: play is "a primary power of improvisation and joy, which I call *paidia* . . . a word cov-ering the spontaneous manifestations of the play instinct" (2001, 27–28). Play, as *paidia*, should thus be read as an impulse, capacity, or spirit. In con-trast, the game, referred to by Caillois as *ludus*, is a system or structure that consists of "conventions, techniques, and utensils" (2001, 29) animated or operationalized by *paidia*. This means that without play, there is no gaming. It also means that the game apprehends or arrests play through the enforce-ment of its rules: "[G]ames explicitly limit and channel the intrinsically pleasurable exploration characteristic of play" (Murray 2007, 13). If play is to be read as the force or capacity that animates gaming, it is crucial to under-stand it.

To do this, the chapter develops a genealogy of play in Western philos-ophy[1] from the Presocratics to modern phenomenologists. It concurs with Tilman Küchler's view that there exists neither an ideal concept of play nor a clear linear history of its evolution. The chapter develops instead a genealogy that is itself "a form of play to the extent that it no longer strives toward the discovery of some original identity or truth" but rather seeks to trace dis-cursive modes through which play is conceptualized and operationalized (Küchler 1994, 11–12). Drawing upon the play literature across a number of scholarly disciplines, the chapter traces two discursive modes of play, the Apollonian and the Dionysian, which have sat in dialectical tension in Western philosophy from ancient to postmodern times.

While the Apollonian mode aspires to forms of play based in, and pro-ductive of, reason, order, being, and presence, the Dionysian tradition emphasizes unreason, disorder, becoming, and the instability of presence. The chapter shows that while the Presocratic notions of play were characterized by a dynamic interplay of the Apollonian and Dionysian modes, Socratic modes of thinking successfully banished much of the Dionysian, effecting

---

[1] I focus in this chapter on play in the Western philosophical tradition, rather than attempting to integrate global theorizations and practices, because this book focuses on wargames in a Western context. As discussed below, important decolonial critiques have been made of key theorists of play, including Aimé Césaire's indictment of Roger Caillios (Césaire 2000). Future work in IR should ex-plore the politics and possibilities of play modes from across the world.

the "malediction of play" in Western philosophy. The chapter then explores the return of the Dionysian, beginning with Friedrich Nietzsche's devastating challenge to modern metaphysics and the limits of phenomenological responses of Martin Heidegger and Hans-Georg Gadamer to this provocation.

Having done this, Chapter 4 will then argue that while late modern play theory rekindled elements of the Dionysian, because it continued to seek origins and Being behind and through play, it was not until the rise of post-structural thinking in the postmodern mindset—in particular the thought of Jacques Derrida—that the Nietzschean promise was realized. The overall aim of this chapter is to show, against much of the dominant literature, that the Dionysian mode contains the seeds of a radical play theory that challenges the ludic and ontopolitical conservatism of the Apollonian tradition.

Accordingly, the chapter opens with an account of the Apollonian and Dionysian play modes, setting out the former's focus on reason, order, being, and presence and the latter's tendency toward unreason, disorder, becoming, and play as the disruption of presence. To do this, it explores key ancient framings of play, beginning with the insights of Heraclitus and turning to the challenges posed by Plato and Aristotle. From there, the chapter explores framings of play in modern philosophical thought, focusing on the German Idealist tradition. Building on Nagel's analysis, it argues that play becomes the "other of metaphysics" in the work of Immanuel Kant and, despite his playful intentions, that of Friedrich Schiller. Having argued that the Apollonian mode comes to dominate in modern thought, the chapter turns to Nietzsche's challenge to the Western philosophical tradition and the accompanying return of the Dionysian in and beyond play. At this juncture, the chapter notes that while there is much to praise in Nietzsche's unsettling of the prevailing Apollonian constraints, he retains a problematic view of the hero-warrior player, reflected in his claim of the "innocence of becoming." My account of deconstructive play developed in Chapter 4 will argue that Nietzsche's hero-warrior player requires reformulation in line with the repoliticization of play advocated in this book.

Having set out the Nietzschean challenge to Apollonian play, the chapter then turns to his (would-be) inheritors, beginning with Johan Huizinga, seen by many as the founder of twentieth-century play theory. The chapter shows that despite his embrace of Dionysian themes, Huizinga nevertheless retains an Apollonian tone through his privileging of some forms of play over others. His reification of "pure" and "holy" play reflects, I argue, a problematic political elitism that has its basis in Apollonian commitments. The chapter then turns to the phenomenological tradition of Heidegger and Gadamer, the focus of which is providing an account of play in itself, as opposed to one mediated through the engagement of a player-subject. Gadamer in particular provides crucial insights for my theorization of deconstructive play, specifically his claim that "all playing is a being-played" (2004, 106). Nevertheless, the chapter shows that despite problematizing key elements of the Western metaphysical tradition, the phenomenologists' treatment of play remains distinctly Apollonian through its search for (groundless) origin, being, and presence.

In contrast to the position taken in much of the existing literature, I "side" in this book with the Dionysian over the Apollonian, welcoming Nietzsche's challenge to philosophical orthodoxy and to conceptualizations of play grounded in the service of reason. This is because while the Apollonian mode constrains and hierarchizes play, operationalizing it in the service of society's conventions and philosophy's metaphysical aspirations, the Dionysian tradition advocates "freeplay," allowing play's ceaseless movements to be generative of multiple forms of becoming, and destabilizing hierarchies of social and political order. My aim is to elucidate a theorization of play that focuses not on *what* we play but rather on *how* we play. In Chapter 4, I do this by developing a third form of play—"deconstructive play"—which is then operationalized through the remainder of the book to introduce fractures in the hyperreal productions of gaming.

Ancient Play

Many accounts of play in the Western philosophical tradition begin with Plato and Aristotle. However, it is necessary to explore an earlier mode of thinking to fully grasp the interplay of the Apollonian and Dionysian elements at work in play (Spariosu 1991, ix–x). In Presocratic thought, notably in the writings of Heraclitus, play features as a fatalistic play-of-the-world in which gods toy with man. As Mihai Spariosu observes, in "Western metaphysics, play has often been employed in the form of a game metaphor that imagines the relationship between divinity and man as one between a player and a plaything." Such an account, he continues, can be traced back to the Sumerians, Hebrews, Hindus, and the Chinese, making it far older than the Hellenic world. In the latter, such play originates in Homer, is developed philosophically by Heraclitus, and then becomes the object of rationalization in Plato (Spariosu 1989, 29).

In the oft-cited fragment B52, Heraclitus states: "Lifetime is a child at play, moving pieces in a game. Kingship belongs to the child" (quoted in Nagel 2002, 18).[2] Here, the child at play is framed as containing the energy and wisdom of man's being, understood as a process of becoming. Interestingly, both Nietzsche and Heidegger refer to this framing. According to the latter, Heraclitus' lesson is that "the *Geschick* of being [is] a child that plays" (1996, 113), while the former concludes that

> only play, play as artists and children engage in it, exhibits coming-to-be and passing away, structuring and destroying, without any moral additive, in forever equal innocence. . . . Such is the game than the aeon [lifetime] plays with itself. . . . From time to time it starts the game anew. An instance of satiety—and again it is seized by its need, as the artist is seized by his need to create. Not hybris [disregard for the rights of others] but the ever self-renewing impulse to play calls new worlds into being. (1962, 62)

While Nietzsche emphasizes here the innocence of this process of becoming and destroying, other commentators have emphasized the tragic-comic quality of this relation. As Nagel explains, "What seems to be a comic chance-play in the gods is truly tragic in human ethical life because such play, or being toyed with by divine puppeteers, is a gambling between life and death" (2002, 2). In this fatalistic drama, people are framed as the object rather than the subject of play; in Plato's words, "man is made God's plaything" (quoted in Ehrmann 1971, 106). Such a framing of play has at its core an agnostic, violent play of nature and gods (Ryall, Russell, and MacLean 2014, 3). As this suggests, Heraclitus' account invites reflection on the question of the often-obscured power relations at work in play.

In his exploration of the seven "rhetorics of play," Brian Sutton-Smith identifies the ancient rhetoric of "play as power." He explains that the "rhetoric of play as power is about the use of play as the representation of conflict as a way to fortify the status of those who control the play or are its heroes. This rhetoric is as ancient as warfare and patriarchy" (2001, 10). In

---

[2] The translation used here is Charles Kahn's. This fragment has been translated in several other ways, including "Time is a child playing draughts. The kingly power is a child's"; "Time (*aion*) is a child playing and making a move with a draughtsman: the play of the kingdom of a child!"; and "Time is a child (*Knabe*) playing the draughts; The child regime!" (Dursun 2007, 70).

this framing, play both reflects and serves the interests of those seeking or occupying positions of power. According to Spariosu, and those who have utilized and developed his work, two distinct conceptualizations of power can be perceived in Presocratic accounts of play: a prerational framing and a rational one. Spariosu writes: "A proper historical understanding of the concepts of power and play in their interrelation must . . . also take into account the divided nature of the Western mentality which, since its birth in ancient Greece, has periodically swayed between a prerational pole and a rational pole" (Spariosu 1989, 6). By this, he means not to suggest that the Presocratics were irrational in the sense of lacking reasoning faculties but rather to identify a mode of thinking and knowledge that was qualitatively different from the rationalist philosophical tradition beginning with Plato.[3]

Spariosu frames prerational play, which he terms "archaic play," as a fatalistic warlike mode characterized as an autotelic activity engaged in by Hellenic nobles (Nagel 2002, 7), who viewed agonism and competition as the basis of key aristocratic virtues such as courage, endurance, and strength (Ryall, Russell, and MacLean 2014, 3). In this mode, Spariosu argues, "power conceives of itself as physical, naked, and immediate. Authority largely depends on physical strength or cunning intelligence. . . . Competitive values prevail over cooperative values, and violence or the threat thereof is commonly employed in resolving conflicts" (1989, 7). "Median play," in contrast, is framed as a logo-rational mode in which competition is tempered by rules and symbolic games (Ryall, Russell, and MacLean 2014, 3) and by laws and justice (Spariosu 1989, 7), which come to lay the foundations for Western ethics and metaphysics. In this mode, Spariosu explains, power does not *present* but rather *re-presents* itself. By this he means that power is increasingly mediated and distributed, that disputes are resolved through argument rather than force or violence, and that greater emphasis is placed on cooperation and consensus (1989, 7).

Alternatively, or in addition, these poles can be framed in terms of the interplay of Dionysian and Apollonian forces, as conceptualized by Nietzsche: "What Nietzsche calls 'Dionysian' and 'Apolline' and I call 'archaic' and 'median' are two faces of the same mentality of power, with one engaging the other in a ceaseless contest" (Spariosu 1991, xvi). As this suggests, these

---

[3] I agree here with Nagel's concern that it is problematic to think of Presocratics as prerational, as this implies erroneously that were operating outside the logos (2002, 4).

forces are not separate in Western analyses of play, but rather interrelated. They can be viewed, as Nagel argues, as a guiding thread operating not in a binary relation but rather "intertwined dialectically in a unity of opposites" (2002, 2). Sicart illustrates this dynamic interplay by describing a process of building a Lego tower simply to watch it fall when pushed over. The impulse, he states,

> is between the rational play of order and creation and the sweeping eu-phoria of destruction and rebirth, between the Apollonian and the Dionysiac ... The order and sobriety of the Apollonian [is] tensely opposed by the embodied, passionate, irrational, and irreverent Dionysiac art. . . . The pleasure of the wasted time, of the pieces scattering as they hit the floor, is the pleasure of destructive play—the Dionysiac ending to my Apollonian world building. Play is this struggle between order and chaos, between the will to create and the will to destroy. (2014, 9–10)

Whether framed in terms of prerational/rational, archaic/median, or Dionysian/Apollonian, then, what is important here is the dynamic rela-tionship between these modes of play. Far from being fixed in a stable bi-nary opposition, these modes of play have dialectically fluctuated in Western thought and culture since antiquity. As Emily Ryall, Wendy Russell, and Malcolm MacLean note, "[T]he history of Western philosophising on play may be understood alongside and in relation to the history of Western men-tality, and . . . this oscillated between a pre-rational and rational pole, with cultural paradigm shifts occurring alongside periods of crisis in established values" (2014, 2).

Key for the purposes of this book is the claim that the Apollonian discur-sive mode began, with Socratic modes of thinking, to dominate and eclipse Dionysian play. Nagel shows that with the rise of rationalism in Plato and Aristotle, the Apollonian tone initiates an ethical polarization of "good" and "bad" play, and a broader malediction of play. The ultimate consequence of this is that "play becomes the Other of reason in Western metaphysics" (2002, 108). Spariosu comes to a similar conclusion, stating that at this time philosophy "sets itself the task of subduing poetry, of imposing upon it a spiritual world of order, clarity, and permanence, a world of rationality and morality—the world of Being in the Platonic sense" (1989, 162). In this Platonic worldview, while a dialectic tension persists between the Apollonian and the Dionysian, the Apollonian frequently has the upper hand (Nagel

2002, 108), and the ultimate outcome is the "eclipse of Hellenic tragedy in the fifth century B.C." (Nagel 2002, 8).[4]

Opinion is divided on the question of whether Plato or Aristotle initiates this banishment of Dionysian play. According to Nietzsche, Derrida, and Gilles Deleuze, it is Plato who is responsible for instigating the domestication and effacement of archaic play (Nagel 2002, 33–35). This view is echoed by Spariosu, who argues that "Plato challenges Homer and the tragic poets because he sees them as influential spokesmen for a prerational mentality. This mentality is based on a notion of unmediated power and presupposes a view of the world as [a] ceaseless, arbitrary play of forces (unlimited Becoming)" (1989, 161). In this reading, Plato stood against the unpredictable and violent elements of play, favoring instead the order and calm of the Apollonian.[5] As Küchler elaborates, Plato advocated play understood as "good mimesis," framed as "the human activity that is able to establish the connection with the divine." In order to attain this authenticity and meaning, according to Plato, "the human being has to overcome the pre-forms of play, that is, not only the irrational desire '[to] utter cries of all sorts,' but also the childish instinct to 'leap and bounce, [to] dance and frolic' without any purpose and without any form." This must be done through "a teleologically oriented process of education in which the human subject has to bring what is essentially irrational . . . under the reign of reason" (Küchler 1994, 13).

Plato's suspicion of the Dionysian aspects of play can be attributed at least in part to the altered, irrational state experienced by those playing. Seeking to temper the unruly tendencies of the entranced or immersed player, as Hans notes, "Plato, in his *Phaedrus*, makes the mistake of judging the ecstasy of being outside oneself from the point of view of rational reasonableness and of seeing it as a mere negation of being within oneself, i.e. as a kind of madness" (1981, 8). There is for Plato, then, a danger associated with the Dionysian. As Spariosu explains, in Plato "what appears on the surface as a rational and objective ontological argument betrays a deep-seated fear of the unrestrainable world of the senses." This is because play is a "borderline

---

[4] This shift is peculiar to the Western philosophical tradition. O'Flaherty, for example, shows how in Hindu mythology, "the world is at play in the hands of the gods, and dreaming and playfulness are forms of reality treated as seriously as the so-called commonsense world. Play, like dreams, is not a secondary state of reality as it is with us but has primacy as a form of knowing" (quoted in Sutton-Smith 2001, 55).

[5] Part of Plato's campaign against the Dionysian sprang from his suspicion of the Sophists. His aim was to challenge the unruly and untrustworthy rhetoric of the Sophists (Egan 2014, 59), which he viewed as "a 'fixed' or crooked game" (Dixon 2014, 71).

phenomenon, hovering between reality and unreality, and because of this undecidability it is potentially disruptive to the self and its identity" (1989, 189). In this reading, it is because of this instability and unpredictability that Plato sought to banish the dangerous Dionysian by subsuming play to the demands of reason and order. As Michael Echeruo notes, according to this narrative it was "Plato, apparently, who perversely introduced the notion that imitation was an inferior version of 'truth,' and so subordinated the arts, until then a respectable medium, to philosophy" (1994, 137). The ultimate result of this, Derrida argues, is that Plato's play is "supervised and contained within the safeguards of ethics and politics" (cited in Küchler 1994, 13).

Other commentators argue, however, that Plato's campaign against the Dionysian was only partial and remained incomplete. Nagel, along with Wendy Brown, has made the argument that Plato's Socrates retained a distinctly playful tone, and that it was Aristotle who presided over the eclipse of the Dionysian. Indeed, Nagel frames Plato as a protagonist against Aristotle's attempt to subordinate the arts—including play—to the rational aims of philosophy. Her argument is that in Aristotle, "play (*paidia*) becomes the Other (of reason) and only leisure (*schole*) is valuable for contemplation" (Nagel 2002, 4). She cites Aristotle's claim "And we can say that serious things [*spoudaia*] are better than laughable things and those connected with amusement [*paidia*]" as the basis for this framing and argues that with this innocuous statement, Aristotle initiates the "malediction of play in Western thought" (2002, 1). Thus, in this reading it is Aristotle who presides over the domestication of play; he "relegates the Dionysian aspects of Plato's play to 'abstract negation' and strengthens the Apollonian motif in play—what Spariosu calls the logo-rational principle" (Nagel 2002, 47).

Aristotle accomplishes this, Nagel explains, by setting up hierarchical relations between higher and lower forms of play and devaluing the activities of all but philosophers by categorizing their play as inferior: "The hierarchies of 'playful' activities are especially pronounced in Book VIII [of the *Politics*], in which *scholia* (leisure) is ranked highest, followed by *ascholia* (work—for sake of leisure), *anapausis* (recreation), and lastly, *paidia* (play, amusement). . . . [A] leisurely activity is associated most of all with the 'work' of the philosopher, which is distinct from the demands of practical life" (2002, 51).

Through this devaluation, then, play comes to be associated with the activities of the masses, women, children, and all those who cannot participate in the serious business of philosophy. For Aristotle, play can be of instrumental value in the education of children, but only insofar as it is purged of its Dionysian elements. This, Nagel concludes, has had lasting impacts upon the way play is perceived in Western societies: "The play set up by Aristotle in his ethical and political writings has significant socio-political implications, insofar as it determines whose play is worthy of philosophical approval. The need for authenticating play has left its traces in Western discourse" (2002, 53). As Echeruo explains, while Aristotle retained a respect for the arts, "he did so on terms that would never again allow the arts to forget their precarious connections with truth" (1994, 137).

One solution to this debate is to simply argue that both Plato and Aristotle had a hand in this banishment because both "convert the violence and arbitrary play of Becoming into the rational and orderly play of Being, but also turn heroic and tragic poetry into a nonserious, speculative, and mendacious discourse, subordinating it to the serious, truthful, and moral discourse of philosophy" (Spariosu 1991, xiv). More important than attributing responsibility to one or the other, however, are the enduring consequences of this challenge.

The first outcome is the development of enduring "paidiophobic trends" in Western thought (Nagel 2002, 59), in which play becomes "ideologically suspect" and finally "abject." This involves a devaluation of play as such. Philosophers came to denounce play as an "unworthy, childish, irrational, superficial activity" (Nagel 2002, 1), framing it as the Other of reason (Nagel 2002, 3). Importantly, as will be discussed further below, this emergent paidiophobia has gendered, racialized, and elitist characteristics. This is because for these philosophers their enterprise "is not a game, not a trivial matter, which can be pursued by women or children or nonpropertied men (i.e. the masses or subaltern subjects)" (Nagel 2002, 1).

Second, this connotes a significant but unstable victory of the Apollonian/median play mode over the Dionysian (Spariosu 1991, xiv; Nagel 2002, 108). Whether one is convinced by those who blame Plato or by those who hold Aristotle responsible, what is clear is that the ensuing "malediction of play" involved the dominance of the Apollonian and the eclipsing of the Dionysian. However, while the result of this is a mode of play that "is purged from excessive, Dionysian elements, i.e. when it is contained in a purely Apollonian framework" (Nagel 2002, 108), this banishment was only partially successful. Despite the dominance of Apollonian play in Socratic modes of thinking, the

Dionysian remains present as reason's a(nta)gonist, haunting the Apollonian into and beyond the modern philosophical era:

> Although Plato and Aristotle convert heroic and tragic poetry into "fiction" or "literature," subordinating it to the serious and moral truth of metaphysics, the ancient agon between the poets and philosophers comes back again and again to haunt Western thought. . . . Faced with this challenge of threat, the modern philosophers may react in two ways: they either reenact the Platonic suppression of prerational values, relegating them again to the realm of "mere" art and play (in the case of Kant); or they wholeheartedly embrace these values, turning literature or art into an effective weapon against their own philosophical opponents (the case of the artist-metaphysicians) [Nietzsche, Heidegger, Derrida]. (Spariosu 1989, 162)

It is to these modern manifestations of this unresolved relation that this chapter now turns.

Modern Play

The ancient malediction of play comes to inform modern Western philosophy. In this mode of thinking, the devaluation is expressed in relation to the rise of rationalism and the scientific method associated with the Enlightenment. Mirroring the Apollonian orientation of the Socratics, dominant modern philosophers either marginalized play entirely or perpetuated the (attempted) banishment of the Dionysian. Hans illustrates this point through a discussion of the changing modes of verification of the period, noting the shift from reliance on experience and judgment to "some variety of the scientific method." He continues:

> Of course, the scientific method itself does not really eliminate verification by common sense, authority, and prejudgment, but it does force these factors underground. . . . Now it is the scientific method itself—and not the experience of an individual—that determines the truth value of a statement. The result of this shift in the method of verification is obvious: those activities and disciplines not amenable to verification through reason and the scientific methods lose their status as having truth value. . . . The arts have been relegated to this status, according to Gadamer, for exactly the same reasons play becomes peripheral. (1981, 3–4)

Hans' claim here is that the rise of reason as a core element of the scientific method corresponds with the devaluation of forms of knowledge resistant to empirical testing and falsification, including play and the arts. The reification of methodological processes as the only legitimate path to knowledge corresponds with the banishment of play as incommensurable with, and a danger to, philosophy's aspirations to reason and truth.

Importantly, as was the case in ancient Western thought, the modern malediction of play corresponds to, and perpetuates, a series of broader power relations: it is linked to the reification of a particular form of philosophy reserved for specific privileged groups and the devaluation of practices associated with subjugated groups. Sutton-Smith notes that play's supposed frivolity is actually political in character because it "may itself be a mask for play's use in more widespread systems for denigrating the play of other groups, as has been done characteristically throughout history by those of higher status against the recreations of those of lower status" (2001, 9). He continues:

> [P]lay is declared frivolous not only because of neglect or because frivolous play is the abstract opposite of some higher-level form of ludic activity. The label "frivolity" is, rather, an abuse of some kinds of play on behalf of other kinds of play, because that is what is politically suitable for some dominating groups. . . . [It may thus be read] as an implicit form of political or scholarly denigration. (2001, 207–208)

Here Sutton-Smith begins a discussion of the ways in which the play of "less powerful groups is implicitly excluded and even ridiculed." The historically dominant forms of play and games of "kings, princes, politicians, colonizing administrators, aristocracies, ethnic groups, heterosexuals, and men," he argues, have been inscribed with a seriousness through association with heroism, military prowess, competitiveness, and organized festivals and contests. The play of marginalized groups, including women, racial/sexual/gender minorities, the poor, and those with less power and wealth, has, in parallel, been denigrated. The former groups have, of course, historically excluded the latter from participating in valorized forms of play, or at best included them in a tokenistic fashion. And yet this devaluation of marginalized play has been only partially successful because it has not, at least not entirely, undermined marginalized participants' seriousness about their play. As Sutton-Smith concludes, "[T]hese denigrated groups are generally deadly serious and righteous about their own play as are those who denigrate them.

They are not frivolous in their own eyes, they are seriously at play" (Sutton-Smith 2001, 205–208).

Apollonian Idealism

It is with the aesthetic turn associated with German Idealism that sustained treatments of play reappear in Western philosophy. As Spariosu notes, following the Socratics' explorations

> play as a major explicit philosophical topic resurfaces with the rise of German idealism and may be connected to the aesthetic turn in Western metaphysics. This turn occurs in the wake of the cognitive crisis accompanying the loss of faith in the ideas of the Enlightenment. . . . Since metaphysics has always regarded art as a form of (serious or nonserious) play, its aesthetic turn in Germany will also bring about extensive reflection upon the idea of play in general, and this idea will be invoked by virtually every major idealist philosopher, beginning with Leibniz. (Spariosu 1989, 30)

This renewed interest is linked explicitly to ancient Greek treatments of play. Kostas Axelos argues that it took 2,500 years until "some thinkers and poets of (German) idealism and romanticism, situated in the sphere of representation and freedom, between the transcendent sense and the physical senses, between the theoretical and the practical . . . once again glimpsed what might be understood as play" (Axelos 1971, 7). While play is treated with a renewed seriousness during this period, its key thinkers are firmly situated in the Apollonian mode. In Nagel's words, they "follow Aristotle's lead vis-à-vis play and its purposefulness and continue to disregard the Dionysian element of play" (2002, 60).

Characteristic of Idealist treatments of play, specifically those of Immanuel Kant and Friedrich Schiller, is an embrace of the Apollonian mode's emphasis on reason, seriousness, sobriety, presence, and truth. In parallel is a disapproval or suspicion of unchecked Dionysian play. Spariosu argues: "[P]lay is gradually stripped of its irrational, violent, and arbitrary connotations, becoming a useful instrument in supporting the ontological and ethical fictions of philosophy." Such a suspicion is especially clear in Kant's treatment of play in the *Critique of Pure Reason*, Spariosu continues: "[T]he explicit goal of the first Critique is to replace the 'mere play' (*blosses Spiel*) of the imagination and thought, in which, according to Kant, philosophy has indulged all too often, with the seriousness of scientific investigation" (1989, 33–34).

Nagel also argues that Kant framed play as a "negative activity," referring repeatedly to the "mere play" of imagination, which "has no import for the objective validity of empirical concepts." For Kant, she continues, play can generate only representation, which amounts to "a random, disorderly, spontaneous, subjective movement of lower cognitive faculties (e.g., imagination) . . . Such play is nothing more than mere illusion (*Schein*) or a false impression (*Blendwerk*); illusory play conjures up chimeras, unicorns but not determinable objects of experience." Thus in Kant, she concludes, "play is held in contempt epistemologically, figuring as the Other of reason and understanding" (Nagel 2002, 61–63).

In this framing, then, play is opposed to seriousness and knowledge. As Ryall, Russell, and MacLean comment, for Kant " 'mere play,' such as the competitive *agon* of metaphysicians, does not have a place in the necessary thoroughness of serious philosophy." While some orderly playful thinking may be used to bridge empiricism and pure reason, Kant "warns that overindulgence in play may lead to laziness, bad habits and a dulling of mental capacities" (Ryall, Russell, and MacLean 2014, 3–4). To be permissible, then, play must be limited and sober. Nagel describes this as a view of play that resembles an "orderly baroque minuet" rather than a "Bacchic frenzy." Restricted thusly, Kant's play is free only "insofar as it does not go beyond the normative boundaries which are posited by understanding. . . . Apollonian, intellectual values not only dominate but do so at the expense of the Dionysian [because] Bacchanalian skirmishes of the imagination are too unruly to be considered, since they would explode the neat, orderly boundaries of his Prussian aesthetic *Spielraum*" (Nagel 2002, 67–69).

Seeming to counter Kant's wariness, Schiller is credited with reestablishing play as a legitimate topic of philosophical study in the modern period (Spariosu 1989, 53), his "emphatic benediction of play in the *Letters [on the Esthetic Education of Man]* . . . inspiring a generation of like-minded play theoreticians, such as Groos, Buytendijk, Huizinga, Bally, and Hartmann" (Nagel 2002, 60). Challenging Kant's framing of play in opposition to, and as a potential antagonist of, reason, Schiller for the first time explicitly calls "the heuristic fictions of philosophy 'play,' relinking art and aesthetics with nonviolent, rational play concepts in their Platonic version" (Spariosu 1989, 30). His oft-cited statement that "man plays only when he is man in the full sense of the word and *he is totally man only when he plays*" (quoted in Ehrmann 1971, 7) epitomizes the seriousness with which Schiller took play.

In contrast to Kant and other contemporaries, Schiller opened up space for play as generative of, and commensurable with, philosophy. He argued that man's reason and sensuous drives could operate not in tension, as they did for Kant, but harmoniously if channeled through the "play drive." In Schiller's framing, this drive can "mediate between the natural, physical drives and logic, between animal sensuous experiences and rational, moral behavior, to create both aesthetic and human potential" (Ryall, Russell, and MacLean 2014, 4). Rather than subordinating the sensuous drive to the rational drive, as did most of his contemporaries, Schiller suggests that they should interrelate reciprocally to generate this third drive, which "would be directed towards annulling time within time, reconciling becoming with absolute being and change with identity" (quoted in Spariosu 1989, 55).

While this certainly pushes against the rationalist trend associated with eighteenth-century Idealist philosophy in general, and Kant in particular, there are limits to Schiller's embrace of play, and his tone remains ultimately Apollonian. Ryall, Russell, and MacLean convincingly argue that Schiller frames play in hierarchical ways that "reveal the elitist assumptions of his project for humanity. Rational forms of play are to be exalted, while pre-rational forms are to be constrained as mere play, a class-based theme which arguably persists today in the concepts of high and low (or indeed adult and child) culture" (2014, 4). Nagel similarly claims that for Schiller physical play is deemed inferior to aesthetic play: "Note that aesthetic play as a higher kind of play is akin to Aristotle's philosopher's leisurely contemplation. In fact, it is an intellectualist (Apollonian) play that Schiller comes to value in the aesthetic education of the self. [Dionysian] drives serve as the 'abject' in Schiller's aesthetic writings" (Nagel 2002, 74). In Küchler's words, Schiller "repeats the (teleo-)logic of Plato's play" by framing it as "a program for an aesthetic education of mankind." The result of this is that

> there is in Schiller no free movement of play. Since there is no play out-side the transcendental grounds of reason, Schiller cannot admit into his project of education and emancipation any kind of "free" and unrestricted play. Any movement or manifestation of play that does not yield to the demands of transcendental reason is dismissed as "mere play." . . . Play becomes "good," that is, serious and productive only when . . . it becomes

an integral part of a metaphysical framework governed by the presence of a final meaning. (Küchler 1994, 15–16)

What is common to Kant and Schiller, then, is a hierarchization of "good" and "bad" play (Ryall, Russell, and MacLean 2014, 4). Nagel similarly notes, "[B]oth Kant and Schiller return to an Aristotelian validation of the Apollonian" (2002, 4). The case of Schiller demonstrates, as Nagel keenly observes, that a malediction can be visible even in those philosophers who endorse play.

The Dionysian (Re)turn

There is considerable debate in the literature regarding the origins of the challenge to Apollonian hegemony and return of Dionysian play in Western philosophy. A key figure of contention is G. W. F. Hegel. Indicted by post-structuralist philosophers including Derrida and Deleuze for logocentrism and *ressentiment*, it is perhaps surprising that others have argued that Hegel "breaks with the Aristotelian malediction of play and thus sets a new ludic agenda" (Nagel 2002, 81–82). Eugen Fink offers support for this reading: "Hegel says for example that play, because of its disinterested and superlatively lighthearted nature, is the most sublime and only true form of seriousness" (Fink 1971, 25). Emphasizing the movement associated with Hegel's dialectical thinking, it has been claimed that Hegel is able to "tarry with the negative," thereby countering Kant's opposition of play and reason. In this reading, Hegel holds that "the True is the Bacchanalian revel," which allows him to employ the "notions of circle and play within the realm of Reason (*Vernunft*) in order to characterize Reason as play" (Nagel 2002, 82). In so doing, he challenges the Apollonian mode and lays the groundwork for a "deviant" philosophical engagement with play in the work of Nietzsche and his inheritors: "[E]ven if Hegel may not totally break with the logocentric, paidio-phobic tradition, he at least deviates from its Apollonian path play-fully" (Nagel 2002, 89).

Greater consensus exists on the question of the importance of Nietzsche's thought in the return of Dionysian play. Ryall, Russell, and MacLean note that "if Plato, Kant and Schiller provide examples of the rationalising of play, then Nietzsche can offer a paradigmatic foundation for the return to pre-rational philosophising on play and power" (2014, 4). Nagel makes a similar case: "Nietzsche is the first play theorist to expose play as the Other of philosophical discourse, and he proceeds to affirm the Dionysian (frenzied, irrational) aspects of play" (2002, 4). Echoing this, Spariosu argues that Nietzsche attempted to free prerational mentality from its rational bonds and reaffirm pre-rational values in modern culture (1989, 11). Importantly, Nietzsche and his inheritors do not ignore rational play but rather "engage in a polemic with the advocates of such play (Plato, Leibniz, Kant, Schiller, Fichte, Schelling, Hegel, and German idealism in general), [and] also attempt to subordinate the rational play concepts to the prerational ones" (Spariosu 1989, 158). The consequence of this is both a reconfiguration of the relationship between Apollonian and Dionysian play and a challenge to the broader malediction of play in modern Western philosophy.

Countering Kant's relegation of "mere" play to philosophical insignificance, Nietzsche treats play as of crucial import. Indeed, in *Ecce Homo* he states: "I know of no other manner of dealing with great tasks, than as *play*: this, as a sign of greatness, is an essential prerequisite" (2007, 202). Nietzsche's focus on play is related to the broader challenges he leveled against philosophy's prevailing metaphysical and epistemological assumptions. As Hans notes, play comes into "the foreground of thought at the same time as our conception of a centered, continuous world has been called into question. One could date this shift to the work of Nietzsche." He continues:

> The playfulness of Nietzsche's writing was a product of his belief that life itself was fundamentally playful. He stated this belief as early as *The Birth of Tragedy*, which attempts to overturn the sobriety of Socrates for the ecstatic playfulness of the Dionysian mode of existence. As Nietzsche refined his view of play he sensed the value of the aphorism's playfulness, its ability to generate a syncretic energy through its concision. His manner of philosophizing and his most significant concepts—the overman, the will to power, the eternal return—are founded in a view of life as a playful exchange of masks. (Hans 1981, ix–x)

For Nietzsche, life's playful quality permeates not only the arts and poetry but also, and to the same extent, thought, science, and philosophy. Recapitulating Heraclitus' famous statement, Nietzsche perceived even in the ordinary play of children "the doctrine of the law of becoming and of play in necessity," and his writings "appear as 'the expression of an intellectual play impulse, and innocent and happy like all play,' as the communications of a playful spirit" (Behler 1991, 94–95). In his wholehearted embrace of unbridled play, Nietzsche was thus the first dancing philosopher (Oriard 1991, 413).

The play impulse is framed by Nietzsche as a self-generating and ever-renewing vitalism based on a "super-abundance that is beyond strict utility" (Homan 2014, 100). He explains that this "ever self-renewing impulse to play calls new worlds into being. The child throws away its toys from time to time—and starts again in innocent caprice" (quoted in Spariosu 1989, 75). Such play is not for some external purpose but is an affirmation of life as process, which emphasizes dynamic becoming over static being. Such a framing reanimates the Dionysian by invoking "play as prerational agon, play as the arbitrary and violent conflict of physical forces or as a manifestation of ceaseless physical Becoming, play as chance-necessity, mimesis-play, play as a. . . prerational mode of being, and play as unrestrained freedom" (Spariosu 1989, 12). In this account, play functions to frustrate the disciplining of the irrational by the rational through a rearticulation of the relationship between aesthetics and philosophy:

> The "aesthetic" perspective that Nietzsche has in mind . . . is exactly the opposite of that of Kant and Schiller, because it concerns the world of the senses and Becoming, rather than that of Reason and Being. This aesthetic view goes back to the original, etymological sense of *aisthesis* (in its traditional opposition to *noesis*, as Kant himself points out in the first *Kritik*, B36), and thereby reverses the Platonic-Kantian hierarchy of metaphysical values: the play of the senses and the imagination gains priority over the play of understanding and reason. (Spariosu 1989, 75)

Thus, Nietzsche challenges the Idealist framing by reversing "the hierarchical polarity of seriousness and play, or ethics and aesthetics, favoring the second term over the first" (Spariosu 1989, 81). The consequence of this is that Nietzsche unsettles the established privileging of rationality over aesthetics. He does this, as Spariosu explains, "by going back, beyond Plato, to the archaic origins of art in the violent exuberant, and innocent play of power, thereby reintroducing the prerational notions of play in modern philosophy" (1989, 31).

In keeping with his broader challenge to conventional morality, Nietzsche frames play as beyond good and evil. Framed as the force animating the "will to power," play is read here as a challenge to the "will to order" characteristic of rational thought and being (Spariosu 1989, 12). For Nietzsche, play is the process by which man, after the death of God, comes to self-author. Indeed, play is the name for the mode of becoming associated with the will to power understood as "a becoming that knows no satiety, no disgust, no weariness: this, my Dionysian world of the eternally self-creating, the eternally self-destroying, the mystery world of the twofold voluptuous delight, my 'beyond good and evil,' without goal, unless the joy of the circle is itself a goal" (Nietzsche 1968, 550). Far from disaster, this situation provides man with the opportunity of a freedom impossible, according to Nietzsche, under established norms. Hans notes: "The death of God is the death of the man who would be god, and it is time we attended to that fact. . . . [T]he death of man does not mean the end of culture, as some would argue, but only its redefinition" (1981, 199–200).

Nietzsche's radical rereading of play thus challenged the hegemony of Apollonian framings by freeing the Dionysian from its shackles so that an interplay between the two was restored. From a denigrated place in Idealist thought, play became central to post-Enlightenment framings of processes of becoming that critique the static accounts of being associated with Kant. As Spariosu notes, Nietzsche's account "is based on an archaic, prerational concept of play as power or as the violent, exuberant, and arbitrary movement of Becoming, whereas the Kantian or the Schillerian kind stems from a rational concept of play as the rule-determined, orderly, and predictable manifestation of Being" (Spariosu 1989, 99). Similarly, Axelos notes that it was "Nietzsche who proclaimed the innocence of becoming, who understood the non-total totality of Being-Nothingness, in a word the world, as a game, this same game linking man in truth-wandering (*errance*) to what imposes itself upon him" (Axelos 1971, 8). This articulation of play as a name for the movement of becoming, as opposed to a static state of being, is perhaps Nietzsche's most important contribution, and has been central to the development of poststructural play theories. This intervention is key to Derrida's notion of "freeplay," and to my conceptualization of "deconstructive play." As will be discussed below, however, while Nietzsche's liberation of the Dionysian paved the way for poststructural treatments of play, his philosophy retains a problematic aristocratic warrior-hero subject that warrants critique.

Homo Ludens

Nietzsche's influence on theorizations of play through the twentieth century was immense. One trajectory this influence took was in the work of Johan Huizinga. His book *Homo Ludens: A Study of the Play Element in Culture* is widely perceived as the foundational text of modern play theory, its protagonist, "man the player," echoing the Nietzschean framing of man as "the playful creator of his own universe" (Oriard 1991, 455). As Ehrmann notes, "In writing about play, it is impossible to ignore Huizinga's book . . . which inaugurates an anthropology of play expressing views of remarkable scope and insight" (1971, 31). Nagel elaborates: "A number of western play theorists have paid tribute to the Dutch historian who introduced their subject into the human and social sciences. It was Huizinga who put forth the original thesis that the activity of playing games is not just part of any civilization but makes culture and civilization possible in the first place" (1998, 19). As this suggests, Huizinga's key contribution was a reformulation of play from the domain of frivolity to no less than the fundamental basis of human society.

Huizinga begins his analysis with an overview of existing perspectives on play. Some definitions, he argues, frame it as "a discharge of superabundant vital energy," while others claim that it provides "the satisfaction of some 'imitative instinct.'" Others describe play as simply a "'need' for relaxation," while for others it "constitutes a training of the young creature for the serious work that life will demand later on." Yet other accounts suggest that "it serves as an exercise in restraint needful to the individual," and further analysis identifies in play "an innate urge to exercise a certain faculty, or . . . the desire to dominate or compete." Still others "regard it as an 'aberration'—an outlet for harmful impulses, as the necessary restorer of energy wasted by some one-sided activity, as 'wish-fulfilment,' as a fiction designed to keep up the feeling of personal value" (Huizinga 2016, 2).

Huizinga insightfully observes that what unites these disparate accounts is that they all frame play as occurring for the sake of something beyond itself. In his words, "[T]hey all start from the assumption that play must serve something which is *not* play, that it must have some kind of biological purpose" (2016, 2). Against this, Huizinga posits that play forms the basis of culture: "The great archetypical activities of human society are all permeated with play from the start. . . . [L]aw and order, commerce and profit, craft and art, poetry, wisdom and science. All are rooted in the primaeval soil of play. . . . [G]enuine, pure play is one of the main bases of civilisation" (2016,

4–5). In so doing, Huizinga identifies in play the "antithetical and agonistic basis of civilisation" (2016, 74).

According to Huizinga, civilization is produced through "major contestive and festival forms of play." This claim offered a direct challenge to the prevailing "puritanical rhetoric that holds play to be useless, even dangerous, to Christian culture" (Sutton-Smith 2001, 78). Sutton-Smith elaborates:

> Huizinga's position is that there is a morphological parallelism between playful contests and the actual contestive conduct of politics, the law, scholarship, and the arts. The forms of culture arise, he says, in such playful antitheses. From sports to crossword puzzles, people who are pitted against each other or who pit themselves against any obstacle in a way that requires skill can be at play or at work. Out of their desire to win or succeed, and the honor of doing so, they lift higher the aspirational levels of human society, even if their contests are to the death. From contest (power) comes the development of social hierarchies (identity) around which society constructs its values. (Sutton-Smith 2001, 78)

As this suggests, Huizinga's framing rests upon the assumption that cultural production is agonistic and competitive, containing a certain "machismo" (Sutton-Smith 2001, 79). Huizinga puts it thus: "Who can deny that in all these concepts—challenge, danger, contest, etc.—we are very close to the play-sphere? Play and danger, risk, chance, feat—it is all a single field of action where something is at stake. . . . Play is battle and battle is play" (2016, 40–41).

Hopsicker and Carlson provide a useful summary of the central properties Huizinga identifies in play. Play must, they argue, be "a 'free activity' which must be undertaken voluntarily"; "absorb the player 'intensely and utterly'" and proceed according to fixed rules in a designated place and time; occur "outside of ordinary life" in the sense that it is not part of "the daily necessities and duties of survival"; and contain "'no material interests' or 'profits' and having its aim only 'in itself'" 2014, 176).

While these principles might at first glance seem persuasive, they have been subject to significant critique. Indeed, according to Nagel, these commitments collectively reflect a "[m]andarin ideology" (1998, 19–29). The German mandarins of the late nineteenth and early twentieth centuries, Nagel explains, subscribed to a pessimistic and conservative theory of cultural decadence that cherished "a nostalgic retreat into the past while decrying the decline and decay of the present" (1998, 27). In Sutton-Smith's words, Huizinga "essentially adopted the aristocratic rhetoric of the late nineteenth century, which sought to see games as being played for the games' sake, just as it saw art as being practiced for art's sake, a point of view that can be sustained in practical terms only by a wealthy elite." The consequence of arguing that "play is outside of ordinary life, that it is immaterial, disinterested, nonutilitarian, voluntary, spatially and temporally separate, childlike, nonprofane, governed by rules, and utterly involving," is that Huizinga "idealizes and sacralizes play" (Sutton-Smith 2001, 203).

In such a view, a pure primordial play is valued over the puerile play caused by "a world-wide 'bastardization of culture,'" leading in turn to "the problem of 'false play' which lacks spontaneity and carelessness" (Nagel 1998, 21). In so doing, Huizinga refuses—indeed, frames as impure or contaminated— any form of play in which the political or economic elements are made explicit. This has important political consequences; as Nagel and Duncan have argued, Huizinga, albeit unwittingly, "sets up rules for what counts as a good life and good play" (Nagel 2002, 2). The ultimate consequence of this is, in Ehrmann's words, that the "so-called liberty of the gift is in fact liberality; the generosity, the gratuitousness of play are ways of acquiring prestige and power" (1971, 43).

Relatedly, Huizinga's account contains a problematic ethnocentrism and a romanticized framing of the "noble savage," for whom being and play are one and the same. "The savage himself knows no conceptual distinction between being and playing: he knows nothing of identity, of image or symbol. And that is why it may be asked whether the mental condition of the savage in his sacred observances is not best understood by retaining play as the primary term. In our concept of play the difference between belief and pretence is dissolved" (Huizinga, quoted in Gadamer 2004, 104–105). This results, as Nagel notes, in a "bad romanticization of a universal notion of play, which, incidentally, displays cultural imperialistic attitudes" (1998, 25). As this suggests, key treatments of play in modern Western philosophy are shot through with, and serve to reproduce, imperial logics and hierarchies.[6]

Furthermore, as Ehrmann argues, Huizinga's formulation at no point calls into question the role of culture. On the contrary, culture is given "a fixed, stable, pre-existent element, serving as a frame of reference in the evaluation

---

[6] See in particular Aimé Césaire's critique of Caillois (Césaire 2000) and analyses in IR of Kant's racism and imperialism (Henderson 2014; Gani 2017).

of play." Underlying this reification is a fundamental epistemological and methodological error: "Huizinga and Caillois erred principally in never doubting . . . that the player (themselves!) is the subject of play; in believing that, present in the game, at the center of play, they dominated it. They forgot that players may be played; that, as an object in the game, the player can be its stakes (*enjeu*) and its toy (*jouet*)" (Ehrmann 1971, 55).

In addition, Huizinga's account of the relationship between play and civilization is contradictory. He begins from the premise that "the play element in culture is on the decline" (Hans 1981, 15); indeed, he can be read as extremely pessimistic about modern play, seeing in it a co-optation and instrumentalization of the culture-generating elements of competition and honor (Sutton-Smith 2001, 79). In this reading, professional athletes and anyone else who plays for reasons other than a game's own sake "perform dirty work *not* noble play and thus contribute to the degeneration to that idée fixe 'culture'" (Nagel 1998, 25). As Sutton-Smith and others have noted, this generates a paradox in that "play contributes to the transition from savage to civilization but . . . as civilization proceeds, play becomes increasingly professional and therefore doesn't contribute to civilization, a contradiction that some have found ludicrous" (Sutton-Smith 2001, 136).

Finally, but no less significantly, Huizinga's play theory rests on a problematic metaphysics of presence. Kevin Flint makes a powerful case by observing that in "Huizinga's discourse, in which he sought to gain mastery and control of understandings of play as grounds for the cultivation of cultures, he did so tacitly by means of the classical metaphysical principle of being . . . [Such] a deferral of the 'is' can be traced back to the philosophical tradition running from Plato to Husserl . . . [serving] to block any possibility of being already unfolding in play" (2014, 155). The implication here is that Huizinga's play theory seeks an origin—for culture, for subjectivity—through its reification of a pure play aesthetic. This has highly problematic consequences: "It seems that his ideal player, namely the Hellenic noble, has to be hermetically sealed off from this threatening life-style of 'everydayness' to devote himself fully to ludic endeavors that are beautiful and sublime" (Nagel 1998, 25). This sentiment has drawn criticism because Huizinga's hierarchization of sacred versus false play rests "on a simplistic and ethnocentric metaphysics of consciousness" (Ehrmann 1971, 41).

As this suggests, both Dionysian and Apollonian tones are in evidence in Huizinga's account of play. The former appears in his exploration of the relationship between play and reason. Play for Huizinga cannot be based in reason: it "cannot have its basis in any rational nexus, because this would limit it to mankind" (Huizinga 2016, 3). The implication here is that because non-human animals play, it must be "supra-logical" and "irrational" (Huizinga 2016, 3). In other words, "play is a form of metacommunication far preceding language in evolution because it is also found in animals" (Sutton-Smith 2001, 7). Relatedly, for Huizinga as for Nietzsche, play falls outside the conventional boundaries of morality: "Play lies outside the antithesis of wisdom and folly, and equally outside those of truth and falsehood, good and evil. Although it is a non-material activity it has no moral function. The valuations of vice and virtue do not apply here" (Huizinga 2016, 6).

In a similar vein, Huizinga challenges the notion that play is the opposite of seriousness, as did Nietzsche: "[T]he contrast between play and seriousness proves to be neither conclusive nor fixed. . . . As soon as we proceed from 'play is non-seriousness' to 'play is not serious,' the contrast leaves us in the lurch—for some play can be very serious indeed" (2016, 5). What is at stake here is less a reversal of the serious/frivolous binary associated with Apollonian framings of play and more a fundamental reformulation of the binary. Huizinga, along with Nietzsche, identifies the seriousness of, and in, play's apparent frivolity, challenging Enlightenment hierarchizations that polarize and devalue:

[T]he consciousness of play being "only pretend" does not by any means prevent it from proceeding with the utmost seriousness, with an absorption, a devotion that passes into rapture and, temporarily at least, completely abolishes that troublesome "only" feeling. Any game at any time can wholly run away with the players. The contrast between play and seriousness is always fluid. The inferiority of play is continually being offset by the corresponding superiority of its seriousness. (Huizinga 2016, 8)

Huizinga concludes: "The play concept as such is of a higher order than is seriousness. For seriousness seeks to exclude play, whereas play can very well include seriousness" (2016, 45).

On the other hand, Huizinga retains some distinctly Apollonian principles, and with these a problematic politics. Against Nietzsche's embrace of the unpredictable and chaotic elements of Dionysian play, Huizinga attempts to limit these in favor of a sober, rule-covered form of play. His is a play of "joyous exultation, not wild hysteria," which is "rid of the violence of the instincts." Furthermore, play must work in the service of "true" culture and civilization: "In order that the play element of civilization be productive of culture or favorable to it, this element must be pure. It must not consist in deviation from or in the repudiation of the norms prescribed by reason, humanity or faith. . . . True play excludes all propaganda. It is an end in itself" (Huizinga, quoted in Ehrmann 1971, 53–54). Thus, while Huizinga dramatically alters play's philosophical standing from "being despised to being idealized" (Sutton-Smith 2001, 203), the Apollonian impulse ultimately dominates his account. As Nagel concludes, for Huizinga, who "follows the logic of authenticity, certain forms of play have to be rejected (such as professional sports, playing for money, for material benefits). Thus in play theories [like Huizinga's] which are under Aristotle's spell, Apollonian play wins out over Dionysian play" (2002, 2–3).

Phenomenological Play

Contemporaneous with Huizinga's anthropological exploration of play was the development of phenomenological approaches associated with Heidegger and Gadamer. Central to their theorizations was an attempt to move away from the subject-centered understandings of the Idealists and their inheritors (Burwick 1990, 63–64). In Gadamer's words:

I wish to free this concept [play] of the subjective meaning that it has in Kant and Schiller and that dominates the whole of modern aesthetics and philosophy of man. When we speak of play in reference to the experience of art, this means neither the orientation nor even the state of mind of the creator or of those enjoying the work of art, nor the freedom of a subjectivity engaged in play, but the mode of being of the work of art itself. (Gadamer 2004, 102)

As this suggests, the phenomenologists' aim was to explore the nature of play itself, as opposed to players' experience of it. They approached this task by giving primacy "not to epistemological issues (logic and reason) but to ontological ones, such as freedom, anxiety, death, and authenticity" (Sutton-Smith 2001, 186). Because of this shift, a new relationship between play and player was to emerge: echoing the archaic fatalism discussed above, man is turned from "from a player into a plaything" (Spariosu 1989, 122).

Unsurprisingly, Heidegger's treatment of play shares a good deal with Nietzsche's challenge to the foundational assumptions and principles of philosophy. As Küchler argues, "Heidegger repeatedly refers to the notion of play in order to mark his departure from many tenets of Western metaphysics." Indeed, he continues, it is precisely Heidegger's invocation of play that "announces the possibility of a post-metaphysical thinking" (Küchler 1994, 23). While he attempts to challenge elements of Nietzsche's framing, Heidegger "thinks of power in prerational terms, as arbitrary, spontaneous, and violent play. No less than Nietzsche's eternal play of forces, Heidegger's play of Being remains groundless while it grounds everything that comes into being. . . . [H]e adopts Nietzsche's prerational perspective not only in his critique of modern rational values, but also in his return to the Presocratics" (Spariosu 1989, 121).

As discussed above, Heidegger read in Heraclitus' exploration of play the force behind being/becoming. Taking from Heraclitus an answer to the question of the energy or momentum of being, he asks: "Why does it play, the great child of the world-play that Heraclitus brought into view[?]" He concludes: "It plays, because it plays. The 'because' withers away in the play. The play is without 'why.' It plays since it plays. It simply remains a play: the most elevated and the most profound. But this 'simply' is everything, the one, the only" (Heidegger 1996, 113). To illustrate this process, Heidegger sets out his notion of the play of being as *Geschick*, in which "Western metaphysics . . . is not some kind of avoidable human misprision, but an arbitrary turning (*Kehre*) in the hide-and-seek game that Language-Being plays with Dasein. Man's fateful mission (*Geschick*) is simply to play along" (Spariosu 1989, 122).

Play as that by means of which man generates Being is thus of crucial import for Heidegger. As Küchler explains, Heidegger posits thinking of "'Being *qua* abyss,' that is, no longer as a grounded notion that denotes presence but as a structural moment within an ungrounded movement of play." Thinking of being as an abyss means that it is no longer grounded but rather formed through play. This means that "play is something that escapes the metaphysical notions of reason and ground," and Heidegger thus posits "a thinking of the notions of Being and ground that takes into account the possibility of play" (Küchler 1994, 26–27). Heidegger seeks a new form of thinking that "takes the risk of thinking 'Being and ground/reason . . . in terms of the essence of play' and not the other way around" (Küchler 1994, 27). To gain access to this "other thinking," Heidegger enacts a radical challenge that "removes[s] the stability of the ground and open[s] up the abyss of a general economy of play," which he describes as a "leap" (*Satz*) (Küchler 1994, 27). Through this leap, which pushes at the limits of metaphysical thinking, a new "ungrounded . . . and unrestricted *grounding* movement of play" becomes thinkable (Küchler 1994, 28).

In this new framework, while games can be used as a "refuge from the real" designed to evade the experience of "being-towards-death" (Webster 2014, 188), play proper refers to the self-generating momentum that animates being despite the latter's ultimate groundlessness: "Being, as what grounds, has no ground; as the abyss it plays the play that, as *Geschick*, passes being and ground/reason to us. The question remains whether and how we, hearing the movements of this play, play along and accommodate ourselves to the play" (Heidegger 1996, 113). The challenge posed by Heidegger, again following Nietzsche, is how to exist under the conditions of foundationlessness described by the death of God. Following the death of God, understood as the removal of all solid foundations for thought, metaphysics, and Being, all that remains is the play of groundless existence. In Heidegger's own words, "[T]he essence of Being is the game itself" (quoted in Axelos 1971, 8). As Spariosu puts it, "Heidegger defines Being itself as play, or as an interplay of Ground and Groundlessness, of sending forth and withdrawal, which cannot be 'rationalized' or thought of in terms of any particular being" (1989, 119–120).

As this suggests, and as his critics have argued, while he certainly problematizes the foundations upon which Apollonian thought rests, Heidegger ultimately fails to break free of the logic of origin (*Ursprung*). Heidegger's is a "de-humanized, ontocentric" philosophy (Nagel 1998, 21), which leads to a paradoxical framing of being as both ground and unground:

> The interpretation of Being as Ground (*Grund*, in the sense of firm land, solid surface, and reason or rationale) always also implies an interpretation of Being as Groundlessness or Abyss (*Ab-grund*). . . . Being as the no-thing is an abyss (*Abgrund*) and as such it does not need a ground; at the same time, however, Being grounds the totality of beings that emerge into presence. . . . Heidegger defines Being itself as play, or as an interplay of Ground and Groundlessness. (Spariosu 1989, 118–119)

This positioning means that the "play of Being remains groundless while it grounds everything that comes into being" (Spariosu 1989, 121). The retention of the logic/structure of origin even as the attempt is made to hollow out its contents means that Heidegger remains within the logic of being.

Heidegger's project is, however, but one of the major contributions made by phenomenologists interested in play. Hans argues that Gadamer's development of a hermeneutic phenomenology is based on play (Hans 1981, ix). Sutton-Smith agrees, claiming that "Gadamer's to-and-fro views of play are probably also a metaphor for his open-ended, ever-recycling theory of the nature of human 'hermeneutic' understanding" (Sutton-Smith 2001, 184). Like Heidegger, Gadamer seeks to leave behind analyses focusing on play through the lens of player experience in favor of getting at the nature of play itself. That is, he argues that play is not generated or confined by players' activities but rather "merely manifests itself (*kommt zur Darstellung*) through them" (Spariosu 1989, 135). Accordingly, Gadamer seeks to develop an ontology of play as a force or mode of being in itself. Framing his exploration of play through the question of art, he states:

> The "subject" of the experience of art, that which remains and endures, it not the subjectivity of the person who experiences it but the work itself. This is the point at which the mode of being of play becomes significant. For play has its own essence, independent of the consciousness of those who play. Play—indeed, play proper—also exists when the thematic horizon is not limited by any being-for-itself of subjectivity, and where there are no subjects who are behaving "playfully." (Gadamer 2004, 103)

This means that play has its own immanent momentum and features, whether or not a person engages in playful activities: The "movement backward and forward is obviously so central to the definition of play that it makes no difference who or what performs this movement. The movement of play as such has, as it were, no substrate. It is the game that is played—it is irrelevant whether or not there is a subject who plays it." For Gadamer, then, play is a movement that exists in itself: "The play is the occurrence of the movement as such." Echoing Huizinga and Nietzsche, Gadamer posits that this vital movement "is not tied to any goal that would bring it to an end . . . [R]ather, it renews itself in constant repetition" (Gadamer 2004, 104).

Gadamer addresses the question of the seriousness of play to justify this claim: "[F]or the player play is not serious: that is why he plays. What is merely play is not serious." This is because players' serious everyday concerns are suspended in play. And yet, he continues, play "has a special relation to

what is serious . . . [P]lay itself contains its own, even sacred, seriousness."
He explains: "Play fulfils its purpose only if the player loses himself in play.
Seriousness is not merely something that calls us away from play; rather, seriousness in playing is necessary to make the play wholly play. . . . The player
knows very well what play is, and that what he is doing is 'only a game'; but
he does not know what exactly he 'knows' in knowing that" (Gadamer 2004,
102–103).

Gadamer seeks to look beyond player experience to better understand the
seriousness of play. This is necessary because "play does not have its being
in the player's consciousness or attitude, but on the contrary play draws him
into its dominion and fills him with its spirit. The player experiences the
game as a reality that surpasses him" (Gadamer 2004, 109). Feezell points out
that for Gadamer "[t]he subject of play is play itself, not the subjectivity of the
player. . . . The experience of freedom from the strains of ordinary life is the
result of play playing itself through the player" (2014, 25).

Citing Huizinga's exploration of the "holy play" in which the difference
between truth and falsehood is dissolved, Gadamer notes that the playing
subject experiences a "curious indecisiveness" that makes it "absolutely impossible to decide between belief and non-belief." This confusing but pleasant
experience is explained by the idea that play has primacy over the consciousness of the player: "The structure of play absorbs the player into itself, and
thus frees him from the burden of taking the initiative, which constitutes the
actual strain of existence." This absorption is experienced by the player as an
enjoyable "absence of strain" and "relaxation," which can be seen in "the spontaneous tendency to repetition that emerges in the player and in the constant
self-renewal of play" (Gadamer 2004, 105). Thus play is characterized by a
"lightness and sense of relief" (Gadamer 2004, 108). In a play experience,
the player "gives herself over to the game, or, if there is some dispute about
speaking of a 'game' . . . the player is taken up by her enjoyable experience of
confronting gratuitous difficulties (or unnecessary obstacles)" (Feezell 2014,
26). In this reading, "play is giving oneself up to the play" (Hans 1981, 185),
the gaming being "a dynamic whole *sui generis* that embraces even the subjectivity of the one who plays" (Gadamer 2008, 53).

Thus the subject is decentered in the experience of play; "play is less a
thing a person does and more a thing done to him" (Vilhauer 2014, 77).
This means, as Barry Dixon notes, that "the game exists over and above its
players. We never change a game by taking part. Rather, it is we who are
changed. We must submit ourselves to the rules of the game, allowing these

rules to shape and move our contributions. We are taken in by the game, becoming part of its world" (2014, 70). In this encounter, the player is simultaneously free and constrained. As Catherine Homan explains, this is because play "marks a negotiation between the boundaries of the game and the free movement of the player, and is always a matter of *with* and *of*. The player thus dramatically and creatively plays with and within this space, or, more strongly, 'the player belongs to the play'" (Homan 2014, 101). Thus, far from an experience of unbridled freedom, as Huizinga would have it, for Gadamer play involves the joy of the game imposing on us (Sutton-Smith 2001, 189).

These observations lead Gadamer to a counterintuitive but powerful conclusion:

> [A]ll playing is a being-played. The attraction of a game, the fascination it exerts, consist precisely in the fact that the game masters the players. . . . Whoever "tries" is in fact the one who is tried. The real subject of the game . . . is not the player but the game itself. What holds the player in its spell, draws him into play, and keeps him there is the game itself. (Gadamer 2004, 106)

Importantly, the consequence of this is that "much of the pleasure of playing lies in the fact that the game plays you; that your reactions are often more reflexive or involuntary than voluntary; that the game takes you out of yourself" (Sutton-Smith 2001, 183). This involves a loss of self-consciousness—in Gadamer's terms, a "self-forgetfulness." Challenging Plato's error of "judging the ecstasy of being outside oneself from the point of view of rational reasonableness and of seeing it as the mere negation of being within oneself, i.e. as a kind of madness," Gadamer viewed this state of being-otherwise as "the positive possibility of being wholly with something else" (quoted in Hans 1981, 8). For Gadamer, "the kind of self-forgetfulness involved in play is really a self-remembering, an awareness of one's world that is not possible in a reflective, mediated view" (Hans 1981, 8). And yet play in this reading is not passive. On the contrary, it involves "the intention, willingness or choice to constrain one's own freedom to the rules of the game . . . [in order] to accomplish something." This is a "profound commitment" in which players "actively approach the game with the seriousness of a fully engaged participant." They must "actively comport themselves in such a way that they become fully involved or immersed in the game. They must have, we might say, seriously playful attitudes and intentions to give themselves over to the game and fully engage in it" (Vilhauer 2014, 77).

As will be explored in subsequent chapters, this has interesting and troubling implications—namely that far from the player playing the game, the game plays the player. Gadamer's own words seem to support this conclusion: "Whatever is brought into play or comes into play no longer depends on itself but is dominated by the relation that we call the game. For the individual who, as playing subjectivity, engages in the game, this fact may seem at first to be an accommodation. He conforms to the game or subjects himself to it, that is, he relinquishes the autonomy of his own will" (2008, 53). Spariosu comes to a similar view: in Gadamer's analysis, "the attitude of the player does not determine the nature of play; rather, the nature of play determines the attitude of the player" (Spariosu 1989, 135–136). In other words, Gadamer defines play as "repetitive encapsulation of the self" (Sutton-Smith 2001, 183). This important argument raises the possibility that play is identity-producing. If a player is changed in and by play, the assumption of an ontologically prior player-subject is challenged. The implication of Gadamer's analysis, then, is that the player is constituted in and through play—an idea core to poststructural play theories.

While this appears to open up the possibility of a radical reformulation of the relationship between play and the player, Gadamer ultimately pulls back from the consequences of this move by positing a pure player-subject: "First and foremost, play is self-presentation. . . . [I]n spending oneself on the task of the game, one is in fact playing oneself out. The self-presentation of the game involves the player's achieving, as it were, his own self-presentation by playing—i.e., presenting—something" (2004, 108). Gadamer bases his theory on the assumption that play, like aesthetic experience, makes possible "pure self-presentation" (Hans 1981, 6). This category of "pure" raises important questions, especially in hermeneutic phenomenology: specifically,

[h]ow could it be—particularly in the hermeneutic phenomenology of Gadamer, which stresses human finitude—that any kind of experience could be pure? Inasmuch as all perspectives are necessarily limited, finite, no such purity is possible. Likewise, Gadamer's model of play and of meaningful experience depends on breaking down the boundaries between world and self, and if this is what actually occurs during play, how could the experience be one of self-presentation? (Hans 1981, 7)

Despite enacting a profound challenge to the malediction of play in Western philosophy, then, in falling back on the production of a pure self-presenting subject, Gadamer ultimately privileges the Apollonian over the Dionysian. While he sought to explore play as an ontological force, he ultimately shied away from the Nietzschean reading in favor of "the rational aspects of play, especially in their artistic guise . . . [specifically] the 'orderly transformation into structure' of a chaotic, arbitrary, and purposeless natural movement." Gadamer is ultimately not prepared to accept the consequences of giving up on Platonic-Aristotelian rationalism (Spariosu 1989, 143), with the result that "his play concept will appear as a forced marriage between rational and prerational play elements" (Spariosu 1989, 133).

According to Küchler, this means that it is not Gadamer but rather Heidegger who provides a powerful point of departure for the conceptualization of a post-modern theory of play (Küchler 1994, 23). This is because "Heidegger's determination of truth as play escapes the permanence and presence implied in traditional metaphysical thinking. . . . The play of Being . . . remains essentially fragmentary and intermittent, the movement of presencing always at the same time presencing its own withdrawal" (Küchler 1994, 39). In other words, "what is at stake in Heidegger's leap and in his transition into the general economy of play is not so much the '*Überwindung*' (over-coming) of metaphysics as its '*Verwindung*' (surmounting), the movement of exposing the restricted field of metaphysical thinking to its non-metaphysical and ungrounded essence" (Küchler 1994, 28). In contrast, he explains,

> Gadamer's play is *dialectical* or *dialogical* in nature. It is a play that plays in the "*inter* of interpretation," that is, *between* the work [of art] and its beholder, both of whom come to lose their individuality in favor of something which is the bipolar structure of dialogue. . . . *[P]lay itself*, as the mediating term . . . now becomes the subject of the interpretive process. . . . Play sublates the individual experiences of its players into the transcending and transcendental structure of its own self. . . . Gadamer's economy of play is consequently of the restricted sort. It is an economy with the clearly defined task of producing continuity and meaning within its own self. For this reason, Gadamer cannot accept the idea of an unlimited free-play. (Küchler 1994, 60–61)

Against this, he concludes, Heidegger provides an interpretation that "escapes the 'horizontality' of a movement of play between two beings, always originating in an abyss. This abyss cannot be bridged in dialogue or the dialectical play of speculation." This framing "ultimately punctuates and suspends the mediating play of dialogue on which Gadamer bases his entire hermeneutic project" (Küchler 1994, 65). As Chapter 4 will show, however, Derrida developed a critique of Heidegger that draws out the extent to which he reproduced the metaphysical thinking he sought to destabilize.[7]

Conclusion

This chapter has developed a genealogy of play in Western philosophy from Presocratic to phenomenological framings. It identified two discursive modes of play—the Apollonian and the Dionysian—that have operated in dialectical tension in Western thought in ancient to modern traditions. It began by exploring key ancient framings of play, specifically the insights of Heraclitus and the challenges posed by Plato and Aristotle. From there, the chapter explored framings of play in modern philosophy, focusing on the German Idealist tradition. Having argued that the Apollonian mode comes to dominate in this period, the chapter turned to Nietzsche's challenge to the Western philosophical tradition and the accompanying return of the Dionysian in and beyond play. It notes that while there is much to praise in Nietzsche's unsettling of the prevailing Apollonian constraints, he retains a problematic view of the hero-warrior player, reflected in his claim of the "innocence of becoming."

Having set out the Nietzschean challenge to Apollonian play, the chapter then turned to his (would-be) inheritors, beginning with Johan Huizinga, showing that despite his embrace of Dionysian themes Huizinga nevertheless retains an Apollonian tone through his privileging of some forms of play over others. The chapter then turned to the phenomenological tradition of Martin Heidegger and Hans-Georg Gadamer, the focus of which is providing an account of play in itself, as opposed to one mediated through the engagement of a player-subject. Thus I showed that despite problematizing key elements of the Western metaphysical tradition, the phenomenologists' treatment of play remains distinctly Apollonian through its search for (groundless) origin,

---

[7] As I have argued elsewhere, I wager it is this tendency to return to metaphysics—rather than accept and work within the foundationlessness of (post)modernity—that underpins his fascism (Hirst 2013).

being, and presence. Key to this is the role of being as presence in Gadamer's analysis. Accordingly, concurring with Hans, we must "look at play outside of the conceptions of pure presence, of *parousia*, of Being, of essence." We must move beyond Gadamer because he ultimately "bases his ideas of play on Being" (1981, 9). Seeking precisely this more radical view of play, Chapter 4 turns to the poststructural tradition and offers a deconstructive theorization of play that resists a grounding in (groundless) being or presence, drawing upon the thought of Jacques Derrida. It is my wager that this third mode of thinking contains useful tools by means of which the hyperreal productions of wargaming in the era of simulation might be destabilized.

4

The Play of Postmodernity

Deconstructive Play

Introduction: Postmodern Play

Building on the genealogy of play traced in Chapter 3, this chapter develops a new theorization of play—"deconstructive play"—that embraces the festival, fun, and freedom of the Dionysian while at the same moment moving beyond it by cultivating critique. Turning to postmodern modes of thinking, the chapter argues that it is in the thought of Jacques Derrida that we see a return to, and graduation beyond, the Dionysian. Noting his inheritance of Nietzsche's challenge to metaphysics in general, and his reformulation of play in particular, it shows that Derrida's deconstructive thinking issues a thoroughgoing challenge to the Apollonian tenets of origin, foundations, and presence. Understanding human subjectivity as a process of "becoming," rather than a fixed condition of "being," Derrida powerfully demonstrates how the play of the world produces meaning and subjectivities, opening pathways to a repoliticization of philosophy and play. This lays the groundwork for my conceptualization of deconstructive play, which embraces the Dionysian tradition's principles of festival, unreason, and groundlessness but seeks to move beyond it by cultivating ongoing reflexivity. Arguing for an autodeconstructive subject who critically interrogates both her play activities and herself, deconstructive play repoliticizes our playscapes by challenging hegemonic power relations. Viewing wargames as one type of hyperreal model that cancels the play of meaning (Baudrillard 1983), I seek through deconstructive play to reintroduce contradiction, tension, and difference such that their ontological totality might be disrupted.

The chapter begins by outlining Derrida's distinctive approach to play and his understanding of its power. From there, it examines his framing of deconstruction as a mode of critical engagement that operates through the movements of play. The core claim is that play is at work in the movements of deconstruction, or rather that play "is" its movements. Having made this

Politics of Play. Aggie Hirst, Oxford University Press. © Oxford University Press 2024.
DOI: 10.1093/oso/9780197629192.003.0005

case, the chapter sets out my reconceptualization of play—deconstructive play—as an addition to the established Apollonian-Dionysian dualism. It makes the case that deconstructive play can be understood as a mode of critical and reflexive thinking that functions as and through play. Against some of the critical literature that frames play as a phenomenon that requires critical challenge as a result of its complicities with neoliberal capitalism (Soderman 2021), I argue that play can be—though is not automatically—precisely such a mode of challenge.

In order to substantiate this argument, the chapter traces how this deconstructive mode of thinking might function through a reexamination of key assumptions about play and games. First it seeks to disentangle play from games to challenge the restrictions on the former imposed by the structures of the latter. Second, it addresses how a deconstructive player might be cultivated, and how this can move beyond the problematic hero-warrior subject of the Dionysian tradition. Finally, it sets out some ways that a deconstructive play mode might interact with existing gameworlds and communities. Having done so, the remainder of this book operationalizes this deconstructive mode of thinking to disrupt the smooth production of hyperreality through wargaming. It does this by first exploring how wargaming produces people by intervening in the cognitive dimension (Chapter 5) and the affective dimension (Chapter 6). From there it identifies two key drivers of wargames—the drive to win (Chapter 7) and the spell of immersion (Chapter 8)—and critically examines their functions and implications for the production of people in an era of hyperreality.

Poststructural Play

The poststructural tradition, of which Derrida's philosophy is a part, is frequently viewed as rule-breaking in its radical reconceptualization of play (Wilson 1986, 75). As Thomas S. Henricks notes, while modern play tends toward individualism, order-making, rule-following, and extrinsic motivation and rewards, and while it operates through the game form, poststructural thought centers play as a force that cultivates "instances of resistance to prevailing cultural patterns . . . [through] act[s] of defiance or reversal, an attempt to undo what is normal" (2015, 195). Poststructuralist thinkers have used the term "play" to connote a resistance to ontological fixing, whether in terms of meaning, identity, or language. John Caputo, for instance, emphasizes the importance of "keeping the play in play, of playing along with the play, of avoiding at all costs the repression of the play . . . [M]etaphysics is the systematic attempt to repress the play, to hold it in check: to create the illusion of abiding truth over and against the flux" (1985, 74).

In this framing, if metaphysics aspires to order and being, play—as a process—emphasizes becoming, changing, and ambiguity. According to poststructuralists, there is an ontopolitics to play; while for Kant and his inheritors play compromises reason, knowledge, and seriousness, for poststructuralists—here in line with Nietzsche's challenge—play resists metaphysical fixing by destabilizing and unsettling totalizing assumptions and principles. The poststructural wager is that through a return to the Dionysian, play can be redefined in order to unleash its political potentials (Galloway 2006, 126) and open pathways to the new (Cremin 2016, 64). While some might fear the excesses of the "libidinal forces of sexuality, excess, play, the artificial and the everyday" at work in the postmodern inheritors of the Dionysian (Giddings 2018, 776), below I make the case for a poststructural retheorization of play.

Writing amid the postmodern revolution, Tilman Küchler argues that accompanying the decline of modernist universalizing discourses was the rise of play: "Within this postmodern and post-metaphysical context the notion of play comes to replace the metaphysical desire to ground things" in unifying principles, laws, and truths. Play's principal achievement in this revolution, he continues, was nothing less than the "liberation of thought from metaphysical a prioris" (Küchler 1994, 1). Such freedom "comes to refer to a certain *praxis*, to a certain performative movement that responds to an ungrounded, unstable ontological condition of play" (Küchler 1994, 3). This liberation is not a simple freedom from constraints, but rather the radically positive insight that thought, selfhood, and truth are themselves generated through the movements of play. Drawing upon Richard Rorty, Küchler outlines the impacts of these changes on philosophical enterprises:

[B]oth form and content of philosophical thinking undergo a fundamental change. . . . "[T]his development has made possible a more playful, more cosmopolitan, less professional tone in which to philosophize. . . ." The "new" epoch of play seems to be one of a general "revaluation of all values," an epoch in which the very ground for any sort of definitive hierarchization and valorization . . . is no longer available. As a result, the epoch of play is

one of contingency and flux . . . the dissolution of the metaphysical ground
in an originary heterogeneity and in a movement of play. (Küchler 1994, 2)

As Ryall, Russell, and MacLean note, "[I]t may come as little surprise that the
continental philosophers . . . have had more to say about the nature and value
of play's pre-rational elements, whereas analytical philosophy has sought to
subordinate the emotional and unconstrained excesses of pre-rational play
to its civilizing role in rational ethics and epistemology" (2014, 2–3).

At the same time, the status of the subject is radically altered in the postmodern turn: "[T]here is nothing stable about the subject any more. Rather,
the subject has lost its ground and essence in the infinite play of a non-ground
and an 'abyss.' " Instead of seeking to reground itself, the postmodern subject
comes to recognize its production through play: "[T]here can be no more
yearning for the end of play. . . . What remains, then, in the post-metaphysical
epoch of play is the movement of play 'itself' and the 'corresponding' affirmation of this play—'in a certain laughter and a certain step of dance' " though
which the subject self-produces (Küchler 1994, 4). As this suggests, there is
a distinctive Nietzschean inheritance at work here in the bid to liberate play
from "the various metaphysical interpretations it has received through the
history of Western thinking." However, Küchler continues, the postmodern
modality of play does not call for a return to the Dionysian: "[T]he postmodern and post-metaphysical *turn* to the notion of play cannot merely be
understood in terms of a *return* to some historically coded interpretation
and form of play" (1994, 4). Neither is play a mere binary opposite to metaphysics or grounding. Rather, play in this framework is a mode of thinking
that occupies, and plays with(in), metaphysics.

Among the poststructural thinkers associated with the postmodern turn,
several are explicitly interested in play. Gilles Deleuze and Félix Guattari
seek to redeem the pre-rational play mentality of Nietzsche through the play
of rhizomes, while Michel Foucault laments the work to which play is put
in disciplinary regimes of schools, prisons, and employment, and Roland
Barthes shows how texts and their readers play in multiple ways (Barthes
1985, 62–63; Cremin 2016, 57–64; Spariosu 1989, 11). And, as mentioned
above, Baudrillard identified the cessation of the play between the real and
imaginary, the signified and the signifier, as the underpinning of the era
of simulation, in which reality has been captured and replaced by models
(Baudrillard 1983). However, arguably no thinker of the tradition takes play

more seriously than Derrida (Derrida 1985, 60; Spariosu 1989, 154). As a metaphor for the movements through which meaning and people are made, unmade, and remade, play resides at the heart of Derrida's thought. This makes it a valuable resource in fighting back against the totalizations of the era of simulation.

Derrida's Interminable Economy of Play

Treating the theme across a number of his works, Derrida sees in play nothing less than an "interminable economy"[1] that can generate the capacity to radically rethink the Western philosophical tradition and its reliance on foundations, origins, and ultimate ends. Asking, "[W]hat is the economy of play?," he advises wariness of accounts that present it as "only a game," merely gratuitous expenditure without meaning. While telling, such obscurantist positions fail to "try to comprehend what play signifies, what strategies, interests, and investments are at work in play" (Derrida 1985, 68). Notwithstanding poor readings that frame him as abandoning meaning (Anderson 2006), for Derrida play is singularly political, powerful, and generative.

Derrida identifies in Plato the origins of the malediction of play that has endured into modern Western thought. He argues that while Plato appears to speak favorably of play, he limits this praise to play "only in the best sense of the word," understood as that which is "supervised and contained within the safeguards of ethics and politics . . . comprehended under the innocent, innocuous category of 'fun.'" Like Plato's idealist and phenomenologist inheritors, far from unequivocally promoting or celebrating play, Derrida continues, its framing as "amusement" or "pastime" actually "helps consolidate the Platonic repression of play" (Derrida 2004, 155–156). This repression occurs because Plato ontologizes play. As Derrida explains:

> [Once] play begins to *be* something . . . its very presence lays it open to some
> sort of dialectical confiscation. It takes on meaning and works in the service
> of seriousness, truth, and ontology. . . . As soon as it comes into being and
> into language, play *erases itself as such*. . . . The point is that there *is* no *as*

---

[1] I borrow this framing from Küchler 1994, 150.

such where writing or play are concerned. . . . They cannot, in classical affirmation, be affirmed without being negated. (Derrida 2004, 155)

Because he only plays at taking play seriously, Plato presides over a progressive neutralization of play, the effects of which were still resounding as Derrida wrote. Consequently, he concludes that "[p]lay and art are lost by Plato as he saves them" (Derrida 2004, 155).

Such a purge of the playful can be explained, as Hans argues, as an attempt to resolve or offset the anxiety produced by the disruption of foundations and groundings in the post-Nietzschean world (Hans 2009, 368). The Dionysian return, with its unsettling of stable philosophical groundings for metaphysics and ontology, he explains, proved for many too much to bear.[2] Rejecting the unruly and risky play that remained in its place, much of Western philosophy has turned back to the Platonic-Apollonian quest for order and origins (Hans 2009). In this quest, play is limited and directed by means of a "reassuring certitude" such as "essence, existence, substance, subject . . . transcendentality, consciousness, God, man, and so on," which serves to master the anxiety caused by the disorienting unending play of meaning (Derrida 2009, 352–353).

Seeking to rekindle Nietzsche's challenge, Derrida is interested precisely in the disruptive capacities of play. He supports "the Nietzschean critique of metaphysics, the critique of the concepts of Being and truth," and favors "the concepts of play, interpretation, and sign (sign without present truth)" (Derrida 2009, 354). This poses a direct and profound challenge to the Apollonian caution surrounding play's disorderly tendencies. In this framing of play, "Plato's nightmare of bad mimesis, associated with immediate power and violence[,] finally comes true. In such contemporary thinkers as Deleuze, Derrida, and their followers play is no longer good mimesis, installing Being and Truth; rather, mimesis is (Platonic) bad play, replacing Being and Truth with the eternal play of simulacra" (Spariosu 1989, 20).

Derrida outlines two forms of play, which correspond broadly to the Apollonian and Dionysian modes set out in Chapter 3. On the one hand, he describes "a *sure* play: that which is limited to the substitution of *given* and *existing, present*, pieces." At work in this framing is a dream of "deciphering a truth or an origin which escapes play" (Derrida 2009, 369). Mapping onto

---

[2] For detailed discussion of this securitizing response to metaphysical destabilization, see Hirst 2013.

the Apollonian mode, in this formulation play is oriented, balanced, organized, and controlled so that something concrete remains in place to provide meaning and certitude. Such limited play is constrained in advance by its desire for a lost origin, saddened and nostalgic in the manner of Rousseau (Derrida 2009, 369), and functions to instill and consolidate order, qua Huizinga (Galloway 2006, 30). Such a play has, as María Lugones argues, a relation of agonism at its root (Lugones 1987, 15), positing an ontologically given subject who interacts—plays—with an object. Here play is limited to "someone who plays" (Anderson 2003, 81; Derrida 1985, 69). In spite of these defensive efforts, however, in this "sure play" elements of the supposedly stable structure remain at play, unsettling the attempt to unify and resolve play (Sawyer 2015, 35–36).

Sitting in tension with this "sure play," and explicitly invoking Nietzsche, Derrida outlines an "unsure" form of play that deviates from, and works to destabilize, order (Derrida 2009, 354; Galloway 2006, 30). Such play resists bureaucratization or instrumentalization, remaining free, minor, sporadic, nomadic, and interstitial (Cohen 1983, 247). In this risky form of play, chance and contingency reign (Derrida 2009, 369; Derrida 1985, 69–70), and rules are not fixed (Lugones 1987, 17). This type of play "substitutes the centrifugality of uncertainty for the centripetality of the Western quest for a transcendental signified," remaining always on the verge of becoming something else—here, the ludic is always possibly ludicrous (Aycock 1993). Importantly, this type of play is not limited to a person's actions; instead, it is the "play of the world" through which meaning and subjectivity are produced (Bitan 2012, 34; Wilson 1986, 81).

This clearly conjures the spirit of Dionysian play. Echoing the fear of the destabilizing potential of the Dionysian evident in Plato and Kant's Apollonian tendencies, it is Derrida's view that "sure" play is a result of existential anxiety. This is because

> [t]he concept of a centred structure . . . is contradictorily coherent. And as always, coherence in contradiction expresses the force of a desire. The concept of a centred structure is in fact the concept of a play based on a fundamental ground, a play constituted on the basis of a fundamental immobility and a reassuring certitude, which is itself beyond the reach of play. And on the basis of this certitude anxiety can be mastered, for anxiety is invariably the result of a certain mode of being implicated in the game, of being caught by the game, of being as it were at stake in the game from the outset. (Derrida 2009, 352)

It is erroneously thought that "[t]hrough centred play, one can master an anxiety" (Spariosu 1989, 156). Arguing that we must set aside this desire for origins and let go of this anxious desire for a lost grounding, Derrida says that "we must *affirm* this, in the sense in which Nietzsche puts affirmation into play, in a certain laughter and a certain step of the dance" (1986, 27). He elaborates elsewhere that this Nietzschean affirmation "is the joyous affirmation of the play of the world and of the innocence of becoming, the affirmation of a world of signs without fault, without truth, and without origin which is offered to an active interpretation" (Derrida 2009, 369). This entails letting go of any stable or given ground upon which to base claims because they reflect not an actual condition but rather a certain anxiety precipitated by their absence. The "desire for this 'reassuring foundation,' as Derrida puts it, is understandable enough, but the reasons why such a reassuring foundation is not possible are more compelling and should place our desire for it in proper perspective" (Hans 1981, 16).

Crucially, for Derrida as for Nietzsche, this shift is not a nightmare but an opportunity: "*This affirmation then determines the noncentre otherwise than as a loss of the centre. And it plays without security*" (Derrida 2009, 369; emphasis in original). What is suggested here is that play is the movement that produces meaning, identity, and difference in a context wherein foundations and origins have been radically disputed. In this framework, play is not an object or concept but rather, as Küchler puts it, "the structural moment of non-totalization itself" (Küchler 1994, 128). The endless play of the world, then, is to be not lamented but embraced as the process by which meaning and subjects are made, unmade, and remade.

Play produces not "a new wholeness" but rather "a permanent state of nonwholeness, 'nontotalization' . . . a permanent agitation of the field, a generative motion" (Galloway 2006, 26). This form of play involves giving up the search for a center or grounding for meaning and subjectivity, as well as giving up any lament for its lack. This is important because when one looks closely—deconstructively—at an apparently given center or ground it turns out to be a "constructive fiction" (Gold 2004, 221). The center or origin we identify comes not from the case in question but from outside, superimposed by a thinking subject so as to organize and make sense of things (Sawyer 2015, 36). Far from encountering an abyss of relativism, when we cease to see the absence of a center as a loss, we can appreciate the generative power of the play of the world. In this serious unseriousness, one can hear echoes of the laughter of Dionysian play (Cohen 1983, 248).

In taking these steps, Derrida draws upon yet moves beyond Heidegger. As Küchler explains, "Heidegger has already gained access to the realm of the post-metaphysical thinking of play. This play now reappears in Derrida's text, however, not without a certain displacement of its movement and without a critique of the *event* of its appearance" (1994, 136). He elaborates that Derrida shares with Heidegger the wager of a leap that pushes at the constraints of metaphysics: "Like Heidegger before him, Derrida also initiates this disruption and brings about the opening of his play by means of a leap (*Satz*)." However, the character of Derrida's leap differs from that of Heidegger's. While Heidegger's leap entails "the leap *out* of the metaphysical domain of science and philosophy and *into* the play of the abyss," Derrida views this as moving "within the structurality of metaphysical thinking . . . that restricts, in an almost metaphysical fashion, the movement of play by centering it around an idea of transcendental presence" (Küchler 1994, 138–139). Against this, Derrida argues for a leap that

> leads him out of what he perceives as the original presence and propriety of Heidegger's notion of the event (*Ereignis*) . . . Derrida's leap has shown that there is no such radical otherness that dispenses property and constitutes Being as presence. . . . Consequently the leap never reaches a bottom and ground beyond the surface (of language). . . . The infrastructural play—the play of the infrastructural conditions of possibility—is ungrounded and decentered. (Küchler 1994, 143–144)

In other words, Heidegger's leap into the abyss is rejected by Derrida as a form of *telos*, which has become obsolete. It is, Küchler explains, "no longer a '*question of jumping with both feet out of a circle*.'" Rather, Derrida advocates "the movement of virtually infinite displacements, a strategy of re-marking and re-writing, of 'scribing [*d'écrire*]' and 'describing [*décrire*]'" (Küchler 1994, 147). Such a strategy is described by Derrida as deconstruction.

The Play of Deconstruction

Derrida is perhaps best known for his framing of deconstruction, which, as Souvik Mukherjee notes, has "as one of its key concepts, 'play'" (2017, 104). Framed in terms of a textual disruption, deconstruction intervenes both at the level of written texts but also in the material world. As Sutton-Smith puts it, deconstruction is a "tactic for endlessly finding further interpretations not yet revealed and thus defeating orthodox understandings" (2001, 147). Indeed, one way of describing the movements of deconstruction is *as* play: "[P]lay is that for the sake of which deconstruction is undertaken; deconstruction is a form of play. When one gives up the nostalgia, not even the search or the hope, for a 'lost native country of thought,' one plays." Understood in this way, "deconstruction is the play-form of metaphysics" (Weinstein and Weinstein 1990, 120). As Sutton-Smith similarly observes, "Because Derrida calls the text a play of signifiers, it might seem appropriate to call it a text at play. . . . If the world is a text, the play is a reader's response to that text" (2001, 144–166).

What plays in the movements of deconstruction is the trace of marginalized or suppressed meaning. Mukherjee writes, "Derrida views the relationship between the centre and the margins to be 'in play'" (2017, 104). This trace haunts apparently stable interpretations, unsettling their (Apollonian) aspirations to origin, being, or presence. This might be described as "the play of the trace. The play of a trace which no longer belongs to the horizon of Being, but whose play transports and encloses the meaning of Being: the play of the trace, or the *différance*, which has no meaning and is not. Which does not belong. There is no maintaining, and no depth to, this bottomless chessboard on which Being is put into play" (Derrida 1986, 22).

While interesting debates have explored the overlaps and tensions between the phenomenological approaches of Gadamer, Heidegger, and Fink, on the one hand, and Derrida's deconstruction, on the other (Michelfelder and Palmer 1989), some clear distinctions can be drawn between their respective treatments of play. While both outline the ways in which play can challenge ontotheological strictures of conventional modes of being, the phenomenologists ultimately rely upon and reproduce Apollonian tenets. Indeed, a residual fear of the Dionysian is perceptible among the phenomenologists, for example in Fink's statement that play "can contain within itself not only a clear apollonian moment of free self-determination, but also the dark dionysian moment of panic self-abandon" (Fink 1971, 25). As this suggests, the phenomenologists sought to ground play in being, or else to use play to explain it. "As Nagel remarks, "Phenomenologists share a predilection for an origin (*Ursprung*!)" (1998, 20). Fink elaborates:

The perplexing world-formula, according to which Being in its totality functions like play, may perhaps make us aware of the fact that play is no harmless, peripheral or even "childish" thing—that precisely in the power and glory of our magical creativity we mortal men are "at stake" in an inscrutably threatening way. Once the essence of the world is conceived as play, the logical consequence for man is that he is the only creature in the entire universe who can relate to and reproduce the workings of the whole of Being. (Fink 1971, 29–30)

Such a tendency is also apparent in Huizinga's play theory: "Play, Huizinga claims, is the origin of culture; it is foundational since it is 'older than culture'" (Nagel 1998, 20).

Contrariwise, Derrida's deconstructive framing of play is not oriented toward origin or order. The subject does not affirm or secure itself through play but rather is produced and disrupted through it. In his words, a deconstructive understanding of play

is no longer turned toward the origin, [but rather] affirms play and tries to pass beyond man and humanism, the name of man being the name of that being who, throughout the history of metaphysics or of ontotheology—in other words, throughout his entire history—has dreamed of full presence, the reassuring foundation, the origin and the end of play. (Derrida 2009, 370)

Play thus serves to punctuate the "*jouissance* of presence" that games and other contained systems provide (Botz-Bornstein 2013, 252). The player-subject is problematized rather than flattered or affirmed (Anderson 2003), and risks getting lost (Aycock 1993). In opening up the self to its playful constitution, the subject risks the loss of stable meaning and identity, but in doing so finds something important and liberating (Laing 2012). This distances the subject from Being—understood as a fixed state of existence—placing them instead in the movements of "becoming" (Harker 2005, 53)

Play read in this sense is a metaphor for non-foundation (Botz-Bornstein 2013) and a fundamental and endless challenge to ontology and metaphysics: "One could call *play* the absence of transcendental signified as limitlessness of play, that is to say as the destruction of onto-theology and the metaphysics of presence" (Derrida 1997, 50). Its movements can be perceived in the language and in writing; as *scriptor ludens* (Wilson 1986), we play with texts so that their limits and tensions are exposed through deconstructive exploration (Derrida 1998b, 5; Derrida 1985, 61). When we do so, the hierarchies and binaries that structure our thinking are uncovered and problematized (Bitan 2012, 31). This deconstructive spirit challenges the search for origin and the metaphysics of presence associated with Apollonian play. In Derrida's words, there is a "tension between play and presence." He explains:

> Play is the disruption of presence. The presence of an element is always a signifying and substituting reference inscribed in a system of differences and the movements of a chain. Play is always play of absence and presence, but if it is to be thought radically, play must be conceived of before the alternative of presence and absence. Being must be conceived as presence or absence on the basis of the possibility of play and not the other way around. (Derrida 2009, 369)

In short, for Derrida, "full presence . . . is beyond play" (Derrida 2009, 353). While Huizinga "hold[s] on to the guardrails of the classical metaphysical principle of 'being as presence'" (Flint 2014, 154) and the phenomenologists "see presence or Being behind freeplay [and consequently] are trying to stop the freeplay by founding it in a presence or origin" (Hans 1981, 10), Derrida's aim is to keep the play in play, without grounding, origin, or end. Along with Nietzsche, Derrida "call[s] into question the centering concepts of Being and pure presence" (Hans 1981, 9). Hans continues:

> If Being or essence or pure presence is to be construed as that which grounds, centres, and presumably ends the play of play, then we must accept that such grounding concepts are arbitrary and false to the very sense of play. Play *never* stops playing, and there is no substratum of Being to which it refers. It is ungrounded, for there is no sense in which we can conceive of the end of play, in which we can dream of its end in the pure understanding of Being. (1981, 16)

Derrida shows "that 'the presence of the present is derived from repetition and not the reverse' . . . For Derrida the signified concept 'play' is never present in itself. Something 'is' according to the unity of an object (or subject) that is brought forth and sustained by repetition" (Flint 2014, 156).

Against this conceptualization, as Hans argues, dominant voices in the Western philosophical tradition from Plato to Kant have sought to "legitimize a ground or an origin for play, something which would remove the anxiety inherent in an activity to which we must wholly give ourselves." He poses a crucial question:

> The need for security and for play regularly come into conflict, with the result that we have tried to ground our play and make it safe. But this desire for a ground is born of an attitude that has always characterized play as a peripheral activity. If one accepts that play is the fundamental activity of man, where does it stand in relation to the ontotheological framework of our culture that Derrida is devoted to deconstructing? (Hans 1981, 15)

Rather than seeking to ground play in being, or seek being behind or through play, Derrida posits that play should always be at play. According to Derrida, "[O]ne only really understands freeplay if one recognizes that its very essence is its lack of foundation—that there is no Being behind free play, that there is nothing behind freeplay, that there is only freeplay." Hans explains that while Gadamer "moves in this direction . . . he nevertheless ends up founding play in Being, in the pure presence of that which is." Derrida's disruption of this is important "in that it removed the notion of play from any metaphysical underpinning" (Hans 1981, 10). In other words, "[p]lay does not play out the song of Being"; rather, it is the mode of becoming that embraces a post-foundational subject position understood in terms of movement, process, and co-constitution. So vital is this play force, he continues, that "to imagine the end of play is to imagine the end of the world, and here pure entropy makes as much sense as does pure understanding" (Hans 1981, 16).

Having set out Derrida's account of play and its role in the movements of deconstruction, this chapter now turns to the retheorization of play offered in this book: deconstructive play.

Deconstructive Play

The deconstructive play mode set out in this book inherits from the Dionysian an emphasis on festival, fun, and freedom but supplements this with a thoroughgoing critical reflexivity aimed at exposing and challenging the enduring hierarchies and inequalities we encounter in games. Rejecting the ordering and hierarchical tendencies of Apollonian play, deconstructive play brings the disruptive movements of Dionysian play to bear in the context of games in order to examine and interrogate their coded-in assumptions and reality-producing capacities. Applying a critical gaze to the Dionysian tradition too, it problematizes its hero-warrior player-subject and argues instead for an autodeconstructive one. The aim is to offer "deconstructive play" as a supplement to the Apollonian/Dionysian dualism explored so far and show how this playful mode can be used to critically interrogate assumptions and power relations at work in gaming. I have argued elsewhere that deconstruction can be read as a mode of resistance to the power relations and totalizations at work in the political realm (Hirst 2013, 2015). In what follows, I examine the resistances and productions it can offer in the context of how we play games.

To do this, the discussion turns first to the relationship between games and play with a view to disentangling them in order to make visible the reification of limits and boundaries imposed onto play through this conflation. Showing that many contemporary understandings of play are limited to "gameplay," it offers a challenge to Ian Bogost's submissive embrace of externally imposed constraints (Bogost 2016), arguing instead for an understanding of play that stresses agency and critique. From there, the chapter explores the ways a deconstructive player might be cultivated. Moving from "gamer" to "player," and from playing games to playing *with* games, this reconceptualization seeks to challenge the limitations of an "implied" or scripted player (Aarseth 2007) and instead augment player agency and reflexivity by encouraging a critical exploration of not just what but also how we play. The discussion seeks to move beyond the heroized subject of Dionysian play and toward an autodeconstructive player. Finally, the chapter reconsiders the role of the game designer and the coded-in imperatives and restrictions they instill in games. By moving away from the pursuit of a game's rules and victory conditions, a player can move closer to the position of a co-producer, at the same moment exposing and, if necessary, challenging the assumptions and politics sutured into a game by its designer.

Deconstructive play thus functions to repoliticize the relationship between game, play, player, and designer, making explicit and contestable the rules, relationships, and outcomes apprehended in the game. It shows that games, no less that the "real world," are texts to be read and problematized. In order to disrupt the smooth working of the modes that produce hyperreality, a deconstructive play mode can introduce tension, contradiction, and difference into the closed systems of games. Important targets of this deconstructive critique in the context of military wargaming include processes of warfighter subjectification, coded-in victory conditions, and the cultivation of a non-reflective state of immersion—these are the respective focuses of Chapters 5, 6, 7, and 8.

Table 4.1 breaks down the respective characteristics of Dionysian, Apollonian, and deconstructive play.

Type of Play	Era	Figures	Subject	Motivation	Features
Dionysian	Presocratic; Nietzschean	Heraclitus, Nietzsche	Aristocratic hero-warrior, child, dancer	Intrinsic; end in itself	Disorder, frenzy, affect, libido, aesthetics, spontaneity, affirmation, creation
Apollonian	Socratic to modern	Plato, Aristotle, Kant, Huizinga, Schiller, Gadamer	Rational man, philosopher	Extrinsic; directed toward edifying end	Order, reason, law, moderation, sobriety, morality, civilization, control
Deconstructive	Postmodern; poststructural	Derrida	Produced through play; reflexive and auto deconstructive	Disruptive and exploratory of hierarchies, power relations, norms, assumptions	Perpetual motion, production and disruption of meaning, truth, values

Disentangling Play from Game

[G]ames are pure rule-governed action. . . . Games, then, are a kind of utopia of rules. (Graeber 2015, 191)

A first deconstructive challenge concerns the relationship between games and play as presented, or simply assumed, in many dominant framings. In the current ludic century (Zimmerman 2013), play occupies an at once reified and obfuscated position in popular consciousness. On the one hand, insofar as it is aligned, or treated as synonymous, with games, it sits at the heart of late capitalism's mechanisms and modes of consumption. As Giddings elaborates, the "accumulative demands and hence moral and cultural superstructure from mercantile capitalism through the factory system to consumer culture have reworked play into its modern forms of consumption and through the monetization and disciplining of precapitalist folk culture into privatized hobbies, commercialized leisure, and morally validated sport" (Giddings 2018, 775). In such a context of "ludic capitalism" (Gekker 2018, 221, citing Galloway), human awareness has become commodified into an "attention economy" in which subjective and cognitive experience is modulated by specific political and economic rationales (Crogan and Kinsley 2012).

On the other hand, however, in our current era play has been subsumed by games. Precisely as games have proliferated apace across our political, social, economic, and leisure activities, they have come to overdetermine play, rendering it synonymous with "gameplay." Stephanie Boluk and Patrick LeMieux explain that we have witnessed the reduction of play into the form of games, a process that "conflates the fantasy of escapism with the commodity form and encloses play within the magic circle of neoliberal capital." As a result, games "operate as the ideological avatar of play" (Boluk and LeMieux 2017, 8). In this reading, play sits in tension with games. While the former typically include rules, laws, space, categories, and objectives, play in this framing does not (Gill 2009, 5). As Derrida puts it, "[T]his play is not like a game" (Derrida 1985, 69) and he indicts Rousseau for transforming play into games (Derrida 1997, 307). In such a formulation games serve to "bottle or contain" the dangerous and explosive essence of play by channeling it into competition, strength, or amusement (Turner, quoted in Giddings 2016, 41).

In such a context, play itself has become gamified and its meaning confined to "gameplay." The game comes in this framework to function as a limiting force exerted upon play. This is perhaps to be expected given that games can be understood as systems or structures that apprehend and direct play. Yet this conflation has the additional effect of conceptually delimiting and constraining play: "Play isn't unique to games—it's just easy to talk about play from the familiar vantage point of games. Play, generalized, is the operation of structures constrained by limitations. Maneuvering a soccer ball into a net without the use of hands or arms. Constructing patterns of lines using only the odd-shaped tetrominoes in Tetris . . . This general act can apply . . . also [to] yard work, parenting, errands and marriage" (Bogost 2016, xi). What is striking here is that play is conceptualized as gameplay, whether or not it takes place in a game: "Play is a way of operating a constrained system in a gratifying way" (Bogost 2016, xi). This suggests that our horizons of play have been significantly narrowed. Moreover, Bogost continues to hierarchize forms of play based on their conformity to the game form. In order to use play as a tool to "slough off all those false fears that keep us from truly living," we need "not selfish, thoughtless play, the play of 'just playing around,' but the deep, deliberate play of soccer and of Tetris" (Bogost 2016, xii).

In addition to being conceptualized as a system or structure that directs play, then, a game can be understood as an artifact that delimits what play can be. Giddings explains, "[G]ames are a more bounded category than the play that brings them into being" (2016, 43). As Turner elaborates, this is because play "is a volatile, sometimes dangerously explosive essence, which cultural institutions seek to bottle or contain in the vials of games of competition, chance, and strength" (quoted in Giddings 2016, 41). In an Apollonian vein, some view this containment and directing as a positive thing. Bogost cautions against unbounded, evanescent play and recommends that players accept the objects, circumstances, people, and structures afforded by gameplay (2016, 6, 18). Contrasting this embrace of limits and boundaries with an ironism of distanced disdain, Bogost fails to pose the question of who creates and patrols any particular game's parameters, leaving power relations and disciplinary forces entirely unconsidered.

By contrast, others lament this state of affairs, arguing that in many forms of contemporary gaming, play is not simply constrained but rather obliterated. As Golumbia puts it, "The question here is not what games provide, but what they replace; for what they replace . . . is often play itself" (2009, 196). In such games the player "has virtually no play in Derrida's sense; rather, the player submits to the issuance of orders and then follows them as precisely and efficiently as possible" (Golumbia 2009, 186). Derrida points to a similar evacuation of play when he indicts Rousseau for advocating forms of festivals and games that exclude it:

> There are many games [jeux] within the public festival but no play [jeu] at all, if one understands by that singular number the substitution of contents, the exchange of presences and absences, chance and absolute risk. . . . At any rate, play is so much absent from the festival that the dance is admitted as the instantiation into marriage and is contained within the closure of the

ball. . . . [It is] Rousseau himself, who transforms play into games and the dance into a ball. (Derrida 1997, 307)

Such a reading is echoed in Baudrillard's account of the era of simulation. In a circumstance of hyperreality—in which reality has been overdetermined by simulation—even the dialectical play of meaning has been overwhelmed. In the past, he explains, the relationship between the real and the represented— the signified and the signifier—produced meaning. In a world of models, this productive difference falls away, leaving a unitary simulated reality devoid of play. This "renders inarticulate every discourse. It short-circuits all that was, . . . the dialectic of signified and signifier, of a representing and a represented . . . The contradictory process of true and false, of real and imaginary, is abolished in this hyperreal logic of montage" (Baudrillard 1983, 122). Insofar as games share the ontological unity of the modes of reality-production of the era of simulation, they can be read as part of the problem Baudrillard diagnoses.

Given the overdetermination of play by games, and the latter's part in the production of playless hyperrealities in the age of simulation, some have argued that we must liberate play from games. This is because "[p]lay is always lost when it seeks salvation in games" (Derrida 2004, 156). While play is often considered frivolous, childish, or useless, it has also been argued that "play will save the day," relieving us from the dehumanizations and violences of (post)modern life (Soderman 2021, 18–19). According to Mihaly Csikszentmihalyi, for example, because games amount to "playfulness tamed" and a mode of "controlled expression," play must be disentangled and freed from them (Soderman 2021, 20). In this reading, while games impose order, structure, and boundaries, play operates through and promotes creativity and agency: "If play has a central quality, it is that this behavior (as action, interaction, and activity), first of all, celebrates people's abilities to craft their own responses to circumstances free from interference" (Henricks 2015, 221). While games have come to function as the "ideological avatar" of play, the latter "can never be reduced to product" (Boluk and LeMieux 2017, 6).

However, others, such as Soderman, claim that play itself cannot be rehabilitated from games because it has lost its innocence and become a product to be bought and sold along with games. In this understanding, "[i]t is not enough to liberate play from games" because the former is part of neoliberalism's attention economy, functioning to prevent us from "noticing capitalism's teeth in our necks" (Soderman 2021, 19–20). His diagnosis is bleak: we live in an era of "playful capitalism" in which "play does not subvert the dominant culture; rather, it *is* the dominant culture" (Soderman 2021, 19). As Boluk and LeMieux similarly note, in our time we have witnessed the "privatization of play," which has served to "gamify intellectual, informatics, and affective labor both within corporate workplaces and within the homes of players across the world" (2017, 4–6). Consequently, we need a deeper, critical assessment of play itself. While play was once offered as a tool to "heal alienation and transform society in an altruistic fashion," today it has morphed into a dominant way of "interfacing with culture and capitalism," coming to fuel the problems it promised to overcome (Soderman 2021, 6).

Soderman's solution is to call for a critical attitude through which we might interrogate the politics and interests at work in games, play, and beyond: "We should be critical of games and how they confine and channel the powers of play . . . but we should also criticize play" by cultivating a critical attitude and mode of engagement (Soderman 2021, 20). This is because "the essence of the human odyssey is not play, but rather critical self-consciousness. . . . With this critical distance, we can stop canonizing flow and play as solutions to our modern problems and see them instead as one site of battle in the historical struggle to free ourselves from alienation and from the illusions and collusions that sustain it" (Soderman 2021, 26). While I am in agreement with Soderman's project of cultivating criticality, my claim is that play—decoupled from games—can function precisely as a mode of critique and politicization.

Disentangled from current conflations with gameplay, play understood as the dynamic movements of thought, meaning, and subjectivity can be(come) a powerful tool in the disruption of contemporary political and social configurations:

> Because they exist primarily as rule systems, games are particularly ripe for subversive practices. A hallmark of games is that they are structured by their rule sets, and every game has its "cheats"—even play itself, pushing at the boundaries of a game, could be said to involve a kind of subversion. . . . [P]lay is associated, at least in part, with transgressive and subversive actions. (Flanagan 2013, 11)

To do this, the cultivation of a playful mode of critical engagement with gameworlds is necessary.

Cultivating a Deconstructive Player

A second deconstructive engagement involves reconsidering the relationship between the player and the game. Crogan and Kennedy pose the question: "[W]hat kind of agents or actors are 'in play'?" (2009, 109). In the field of games studies, this question has generated some sustained attention. If a game consists of boundaries and limits, how do or should players relate to them? While the dominant view is that of the "active player," who is not captured or interpellated by game designers but rather creates the play environment through engagement with it, this depiction has been critiqued for being "naïve, celebratory, misguided and romantic . . . given the clear bias such a view represents in favor of the statistically marginal subversive or truly innovative play styles" (Aarseth 2007, 131). Espen Aarseth reflects: "Most players simply follow the directions and play to win, so why put the focus on those few who don't? Are game studies researchers really unaware of what typical players actually do, or are they just bored by it, and look for more colorful examples to liven their writing?" (Aarseth 2007, 131).

Counterposed to the active player, and accounting for the vast majority of players, is the "implied player," which can be understood as a "role made for the player by the game, a set of expectations that the player must fulfill." Linking this to "Gadamer's notion of the unfree player subject," he goes on to suggest that the implied player is "a boundary imposed on the player-subject by the game, a limitation to the playing person's freedom of movement and choice" (Aarseth 2007, 132). For most "players of a game, their goal is pursued by seeking preemptive mastery of that environment"; for such "power gamers" the play experience is one of "permanent combat between the separate worlds of each player's fragment of the whole" (Crogan 2011, 122–126). At the very least, then, the notion of an unencumbered a priori player becomes unsustainable: "[P]layers are acted on as much as they act; . . . they must work out what the machine wants them to do (or what it will allow them to do) as well as engage with it imaginatively" (Giddings 2009, 151).

Importantly, this process is both cognitive and corporeal. James Ash explains that it can be understood as a "process of attunement" that is "central to the production of captivated bodies . . . [A]ttuning oneself to the game involves a self-management of the affective and emotional state of being of the user." Games, he continues, "actively sensitize users to open their bodies to a variety of affective states to become skilled at the game." This "points to a politics of captivation in which the sensual and perceptual relations of the body are organized and commodified by these games in order to create attentive subjects" (Ash 2013, 28). Bogost seems to advocate this mode of relating to games: "When designing a game, the point is not to make it taste sweet, but to fashion a structure. And when playing a game, the question is not how to overcome the structure, but how to subject oneself to it" (Bogost 2016, 94). In short, "play is submission, not liberation" (Bogost 2016, 104)

While it may appear to compromise or curtail player autonomy, this situation provides an opening through which critique can be cultivated. This is because play "problematizes the traditional concept of the subject" (Anderson 2003, 73). As noted above, play disrupts the aspiration to full presence of the subject. Indeed, we can understand "play as a system of differences able to disrupt presence" (Botz-Bornstein 2013, 257). Far from existing as an autonomous, fully formed subject, then, players are produced—and self-produce—in and through games. The subject is always in the process of formation and re-formation, never arriving as a complete entity or totality.

There is, as Derrida puts it, a "tension between play and presence." This is because "play is the disruption of presence. . . . Play is always play of absence and presence, but if it is to be thought radically, play must be conceived of before the alternative of presence and absence. Being must be conceived as presence or absence on the basis of the possibility of play and not the other way around" (Derrida 2009, 369). The subject is produced, disrupted, and produced anew through play: "There is, then, no absolute truth; no foundation or origin behind interpretation and therefore no true essence under lying the subject. . . . The multiplicity of the subject is an effect of the movement from one interpretation to another, and this is, in other words, the play of ever-changing surface. . . . [T]he subject is not only the 'play' of multiple interpretations but also the difference that this generates" (Anderson 2003, 81).

This understanding of subjectivity as (at) play makes possible various forms of contingency—for example, of the intelligence of players and the interaction of that intelligence with game environments in ways not predicted or sanctioned by designers (Ash 2010, 660–661). The cultivation of this kind of contingency and unpredictability is central to a deconstructive play ethos. As Crogan notes: "However powerful the logistical impulse to preempt control of experience realized in the game design, players open up the possibilities for specific, idiosyncratic adoptions of its entertaining playtime." He concludes: "The critical potential of inhabiting the suspension of the serious must be realized in a battle cry for criticality against the over-arching tendency of the program industries to standardize and predetermine the nature of access and utilization of their products" (Crogan 2011, 174).

In order to do this, it is vital to reconsider the concept, and prevailing configurations, of player agency. In games studies, debates and definitions of agency are frequently rooted in Janet Murray's conceptualization: "Agency is the satisfying power to take meaningful action and see the results of our decisions and choices" (Murray 1997, 126). Variously associated with flow and immersion, and construed as both experience and capacity, the term retains a lingering fogginess (Jennings 2019, 88–89) and remains contested (Tanenbaum and Tanenbaum 2010, 11). Many accounts link agency to in-teractivity, differentiating them from other cultural products and media by emphasizing their participatory, rather than simply consumptive, qualities (Muriel and Crawford 2020, 138–139).

As this suggests, some celebrate games' unparalleled capacity to furnish players with agency. Giddings notes that games "are often celebrated as inter-active media, as facilitating human activity and agency in media culture and on the screen" (2009, 151). Others go further still, arguing that "[g]ames are about agency. They are about giving players choice and opportunity" (Tulloch 2014, 345). Interpreted in this way, in a game (and unlike with media such as books or film, which tend to have linear narratives), the player "has rela-tively great *freedom* to determine the sequence of actions himself. The game, therefore, is necessarily *multilinear*; if the player cannot choose between various options there is no game at all" (de Mul 2005, 258). Accordingly, in this understanding games can take players from scripted environments to simulated ones, situating them as performers improvising in a story and thereby generating experience and meaning (Tanenbaum and Tanenbaum 2010, 13–14). In such a dynamic, players can use games as "a springboard for self-reflexivity" (de Zamaróczy 2017, 168) and experience "play as a space of control and mastery, a space for player empowerment, choice, and agency" (Tulloch 2014, 336).

Others argue that player agency is an illusion (Tanenbaum and Tanenbaum 2010; Jennings 2019). Far from enabling freedom and choice, play is "a process of submission and of voluntary obedience to the rules of the game" (Tulloch 2014, 336). In this reading, rather than enabling interactivities through which players might produce meaning and identity, "the human-machine interface made possible by gaming" is better described as "an aggres-sive form of 'interpellation'" that serves to discipline player behavior (Garite

2003, n.p.). In accounts that stress understanding, players are fooled into experiencing agency when it is really not present: as Jennings explains, games "invite players to engage with them interactively, but they grant only illusions of agency. They only satisfy players' desires for agency by sublimating those desires." Such a process amounts, she continues, to "forced obedience" in which players give up meaningful control, and experience its mere illusion. The upshot of this is that games offer nothing more than an "interactive fallacy," convincing players to suspend their disbelief and that they are in control at the same moment as their control is given up (Jennings 2019, 95–96). In such a system, "[t]he game is what grinds. It shapes its gamers, not in its own image but according to its algorithms" (Wark 2007, 221). In short, the most that players can hope for in games is "empowerment-through-obedience" (Jennings 2019, 102).

This reading allows for precious little room to maneuver. In such a protocological system, simply taking part entails the adoption of its ideology (Gekker 2018, 226). This interpretation would seem to evacuate all meaningful play from the gaming experience. While play celebrates subjective agency (Henricks 2015, 226), games provide only the choice to relegate choice to the system (Gekker 2018, 225). After all, as Factor observes, "[i]t's only play if you get to choose" (quoted in Henricks 2015, 222). Such a reading implies a submissive disposition on the part of players. Bogost, for example, argues that players should surrender control and make do with what is given rather than trying to change their environments (2016, 2, 4, 236), while McSorley shows how a dispositif of resilience is encouraged such that the player seeks self-improvement in line with the game's parameters rather than engaging in structural critique (2020, 43–47).

This reading also implies a politics of trust in the game and designer on the part of the player. As Bogost puts it, players should "embrace the [game's] conditions rather than mistrusting or rejecting them" (2016, 151). He takes this position because in his view creativity and meaning are generated from the rules, limits, and boundaries set in the game: "Play is an activity we associate with freedom, being able to do what we want. . . . In fact, play and games offer the opposite: an invitation to do *only* what the system allows, for no reason other than the fact that it was designed that way. Games are built out of constraints, and play arises from limitations" (Bogost 2016, 138). Indeed, the pleasure of gameplay arises precisely from these limits (Bogost 2016, 172).

And yet the polarized options of unlimited agency versus illusory agency raise a number of problems. In both accounts, agency is conflated with notions of choice and freedom. Critics argue that such an understanding is grounded in neoliberal political rationalities: "The hegemonic discourse in video game culture . . . prioritizes the idea of the player as being *in control*, in control of their actions and the outcomes of these actions in the game" (Muriel and Crawford 2020, 139). In this framing, agency is viewed as "a solitary experience of individual player control," a conceptualization that can lead to problematic "idealizations of player agency, control, and activity [that] abstract the potency of the single player-character into a hyper-individualistic actor whose choices can and should have resonating consequences ranging from the personal to the world-historical" (Jennings 2019, 101–102).

At the same moment, such framings pit players against the game and its designer(s) in a struggle to maintain control (Tanenbaum and Tanenbaum 2010, 11), situating the liberal player-subject in a web of rules and restrictions that compromises their agency (Tulloch 2014, 335). They also invite a problematic binary in which the "false" agency of games is counterposed with an assumed yet unspecified "true" agency in the non-game world (Jennings 2019, 97). In addition, they fail to answer the question of whether agency is an experience or a capacity, and whether a violation occurs if players believe themselves to have agency when the game precludes it (Tanenbaum and Tanenbaum 2010, 13). They furthermore fail to consider agencies beyond the human (Muriel and Crawford 2020, 140) and impose an ultimately unsustainable binary between "active" and "passive" player-subjects (Jennings 2019, 99). Such a binary is problematic because, as Giddings explains, to play games "by their rules is not to succumb to ideology but it is to render oneself passive—though partially, incompletely and interestingly . . . [At] the very least we need to rethink the terms 'active' and 'passive' " (Giddings 2016, 157).

Perhaps more fruitful is to recognize, but not seek to resolve, the paradoxical quality of agency. Rather than being either an autonomous, rational, and fully formed subject or an overdetermined and interpellated dupe, the player is produced as both agent and prisoner in games (Tulloch 2014, 336; Jennings 2019, 102; Muriel and Crawford 2020, 146). Read in this way, gameplay is contingent upon both control and compliance (Tulloch 2014, 336), both mastering and being mastered (Jennings 2019, 102). As such, it is both emancipatory and alienating, involving at the same moment autonomy and submission (Muriel and Crawford 2020, 153). Faced with this paradoxical simultaneity, many commentators seek to resolve the problem. Tanenbaum and Tanenbaum, for example, attempt to reconfigure agency into meaning-making in order to resolve the tension between narrative constraints and interactive freedom (Tanenbaum and Tanenbaum 2010). Tulloch takes a different route, seeking to reconstrue the game as a Foucauldian dispositif through which player agency is produced rather than restricted (Tulloch 2014). Gekker sees no possibility of such resolution and opts instead for a mode of resistance to the attention economy by means of withdrawal through interpassivity and non-play (Gekker 2018). While these accounts offer important reconceptualizations of entrenched assumptions, my wager is that in seeking to resolve or step outside the paradox, they pursue an illusory resolution to the inherently tension-ridden quality of player agency. Rather than seeking to synthesize or withdraw, a deconstructive player mode allows an exploration of this paradox and its politics.

Rejecting a binary in which the player is either the autonomous, rational, and fully formed subject of a game or a passive object ensnared by it, a deconstructive player would cultivate reflexivity about the expectations, roles, and norms they embody and perpetuate. For example, there is a tendency among players—actively promoted in many mainstream games—to self-heroize. As Jane McGonigal describes, games provide players a "feeling of power, heroic purpose, and community" (2012, 3). Indeed, according to Bogost, they can facilitate the "heroism of ordinary life" (2016, 70–72). As Murray notes, military shooters in particular "presume the heroic and moral rectitude of their protagonists" (2016, 321).

Perhaps surprisingly, versions of the hero trope are at work in both Apollonian and Dionysian play modes. The former maps broadly onto the liberal conceptualization of the rational, unitary, and self-possessed subject, while the latter invokes Nietzsche's anarchic hero-warrior who brings about the revaluation of all values. What is common to these diverging autoheroizations is a tendency of players to view themselves as protagonist. Problematizing the conservatism and conceits of this, a deconstructive player might reflect upon the legitimizations and marginalizations this may generate.

In addition, such a deconstructive player might seek to reconfigure their relationship with game designers. In conventional gameplay, Sherry Turkle explains, the game requires players to "decipher its logic, understand the intent of the designer, and achieve a meeting of the minds with the program behind the game." This means, she continues, that "most players carry ideas about a [game] world one does not so much analyze but inhabit" (Turkle 1995, 67–68). Far from cultivating critical engagement, much mainstream game design encourages acceptance and player conformity. As Warren Spector reflects, game designers often "go for the adrenaline rush (because it's easy) rather than forcing players to think about what they're doing (which is hard)" (Scholder and Zimmerman 2003, 81).

Against Bogost's argument that a player can choose either to submit to and trust the game or take an ironist stance of disengagement or disdain (Bogost 2016), a deconstructive player asks earnest questions about the politics and power relations at work between player and designer. While Bogost encourages submission to the rules, constraints, and directives of games in general, failing to distinguish at all between those in which players have capacity to influence any elements (or even choose whether or not to play at all) and games in which they have none, a deconstructive engagement would seek to orient the player in the world of the designer, consider and reflect upon its characters and composition, and become conscious of its directives and incentivizations.

Considering the power relations at work between the player and designer can also encourage more critical and reflexive forms of game design. As Miguel Sicart notes, designers should "dare to engage players beyond the pleasures of conflict, in reflective practices of gameplay" (2016, 310). Mirroring the Dionysian here, such accounts emphasize the scope in games for subversion (Flanagan 2013, 10–13) and new times, spaces, assemblages, and realities (Giddings 2016, 139). Wark writes: "The gamer's God is a game designer. He implants everything in a hidden algorithm" (2007, 013). In a post-Nietzschean world in which for many God is long dead, a politics of skepticism and reflexivity is preferable to one of blind trust.

Deconstructive Play in Gameworlds

A third deconstructive intervention concerns concrete practices that operationalize play liberated from games and the critical engagements of a deconstructive player-subject. While deconstruction, and Derrida's thought more broadly, are often indicted for being overly abstract and removed from concrete political praxis, in this final section I offer some further suggestions about what deconstructive play could involve in practice. Deconstructive play problematizes the narrative of player empowerment through mastery.

It advocates, in contrast, a mode of play that stresses critical engagement, increased self-consciousness and awareness, and a reflexive exploration of games as textual artifacts and embodied experiences. My claim is that we should bring more play—as distinct from conventional forms of gameplay— into our gaming worlds and practices in order to deconstruct and make visible their assumptions, incentives, and politics.

In her influential analysis of the cultural impacts of simulations, Turkle argues that there are three possible modes of engagement. The first, she explains, goes along with whatever the game or simulation directs; the second involves avoiding and disengaging as far as possible; the third involves "a more sophisticated social criticism" by means of which "players challenge the model's built-in assumptions" to expose their function as a "key element of political power" (Turkle 1995, 71. See also Bogost 2008, 108; Frasca 2001, 169). Such critical scrutiny, which rejects the justification that "it's just how the game works" and the "abdication of authority and acceptance of opacity," is especially important when it comes to wargames because "[w]e turn games into reality and reality into games. Nowhere is this more apparent than in games of war." The key question, she posits, is whether a player is merely "playing along" or using their brain to become "simulation savvy" (Turkle 1995, 72). What Turkle advocates here is the examination of games as cultural artifacts. As de Zamaróczy notes: "Once one begins to think critically about the assumptions built into . . . games, ever more assumptions come to mind" (2017, 162–166).

Accordingly, more important than *what* we play is *how* we play. More specifically, by bringing more play—as opposed to gameplay—into our gameworlds, a greater awareness of the limitations, production, and politics at work is made possible. DeKoven counterposes the "playing mind— innovative, magical, boundless" with the "gaming mind—concentrated, determined, intelligent" (2002, 49); deconstructive play would seek to extend the former so as to expose and alter the rules directing the latter. As Sutton-Smith explains, we can think of a continuum, "one end of which has play genres that are framed, follow the rules, and have relatively predictable expectations (as in games or sports), and the other end of which doesn't play within the rules but with the rules, doesn't play within frames but with the frames, as in farce or comedy" (2001, 150). This is not about breaking the rules in the sense of destroying the game but rather about playing *with* them—testing, bending, substituting, removing—to see what insights and effects emerge: "A crucial component of minor or avant-garde practice in the digital era is the interfering with codes to produce works that are simultaneously distorted and tangibly familiar, but never in a way that irrevocably demolishes the functionality of the final work" (Franklin 2009, 169).

In concrete terms, this mode of engagement with our gameworlds can take many forms. First, designers can be encouraged to create more space for players to engage critically and reflexively with their games. Sicart, for example, suggests the cultivation of "player complicity," through which designers can force players to interpret the ethics of the game through emotional engagement and opportunities "to reflect critically about their play experience" (2016, 313). Going further, Boluk and LeMieux propose "metagaming," understood as a design philosophy that takes the form of "a critical practice in which playing, making, and thinking about" games occur simultaneously. In such a play mode, the original governing logics and structures of a game are experimented with and subverted (Boluk and LeMieux 2017, 2). While fruitful in its own terms, this approach is perhaps limited by its focus on opportunities for critical engagement offered within the game, by its design(er).

Second, new forms of player engagement can be cultivated without license from designers or their games. McKenzie Wark poses the question: "Could a more intimate relation of gamer to game yet be the condition of possibility for the autonomous self-creation of something beyond the gamer?" (2007, 194). She suggests the hacker, a figure who engages in "a free, self-directed activity that makes its own rules, its own conditions of completion, and its own protocols of success. It is an algorithm that writes itself. It is a practice beyond work and apply, and against the game" (Wark 2007, 198). Alexander R. Galloway proffers the notion of "countergaming," in which modders and hackers alter some element of a game's design, rule set, or software in ways that can "conflict violently with the mainstream gaming industry's expectations for how games should be designed." Some specific forms of artistic mod creations, he argues, "seem to contradict their very existence . . . [because] the game loses its rule set completely and ceases to be a game after all" (Galloway 2006, 107–108). In addition, Mia Consalvo identifies the cheat, a figure whose disruption of a gameworld "lays bare [the] player's frustrations and limitations. It points to ludic hopes and activities, and it causes us to question our values, our ethics" (Consalvo 2009, 408).

In addition to altering games themselves, deconstructive play encourages alternative ways of playing games, building on existing conceptualizations. Flanagan, for example, argues for "critical play," which involves questioning some aspect of a game's content or play environment "that might otherwise be considered a given or necessary" by means of a "careful examination of social, cultural, political, or even personal themes . . . using the intricacies of critical thinking . . . [and] critiquing the status quo." In so doing, she continues, players can derive considerable pleasure from "subverting set interaction norms," exploring "what is permissible and what pushes at the boundary between rules and expectations" (Flanagan 2013, 6–13). Such disruption to rule systems is also in evidence in Katie Salen and Eric Zimmerman's framing of "transformative play," in which "the free movement of play alters the more rigid structure in which it takes shape" (2003, 305). Aarseth outlines his notion of "transgressive play," which involves a "struggle against the game's ideal player" and a "symbolic gesture of rebellion against the tyranny of the game" (2007, 130–132). Giddings seeks to explore the possibilities of "free, imaginative play" that can occur even within "the rule-bound, mediating structures of digital media" (2016, 9). And Boluk and LeMieux propose metagaming to describe the processes by which players move beyond simple gameplay, exposing the colonizations and enclosures games impose upon play, and turning themselves from consumers into co-creators/designers (2017, 2–9).

The framing of deconstructive play offered here shares these commitments, drawing them together and further radicalizing them into an autodeconstruction play mode that puts the game, play, and players under ongoing critical scrutiny to show how they are produced and reproduced, and their political effects. Crucially, however, deconstructive play adds further critical maneuvers to existing frameworks. As a mode of critique that, in Derrida's words, is "always a matter of *undoing, desedimenting, decomposing, deconstituting* sediments, *artefacta*, presuppositions, institutions," deconstruction radicalizes critical engagement by being unending both in scope and temporally (Derrida 1998a, 27).

Such deconstructive play might involve hacking, modding, or indie design, taking the game experience from smooth to bumpy (Galloway 2006, 110). It may directly contravene the oft-repeated mantra "don't fight the scenario." It may involve reading games through alternative lenses, such as queer, feminist, or post/decolonial frameworks (Dyer-Witheford and De Peuter 2009; Condis 2018; Ruberg 2019). It calls for a reconceptualization of agency that goes beyond arbitrating between in-game options and algorithmic scripts, insisting instead on taking account of the meaning-making at work in play. In deconstructive play, players play like testers, pushing at a game's hidden assumptions and black-box cause-and-effect arrangements—only with the aim not of ironing out these glitches but of interrogating their impacts. It pushes at problems of ludonarrative dissonance, exposing the politics and power relations at work in design and coding choices.

Through consistent critical reflection on both the game and the player, an autodeconstructive engagement seeks to empower the play of the player to problematize games' capacity to direct, manage, and subjectify them. To this extent it is interested in cultivating players rather than gamers, insisting that players are the subjects, rather than objects, of the games they play. Crucially, and in contrast to critics who argue that certain forms of games should not be produced and played, in this framing *what* we play is less important than *how* we play. Following Derrida, an ethical concern animates this deconstructive mode and the Dionysian tendencies at work in it (Anderson 2006; Sawyer 2015, 45–46). It seeks to continue this ethically motivated destabilization— through which exclusions and totalization are resisted—by turning the deconstructive effort on potentially all elements of the game, its designer, its purpose(s), and the player herself on an ongoing basis.

A deconstructive play mode can, by reintroducing tension, contradiction, and difference to the closed system of the game, playfully interrupt the smooth running of a game's contribution to the production of hyperreality. While of course it cannot allow us to step outside of the hyperreal productions within which we are situated, and with the caveat that individual and even collective subversions do not bring the era of simulation to an end, deconstructive play can occupy and destabilize the processes by which hyperreality is produced and maintained, thereby exposing and challenging the hidden politics and power relations at work.

Conclusion

This chapter has engaged with the poststructural tradition and set out this book's theorization of deconstructive play. This radical form of play inherits from the Dionysian tradition a rejection of origins, grounds, and Being, and challenges the Apollonian emphasis on play as a tool or instrument of reason, order, or presence. It rejects the hierarchical orderings of play associated with Kant, Schiller, Huizinga, and the phenomenologists, and embraces the Dionysian qualities of festival, unreason, and groundlessness, emphasizing the becoming-as-process understanding of subjectivity. However, it also seeks to problematize the Dionysian reification of a hero-warrior player and distance itself from the license that Deleuze's Nietzsche offers, which claims innocence for playful becoming. Siding here with Derrida over Deleuze, my conceptualization of deconstructive play emphasizes a normative imperative for endless critical reflection on both play and player.

Beginning from the idea that *what* we play is less important than *how* we play, deconstructive play calls for the cultivation of an autodeconstructive player who self-consciously and consistently punctuates the dreamlike immersion of gamespace with questions and reflections. Such a player moves from being a consumer to being an interpreter of game artifacts (Sicart 2016, 316). They query the incentives and constraints that direct play in games, asking, "Why am I playing this game the way I am playing it?" (Murray 2016, 323). They problematize the hero-warrior protagonist construct, which often obscures rather than cultivates this critical disposition (Murray 2016, 321). And they take seriously the ways in which games are productive of realities and people, including their own identities, values, and subjectivities.

Such reflexivity and self-problematization are intended not to aim at Apollonian goals of truth or Being but rather to mark and act upon enduring hierarchies in gameplay falling along colonial, gendered, heteronormative, and myriad other exclusionary lines and interrupt the closed models that produce hyperreality. It is my claim that such interrogation does not undermine the joy of play but makes possible another Nietzsche's creative self-authorship in an ungrounded landscape. Seeking to address Baudrillard's diagnosis of the end of the play of meaning and representation in the era of simulation, it wagers that in play we can find powerful means of subversion that push against the smooth running of the models that produce hyperrealities.

The remainder of this book operationalizes this deconstructive mode of playful thinking to introduce cracks in the hyperreal productions of military wargaming. It does so by first exploring how wargaming produces people by intervening in both the cognitive and affective realms. From there it identifies two key drivers of wargaming—the drive to win and the spell of immersion—and critically examines their functions and implications in the production of hyperrealities and subjectivities today.

5

Play as Pedagogy

Gaming the Cognitive Dimension

Introduction: Play as Pedagogy

Chapters 3 and 4 traced a genealogy of play in Western philosophy and offered a theorization of play grounded in the thought of Jacques Derrida. Having laid these theoretical foundations, this chapter and Chapter 6 examine how wargaming produces people by intervening in both their cognitive and affective registers. In doing so, the chapters seek to operationalize deconstructive play in order to expose the subjectifying process at work in wargaming. In 2011, leading wargame designers Peter Perla and Ed McGrady published an article in the *Naval War College Review* titled "Why Wargaming Works." In it they stated: "If we wargamers—we who create and employ these tools—are to fulfill our responsibility to our agencies, our companies, our nation, and yes, our species, we must first recognize why wargaming works and then apply its power in constructive and helpful ways to address the complex and uncertain issues that we face now and will face in the future" (2011, 129). As this suggests, the wargaming CoP has placed a good deal of emphasis on demonstrating *that* wargaming works, understood in terms of its efficacy as a research, analytic, educational, or training tool.

In order to sustain the momentum generated in the first decade of the wargaming renaissance, the CoP deems it imperative to demonstrate robust proof of wargames' utility as a key element of fourth-generation warfare. Such a task has proven difficult, however, not least because wargaming is not readily amenable to quantitative or statistical analysis. As things stand, "we do not have great, systematic, rigorous, definitely not empirically tested theory that any of this is helpful" despite a good deal of anecdotal evidence of wargames' efficacy, as Yuna Hua Wong—then a researcher at the RAND Corporation—put it (interview 2017).

This chapter takes two analytical steps to explore wargaming's functional logics. First it examines the claims made by proponents regarding *why*

Politics of Play. Aggie Hirst, Oxford University Press. © Oxford University Press 2024.
DOI: 10.1093/oso/9780197629192.003.0006

wargaming works, building on the accounts of Perla and McGrady and extensive interview testimony. It establishes a series of benefits the wargaming CoP claims for its craft, that set wargaming apart from other methods of research, education, and training. Having set out the CoP's case for *why* wargaming works across these applications, the chapter moves beyond questions of efficacy to explore the question of *how* wargaming works. Acknowledging clear variations in design, intent, and objectives across research, education, and training applications, the chapter argues that *all* wargames have a pedagogical element through which their players—and indeed facilitators, designers, and sponsors—learn something. As Chapter 1 concluded, whether through "process" or "product," all games impart information and experience that remain with players long after the game ends. The core aim of this chapter is to demonstrate how this learning takes place by intervening in players' cognitive realms.

The chapter begins by setting out the benefits proponents of wargaming claim for their craft, specifically that wargaming saves lives by reducing conflict, mitigating risk, building cohesion, and providing safe-to-fail learning and experimentation environments that can hone a range of skills including abductive reasoning, procedural literacy, psychomotor skills, systems thinking, and cultivating reflexes. From there, the chapter turns to the question of how the CoP seeks to demonstrate these benefits, noting the difficulty of demonstrating the efficacy of wargaming. Having established these fundamentals, the chapter shows how wargaming functions as a pedagogical tool. It does so by setting out four stages through which wargaming interacts with its audience: (1) by generating buy-in and engagement; (2) by encouraging consolidation through iteration; (3) by encouraging consolidation through critical thinking; and (4) by promoting retention. It draws a broad distinction between research and education games, which include all four of these steps, and training games, which often, though not always, skip the third of these processes.

Having demonstrated this, the chapter goes on to examine how wargames function to produce realities. It shows that despite its ostensibly "unreal" status, wargaming imparts real-world lessons that intervene in players' cognitive registers long after a game is over. It shows that while some wargames seek to closely emulate reality, and others engage players using deliberately unreal or fantastical content, the unreal worlds of wargames serve to produce people by leaving their mark on their ways of thinking. The chapter then takes the argument a step further by showing not just how wargames affect specific elements of reality, but also how they function as one sort of model that has turned reality into hyperreality in the age of simulation. Returning to the work of Der Derian and Baudrillard, it argues that a "forever game" is underway that has fundamentally altered the character of war in ways that permit no "game over."

Why Wargaming Works

Wargames proponents claim that their craft imparts a wide range of valuable skills, including "abductive reasoning" and "procedural literacy" (Harrigan and Kirschenbaum 2016, xvii, xix), "systemic thinking" and "occupation-specific reflexes and cognitions" (Ghamari-Tabrizi 2016, 347, 351), and "analytical and spatial skills, strategic skills and insight, learning and recollection capabilities, psychomotor skills, [and] visual selective attention" (Susi, Johannesson, and Backlund 2007, 8). Wargames are especially good, it is argued, for developing "'higher order' or 'domain general' skills, including flexibility, problem-solving, probability judgments and negotiation skills" (Neale 2018, 22).

When it comes to games explicitly designed for education, argues James Lacey of the Marine Corps War College, "gaming can fundamentally transform the classroom when it comes to teaching strategy, history, and theory. In fact, wargames provide the most cost-effective means of bringing 'experiential learning' into the classroom." Specifically, he continues, they teach important substantive lessons about the character of global foreign and military affairs, such as, "[f]or one: 'Nations have no friends, only interests.' And for another, they learned just how hard it is to conduct long-term strategic planning in a 'low information environment, where you can trust no one.'" Accordingly, he concludes, "I cannot see any reason why such games and simulations cannot be employed to improve virtually every aspect of war college education" (Lacey 2016).

In the context of strategic and research gaming, as Philip Sabin explains, wargames "convey a vicarious understanding of some of the strategic and tactical dynamics associated with real military operations." Once they have accrued sufficient experience, players "acquire an intuitive feel for more generic interactive dynamics associated with warfare as a whole" (Sabin 2014, 31). As he notes elsewhere, wargames thus assist with the development of an "intuitive understanding of the force-space-time dynamics" in conflict (Sabin 2016, 424).

As this suggests, the wargaming CoP claims for its craft a series of benefits across research, teaching, and training in the US military. As Lademan reflected, "I think of wargaming as being a powerful technique that has an applicability across the spectrum of activity. All the way from, say, training junior officers, up to providing senior leadership with insights into operational problems and future force structure and the concepts and technologies needed to support that" (interview 2017). Chief among these is the idea, as discussed in the Introduction, that wargaming saves lives (Harrigan and Kirschenbaum 2016, xxvi; Compton 2018, 25; Robinson 2018, 79). This is because, proponents argue, wargames allow players to "climb inside" scenarios to explore strategies, tactics, and operations without the risk of injury or loss of life. This makes them safer than both real-world conflict and conventional field training. As Downes-Martin and Pellegrino explained: "[I]f you go to war, it's to kill people and break things. Wargaming maybe can reduce the amount of people who die and the amount of stuff that gets broken, so it's a very, very serious activity" (interview 2017).

Taking this logic a step further, many proponents argue that wargaming also serves to reduce the risk of violent conflict by promoting a better understanding of its causes and conduct. In this vein Perla notes: "In today's world, where another Great War could well mean the end of mankind, wargaming is not just a hobby for the over-educated or a toy of the military-industrial complex, it is a way to help us understand the nature of the beast, and through that understanding to, if not tame it completely, at least prevent it from devouring us" (1990, 179). This rationale reflects a broader framing by the wargaming CoP of the non-belligerent, and sometimes pacifistic, character of its members and enterprise. Wargamers tend to be "peaceable, intelligent, and often rather apolitical individuals who read widely about all aspects of military affairs" (Sabin 2014, 163).

This account is often traced to the wargaming activities of H. G. Wells. In addition to his science fiction works, Wells published on wargames and strategies, specifically those using miniature figures and artifacts (Perla 1990, 34, 178–179). A committed pacifist, Wells saw wargaming as compatible with an anti-war stance: if "Great War is to be played at all, the better it is played the more humanely it will be done. I see no inconsistency in deploring the practice while perfecting the method" (Wells 2004, 27). Harrigan and Kirschenbaum elaborate: "Wells remains perhaps the most frequently quoted proponent of the piety that the playing of wargames is redemptive because they teach us what a 'blundering thing' real war is" (2016, xxvi).

Interestingly, however, his love of wargames appears to have compromised Wells' pacifism in the end. As Tyler McBrien points out, while "Wells sought to reclaim the Kriegs[s]piel for the side of peace," and even replace war with game entirely, his book was warmly received by the British Army, and he corresponded with a colonel whom he advised about adapting it for military training. Thus, "[i]n the end, the playful seduction of wargames seemed too great even for Wells. . . . Even the great pacifist got a thrill from war's simulacrum" (McBrien 2022)

A peaceable framing of wargames is further reflected in claims that they often promote non-violent options in dealing with contemporary conflict. As Brynen has argued, in the post-9/11 context the salience of operations short of full-scale war has increased, necessitating wargames "that addressed the political, military, economic, social, informational, and infrastructural dimensions of a situation ('PMESII' in Western military jargon)" as well as those "examining the various nonkinetic actions that military forces might take" (2016, 488–489).

One key dimension of this is that, according to the CoP, wargames allow you to mitigate risks associated with training and combat. Games allow you to train for things that are too risky to rehearse in a live environment. As one instructor explained: "You're able to represent environments that you may not be able to in regular training environments. So you can actually do the high-risk training" (interview 2017). As two instructors elaborated, "It's powerful also for the ability to create a safe space. The military can be very risk-averse and it is always a challenge for us to build a space where [service members] are somewhat forced to take risks and understand risk/benefit decision-making. . . . If they are forced to make a risky decision by virtue of a given scenario, how do they mitigate that? How do they communicate that? How do they, what are the sort of other planning elements that they need to take into account if they're not just going by the doctrinal standard?" (interview 2017). At the same moment, wargaming can better attune players to risks and their consequences. Noted Lademan: "I don't mean to suggest that you become immune to the idea of what risk is and the consequences of risk, but perhaps you become a little more sensitive as to what possibilities lie in taking risks" (interview 2017). One wargames designer similarly argued that "the blessing is that people get used to making these decisions, especially in very difficult situations. They are less afraid of taking risks" (interview 2017).

Relatedly, the CoP argues that wargames provide a vital safe-to-fail environment in which trainees or leaders can make mistakes without the real-world consequences. In non-games training, as two wargaming instructors explained, "which, in theory, is intended to be a chance for you to flush out and make mistakes, in fact if you make mistakes, there is somebody watching and that ties back in later down the line." Games, in contrast, provide "a nice break out of that in a lot of ways and oftentimes, even if it is a short opportunity, the most free space a lot of students have to sort stuff" (interview 2017). One of the key benefits of gaming "is the ability to make mistakes," another instructor reflected. "We always tell the students that when you get out into the operational environment you have to have your game face on because lives are on the line. This is the environment where you can experiment and make mistakes, maybe try a different approach, experiment with different perspectives and lives are not on the line. Maybe it gives them a bit more academic freedom too to explore things" (interview 2017).

A further benefit is cohesion both inside and between institutions, services, and units. As Moreland commented, "[T]he benefit of game-based learning, one of them, is that you can connect people across vast distances, use some of the other enablers like translators and data repositories to share information and approved communications across staffs that really can't get together all that often" (interview 2017). An instructor said much the same thing: gaming is "a way of educating students instilling an appreciation for students at one service for the capabilities of another service which is in our mission statement here at the staff college" (interview 2017).

Despite these claimed advantages, many in the CoP note that it is difficult to empirically demonstrate the efficacy or "added value" of wargaming as compared to other methods of research, education, or training. As Wong wryly noted, "All babies are cute, all birds are beautiful, and all the wargames are a success" (interview 2017). Two wargaming instructors discussed why this poses such a challenge: "It is so brutally hard . . . to show demonstrable proof of game-based learning because unless you have some kind of completely bizarrely clinical situation, you cannot show that mental linkage that is occurring . . . much less control for any of the other elements that may affect that" (interview 2017).

Several in the CoP note a dearth in academic studies dedicated to wargames' efficacy. One designer, for example, pointed out that "the research on whether gaming teaches people better than other methods is surprisingly thin and surprisingly inconclusive. . . . It's a bunch of people making claims because they feel right, but without any real way of testing them. And part of the problem is that what they're testing is what they can't test. . . . What they find very difficult testing is exactly the sort of thing that we want the most to be accomplishing" (interview 2017). Bartels similarly reflected that "the academic literature . . . [is] not very satisfying. You have a couple of small and quasi-experimental kinds of things, where you don't get very large effect sizes. Or, you know, there are reports I've seen. They're, sort of, 50/50 of small effect size that gaming works, or no results, or small effect sizes that gaming is inferior to a normal discussion session. And it doesn't seem like we're really making any progress with that approach. The results don't seem to be really clarifying themselves at all" (interview 2017).

One sticking point is the question of how wargames' efficacy can accurately be measured. Explained one designer: "The goal of coming out of a game here is not necessarily to improve your mastery of the material. . . . It's also supposed to give people an opportunity to practice skills, modes of thinking, and these other things that are a lot harder to measure, and frankly harder to say anything meaningful about. . . . So then you get into the question of can a game or a series of games have any meaningful impact on someone several years out or not? I mean, maybe. But how do you study that?" (interview 2017).

Some note that post-game surveys and after-action reviews (AARs) can be fruitfully used to track success. Goodwin reflected:

Instead of simply going "Yes, the game was a success" we would actually go in and do surveys after the game, usually immediately after the game, [and] electronically corelate that data and come up with conclusions as well as graphics to demonstrate our success. Then you really have evidence if you have an external source asking, "Was that successful?" I see across the board in military gaming that very seldom is there an honest delineation of the findings. AARs or hotwashes are usually limited to a few people, all of whom have a stake in the success of the exercise or the outcomes of the exercise. (interview 2017)

Thus, a solid scholarly demonstration of wargames' efficacy is wanting, despite extensive anecdotal and experiential testimony. As one designer put it:

The problem we have is that people really feel when they're playing the game that they are learning stuff but it's very hard to measure. So when you're trying to compete for funding, you have a really hard time proving learning outcomes. It could be done if you took a control audience doing

things the same old way and took another audience with a gamified curriculum and over multiple sessions tested them on what they are supposed
to know. I may be wrong and there may not be an improvement, but my
guess is that the gamified people would feel that there is an improvement,
whereas the more traditional side may not feel that way. (interview 2017)

Having set out the CoP's claims as to why wargaming works, the following
section turns to the chapter's core concern: *how* it works.

How Wargaming Works

Games work by taking mundane things that may not be a lot of fun to study
on your own and giving them a spin. That helps. It's the candy-coated shell
on the bitter pill of knowledge.
                                                          —Machuga (interview 2017)

The literature on game-based learning (GBL) echoes many of the claims
of the CoP surrounding the efficacy of their enterprise. As Tarja Susi, Mikael
Johannesson, and Per Backlund summarize, proponents argue that games
have the potential to improve teaching and training because of their power
to promote engagement, motivation, role playing, and repeatability (2007,
2–3). Furthermore, they "captivate and engage end-users for a specific purpose, such as to develop new knowledge and skills" (Corti, quoted in Susi,
Johannesson, and Backlund 2007, 2–3). James Paul Gee comments that
games generate a state of " 'embodied empathy for a complex system' where
a person seeks to participate in and within a system, all the while seeing and
thinking of it as a system and not just local or random events" (Gee n.d., 5–6).
    According to educational psychologist Dave Neale, wargames can be pow-
erful pedagogical tools in two key ways. First, he explains, they can "provide
important learning and development opportunities for the players themselves, by allowing them to think about the situations they face in new ways,
and to practice applying a range of important skills that can later be applied
to real-world situations." Second, wargames "allow a real-world situation to
be simulated, and so it is possible to learn about that real-world situation, and
the potential effects of different human actions on outcomes. This kind of
learning is available to the players of the game, but also to spectators or other
individuals who read a report of how different scenarios played out" (Neale

2018, 21). Wargaming is thus of pedagogical value both to players themselves and to those evaluating player behavior and decisions for research, analysis, or experimentation purposes.

Members of the wargaming CoP frequently appeal to Bloom's Taxonomy of Learning Domains, which outlines three levels at which people learn: the cognitive, affective, and psychomotor domains. As Markley put it, "We're fond, here at Army War College, of associating learning objectives with Bloom's Taxonomy. And I think that the higher you go in the taxonomy, the more gaming works . . . When you put somebody in a game, they are almost immediately at the synthesis and evaluation level. They've learned something ahead of time about the subject matter but now I've got to figure out, how do I take what I've learned, evaluate the situation I'm being put in, see if I can figure out how to apply what I've learned before? How do I combine or synthesize the previous things, given the current set of circumstances in the game?" (interview 2017). The following sections set out four key dimensions of how wargames subjectify players by intervening in their cognitive domains and show that while "process" games involve all four of these steps, "product" games often skip the third.

Step One: Attention and Engagement

Proponents claim that wargames capture and retain the attention of those who play them in ways that exceed what is possible with other methods of research, education, and training. As Ghamari-Tabrizi explains, advocates argue that games can "improve student motivation, learning, and retention" because they promote "exploration and discovery." They further claim that such learning is particularly effective when it is "experiential, graphically dynamic, event-based, and when didactic material is embedded in a story" (Ghamari-Tabrizi 2016, 342). Many in the CoP share this view. Lacey notes: "There is nothing else I have done or have seen any other professor do that creates anything near the level of student participation that wargames and simulations do" (2016).

This is in part because games, unlike other methods, allow players to "learn by doing." As Perla and McGrady explained, "The main mode through which gaming helps people learn is through the creation of something they can experience and learning by doing. You have to make decisions. You can't just sit idly by and observe as you can in a lecture class. If you're in the position where you have to make a decision, you have to somehow come up with the reason for making the decision" (interview 2017). Another designer made a similar point: "There's real value in learning by doing, essentially getting a chance to practice a skill before you're called on" (interview 2017). This is because, as Casey and Martin explained, "gaming is just a unique medium because it actually actively engages the user versus just sitting there and just watching something. You get to do something, and it is active. They always say that just writing down notes helps you remember, but doing stuff and participating is just a way to keep your brain happy while you are learning, which is just going to help even more" (interview 2017).

One important effect of learning by doing, one designer observed, is that it encourages learners to stick with the task at hand: "The gamification of training skills, learning a process, especially if it's a boring process, is a neat thing because it makes people want to keep doing it. That's useful because you're taking something that would otherwise be dull and make it a bit more interesting for those monkey rote-learning-type tasks. In terms of learning to shoot weapons, employ weapons, that's often useful. People will learn and internalize much more quickly" (interview 2017). It also promotes engagement by providing applied and contextualized learning. Noted Moreland: "Gaming in particular is useful because it allows students or learners to apply the knowledge they're getting in a didactic environment. It reinforces what they're learning in the lecture hall with a hands-on activity, so it also validates or gives students an opportunity to confirm that what is being taught is indeed valid and stands up to some rigorous experimentation" (interview 2017).

Because of this, many in the CoP argue, games are more engaging than conventional teaching, learning, and research activities. As James Sterrett, chief of simulation and education at the Army Command and General Staff College, described it: "[L]ecturing is time efficient and it is instruction ineffective. We know this, but it is time efficient, so we do it; we cover the material until it has 'been delivered.' But how well does it sink in? Not very well, often. I mean, there are spectacular lecturers out there who will drive the stuff into your head with wonderful ease, but they are few and far between. We can opt to teach people with games: '[H]ey, here's the situation— learn to solve it'" (interview 2017). Paul Tappen, Ryan Kennedy, and Paul Maher of the National Guard Bureau Joint Exercise Branch made a similar point, observing that "the military is completely saturated with different PowerPoint or online-based training between just administrative stuff, for other jobs, security training, all that stuff. So, putting them [trainees] in an environment where they're kind of learning more by doing can add that level of fun at a level of realism and kind of show that importance, and from an educational point it's easier to get everybody's attention" (interview 2017).

This increased attention and engagement is due at least in part, the CoP argues, to the fun often associated with gameplay. As one designer noted, when it comes to conventional lectures "the students are forgetting what they just learned fifteen minutes after they have the lesson. . . . I have done matrix games now with a bunch of local universities . . . and in each case, the students have come up to me and commented that this was one of the fulfilling experiences they have had and they have learned more and done more within that three-hour session than what they had done for the entire semester. That they need more of that because that is how they want to learn" (interview 2017). Casey and Martin took a similar view:

> All the different stuff that goes into making games enjoyable and engaging render themselves all quite well to education. What you typically find in a lot of educational situations is they are trying to teach things, but they are not engaging students. What we find is games have the ability to engage the students because of those reward mechanisms, because it's fun. It's something different and it is a way to get their attention and hold it and then teach them either directly or indirectly through that. . . . We see a lot of kids learn so tremendously better and faster and more efficiently and teach themselves.(interview 2017)

As this suggests, one of the advantages of wargames is that they are experienced as more enjoyable than other forms of research, education, and training. A wargaming instructor explained, "I think that our audience is generally fairly predisposed to understanding and appreciating and being familiar with the use of a board game or an exercise in the educational environment. . . . Overall, I think our students are probably more disposed than general civilian audiences to dealing with games well and getting things out of them, but it comes down to design at the end of the day" (interview 2017). Lademan concurred: "It's very, very popular. . . . I've never really been in a circumstance where I didn't find that converting an idea or a lesson or a lecture or even free time into some sort of a gaming experience wasn't both productive to one degree or another but certainly attractive and found, you know, a resonant interest in the participant we were trying to work with" (interview

2017). Downes-Martin and Pellegrino made a similar point: "The preponderance of feedback tends to be 'it was generally a positive experience.' . . . It can be incredibly engrossing" (interview 2017).

That said, several in the CoP noted that players sometimes resist engaging with games. This may be because in part, as Wong suggested, "people who are not used to gaming but find themselves needing to participate in a wargame . . . can be intimidated because they're not really sure what to do" (interview 2017). Kligge estimated that "one-third [of those taught/trained with games] find it very relevant, very useful . . . one-third recognize some value but just aren't into gaming, therefore they come in already a little underwhelmed by the process or the prospect of having to go through the process. And then one-third are just reflexively disinclined to suspend belief and operate in that environment" (interview 2017). Another instructor noted: "I've never had a group that at the end of it said, 'That was a complete waste of time, we never should have done it, I hated it.' Even the ones who are a little nervous up front usually find there was some benefit, I think" (interview 2017).

Some identified analog platforms as a barrier to engagement. Explained one designer: "There's a lot less enthusiasm to playing board games and I think the reason for that is in the military culture, a lot of people see sitting around playing board games as a passive activity versus an active one. But like I said, when you couple it with some sort of interface so that it doesn't seem like a game so much, then they tend to respond very well. That's why the computerized versions tend to be a lot better" (interview 2017). Others highlighted a generational divide, like this designer: "There are pockets of resistance at the senior level, but certainly the young soldiers coming in buy into it" (interview 2017). Notwithstanding these limitations, the prevailing view in the GBL literature and in the CoP is that wargames improve student engagement with subject matter.

Step Two: Consolidation Through Iteration

In addition to increasing player attention and engagement, wargames impart information through iterations. Indeed, the importance of playing a game multiple times is frequently emphasized in the CoP. Pournelle explained: "It has only recently been realized [that] you have to play the game again, multiple times, if you want to have any personal and organizational learning occur. Repetition is crucial" (interview 2017). An instructor expanded: "[The] other thing we explore is repetition. When you get to [play the game] again, maybe with some variables changed or with the roles flipped, oftentimes it's the second iteration where the learning is the strongest. I think it's because now [players] get to crash their original theories into what they learned. . . . The iteration of that allows them to evolve their thinking over time, and maybe if they learned a false lesson in the first iteration, it clarifies itself in the second iteration" (interview 2017).

Other CoP members agreed. Goodwin confirmed: "You have to be able to do a whole game multiple times within the time allotted, so that you can do learning by doing. . . . Real learning through gaming takes repeated play, so that once you learn the rule set you really start to apply them and in this environment the rule set should be based on the principles taught in the classroom. . . . How many people play one game of chess and they can draw all of the lessons?" (interview 2017). Markley made the same point: "Depending upon the design of the game and the intent of the game, you may play the same game a number of times, with the idea that each iteration of play is an opportunity to practice and refine, to hone and improve" (interview 2017).

Some in the CoP draw a distinction between different types of gaming and the importance of iterations. Hall noted that "repeatability is more important at the tactical level, and it reduces as you go higher." He continued:

> We use a simulation game called VBS3—Virtual Battle Space 3—for squad and platoon level training. . . . We would take cadets, put them in that simulation, and they would have to do a squad or a platoon attack. The beauty of it is, it's absolutely repeatable. . . . It may only take thirty minutes to run that, but you do a quick AAR and then you have them do it again. So in the space of an afternoon they could do the same mission four or five times, and you can see a definitely verifiable improvement in their performance over that time period. (interview 2017)

He confirmed that that cadets trained with VBS3 were shown to do better than those who were taught with other methods: "There was a quantifiable difference in performance and improvement between the sim group and the non-sim group. Obviously, the sim group did better" (interview 2017). In training of this kind, iterations are key, as de la Vega observed, because soldiers can "use a simulation to practice their craft, to practice their skill set and in an environment that may not be as hazardous to equipment, to personnel, such as engagement with the weapon systems. You can identify any kind of hazards and mitigate those risks when you're going with a simulation so therefore they can practice good training habits, safe training habits, and work on their skill set before they actually do the real thing" (interview 2017).

The suggestion here is that that iterations generate synthetic experience that can be drawn upon in real-world situations. One instructor summarized: "The key to repetitions is that it builds up the experiences so that you have something to pull from. It might not be a situation where it's exactly the same. . . . [But] there's enough for you to make that decision, so you can constantly make decisions and don't get stuck on one decision" (interview 2017). This is because of the active learning that takes place, argues the CoP. In the words of a designer, "When you read about something, you become aware about the relationships. When you play a game about it, you get put in a role of one of those people, you experience the context of the decision-making, I think sort of more viscerally than passively reading about it, I think the idea of practicing decision-making . . . is an important one . . . particularly for a military education" (interview 2017).

The learning that takes place in wargames is multilayered. Indeed, beyond the explicit game objectives, various other forms of learning take place as well. Casey and Martin explained: "There are games that will have things that you learn indirectly, meaning you will play the game and you will go through the different game mechanics and it will seem like a game to you but while you are doing that, you naturally have to learn little bits about it" (interview 2017). This is because, according to Squire, in games "knowledge is not presented to the learner but arises through activity—activity that occurs in relation to preexisting knowledge and beliefs and the projected identities that are established for players" (2008, 20). A key feature of wargame learning, then, is the management of information. "Lots of people talk about managing knowledge, but the reality is that what you really have to do—and I don't care whether it's in a family or in a business or in the military—you have to maneuver knowledge," said Lademan. "That is, you have to get knowledge to the individual who is capable of acting on it *and* you have to expect that individual to make a decision that reinforces the, you know, the solution to the problem, whatever the problem is. So in other words, maneuver involves the movement of knowledge for a purpose" (interview 2017).

One reason iterations are important is that players, and other game participants, can learn from failure. Bartels pointed out that "you learn more from the paper that you write and screw up than the paper that you write really well. The experience of realizing that you've misstructured your argument, and this has all come down around your ears, is a really informative. I think gaming has some of that same kind of feedback . . . 'Well, that did not work. I did not expect the adversary to completely trans me in this way. I guess I have to go back and rethink that.' It's got that sort of learning-from-failure to it, which I think can also be helpful. And I think that's a little bit different from the sort of learning-through-doing argument that you often see in the experiential literature" (interview 2017). Markley observed, similarly: "I think each game experience should force you to reflect on that decision-making process, whether or not you change maybe a function of how well either you or others judge your 'success'" (interview 2017). Iterations are thus key to the pedagogical impacts of wargaming in the cognitive register.

Step Three: Consolidation Through Critical Thinking

In addition to consolidating learning through iterations, the CoP often claims that wargames promote "critical thinking." Bartels commented: "One of the things gaming was really specifically helpful for was that it was a way for me to get them [players] to be very explicit about what assumptions they were making in how the world worked without having to get them to embrace formal theory and academic discourse and language that was really quite difficult for them" (interview 2017). She continued: "If I built a world that has religion as a major driver of conflict, and embedded them and immersed them in that environment, the students could articulate to me, 'Hey, this doesn't feel right. In my country the reasons people are taking out their grievances has way more to do with social status and economics than they do with this religion framework that you seem to be pushing.' But they were doing that based on their intuitive sense of how the world works in their mental models . . . They could just, sort of, convert directly from mental model, observation of the game, and then describ[e] this mismatch between the two" (interview 2017).

Such critical interrogation is important, as Downes-Martin and Pellegrino explained, because people need help "evaluating options and, of course, evaluating means critical thinking, handling uncertainty. Humans are very bad [at this]; if not, they find it impossible . . . Humans in general are not just bad as in their answers are random. They're bad in that their answers are usually wrong if they try to intuitively answer probability questions. . . . We have not evolved to be very good at it, and all sorts of games are based on that" (interview 2017). Wargames are, as one designer described, "effective for teaching critical thinking skills . . . precisely because it's sharing an experience many thinkers probably model. It's the simplification of a very complex reality and it's allowing the student to explore that, interact with it, see what happens, try things out and get familiar. And then hopefully compare that model to their own view, their own mental model and therefore get a better understanding of the complex environment. So for thinking skills I think they really shine. They're almost irreplaceable" (interview 2017). As another designer put it, gaming helps address this problem insofar as it presents "a dynamic situation that allows students to come to their own conclusions, mapping that against their own personal mental models . . . You'll hear the term 'mental model' used a lot, and that's kind of a key element of gaming. Not just developing your own but trying to understand other people's" (interview 2017).

As discussed in Chapter 1, many in the CoP draw a distinction between training, education, and research games, situating the first as the most deterministic and the last as the most open-ended. This conventional wisdom implies that critical thinking in the military is the preserve of higher ranks alone, which would suggest that step three is bypassed in rote training. As a wargaming instructor noted, games "can be used as an educational or instructive mechanism for things that are not critical thinking . . . [They can be] a problem-solving tool and not a critical thinking tool" (interview 2017). In this framing, critical thinking is the preserve of high-level, research, and strategic gaming. An instructor explained: "As you go higher up on the spectrum towards the strategic side, the doctrine itself is much less specific or clear about how to deal with those sorts of things. You need to be able to think critically about this, apply your own judgment in forming an assessment. The US military embraces the concept of mission command. You give people objectives, and within a set of parameters they are responsible for working out how to accomplish them. That is critical thinking to my mind" (interview 2017).

This focus on critical thinking at the highest level of rank reflects, as Downes-Martin and Pellegrino acknowledged, the changing character of war in the digital age: "The world has changed. So critical thinking—thinking about thinking, thinking about being reflective, thinking about your own biases—has been brought into the service amongst other things of problem solving" (interview 2017). Bateman made the same point: "At the strategy level—that's the big emphasis that we focus on from the very beginning of the year—we want the students to become critical thinkers. . . . [We tell them,] 'I'm not interested in your opinion. Show me. Make an argument and show me the evidence that supports your argument. Convince me that what it is that you are laying out has merit and is the right way to go about doing something'" (interview 2017).

Wargames, the CoP argues, can be used for precisely such critical thinking. Said an instructor: "If you put a game in front of a bunch of students and they vehemently disagree with the model—they think it is incorrect and they are pointing at all these flaws and then they are like, 'No, in my country, this is how the actor in this place would be behaving'—I would stand up and start clapping and say, 'Mission accomplished! You guys had some really insightful learning points, dissecting this model and actually going through some really critical thinking.' All models are bad, some models are useful. Some games, even ones that may not be perfect, can still cause some fantastic discussion and learning to occur" (interview 2017). Hall elaborated: "Often it's a style of thinking that we're really training" (interview 2017).

And yet others in the CoP posit that critical thinking is no longer the preserve of commanding ranks and research gaming alone. As Wong noted, "There is a push for better critical thinking skills, there is a push for really looking at military officer education. . . . [F]rom what I saw in the Marine Corps, [there's also a push for] critical thinking skills, creative thinking skills, down to being enlisted at lower and lower levels . . . Even people at the enlisted professional military curriculum level are being told you need to put critical thinking skills in" (interview 2017). Moreland indicated that this emphasis on critical thinking in lower ranks began several decades ago: "[T]hat shift really occurred when we professionalized our non-commissioned officer corps, and we really started investing in their education. This was back in the analog days. The military was investing significantly in the mid- and early eighties in educating their enlisted ranks and making them more professional, more capable, more critical thinkers. . . . That actually predates the advent of the network-enabled technologies. It's more of a deliberate choice to invest [in] professionalizing that corps" (interview 2017).

One example of this lower-level critical thinking push is the "cultural sensitivity" training that has proliferated in the post-9/11 context. One military wargames researcher recounted, "We here in America, we get this pioneer spirit and we can kind of wander out into the unknown and make it conform to our vision of the way it should be. That particularly doesn't work well with stability operations, where, if you're trying to come off as being supportive, you've really got to get into a mindset where you're really listening as much as you are acting. . . . You're trying to get people to think about this problem differently, but a lot of the people that we're trying to convince to use these new techniques don't fully understand the notion that this is a complex new way of thinking about the world" (interview 2017).

In this new operational environment, as de la Vega indicated, the military is currently pushing "critical thinking right from your basic knowledge and understanding all the way up to synthesis or innovation" (interview 2017). And a wargaming instructor noted, "Even enlisted service members are frequently expected, as part of doctrine, to be able to exercise critical thinking about a given range of things depending on what their position is and what their responsibilities are" (interview 2017).

This disagreement may, to some degree, be a result of terminological differences. Some view "critical thinking" as a catch-all term that encompasses problem-solving and out-of-the-box solutions. Noted Downes-Martin and Pellegrino: "Broadly speaking, critical thinking seems to have become the buzz word for just thinking" (interview 2017). They expanded: "[A]n aspect of critical thinking is techniques for problem-solving. Not just problem-solving; techniques for diversion thinking, and all that sort of thing. But if you want to go deeper, then it's thinking about thinking—you know, what is it about thinking that works? . . . I mean, critical thinking is also very creative. It's how do you think about the world around you, and that includes using intuition and creative jumps, as long as you've thought about what does being intuitive mean. We know from research experiments that intuition is sometimes brilliant—very often, however erratic" (interview 2017). In this framing, critical thinking and problem-solving are very similar.

Others in the CoP draw a clearer distinction between these types of thinking. Wong suggested that if "you define problem solving as coming out with a solution when none is evident, then it can be divided into two pieces. One is creative thinking, which generates potential solutions, and [the other is] critical thinking, which evaluates the potential solutions" (interview 2017).

Whichever understanding of critical thinking one accepts, the key point is that wargames cultivate specific cognitive processes that produce new ways of thinking. As a former Marine Corps staff sergeant explained, "You're training these young guys to react to real-world critical thinking. Fast reaction, very split-second life-or-death situations in a simulated environment. And, again, while there's never any substitute for the real thing, it's our duty to get people as close to that as they can and stress them out as much as we can so when they do go out there, there's an element of 'Okay, I've been through this in training, I know how I need this thing.' And we can identity any major flags with the person's decision-making process" (interview 2017). Lademan had a similar perspective: "You begin to fashion and inform and maybe even instill a kind of a culture in participants in wargames. They begin to look not for the expected but for the unexpected. They begin to [adopt] courses of action that don't rely on conventional wisdom. And consequently they allow you to explore dimensions of warfare without the risk that warfare entails" (interview 2017).

One element of such thinking processes is, as Downes-Martin and Pellegrino posited, quickly identifying pathways to success through pattern recognition: "People who are comfortable in gaming environments and are 'gamers' . . . very rapidly engage on a problem. Games are problems. Someone once described gameplay as my willingness to solve an unnecessary problem. . . . The willingness to do that produces a group of people who very rapidly structure problems because they're used to looking at a game situation . . . [and] learn to figure out a pathway to success. Why, that sounds like a pretty handy skill set if you're a military officer. If you're anybody . . . It's problem-scoping and identifying the solution space" (interview 2017). They continued: "You could postulate that people who game are more quickly able to recognize where a pattern has shifted because games are very different. . . . I'm going to rapidly abandon a strategy or abandon an approach when it doesn't seem to be working" (interview 2017).

As things are currently organized, the main forum in which to examine and consolidate this critical thinking in wargaming is the "hotwash" or after-action review (AAR). In the words of a designer:

> A hotwash is a touchpoint specifically with that observer-controller and a training audience in order to be able to look back and look at what they have been doing, see if it was the best technique that they could have applied, and then reset as they go into the rest of the remainder of the exercise or until the next, that evolution is over. And then at the end of that event, every training unit will hold an after-action review which will look back and they will analyze what they have done so they can encapsulate those

lessons and then bring them forward and then actually, if they're important enough, they will pass them onto the next units so they will be retained in that unit's collective memory for such time as it is, until they have all rotated out. (interview 2017)

This is important because, as Bateman explained, "it's not enough just to play the game. We've got to have the discussion afterwards [to explore] what happened, why did it happen this way, just like you would in a real-world operation. You've got to come back and do the after-action review, and talk about what happened, how did it unfold, where did we make mistakes, what do we need to do differently next time? What was successful, so that we keep doing that? We reinforce the success and we mitigate the places where we had problems" (interview 2017). Indeed, the AAR is not an add-on or optional extra after a game, but rather an integral part of it. Markley emphasized: "The game is not complete until the instructor has had an opportunity to have the student reflect on what happened and why. . . . If you leave it for the student to walk away without having had the opportunity to actually reflect post-game, then you can't be certain that [they haven't] learned all the wrong things. Because each game is a unique instance of whatever is being played; as long as there are human decision-makers involved, one should not expect the outcome of the game to be the same twice" (interview 2017).

Some in the CoP argue that AARs should be expanded. Goodwin is among these, stating, "We do not spend adequate time assessing the exercise or gaming experience, the so-called hotwash or after-action review. . . . We actually used to have classes on that, where we would almost set up the students to see, do they take what they've learned, or do they fall back on the devices that they've used through much of their career?" (interview 2017). Markley concurred: "I'm of the view that you complete the learning process, if you will, by that forced period of reflection at the end of the game. So, again, there's a thinking in the game while you're playing it, [and] there's the thinking after the game to examine your own thinking and to reason about the decisions that you made at the time . . . I think you sell the educational experience a little bit short if you just play the game, shake hands with the 'winners,' and everybody goes home" (interview 2017). As Tappen and colleagues similarly explained, "The players will walk away and they may have some personal insight, but if you really want to make an impact, those hotwashes and after-action is really why we do this, and that goes between the gaming world and the exercise world" (interview 2017). They continued: "It's one thing to pull everybody into a room and do your wargame on the spot, but then to have them stay engaged for the next month to do that after-action stuff is tough . . . I think it could go on longer, frankly, because it's not just your after-action, it's your improvement to win, if you really want to go full circle with it. Making changes to the plans, policies and procedures" (interview 2017). The implication of this is that in rote or deterministic gaming, most often used for lower rank training purposes, this step is often skipped. Since the DII and associated 3OS, however, even gaming of this kind emphasizes consolidation through critical thinking. The key question that remains involves the difference between thinking critically *within* models in order to succeed in their terms and thinking critically *about* models disaggregated from their goals or ends.

Step Four: Retention

Having generated attention and buy-in, and consolidated through iteration and/or critical thinking, the final step of wargames learning is retention of information and experience imparted. Many in the CoP claim that wargaming allows for better retention than conventional teaching methods. As one designer noted, "A wargame in an immersive environment allows you to learn things better as far as you remember environments you're immersed in versus trying to memorize facts from a textbook" (interview 2017). This is because, another designer explained, "the retention of what you just learned during lectures is going to be minimal . . . I have no recollection of what I learned about Clausewitz when I was in the Naval War College. But I can tell you almost everything that has gone on with the matrix games that I have run in the past two years, and almost every move I can recite verbatim because they are good moves and they led to something and I learned from every move, even if I was a facilitator. Even as the facilitator, I have learned more in the past two years than I learned in the last ten years of my career" (interview 2017).

As Chapter 6 will explore in detail, this retention is facilitated in part by wargames' competitive dimension. Noted one designer: "When you play a game, you are going to remember everything because you are competitive. I am really competitive, so I'm going to read the rules, I'm going to 'be the scenario', I'm going to read what my goals are, and then I'm going to attempt to determine what the goals are of my adversaries or even my allies because not every goal for your allies is the same as yours. And so, personally, I have seen this in about all of the students we have run our games with—they are more interested, and they will retain more because they are playing it, because it is more tactile, and a lot more people they learn from more of a tactile experience" (interview 2017).

Key also to this capacity for retention, according to the CoP, is the experimental elements of gaming. Pournelle explained why: "The key thing that I think games bring are context. You can have all the training you want on any particular topic you discussed there, but it can be very dry if you don't have some sort of context, and the training may not adhere if it's that dry. A good game design will be more memorable" (interview 2017). An important dimension of this experimental aspect, many in the CoP note, is the "lightbulb moment" of understanding. As Goodwin described it, the "ultimate goal of any exercise developer or game designer is to create the so-called aha moment for the gamer." This is because students "may not remember anything from their educational experience except maybe three or four major moments of experience or exchange. And, in that respect, that's what we're all striving for, that's to us an indication that we're actually achieving the desired effect, as long as they're taking away the right lesson" (interview 2017). Such "eureka moments" are important, as Merle S. Robinson notes, because they allow players to "articulate a new understanding of relationships/opportunities, and consequences for their actions" (2018, 79). These moments feed directly into the games' real-life utility. Said a designer: "I want them getting that aha bit so that then feeds back into their decision cycles and their choices" (interview 2017).

As Chapter 8 will explore, key here is the experience of immersion in the game environment. Hall elaborated: "[I]f you immerse [players] in the frame of reference of the combatant, then that inherently increases your understanding, because now you have to be them. So you get a player briefing with the background and then, here's your objectives for the game, and now play the matrix game. And then you play it and you're like, 'Holy crap, now I understand why they do this and why they want this'" (interview 2017). Another designer similarly pointed out that when playing a game, "I have that 'aha' moment where suddenly I see what I need to do, how does that happen, and having the players experience that moment is where a game will be meaningful" (interview 2017). A good games instructor, de La Vega reflected, "observes their students to see if they've got that aha moment where they get it and '[O]kay, let's see if we can then see how well they do at reproducing that information, that feedback in practice where you're looking at doing it' and then a little bit further back the teacher pulls back a little bit to say, 'Okay, let's see if you can do it on your own without my guidance'" (interview 2017).

One danger associated with this, highlighted by many in the CoP, is the possibility that a wargame can result in "negative learning." One designer offered this perspective: "We have flight officers who see *Call of Duty* and go, 'Okay, that's going to be a great training tool. Why haven't we taken that and made it into an Army training tool?' The problem is those visuals are not linked to the laws of physics, so you get what we would call negative training value" (interview 2017). And an instructor explained, "If the avatar that is being controlled by the gamer can do things that a regular human can't, that's negative training. If their weapons aren't accurate, that's negative training" (interview 2017). Similarly, Robinson noted, "if people are allowed to set unrealistic probabilities for the success or failure of different units, that's negative learning. If they are supposed to be performing a critical task, [and] if in performing that critical task they skip critical elements, then that's negative learning. They have to perform the task to the standard that has to have relatively realistic outcomes" (interview 2017).

In some cases, such negative learning has to do with the algorithms and mechanics of a particular wargame. "We used to do a lot of rehearsals using computer games as command post drivers leading up to the invasion of Iraq," reflected a designer. "And one of the things that got me at that time was that I was very aware of the limitations of those simulations. I used to do a lot of simulation design in these exercises and I was trying to be very careful, telling people, 'Be careful about this because it doesn't work that way, there are some algorithm issues,' but I couldn't really get that to stick" (interview 2017). Another designer commented, "There's always the danger of taking what worked for a simplified model and trying to apply it to a case that it wasn't necessarily designed for. . . . There's certainly some things you can carry over in terms of the way of thinking, but you've got to be a little careful of what was the game designed to do, or what idea was it designed to explore, and how are you extrapolating those lessons in something else" (interview 2017).

In other cases, negative learning is due to a lack of good game facilitation and control. This wargames designer agreed: "There are problems with negative learning outcomes without a moderator. . . . Without a moderator, a person can go through multiple iterations of a game and take out the wrong lessons without having a means to have an objective basis for their experience" (interview 2017). To avoid negative learning, as another designer explained, you need expert controllers who "don't go into a training event and specify a particular way that the person should do something. What they do is, they kind of put some boundaries on the training audience and just assist them along to some degree" (interview 2017).

A further source of negative learning is the assumption that game results are readily applicable in the real world. Guillory cautioned: "The biggest danger . . . is extrapolating too much from the wargame, thinking, 'Hey, it worked in the wargame, so it will work in the real world.' Well, the real world gets a vote too. Because something worked in the wargame doesn't mean it has to work in the real world too, or because it didn't work in the wargame we should automatically discard it" (interview 2017). Lademan noted that people "will say that 'well, the wargaming showed that we have to do this.' In other words, to take the results of a wargame in too literal a fashion. And that somehow the board game proves and validates something, which it emphatically does not" (interview 2017).

One element of this is the adoption of advanced technologies for inappropriate purposes. In a designer's opinion, the military is "trying to adopt things too quickly. One of those would be Oculus. You can now strap [goggles] on and get to a virtual environment with a cellphone without giving real thought to how that would be used. It's more of a 'Look, we're using the technology, aren't we great?' instead of a 'We've put some real thought into how we're going to use this technical tool and we've done the instructional design to take advantage of it'" (interview 2017).

A popular mantra among the wargaming CoP is that "all simulations are wrong but some are useful." This utility depends on a clear and purposeful application of gaming for specific ends and objectives. Perla explains: "Well-defined objectives are essential to a professional game. In specifying the objectives, game sponsors, designers, and analysts must clearly identify how and in what ways the game can provide the type of experience and information needed to achieve them. . . . A wargame's objectives should be the principal drivers of its entire structure" (1990, 165). Similarly, Sabin notes, "[T]he first priority when deciding to employ a wargame in class is to have a clear sense of the educational objective" (2014, 37).

If negative learning of various kinds is to be avoided, as Hall explained, commanders should be mindful that "we have shaped this simulation to support your training objectives, so be cautious of what lessons you learn, and try to apply to the real world. . . . We're using training simulations that are not physics-based, so don't think that because you used a certain weapon system in a certain way in this command post exercise that you will be able to do that in the real world" (interview 2017). Lee offered a similar caution: "There is a lot of potential use for a simulation, but the simulation itself is only a computer-generated environment that is going to be fraught with error. And so results need to be taken with a grain of salt so that you don't walk away from it going, Wow, I won that battle, I really know what I'm doing' when in reality, maybe you did but maybe you didn't" (interview 2017). One designer commented, "We tend to take solutions from a game and try to apply them absolutely, without taking into context that it's actually an abstract representation of whatever it is we're representing" (interview 2017). While wargames have the capacity to improve information and experience retention, the risk of negative learning must be constantly mitigated.

Producing Realities with Wargames

The issue of negative learning draws into focus the degree to which the synthetic experience generated in wargames functions to construct realities for their audiences. Indeed, it is by means of this process of reality construction that wargames intervene in the cognitive registers of players. This final section examines how this synthetic experience is imparted, noting that the realism of a game's content is not necessarily key to its capacity to produce realities that intervene in players' consciousness long after any given game is over. It concurs with, but also builds upon, Der Derian's account of the hyperrealities of virtual technologies.

Historically, wargames have been utilized to cultivate real experience via a synthetic environment (Ghamari-Tabrizi 2000, 180). And yet even in these early days the problem of the relationship between games and the realities they represent was noted (Ghamari-Tabrizi 2000). As Banks, Groom, and Oppenheim cautioned almost five decades ago, "[G]ame- and simulation-based propositions are propositions about a model—not about reality" (1968, 13). Indeed, at this early stage the term "real" was shown to be ambiguous when discussed in the world of wargaming. Sidney Verba wrote: "The use of the term 'real' in contrast to the simulated world may be a bit misleading. The simulation is, of course, also real—there are real people interacting or real

computers computing. And we all know that 'games' may be deadly serious"
(1964, 495n6).

Today, some in the CoP argue that advanced technologies allow for greater
realism, in the sense of fidelity to the real world. Multisensory technology is
useful, one instructor thought, because "people tend to get drawn in faster.
In gaming technologies that concentrate on the three-dimensional aspect,
realistic environments, [players] respond much better. . . . In order for that
to happen, they do have to be able to suspend their disbelief. So it . . . has to
have the right representation of effects that they would see in the real environment" (interview 2017). The rapid pace of technological development has
accelerated this process in recent years. Moreland highlighted: "In the past
one of the main concerns about using simulations and e-learning was that
you lost a certain amount of fidelity, a certain amount of realism and rigor in
the training. I think as the tech improves, you're finding that they can more
closely and closely approach realistic scenarios for education and training"
(interview 2017). Accordingly, for many in the CoP, capturing reality as accurately as possible is key to wargaming's capacity to impart valuable lessons
for use in the real world. A designer commented, "In the military simulation
, . . . your goal has to be to make it as real as possible. In a commercial game,
you're entertaining someone, so it doesn't matter how perfect your reality is if
they didn't have a good time" (interview 2017).

As this suggests, digital and virtual games often put a premium on such
realism. A designer acknowledged: "The attempt is made in a virtual simulation to make it as physically real an experience as it can be. . . . We are
doing things with smells, with sound and lighting, that are trying to make the
experiences as real as possible. In a combat vehicle or an aircraft simulator,
your seat position is on a motion platform, the movement of the vehicle is as
realistic as it can be to the terrain it is moving across so that the altitude of the
aircraft, the sounds of the weather and the action of weapons is as real as we
can make it. I do think that is important from a psychological standpoint."
Such games, he continued, can be "so realistic—and I have actually seen this
myself—where the players or the training audience will get so wrapped up
into the game that they think it is real" (interview 2017).

One advantage of this, as Robinson explained, is that "instead of interacting
directly with a manual game board like we had to do in the early 1980s, now
all the data from the wargame is sent via the standard communications
devices. In other words, we have an added benefit of reality. Now that we use
digital devices, we send the results to the digital devices rather than having

them displayed on a train model or map board. And this, second only to actual combat experience, gives them virtual experience. Experiential learning is a lot better in most cases than just static learning" (interview 2017).

While many in the CoP acknowledge that games and simulations can never capture reality completely, recent advances have come a long way. Robinson reflected: "Nothing's 100 percent real. . . . But it's the closest thing you can get, particularly when you're dealing with crude systems like helicopters, etc., in the virtual-reality side. And when you're dealing with the command levels of war, command posts like battalions and above, it's extremely real for them because they're responding now not just to the roll of dice but rather to watching a virtual battle unfold on their command-and-control devices. . . . They're not perfectly real but it's a lot more real than any other option" (interview 2017). One instructor commented, "I would say that we're at a fairly sophisticated level, but there is always room for improvement. It's hard to represent certain of the senses, smell being one of them" (interview 2017).

For others in the CoP, advanced multisensory simulation technologies are not vital for the cultivation of an experience pertinent to the real world. Instead, analog artifacts can serve this purpose just as well. Goodwin argued: "In our world—education—if you think of some of the products that we use to drive games, such as taskings from the National Security Council or from the president, we always try . . . to make them look as realistic as possible. Because, in government, that's part of the education. You have to know in a document where the real information is, the actionable information, as opposed to the preambles or just fluffy stuff. So there's multiple levels of learning—not only the exercise itself, but how do you take your gaming tools and exploit them for maximum benefit? . . . So, part of it is teaching them 'This is what a policy decision directive looks like' and 'This is where you go to look for the real meat of this kind of thing' so that when they go back to their day jobs, it's not the first time they're seeing it" (interview 2017). Such objects can be important for games learning, one designer remarked, because they provide "something physical that they [players] can put their hands on and see. That aids them in understanding something that's actually significantly more abstract" (interview 2017).

Yet others in the CoP believe that such claims about the importance of realism for wargames' pedagogical efficacy, whether achieved virtually or by analog means, are overstated. Some suggest that too much realism can undermine players' engagement. The opinion of one designer was that "there have been some incredibly good commercial simulations but they are a bitch to play because they are just not fun, you know, because they go into so much agonizing detail and they look at so many different realistic variables that the designer can claim, '[H]ey, my game is super-realistic,' and okay, it is sitting on a shelf because it is not fun to play" (interview 2017). Accordingly, as Perla and McGrady explained, "some players emphasize playability as more important than realism, [while] others put it the other way around. There is a theoretical notion that you want to shoot for the sweet spot in the middle, but in my experience there is no sweet spot in the middle" (interview 2017).

Some in the CoP argue that the reality or otherwise of a game is important not in its own right but rather insofar as its purpose is realized. Downes-Martin and Pellegrino pointed out that a number of those in the wargaming CoP "say unless that game is highly representative of the actual situation that I'm trying to make you smarter about, whatever that means, then it is of no utility. So that's one end of the spectrum. The other end says it's not about the specificity of it, it's about the transferable skill set that the game introduces" (interview 2017). As Perla and McGrady explain, "[G]aming, as a story-*living* experience, engages the human brain, and hence the human being participating in a game, in ways more akin to real-life experience than to reading a novel or watching a video. By creating for its participants a synthetic experience, gaming gives them palpable and powerful insights that help them prepare better for dealing with complex and uncertain situations in the future" (2011, 112).

In this framing, synthetic experience useful in the real world can be generated by means other than realistic gaming. Some members of the CoP argue that it is preferable not to use real-world countries or scenarios. Rupert said, "I never use real places. . . . I always use Lilliput and the Land of Oz, then I say, 'Take what you've learned and apply it. How would you do X, Y and Z?' . . . That opens them up because now they're thinking about the concept. [If I] use Afghanistan, some guy will always go, 'Well, when I was in Afghanistan . . .' So it kind of allows you to break out of that a little bit" (interview 2017). Commented a wargaming instructor: "I don't think that immersion is a question of how realistic something is. An experience does not have to be realistic to be immersive" (interview 2017).

One common deviation from reality is to make the game more challenging than its real-life equivalent. One designer described it this way: "The conditions under which they train are always harder than real-life conditions. The enemy is better equipped . . . [or] as well-equipped as they can be, as well trained as they can be, as well organized as they can be, as dangerous as they can be, so they can experience all that. If the training side wins a lot of battles, they don't learn a lot of lessons." This is important because "when I go to do it for real, I have seen all of it before. I have fought something that is harder and the procedure is in my muscle movement, my reactions to what is happening is honed because I have been through it four or five times with someone who was even tougher before I experienced it for real" (interview 2017).

A further benefit of games' unrealness is a greater degree of freedom to experiment and make mistakes. As Perla notes, because it "emphasizes human interaction and role-playing, wargaming can be a powerful learning tool. Participation in a game allows players to 'practice' the roles they assume in the game" (1990, 250). Importantly, such practice differs from the equivalent real-world activity because "one is freed from many of the normal constraints and consequences of actions, and so you can try actions you would never have attempted in the real world" (Neale 2018, 21). This allows greater readiness for equivalent real-world challenges. One designer summarized: "If I'm going to send people into harm's way, what we want to do is have them experience these things in simulations and in training before they have to encounter it for real. So, what the outcome we are looking for is not necessarily for them to win but for them to experience something that . . . is [as] challenging as we can possibly make it so that these challenges are experienced, and they learn lessons from them" (interview 2017).

In this framing, games can help manage and produce solutions to realities even as they remain unreal. Lademan explained that in a game you

begin to understand the points of reality that exist within that solution space—things that you know, that the intellect can absorb, can understand, or that are presented to you as facts by the problem itself or by the circumstance you're dealing with. In other words, reality. Once that reality is understood you begin to develop the context in which that reality exists, in other words, what things does that reality influence, what is influencing that reality? Based upon the context that it's positioned in. You establish those points on that solution space and then you go through the . . . process of combining and arranging those points of reality and their context, and the consequences, into something that, that really mimics the art of the possible. (interview 2017)

Indeed, the unrealness of gaming can itself be pedagogically advantageous as compared with real-world equivalents. As Robinson suggested, "[G]aming provides a virtual experience in the absence of actual experience. For teaching, it's better than actual experience because you can go back and do a replay and you have time after you've done a war game to sit down and critique the results in detail" (interview 2017).

Most important from the perspective of how gaming works by intervening in the cognitive register to produce subjectivity, the experience generated in the game is real and stays with players after the game whether or not the game emulates reality. In this unreal reality, trainees' physiological responses engage as they would in reality. Gaming may be an artificial environment, but "the juices flow" (Resnick, quoted in Allen 1989, 319). Robert C. Rubel explains that in command-and-control games, for example, "players are organized into cells, each of which represents a command or perhaps an element of a staff organization. These cells are provided with communications devices (most recently networked computers) and command and control (C2) doctrine. The war game provides a venue in which command and control processes can take place. The point here is that within the context of the game, *actual—not simulated—*command and control occurs" (2006, 114; emphasis added).

The realness of games comes, then, from the experience and cognitive processes involved in playing them. As Lee elaborated, through gaming "we develop those memories, those thinking skills, so that it's not the first time a leader has seen something occur—he's experienced it before, he can mentally map out what to do next. And it also allows him to get ahead of the pace in terms of thinking, so that he doesn't have to spend a lot of time and effort figuring out a solution—he's already experienced it once before, so he can make that set of decisions earlier in his decision-making process and get inside the enemy's decision cycle as well" (interview 2017). And Allen similarly notes: "[G]ame playing can be a dress rehearsal for this reality of crisis. In a game, as in a crisis, participants feel time and events tightening on them. . . . Game playing gives potential crisis managers that desperate feeling. . . . What appears to be the *unreality* of gaming—the vise of time, the lack of solid knowledge, the dominating influence of Control—is the *reality* of crisis" (Allen 1989, 238).

The very unrealness of games, then, can be key to how they intervene in the cognitive realm to produce new ways of thinking and acting. As Downes-Martin and Pellegrino explained, "If you're about to criticize what we're doing by starting off with the words 'It would be more realistic if . . . ,' I've stopped listening . . . because it's not about creating realism. If realism worked, then you would have solved this problem already by looking in the mirror. That's as real as it gets. Apparently you need some other environment, some abstracted thing that concentrates the mind in certain factors, that discounts other factors. Potentially that approach will shed light on something you have otherwise not been able to figure out" (interview 2017). This is the unique purchase of a game: "This is called a game. Not an exercise. Not a simulation. Not real world. Not a rehearsal. It's a game. . . . I have a completely realistic simulation: it's called real life. There's a simulation that simulates everything. A computer that simulated everything, it's called the universe" (interview 2017).

Games are thus best understood as having enduring real-world effects on how players think, whether or not their subject matter is realistic. "It's a metaphor," said a designer. "You're abstracting reality in a way to get at the kernel of the decision conundrum and you're leaving a whole lot of things out" (interview 2017). Another noted: "If it's not real, it's an abstraction. What we're arguing is over the degree of abstraction we're comfortable with" (interview 2017). This unreal realness can sometimes become more real than the reality simulated. As Downes-Martin and Pellegrino explained, at some stage "the games begin to substitute for a real-life experience. If I failed in the game, it wasn't so that I would learn so that I will know that when I get in the field not to make a similar mistake or at least I'd been exposed to some potential consequences of certain actions. [Instead] it became 'You failed in the game. I'll make a note of that for your report' . . . If people start to use the games as the substitute for performance evaluation, that's a chiller" (interview 2017).

Games have the power to construct realities. Explained one wargames designer: "The curse is—as Jean Baudrillard, the philosopher, would say—you get that simulacra-versus-simulation effect. Your imagined reality becomes more real than the reality you're actually involved with, so your wargaming experience can create false impressions or negative learning that you are going to rely on more than on real-world experience, and that's a problem" (interview 2017).

The final section of this chapter examines the implications of this as regards the production of subjectivity through wargames' intervention in the cognitive dimension.

The Forever Game

Within the CoP, debates about games' relationship to reality usually stop short of an engagement with the hyperreal (i.e., reality-producing) properties of wargaming. This is because, for the most part, the CoP implicitly accepts a clear distinction between reality and non-reality. However, in the era of simulation—as Baudrillard argues—such a distinction is rendered problematic. Building upon Baudrillard's diagnosis, over a period of three decades Der Derian examined the relationship between simulations[1] and the realities they purport to represent, asking: "Can a simulation overpower a reality which does not conform to it?" (1990a, 189). Answering in the affirmative, he suggests that "the power of simulation, magnified by a fear of the future or a nostalgia for the mythical past, comes to dominate all other forms of representation" with the result that "the lines between war and game, pain and pleasure, fact and fiction do not blur: they pixelate in hyperreal detail onto the same screen" (1997, 208–212).

Since at least the era of *Kriegsspiel*, Der Derian posits, simulations have worked in defense of the reality principle they themselves transgress, culminating in modern military wargaming, experimental research at think tanks like RAND, and the global proliferation of commercial-reactional gaming (1990b, 300). Insofar as they function as "the continuation of war by means of verisimilitude" (Allen 1989), he explains, simulations have displaced and replaced the realities of the political world. They thus have at least three concrete effects: the implosion of the distinction between image and reality, the hyperrealized enemy more other than any real other, and the mediation of the estrangements precipitated by these ruptures through projects of security and truth-seeking in a post-foundational political landscape.

In work that speaks to broad meta-theoretical debates between rationalists and reflexivists, Der Derian documents a disciplinary shift from geopolitics to chronopolitics and charts the field's course from realist modes of representation ("in which world-historical figures meant what they said and said what they meant") to neorealist framings ("in which structures did what they did, and we did what they made us do, except of course when neorealists revealed ... what they 'really' did") and finally to a hyperrealist (post)modernity ("in which the model of the real becomes more real than the reality it models, and we become confused") (1990b). Such a trajectory, he argues in a later work, marks "the passage from material to immaterial forms of war, where simulations and substitutions proliferate with plug-and-play worst-case

---

[1] Der Derian notes the terminological differences between "simulation" and "(war)game" and clarifies that he uses those terms interchangeably in spite of this, in line with the practices of his interviewees (1990a, 300–301).

scenarios" (1997, 211). Tracing the operation of a MIME-NET, he argues that through the use of "networked information and virtual technologies to bring 'there' here in near-real time and with near-verisimilitude, virtuous war exercises a comparative as well as strategic advantage for the digitally advanced. It has become the 'fifth dimension' of US global hegemony" (2000, 772).

Reflecting on the metaphysical void opened up by Nietzsche's killing of God, and thereby also of Man, Der Derian notes Baudrillard's claim that the central purpose of modernity is to "save a principle that has lost its object"; that is, reality's loss of realness must be concealed (1990b, 299). In the (post) modern condition, in other words, reality has been replaced by simulations. Just as Disneyland is presented as imaginary in a way that masks the irreality and hyperreality of Los Angeles and the broader United States, so do military simulations come to produce particular realities of militarism and war that substitute and compensate for the latter's mutability. As Jef Huysmans explains, in a simulation

> the model becomes more real than the real. It becomes hyperreal. It no longer produces images but simulacra which have no referent, or have lost their relationship to it. That means that the exchange of signs which simulation produces is not a matter of favouring the sign over the real. It is not an inversion of the sign-referent relation but rather an implosion. When the model becomes more real than reality, the relationship between sign and referent implodes. The main task of the production of such simulacra is to mask the absence of reality and thus to save the reality principle. (quoted in Neumann and Waever 2005, 376)

Back in 1990, Der Derian noted two examples of this reality-producing capacity: the shooting down of an Iranian civilian airliner in 1988 due to a misrecognition caused by simulator training, and the national security impacts of the novels of Tom Clancy (1990b, 301–302). Today we might point to the ways in which tensions between the US and China have been exacerbated by wargames in the Taiwan Strait (Peer 2022), or the degree to which diplomatic efforts between the US and North Korea have been renewed by the cancellation of wargames on the Korean Peninsula (Seo and Griffiths 2019). We could refer back to the Desert Crossing and Millennium Challenge exercises mentioned in Chapter 1, which could—and should—have been taken seriously by policymakers in the run-up to the invasion of Iraq.

However, the argument can be taken further still.[2] In addition to the capacity of wargames to influence or change real-world events, in the era of simulation—as Baudrillard diagnosed forty years ago—reality itself has given way to hyperreality generated by closed models (Baudrillard 1983). As discussed in Chapter 4, Baudrillard showed how the play of real and imaginary, of thing (signified) and word (signifier), has been obliterated in an age dominated by models that operate as closed systems. Leaving in their place an ontologically unitary system, devoid of contradiction, tension, difference, the play of meaning-making is replaced by a hyperreality characterized by uniformity and repetition. We have thus moved from the era of representation—understood as a relational mode involving interaction between reality and construct—to full-spectrum simulation in which there is no outside. In such a system, the binary of reality and model falls away; in its place is the forever model that has produced a totalized always-unreal reality. As Baudrillard puts it, "[T]he contradictory process of true and false, of real and the imaginary, is abolished in this hyperreal logic of montage" (Baudrillard 1983, 122).

It is striking how well Baudrillard's description of the models that produce this substitute reality maps onto wargames. He argues that such systems have "broken down reality into simplified elements that they have reassembled into scenarios of regulated oppositions." These scenarios, he continues, are then "presented today in a spread-out series, or as part of a line of products, and this fact alone tests you already, because you are obliged to make decisions" (1983, 120–121). Along this pathway, "[n]o contemplation is possible. The images fragment perception into successive sequences, into stimuli towards which there can be only instantaneous response, yes or no" (Baudrillard 1983, 119). Such systems are constructed, he posits, on the basis of the "active response" of the subject, its "ludic participation" in "a total environmental model" (Baudrillard 1983, 139). Tellingly, he describes this as the "euphoria of simulation" in which life's most serious and intense experiences "can be substituted for the total joy of the signs of guilt, despair, violence, and death'" (Baudrillard 1983, 148).

To illustrate how the production of hyperreality happens in the age of simulation, the example of warfare in instructive. While clearly operating at the heart of military wargaming, the reality of war has become more complex than it perhaps once was. On the one hand, scholars such as Nordin and Öberg have argued that war—usually understood in Clausewitzean terms as

---

[2] I am grateful to Dan Öberg for encouraging me in this direction.

fighting—has morphed into a much more distributed and processual series of phenomena and relations. In this reframing, war is no longer carried out by commanders and warfighters alone; rather, war takes place across economies, civilian populations, and—most importantly for the present discussion—technologies and procedures. Drawing on Baudrillard's analysis, Nordin and Öberg argue that such technologies and processes "attempt to synchronise, coordinate, and make warfare more efficient through staff procedures. They are all based on the idea that perfect operationalisation generates a war in which all means and capabilities are interconnected in ways that aim to create a seamless economy of violence." Consequently, they conclude, "as part of a symbolic disappearance through the fulfilments of technological processes, warfare strives towards perfection and symbolic aspects disappear through a model which is being operationalised as if it is war." Thus, war understood as fighting has "disappeared into the *processing of warfare*" (Nordin and Öberg 2015, 399–400). In this framework, the reality of war as we usually understand it has all but fallen away, replaced by networks, models, and processes—some deadly, some recreationalized, and some both—that have fundamentally changed its character.

On the other hand, the reality of war has proliferated to such a degree that it seems to be everywhere and occurring all the time. As Mary Dudziak has proposed, while in the past it was arguably possible to point to a temporally bounded state of war that differed from times of peace, in the twenty-first century we are faced with a unique situation: "We find ourselves in an era in which wartime—the war on terror—seems to have no end point. This generates an urgent problem in American law and politics: how can we end a wartime when war doesn't come to an end?" In such a "forever" war, as she continues, the idea of combat as a state of exception is replaced with that of war as norm (Dudziak 2013, 3–4).

As part of the forever war, military processes and practices have expanded well beyond the confines of warfighting individuals and institutions. From popular culture to fashion, and from recreation to education and training, codes and artifacts of war pervade our everyday and aspirational lives. While some in IR have argued that this militarization of civilian spaces can be charted and opposed, others have convincingly claimed that we should "forget militarization'" because it "obscures the constitutive nature of warlike relations of force perpetrated against populations deemed to be a threat to civil order or the health of the population" (Howell 2018, 118). This is because the concept of militarization itself "serves to reify the putatively discrete spheres of the military and the civilian" by positing a temporally prior non-militarized civilian realm (Bousquet, Grove, and Shah 2020, 102). In this framework, militarism and war have become so entrenched in everyday civilian life that their respective realities are impossible to disaggregate.

Taking these two examples of the changing reality of war together, we can see that, far from being bounded in specific actors and times, war has become something that is at work everywhere and among everyone. What this means is that through changing the processual relations of war, the simulations that seek to model and explain it have altered its character. Understood in this way, the issue is not our engagement or otherwise in specific games, but rather the place of games in the production of hyperreality in the age of simulation. Insofar as they contribute to this production, in which "the real and the imaginary are confused in the same operational totality" (Baudrillard 1983, 150), wargames are not productive of specific themes or elements of reality but rather—in a collective forever game—contribute to the replacement of reality by hyperreality writ large. Just as the forever war and the permeation of military artifacts and practices into all aspects of life entail that war cannot no longer be understood simply as fighting between combatants, the forever game marks the extent to which games have cumulatively produced a new hyperreality of war in which there is no "game over." What is necessary, then, is the extension of critical thinking from within—and in pursuit of the goals of—particular game models to a more thoroughgoing investigation of how such models produce our realities and subjectivities.

Conclusion

This chapter has shown how—using play as pedagogy—wargaming intervenes at the level of players' cognitive registers in ways that are productive of people. It began by setting out the benefits proponents of wargaming claim for their craft, specifically that wargaming saves lives by reducing conflict, mitigating risk, building cohesion, and providing safe-to-fail learning and experimentation environments that can hone a range of skills including abductive reasoning, procedural literacy, psychomotor skills, systems thinking, and cultivating reflexes. From there, the chapter addressed the question of how the CoP seeks to demonstrate these benefits, noting the difficulty of demonstrating the efficacy of wargaming. Having done so, it examined how wargaming functions as a pedagogical tool, setting out four stages through which wargaming interacts with its audience: (1) generating buy-in and engagement, (2) consolidation through iteration, (3) consolidation through critical thinking, and (4) retention. It drew a broad distinction between research and education games, which include all four of these steps, and training games, which often skip the third.

The chapter then picked up where Der Derian's analysis of games' hyperreal properties left off, showing that despite its ostensibly "unreal" status, wargaming imparts real-world lessons that intervene in players' cognitive realms long after a game is over. While some wargames seek to closely emulate reality, and others engage players using deliberately unreal or fantastical content, the unreal worlds of wargames serve to produce people by leaving their mark on players' consciousness long after a game has ended. The chapter then took the argument a step further by showing not just how wargames affect specific elements of reality but also how they function as one sort of model that has turned reality into hyperreality in the age of simulation. Returning to the work of Der Derian and Baudrillard, it argued that a "forever game" is under way that has fundamentally altered the character of war in ways that permit no "game over." In order to understand the implications of military wargaming, then, it is vital to move beyond debates about realism versus abstraction and instead begin from the understanding that gaming produces realities that remain at work in the cognitive domain of players long after a particular game has ended. These productions play a part in the broader replacement of reality with hyperreality characteristic of the age of simulation. With the preceding chapters having shown how wargaming produces people by intervening at the cognitive level, and having demonstrated its reality-producing properties, Chapter 6 will examine the ways in which wargaming also intervenes at the level of player affect by targeting values, feelings, and even identities.

6

Playing the Player

Gaming the Affective Dimension

Introduction: The Problem of Player Agency

Moving beyond the cognitive domain explored in Chapter 5, this chapter provides a critical account of ways wargaming produces people by intervening at the level of affect. In so doing, it evaluates wargaming not in terms of its efficacy but with a view to excavating its functions as a non-linear communication device and its impacts on player values, emotions, and subjectivities. The CoP argues that the active learning enabled by wargaming is powerful because it engages players not just at the level of cognitive processes but also at the level of affect and imagination. As Ghamari-Tabrizi relays, quoting Robert Specht, wargaming "teaches both intellectually and emotionally—it is an experience one lives through" (Ghamari-Tabrizi 2016, 340). H. G. Wells, too, notes that military wargaming is "an important tool for training and education, and ideal means for 'waking up the imagination'" (quoted in Perla 1990, 179).

The aim of this chapter is to show that while many designers and practitioners emphasize wargames' capacity to encourage critical thinking, reflexive decision-making, path selection, and post-game analysis, it is also clear that players' choices, beliefs, and even identities are deliberately targeted as part of military wargaming. Accordingly, the key claim elucidated is that, by means of processes of affective subjectification through which individual and institutional goals are aligned and ideological and institutional values are imparted, players are often treated as the *objects* rather than the *subjects* in military wargaming. The consequence of this, the chapter shows, is that, far from promoting agency and reflexive engagement, the players of wargaming are the terrain upon which a human-dimension battle is waged across the military's research, teaching, and training regimes.

The chapter begins with an examination of the politics of game design, exploring the power relations at work between the designer, sponsor,

Politics of Play. Aggie Hirst, Oxford University Press. © Oxford University Press 2024.
DOI: 10.1093/oso/9780197629192.003.0007

facilitator, and player. It notes that while the CoP emphasizes the power of wargaming to promote skills, knowledge, and wisdom, very little consideration has been given to normative questions surrounding its affective effects on players. From there, it turns to the ways in which games mobilize emotion in order to impact powerfully upon players in both their conscious and unconscious registers. The chapter then explores the ways in which, by promoting Apollonian play (as elucidated in Chapter 3), forcing player decisions, and generating synthetic experience, gaming subjectifies players by intervening at the level of affect. Echoing Gadamer's caution set out in Chapter 3, this chapter shows that military wargaming plays its players. To recapitulate his words: "[W]hatever is brought into play or comes into play no longer depends on itself but is dominated by the relation that we call the game. For the individual who, as playing subjectivity, engages in the game, this fact may seem at first to be an accommodation. He conforms to the game or subjects himself to it, that is, he relinquishes the autonomy of his own will" (Gadamer 2008, 53).

The Politics of Game Design

James Dunnigan argues that a wargame is best understood as a "non-linear communication device." He explains:

> What makes a simulation such a powerful form of communication is that it is, like most events, non-linear. A book or a film is linear. The author leads you from point to point, with no deviation allowed. Simulations, games in general, and analytic history, are non-linear. That is, you can wander all over the place and still be somewhere. Flip through a book, and you pick up pieces out of context. Make different moves in a game, and you have a context, because the game allow[s], even encourages, deviating from the historical events. . . . You can wander around a piece of analytic history and still get a lot of useful information. (2000, 219–220)

Ghamari-Tabrizi develops this framing, arguing that "wargames are gestalt inscriptions," understood as "a language in which non-sequential ideas could be expressed." She cites Jaron Lanier's 2010 prediction that games would become "compact semiotic packages exchanged as 'tokens' of communication," rendering "contingents that aren't present"—that is, words—unnecessary.

This is because when one has "fluent control of concreteness," abstractions such as categories are no longer useful. Consequently, wargames may helpfully be regarded as "semiotic packages—multimodal, multisensory writing systems of wholes, gestalts, systems" (Ghamari-Tabrizi 2016, 349). The intricate and non-linear character of wargames' communicative elements makes them at once difficult and fascinating to appraise. Their capacity to model holistic systems, stripping out some of reality's muddling inconsistencies and tensions while attempting to render others, makes them a singularly powerful—and problematic—means of representation.

Notwithstanding their non-linear quality, wargames can be understood as a system of organizing, representing, and operationalizing elements of reality in ways that are generative of meaning. As Harrigan and Kirschenbaum argue, the wargame design process "encodes assumptions about historical events (or contemporary real-world situations) into the mechanics of the game itself. In this they are no different from any other system of representation" (2016, xviii). Perla offers a similar analysis, emphasizing that wargames can "impose a structure and discipline that force game designers, players, and analysts to organize . . . facts into operationally meaningful packages" (1990, 9). As Koster also suggests, games can be conceptualized as "iconified representations of human experience that we can practice with and learn patterns from" (2013, 36). By distilling down such human experience into playable artifacts, then, wargames "reduce history to a lovely thick sauce" (Vasey 2016, 456).

As with all forms of representation, such a reduction is necessarily selective and hence necessarily political in the sense that specific power relations influence what is included/excluded, visible/hidden, and condoned/condemned in the game and its goals. Reflecting this point, and building on the insights of Clifford Geertz, Jeremy Antley suggests that a game promotes particular values, norms, and assumptions by actively placing cultural sensibilities on display, "and in so doing helps maintain those sensibilities within that cultural group" (2016, 465). In addition to promoting particular values and ideas, games at the same moment obscure or hide themes, histories, or principles that may be uncomfortable or unwelcome. As Brian Train and Volko Ruhnke explain, "As artifacts of the culture that produced them, wargames serve in the continual exercise of historical revision and socially useful amnesia. . . . Like all human creative endeavors, a wargame is not and cannot be a neutral object" (2016, 515). Read in this way, wargaming contributes to the maintenance of prevailing social tropes and the elision of less popular or palatable themes.

While the necessarily political character of wargaming is thus acknowledged by some in the CoP, the normative and subject-producing implications of this are rarely reflected upon. This is surprising given the intensity with which practitioners affirm the power of wargames to impart skills, knowledge, and values. As Sabin notes, "Wargamers rarely reflect on the morality of their activities, except to point out that their simulacra do not themselves cause suffering, and are more likely to dampen than to inflame combative urges" (2014, 161). Perla offers a similar framing, noting that wargames have traditionally "provided a harmless setting in which human beings could face some of war's challenges without destroying lives, property, or nature." Following Wells' analysis of playing war, Perla suggests there is "no inconsistency between deploring the practice while perfecting the method" (Perla 1990, 179).

Where normative and affective concerns are explored, they tend, not unreasonably, to focus on two issue areas. First, they relate to the question of the morality of abstracting the military and civilian targets of war, who are represented in artifacts like counters or excluded entirely from the scenario. Sabin explains: "[W]argames by their very nature give little if any sense of the human consequences of the actions they model," but in this "they are no more intrinsically immoral than are the many other ways in which the dreadful but compelling and fascinating reality of warfare is represented for our interest and enlightenment." Rather than spending time worrying about the perpetrators and casualties of war, Sabin reflects, players' decisions follow a logic of "cost-benefit choices framed by the designer in terms of an abstract currency of victory points, and they give little feel for the moral burdens borne by the real combatants" (2014, 162–163).

Second, where normative issues are raised they concern the possibility that games exploring themes of war and violence will lead players to become aggressive and/or desensitized to violence in the "real world." This possibility is widely discounted in the wargaming CoP. As Sabin puts it, There is no sense, as some have argued with violent video games, that playing simulations fosters real-life aggression and desensitises users to the moral gravity of actual warfare and killing" (2014, 161–163).

Beyond these two issue areas, which themselves receive scant attention, little else is deemed of concern in normative or affective terms as regards professional wargaming. An as yet unposed question in the CoP involves the impacts of wargames on those taught and trained with them, beyond the questions of desensitization and real-world aggressivity.

Having established that there is a politics to wargame design, and having noted the broad elision of normative questions surrounding the impacts of wargames on those who play them, the discussion now turns to the power relations at work between designers and other game participants. Examining the roles of designers, facilitators/adjudicators, and players in turn, it shows that in promoting particular forms of subjectification, wargaming compromises player agency at the same moment that it is productive of people.

Designers

Wargame designers emanate from a range of scholarly and practitioner backgrounds. This is because, Bartels explained, "there's no degree in wargame design within the US. Designers are political scientists and operations researchers. They've got military experience, they're hobby gamers, so they're coming with all these different research design paradigms in the back of their mind. Gaming doesn't have its own research design paradigm that it puts on top of you, so you tend to carry in whatever you started [with]" (interview 2017). That said, it is widely accepted that there are three main styles of design among the CoP: the artist, the architect, and the analyst. Perla and McGrady provided a helpful overview of these approaches to design: "The artist creates the story and he's really trying to get the players to live the story that he's envisioned. The architect creates the universe and is trying to turn the players loose in the universe to see what they do. The analyst is trying to build a model of the real world and see how the players interact with that model as if they were interacting with the real world" (interview 2017).

In a necessarily selective process of representation and distillation, a designer must apprehend a version of reality in their game's scenario, mechanics, and objectives. As Train and Ruhnke explain, "[T]he designer, through the processes of research, conceptualizing, testing and production of a game, must make a series of choices of what to include in his design and what to leave out" (2016, 515). Such a process always involves trade-offs and compromises because reality is far too complex to be grasped and modeled in its fullness. As Brynen argues, all wargame designers "face a trade-off between accuracy and parsimony, and must also adapt the employment of models to suit particular analytical or educational needs—focusing on some areas and abstracting or even ignoring others" (2016, 491). Harrigan and Kirschenbaum similarly note: "[I]t is in the nature of a model to simplify the complexity of the world" (2016, xviii). Games are thus necessarily per-spectival and subjective: "Consciously or unconsciously, a wargame designer transmits specific messages, concerns, and even conclusions to the players of the game through the medium of its structure and procedures" (Perla 1990, 185).

These subjective judgments and selective representations can manifest in a particular game in many ways. One example, provided by a military wargames researcher, involves biases in assumptions about human behavior. He reflected that if you ask a designer to build a model of a crowd, "he can do a pretty good model of what a crowd looks like . . . but they won't actually behave like a crowd does. And people won't recognize that that's true . . . In a way they have . . . a dangerously high level of influence sometimes. In the absence of anything better to make a decision people will rely on the model. [But] the model can have some systematic biases that reflect biases within the creator" (interview 2017). He continued:

> It takes a long time to really get into what are the assumptions that are being made here and how are they driving the behavior of the system that you're looking at. . . . When you're really sitting down and you're looking at one of these complex emergent behavior social systems, groups of people, there are times in which I'll eventually get down and say, "That assumption is just not backed up by anything empirical," [or] "This is arguably a bad assump-tion." But it's in the system and nobody sees it . . . We have made decisions on the basis of these models that I would say . . . were bad decisions because the underlying assumption was a bad assumption, and nobody could see it. So they have a lot of power. And that's kind of a problem. (interview 2017)

As this suggests, wargame design involves a series of trade-offs, perhaps most significantly that between accuracy and simplicity (Sabin 2014, 19–30; Brynen 2016, 491).

Indeed, periodic dips in wargames' popularity—explored in Chapter 2—can be in part explained, as Perla suggests, by designs that were either insuf-ficiently realistic or too complex. The former lost their appeal because they appeared as mere abstractions, while the latter alienated players through highly specialized and complicated rule sets. The key, he concludes, is finding the right balance between complexity and playability (1990, 317). In this vein, Allen notes that "wargaming covers a spectrum of reality and make-believe." He elaborates:

> At one end is the pale abstraction of analytical gaming. Moving through the spectrum from that faint shade of reality, gaming next appears as electronic simulations, then as people-around-a-table games like the one in the Pentagon basement. The spectrum next begins darkening with the reality of exercises—games played with real warriors and real weapons, real warships and real warplanes. At that end of the spectrum, right next to the exercises, is the dark of war itself. Wargaming is a simulation of war, a horror show without props. Actors, chosen for the real war, walk the stage in rehearsal, ad-libbing to a script that keeps them bound by reality. (1989, 3–4)

As such, wargaming is a marriage of fantasy and reality, its players "strategists-in-waiting" (Allen 1989, 88, 158).

According to many in the CoP, however, the subjective and selective character of game design is not necessarily a problem. As Rubel explains, "All wargames have explicit purposes, and rarely are these purposes so holistic as to demand unsparing investment in fidelity. Bringing the purpose of a game into focus leads quite naturally to distillation; many games are able to set aside significant aspects of reality. To the extent that distillation promotes clarity, highlighting relationships in the aspect of warfare we are studying, the epistemological damage of failure to include all possible factors is counterbalanced." This is defensible, he argues, because too much reality is as problematic as too little; since "knowledge gained from a war game is in the eye of the beholder (player or analyst), obfuscation caused by excessive comprehensiveness is at least as damaging as the omission of some significant element."

Thus we can conclude, he argues, "that a war game should be designed with as much fidelity as possible without including factors that, because they are not clearly related to its purpose, risk diluting or masking valid knowledge that might legitimately be gained" (Rubel 2006, 114). What is key here is that the game's objectives should take precedence over fidelity to reality in game design. As Perla and McGrady reflected, rather than representing reality as faithfully as possible, "the objective of the game is to allow the designer's point of view to come across" (interview 2017).

Thus, the choices made by the designer are governed not by a commitment to accurately apprehend the real world but rather by the game's objectives. In military wargaming, this will be a specific training end-state or an education or research process. In the professional gaming sector, these objectives are, however, usually not set by the designer. Instead, the game will have a sponsor who specifies the aims and end-states to the designer for integration into the game, a process that often takes skilled translation. Bartels elaborated:

> When you do have a sponsor who has written extensively on the topic, you can read what he's written, you can talk to him about how he sees this problem working. And then, you're, really, just figuring out how to create the game environment that mimics those factors . . . The value-added of a game designer is being able to work with the sponsor to figure out what it is that you actually really want. I don't think this is, actually, any different in the educational gaming space than it is in the analytical space. . . . It really boils down to: Can you formulate what the purpose of the game that the researcher actually wants is? What do they want and why do they want it? (interview 2017)

The sponsor commissions and funds the game with a specific purpose in mind, then, and it is the job of the designer to understand and encode this purpose into the game in the form of learning objectives so as to stimulate player engagement (Perla 1990, 185–186).

Wargames, and the designers who make them, thus enjoy a particular and powerful capacity to impart ideas, values, and assumptions to players. Indeed, some in the wargaming CoP acknowledge that in addition to serving as a formidable mode of learning, "[t]he power of a wargame to communicate and convince, however, can also be a potential source of danger. Wargames can be very effective at building a consensus on the importance of key ideas or factors in the minds of participants. They attempt to create the illusion of reality, and good games succeed. This illusion can be a powerful and sometimes insidious influence. . . . The designer of a game has great power to inform or to manipulate" (Perla 1990, 182). As another designer similarly noted, "It's easy to design a game so you get the outcomes you want" (interview 2017).

This power wielded by game designers is often referred to among the wargames CoP as being "godlike." Bartels recounted: playing God "is certainly a joking line that we almost all use. I think some of it is the world-building aspect, and I think it is also the level of control you have. . . . You quite literally get to be fate. If you don't have a transparent adjudication system, you can entirely rig what happens in the game" (interview 2017). One military wargames researcher similarly reflected: "Especially when you're building cognitive systems that generate a certain emergent behavior, there's a kind of intelligence you see that emerges out of these things. It's easy to find myself thinking that God is a modeling and simulation guy and he created this simulation that we live in. And eventually we all wake up and realize we must be created and we go looking for the modeling and simulation that created this" (interview 2017). Another designer suggested you can "think about it like the Greek gods . . . You're looking into your little dish, and you're standing on Mount Olympus, and you're periodically interfering with the little humans. Being a game designer is like that" (interview 2017).

Echoing this framing, Nieves commented on the role of the game designer: "They are creating a world. They are literally looking down at this scape and they've created everything from start to finish and that is a powerful feeling. . . . I imagine that game designers when they create their worlds feel a sense of love for their products because they have just created life. Those games do take on a life of their own" (interview 2017). Rupert similarly said: "If you're designing a game, you're designing the world. You're designing the scenario. You're designing the rule set. You're designing who the opponent is" (interview 2017).

Some in the CoP joked about the temptation to become a vengeful god if players do not engage with the game as instructed. As one designer relayed, "When I have a student who is being disruptive and obnoxious, it is always tempting to kill them off or move them to a different role where they will be less disruptive. And there are times when I've done it because it's just hit the point where no one else is learning because this person is not coping with the position I've put them in. But there is something slightly disturbing about the notion that the solution to a disruptive student is to kill them" (interview 2017). Voicing caution about such measures, Bartels explained that "there are consequences if you get overly enamored with the God metaphor. If it feels like you are playing God and not that there are a set of rules, you're not going to succeed in teaching the students the rules. You're going to teach them that you're a capricious God and not to live in your world. . . . Designers have to fight their desire to play God" (interview 2017).

Thus, there is an unequal power relation between the game designer and the player, which to date has been underexplored in the professional wargaming

CoP. While steps can surely be taken to reduce the starkness of this power relation—by having players challenge rule sets, modify or hack code, or challenge design assumptions—when it comes to being a player in play, the designer holds all the cards. There is also, however, an underacknowledged power relation at work between players and the adjudicators and facilitators who direct wargaming.

Facilitators and Adjudicators

In addition to the unequal power relations at work between designer and player, wargame facilitators exercise considerable influence as they direct and oversee player action. As Chapter 1 established, wargames require skilled facilitation and careful adjudication. As Turnitsa explains:

> [T]he game presents a situation to the player, the player studies that situation and selects a desired future state to achieve, decides on a course of action that he/she believes will result in that future state, and executes that course of action within the game. The game responds (based on input from other players, the environment, game systems controlling non-player factions, etc.) by adjudicating the opposing actions, and presenting a new situation. The chief task of the game system, whether it is an analog system for a tabletop or seminar wargame, or a computerized system, is the ability to evaluate the results. (2016, 30)

The wargaming CoP frequently raises the issue of game facilitation and control, citing a lack of skilled adjudicators as a key reason games can fail to generate player buy-in or to realize their objectives (Pournelle 2017, 26). As with game design, however, processes of game facilitation and adjudication are distinctly subjective and selective, functioning in a political rather than a neutral manner. The following explores how, despite this, facilitation and adjudication are frequently presented as objective in ways that mask this political character.

As discussed in Chapter 1, games can be adjudicated on a spectrum between "rigid," understood as a game in which the outcomes are determined by the game rules, and "free," in which a referee or game staff observe "the decisions and executed actions of the players, and through analysis and subject matter expertise, are able to determine results, and describe them to the players (in essence, creating the next situation in the wargame, for the players to react to)" (Turnitsa 2016, 31). Whether it is decided by the game system itself or by an individual or a group of game staff, adjudication is central to wargaming's structure and purpose: "[I]f wargaming, as distinct from combat modeling or simulation, is to allow for players applying decisions to control forces engaged in operations against each other, then the ability to judge which set of decisions, and which course of action, results in victory is key to the wargaming event" (Turnitsa 2016, 34). Skilled adjudicators are often held in high esteem. As Downes-Martin notes, the adjudicator is a "super player" in complex games (cited in Wong 2016, 537). In Sabin's words, an adjudicator is thus a "God-like figure" (2014, 31), while according to Banks, Groom, and Oppenheim, they act as "God and Nature," in part playing the game and in part shaping it (1968, 6).

This raises the question of who is fit to adjudicate. Wong asks: "Who really is expert enough to understand what outcomes would arise from player moves in a game about Syria? Adjudication is futures thinking, and the more complex the judgment, the easier it is for it to go awry" (2016, 536). As with game design, some in the CoP acknowledge that subjective judgments in facilitation and adjudication are unavoidable. Perla notes that it is wrong to assume the CoP need not worry about the possible biases of game staff: "[B]iased direction can teach invalid, and potentially deadly, lessons" (1990, 33). Another designer discussed this point at some length:

> There are problems with negative learning outcomes without a moderator. A game has to have a moderator to be able to draw out those lessons and keep the entire experience as an objective basis, to allow a player or participant to actually visualize what they have done in there and how they could have done things differently. Without a moderator, a person . . . can go through multiple iterations of a game and take out the wrong lessons without having a means to have an objective basis for their experience. (interview 2017)

While it is certainly true that without oversight players may learn lessons other than those intended, what is interesting and problematic here is the presentation of the adjudicator's judgment as objective. While they may well be more knowledgeable than players about the specific region or conflict explored in a game, this does not mean their judgments are objective. Because adjudicators are fallible humans, their interventions can be no more than subjective, even if they are as well informed as it is possible to be.

The difference between objective and intersubjective facilitation is often fudged when discussing facilitation and adjudication among the CoP. This is evident in Hanley's account:

> Objectivity is a result of inter-subjectivity; i.e. all using their subjective perceptions in observing an object agree on its attributes. For example, observers could observe a coffee cup and agree upon its color, size, weight, etc. The validity of games [is] enhanced by having teams of subject matter experts involved in the design, play, adjudication, and findings from a game who can question aspects upon which they agree and disagree to arrive at more objective judgment. A way to check the objectivity of campaign and combat simulations is to have different teams model the same contingency, or have a team use different models. Should different teams model the phenomena the same way, their simulation satisfies the criteria for objectivity. Should they differ substantially, their simulated "world" is not objective. (Hanley 2018, 55)

In this framing, objectivity is presented as synonymous with the concurrence of several subjective evaluations. While there may be a case for this if one subscribes to Karl Popper's or C. S. Peirce's conceptualizations of objectivity as intersubjectivity (Freeman 1973), in the wargaming debates this has not yet been fully elucidated.

Instead, game facilitators and adjudicators are often assumed to enjoy superior wisdom to players, while in reality their decisions are based on their own subjective understandings to no less a degree than is the case for players. Where there are adjudication teams, these are often marked by dissensus, with results decided on the basis of who insists most strongly that their view is correct, rather than its demonstrable superiority. The consequence of this is often an instantiation of the status quo or a particular perspective rather than an objectively mediated outcome. Importantly, these views will be influenced by intellectual and affective predispositions.

Having explored the privileged positionalities of designers and facilitators, the remainder of this chapter interrogates the impacts of wargames on those who use them. Leaving aside well-trodden debates about the moral issues of abstracting war's participants and casualties, and about encouraging violence and desensitization on the part of players, the following sections address the question of how wargames as tools of learning subjectify players in ways that circumvent their reflexive capacities and intervene in their affective registers. In doing so, it affirms that a normative concern for player agency should receive considerably more attention in wargaming and scholarly circles than it has hitherto.

Players

The account of players and their agency proffered by the wargaming CoP is fraught with tensions. On the one hand, designers and practitioners are at pains to emphasize the extensive freedom enjoyed by players to make decisions and choose their paths in games. As Perla puts it, the designer builds the game world and "provides a set of maps and instructions for exploring it. But it is the player, not the designer, who dictates which paths will be taken. Indeed, it is often the case that players will discover paths through the game world that even the designer did not perceive. . . . [T]he game's designer cannot dictate more than the broad limits of its player's explorations" (1990, 184).

Many in the CoP echo this framing, emphasizing the mutual exchange of knowledge and wisdom that occurs between wargame sponsors, designers, facilitators/adjudicators, and players. When it comes to the inherently pedagogical character of wargames, Perla argues, the game "must be designed to allow the players not only to learn, but to teach as well." In this vein, the design process should address the question "What does the sponsor want to learn from the players?" (Perla 1990, 190). In this way, he concludes, gaming is a communication device characterized by the flow of information "from a sponsor through the designer to the players, and from the players, through the analysts, back to the sponsor" (Perla 1990, 191). Read in this way, wargaming involves the free and fair exchange of ideas, information, directives, and feedback between the architects and players.

Such a framing affirms that wargames provide an unusually open context within which the player can explore and learn. Indeed, some suggest that such openness is excessive. Jeremy Antley relays the possible objection to wargames that they call into question the pedagogical role of the instructor: "With their emphasis on the player as the producer of knowledge, games undercut the instructor's authority as a gatekeeper of interpretation," he writes (2016, 463). Others in the CoP share this view. As a designer reflected:

> What we're really asking you to do when you learn anything about complex human affairs by playing a game [is to] understand the designer—his or her model—and critique it, evaluate it, by comparing it to your own and end up with something better. . . . We know that models are simplifications for a specific purpose and whatever the purpose of the simulation game, fun or teaching or otherwise, the designer simplified things in a certain way and that is imperfect. Every simplification is imperfect, is wrong. But the designer is presenting to you what he or she thinks is important and now you have to take from that what is important to you and your application of it. How does that compare to everything else you know? That's learning. (interview 2017)

Several CoP members emphasize that manual games best provide scope for this agential engagement. One designer pointed out that you can "modify your environment in a tabletop game because the rules are yours. Now that they are yours, you can do whatever you want with them. Whereas [if] they are coded into the system in a videogame, they are not able to be manipulated by the common person. Anybody can manipulate a set of tabletop rules. . . . We call them 'tinkerers'" (interview 2017).

This reading is tempered, however, by a counternarrative in which players are framed as the objects or targets of wargaming, to be attracted, directed, and influenced in both their cognitive and affective registers. The actions proposed at the end of the MORS 2017 Wargaming Report, for example, include developing links with the discipline of psychology because of "the fact that the minds of the players are the main instrument within a wargame." Such a link could, the report continues, help explore "what we are really achieving in the minds of the players" (Pournelle 2017, 94). As Chapter 5 explored, part of this intervention concerns the cognitive realm. Allen notes, relaying William Martel's view, that wargames teach players how to think in a crisis mode (Allen 1989, 297). Neale similarly claims that "[t]he game context, precisely because it has a specific effect on human thinking and behavior, can lead to more creative and sometimes more effective solutions to problems than would be identified by the same people in a real-world context" (2018, 22).

In some games, the effect might be a particular skill, such as proficiency with a weapon or vehicle. In others, it might be serving as a data point by means of which institutional decision-making trajectories may be mapped. In both cases, however, the player is the object or target of the game. An uneven power relation thus persists by which sponsors, designers, and facilitators/adjudicators are able to script, encourage, and obstruct players' activities and decisions in myriad ways. The following sections explore three key ways in which games, and their designers, influence players at the level of affect: first, through a combination of persuasion, emotion, and coercion; second, by promoting an Apollonian play mode that directs how players play; and, finally, by aligning players' goals with those of the game.

Persuasion, Emotion, Coercion

Among games studies scholars, the affective and embodied qualities of gaming are widely acknowledged. As Jon Dovey and Helen W. Kennedy put it, games often "involve a very strong emotional effect in the player; often adrenaline-based, fight or flight reactions are physically provoked. In all, the activity of playing a game offers the sensorium a greater range of inputs that novel reading or film viewing" (2006, 8). Among the CoP, the ways in which games, and their designers, seek to influence players are expressed in more and less stark ways. Some statements suggest that gaming *assists* players. Perla, for example, notes that games "must be structured to *help* human players make decisions and to allow them to learn about the effects of those decisions" (1990, 164; emphasis added). Other statements are more candid in their acknowledgment that players are subject to forms of persuasion. As Charles Vasey puts it, for a wargame to be successful the player "must be persuaded into your web" (2016, 456). Train and Ruhnke make a similar point: "[T]he artwork, images, and content are chosen to entice the player/consumer" (2016, 515). In Perla's words, the designer must find ways of "grasping and holding a player's interest in performing his game role" (1990, 199).

Specifically, players must be persuaded to trust the games they play and the design teams that make them. Indeed, many in the CoP argue that for a game to yield trustworthy insights, those involved in playing the game must trust it. McGrady and Vebber explain:

[G]ood games are games that people trust. From the perspectives of the sponsor, participants, designer/developers, and implementers, there are always issues with the various aspects of the gaming process. Identifying, rectifying, or mitigating those issues develops trust among those involved in the gaming process and results in trustworthy insights emerging from the play of the game. This leads us to the question of how do we build that trust and what technologies are available to enhance trustworthiness. (2017, 33)

As this suggests, considerable emphasis is placed on the power of affect and emotion to influence player behavior and engross them in a game.

Some in the wargaming CoP affirm gaming's affective dimensions. Perla, for example, notes that for Wells, gaming has an "emotional side [which] . . . provides an opportunity for glory without gore and defeat without destruction" (1990, 4). Others in the wargaming community are more "squeamish" about the emotional dimension of gaming (1990, 4). Still others are more candid about wargaming's capacity to impact upon players' affective registers. Downes-Martin and Pellegrino explained:

People learn through repetition or trauma. Now, repetition is tough because it takes time and it's boring if you keep doing the same stuff and so on. Trauma sounds terrible, but a wargame involves emotions, intense emotions. You want to win. You want to avoid the humiliation of losing. There's time stress. . . . It doesn't matter what the game is for: the people playing it, if they're emotionally engaged in the game and suffer emotional elation and despair during the game, they will come away—they may not have accurate memories. I don't know what the effect of emotional stress is on accurate memory. They're not traumatized in the sense of PTSD, that's not what I'm talking about. But there's this emotional engagement and I think gaming taps into that. (interview 2017)

In this account, gaming precipitates a wide range of player emotions. Such emotion is important not just to generate initial buy-in to a game but also to ensure enduring and enthusiastic participation such that the objectives might be realized. In this way, affect is a key play incentive. One designer put it this way: "Emotion can be powerful for lower-level people to say, 'I want to do this again.' To me, that's always the key. The minute you stop saying 'I want to do this again,' we've got a problem" (interview 2017). A wargaming instructor similarly notes, "You want to give them some wins. You want to give them enough stuff that they feel good and they keep being engaged so that they want to keep learning" (interview 2017).

In addition to relying upon persuasion and affect, wargames use coercion to obtain and maintain player engagement. One key example of this is the prevalent use of the term "force" when it comes to players' in-game activities. The language of "force" is pervasive in the CoP's accounts of the benefits of wargaming. Perla, for example, notes that "the operational implications of advanced weapons systems can be portrayed vividly by forcing players to deal with the opportunities and difficulties they present" (1990, 181). Kligge reflected that "the largest benefit is students are forced into potentially uncomfortable situations where they don't have a lot of experience" (interview 2017), while Sterrett argued that gaming is useful "because it forces you to put what you're learning into action" (interview 2017). The force in question is most often associated with compelling a player to make decisions in-game. A designer elaborated: "Gaming forces you to complete the decision process. If . . . the three of us talk about what should the United States do in Syria, we can have a really good conversation. We'd bring all sorts of ideas to the table. But one of the things a game really forces you to do, at some point, at some level, is to reach some kind of a decision" (interview 2017).

This theme of force is reflected in the high-pressure environment designers often seek to cultivate in games. As one wargames designer noted, "[T]here's no doubt that these kind of wargames that happen are focused very much on procedures and stress, and really performing those procedures under stress" (interview 2017). Hall explained that "you've got to place the player in an uncomfortable position. The best way to make it uncomfortable is to have his commander watch him play the game." He went on to provide an example of how pressure and stress are applied to players in military wargaming: "One of the tools I used is . . . a tactical decision game. It's usually a simple map with a scenario. . . . And then I would bring my lieutenant into our conference room, turn the lights off, turn on loud music, have them have their flashlights and their notebooks. And then I would say, 'Okay, here's the situation. You have ten minutes to write a fragmentary order and brief me on it.' And then I would critique them on it" (interview 2017).

Practicing skills and tasks under such stress conditions is, many in the CoP argue, an important part of military training and education. Wargames are a key resource here, Lee noted, because they "allow you to generate these long-term events so that people can become more exhausted and have to learn how to work cognitively through the challenge of fatigue in order to make good decisions. So that immersive environment, that immersive state, those emotions, are important for setting conditions within a simulation to improve the quality of the training" (interview 2017). Such wargames can be extremely demanding of players. An instructor commented: "It's a very tough environment to be in, or it can be, especially if there are mechanics that force them to participate" (interview 2017).

Having identified the mechanisms of persuasion, affect, and coercion employed in wargames to attract and retain player engagement, the following section demonstrates that designers, facilitators, and adjudicators actively seek to influence how players play wargames, promoting a distinctively Apollonian play style.

Promoting Apollonian Play

As Chapters 3 and 4 demonstrated, the history of play in Western philosophy and culture has revolved around a struggle between Apollonian and Dionysian modes. This section argues that the form of play promoted in US military wargaming is distinctively Apollonian in character. As compared to the irregular, compulsive, changeable, and unpredictable characteristics of Dionysian play—and, indeed, the "deconstructive play" advocated in this book—Apollonian play is characterized by reason, seriousness, presence, order, and unity. Unlike Dionysian and deconstructive framings, in which play is an end in itself, Apollonian play is directed, mediated, and channeled toward a purpose, whether the upholding of modern Western philosophical assumptions or the promotion of US military research, education, or training objectives. Accordingly, the following shows how this Apollonian mode is promoted through wargame designers', facilitators', and adjudicators' attempts to influence how players play wargames.

According to its advocates, wargaming creates a safe-to-fail environment in which players can rehearse skills and plans without the risk of injury. In Hanley's words, gaming "stimulates creativity through play in a safe environment and discovery of approaches that were unknown or unanticipated" (2018, 64). Koster elaborates: "This is what games are *for*. They teach us things so that we can minimize risk and know what choices to make" (2013, 120;

emphasis in original). For a wargame to succeed in this aim, however, several conditions must be met. First, players must not "fight the scenario." As one designer explained, "The classic thing people say is 'don't fight the scenario.' A lot of times it's 'don't even fight the game' because everyone comes into the game [with] their own perception of how things are supposed to be and it's almost impossible to not offend their sensibility in one way or another in the gameplay" (interview 2017). Another designer similarly noted, "The term we use a lot—I'm sure everyone else does too—is 'don't fight the scenario.' We're trying to encourage them to set whatever reservations they may have about the specifics aside and take this as seriously, be as immersed as possible" (interview 2017).

Key to the success of pedagogical gaming is players' acceptance of the scenario. This sits in tension with the claim that gaming promotes critical thinking. As one instructor explained, gaming "develops different kinds of critical thinking. Because you always get the player who wants to break the game. You know, 'How do I get around the rules, how do I do something that wasn't intended?' For them that's the challenge: 'How do we get out of this constraining environment and gain advantage over the player who hasn't figured that out yet?,' which causes a level of creativity that is interesting to watch sometimes" (interview 2017).

It should be noted that a few in the CoP resist this imperative to prevent players from challenging elements of a wargame. Wong, for example, affirmed: "I see a lot of games run where the participants are told not to fight the scenario and I think that's very damaging. So I disagree with this idea that the researcher or the wargamer comes up with this great scenario and then you [are] just supposed to browbeat the player into this scenario. I think it's much more effective when the participants have been involved in a longer process of developing this scenario themselves. Then they have a level of interest and investment and sort of belief that I think improves play" (interview 2017). However, such reservations remain rare in the CoP.

Second, and relatedly, in order for players to accept a game's scenario, they must experience a suspension of disbelief. As Markley reflected, the designer must "create an environment that allows participants to suspend their disbelief. Your scenario, a problem being examined, has to be perceived as at least plausible for people to want to leave behind their disbelief, because they have their own mind, what they believe is more probable circumstance or situation" (interview 2017). Perla comments that a wargame "must be interesting enough and playable enough to make its players want to suspend their inherent disbelief, and so to open their minds to an active learning process" (1990, 8). He continues:

> Because the players are the critical elements of a game, the game's designer must build his game to help the players suspend their disbelief, much as a novelist would. But the game designer must go even further, getting his players to contribute actively to building and participating in the fiction. In order to accomplish this, the designer must, of necessity, make the players want to play the game, or at least to want to play it well once they are involved. (Perla 1990, 202–203)

Gaming must surmount players' potential skepticism or reticence by generating buy-in. As Casey and Martin explained, "It really just comes down to, can you capture somebody's imagination? You could call it a suspension of disbelief . . . but essentially what you're doing is you're getting them to buy into whatever they are doing" (interview 2017).

The suspension of disbelief must be carefully cultivated by game designers and facilitators. Perla writes: "[T]he key point is whether the structure of the player roles contributes to or is detrimental to the game's realistic representation of the operational situation, and also to the player's willing suspension of disbelief. If the player's role is too limited in scope for decision and action, the player will lose interest and remember that 'it's only a game.'" He cautions that poor role development and untrained game staff can "break the spell and allow the players to return too far back to real reality instead of remaining focused on the game reality. [This] must be avoided at all costs if the players are to continue suspending their too readily resumed disbelief" (1990, 248–250). The implication here, then, is that players must come to identify with the roles and mechanics of the game in order for it to function as desired and realize its objectives. The following section argues that this convergence is self-consciously sought by game designers, facilitators, and adjudicators by endeavoring to align players' goals with those of the game in ways that intervene in their affective domains.

Aligning Player Goals with Game Goals

In addition to promoting a distinctively Apollonian play mode that encourages player conformity—and the realization of specific objectives—designers, facilitators, and adjudicators aim to align the goals of players with the goals of the game. As one designer explained, wargaming is about the pursuit of a set of goals different from, and at odds with, the goals of opposing player(s):

> The goals for that person on the other side aren't the same as your goals. The competition is to try and attain your goals. [If you] come out [of] the game feeling that . . . you have attained your goals, [then] you pretty much won that event. And so it pushes the students to try to get to their goals, which means that they have got to study more because in order to get your goals, the way the matrix game is run, . . . you've got to know fact. A matrix game is an argument-based game in which you gain bonuses by covering more facts than your opposing teams. And it is run by a facilitator who adjudicates using those facts. (interview 2017)

What is suggested here is that games are won or lost on the basis of the attainment of specific goals as directed by the game's objectives. By virtue of the pursuit of such victory conditions—as will be explored in more detail in Chapter 7—the game's momentum is generated.

What this ultimately means is that players are compelled to align their personal goals with those of the game. In his discussion of the six features of gaming, Jesper Juul posits that "the player invests effort in order to influence the outcome . . . [And] players are attached to the outcomes of the game in the sense that a player will be the winner and 'happy' if a positive outcome happens, and loser and 'unhappy' if a negative outcome happens." This, he continues, "is part of what we may term the 'game contract' or *lusory attitude* . . . that the player agrees to by playing. The spoilsport is one who refuses to seek enjoyment in winning, or refuses to become unhappy by [losing]" (Juul 2003, n.p.).

In other words, in gameplay, players should and do adopt the game's goals as their own and seek to realize them. As Perla puts it, games should be designed in light of the question "How can the game best assure that the goals of the sponsor and the goals of the players will reinforce each other?" (1990, 190). Such a melding of personal and game goals is a powerful driving force for in-game engagement and learning. As James Paul Gee candidly explains:

> [T]his marriage of personal goals and "in game" goals is a highly motivating state. . . . When I have married my personal goals and values to the virtual

character's "in game" goals, I see the game as both a *project* that the game designers have given to me and, simultaneously, I *project* my own goals, desires, values, and identity into the game world, melded with the "in game" identity and goals of the virtual character. The "project" now becomes "mine" and not just something imposed on me, because I have "projected" myself into it. (n.d., 19)

Ultimately, designers and instructors affirm that players should refer to their in-game roles in the first person, signally an alignment of role and game goals with their own. As one designer put it, as discussed in Chapter 5, before playing a game "I'm going to read the rules. I'm going to *be* the scenario. I'm going read what *my* goals are, and then I'm going to attempt to determine what the goals are of my adversaries or even my allies because not every goal for your allies is the same as yours" (interview 2017; emphasis added). This process of goal alignment entails an impactfulness beyond the realm of conscious and reflexive thought. The final section of this chapter argues that this process can be read as one of player subjectification.

Producing People with Wargaming

A wargame is, in effect, a conflict simulation run on the human brain rather than a computer. (Perla 2018, 77)

The topic of subjectification has received wide-ranging analysis in IR and beyond. Often associated with Foucault's account of the generation of self and identity, it refers to the continuous processes by which a subject is produced as such. Foucault relates this process to the notion of play: for him the "self emerges in an agnostic play of forces" (Bogue 1994, 7). As this suggests, play and games can be potent forces in subjects' becoming. In the words of Luke Caldwell and Tim Lenoir, "[T]he interactivity of gaming serves as a vector for subjectification" (2016, 254). N. Katherine Hayles similarly argues that the "construction of subjectivity is increasingly entangled with algorithmic procedures governing the game world" (2004, 315).

As Chapter 4 explored, the deconstructive play mode advocated in this book amounts to a reflexive form of subjectification in which the subject critically mediates the forces and power relations through which they are produced and reproduced. The discussion in that chapter emphasized the ways in which games and their players generate complex and contradictory forms of agency. To recapitulate, while some follow Murray's view that agency is the satisfying power to take meaningful in-game action and see the results of our choices (Murray 1997), others argue that games offer at best an interactive fallacy (Jennings 2019) that amounts to submission or voluntary obedience to the rules of the game (Tulloch 2014) and results in aggressive forms of player interpellation (Garite 2003). The deconstructive play mode proposed, it has been argued, can push toward a more dialectical understanding in which the player is—and is self-consciously—both agent and prisoner in games, engaging in the dynamics of control and compliance at work.

The remainder of this chapter examines the ways in which military wargaming functions as a mode of player subjectification that leaves considerably less scope for critical reflexivity and mediation on the part of the player. Indeed, it argues, wargaming facilitates a form of subjectification that seeks to circumvent player reflexivity and conscious mediation. It makes this case by tracing the identity-conferring properties of three key elements of the wargaming process: generating synthetic experience, cultivating mental and physical muscle memory, and targeting players' unconscious registers. The conclusion drawn is that players' subjectivities are the target or object of wargaming as part of the production of people in the age of simulation.

Generating Synthetic Experience

Inherently designed as they are to teach their players, wargames seek to generate synthetic experience. As Ghamari-Tabrizi explains, "Wargames are synthetic experiences—substitutes for real life. . . . Wargames are training mechanisms for inducting specific modes of embodied attention, concentration, and endurance" (2016, 331). Perla echoes this framing, observing that "wargaming works to create a shared synthetic experience among its participants" (2016, 175). Such an intention predates contemporary advanced technologies with which synthetic experience might normally be associated. Notes Hanley: "Following World War II, simulation using both wargames and computers became important to provide synthetic experience to prepare for conflicts" (2018, 65).

Synthetic experience involves the cultivation of "real" experience using synthetic means. As a wargaming instructor suggested, "Gaming can create experiences that people will use later on" (interview 2017). A designer similarly noted, "It's about developing scar tissue. It's about having a formative experience that one can relate to at a later point. . . . The real benefit of gaming is being able to think back to prior experiences and then draw those forward" (interview 2017). Lademan offered a similar framing, suggesting that "what an officer would carry away from his experience in wargaming is the attempt to apply that kind of method of thinking to his real-world situations. You know, being able to investigate a problem, being able to discover the risks and the implications and the parts and the relationships of a problem, and being able to draw all that together into a synthesis, which informs how he reacts to a problem" (interview 2017). Synthetic experience, then, is intended to be of use in real military activities. Indeed, as Robert Sparrow and colleagues note, "The aim of such games, according to the simulation designers, is to create 'synthetic experiences so compelling that participants react as if they are real.' . . . Their goal, as David Ayer puts it, is to 'create veterans who've never seen combat'" (Sparrow et al. 2018, 6).

However, there is a politics to this cultivation of synthetic experience. Specifically, what is to be included in this synthetic experience is mediated by sponsors, designers, and facilitators through game design and execution. Perla explains: "[A] scenario should include all essential information about a game's setting and subsequently planned modifications to it, and should contain no superfluous information. . . . The trick for the designer is to determine what is essential and what superfluous" (1990, 205). What this ultimately means is that the experience cultivated in the game is of a different character than "real-world" experience insofar as the complexities and tensions have been filtered. As a non-linear communication device that presents a given system as a whole, a game filters out reality's necessarily tension-ridden complexity. This means that making decisions is easier for the player. The problem is that this ease is achieved by the designer by withholding information that might have led to a different course of action. In other words, this means that rather than the individual drawing their own conclusions by mediating the details of an event or experience, their perspective is narrowed and directed in advance by the designer's evacuation of "superfluous" information from the game system. Given this, the capacity of players to make an agential decision is circumscribed by designers' view of the scenario and courses of action.

Mental and Physical Muscle Memory

Central to this process of generating synthetic experience is the cultivation of mental and physical muscle memory. As de la Vega explained, "You can use a virtual trainer that looks just like a real piece of equipment and you'll be getting the same feedback, you'll be establishing the same muscle memory, and if your simulation is just like reality, you're going to be establishing the same skills, the same reactions, the same critical thinking requirements to respond" (interview 2017). A wargaming instructor elaborated: "It is about that muscle-building so that when they are, in real life, in a situation with incomplete information they can work through these processes. . . . That is absolutely what I mean by mental muscle memory: you are building mental agility to use this practice you have been afforded to help you more rapidly and effectively process information and make decisions, if you move through your OODA loop faster and better" (interview 2017).

When it comes to training games in particular, such a process is repetitive and interactive. As Moreland explained, "Where you're talking about muscle memory—practice-makes-perfect types of things, like flight simulators or weapon systems simulators, where it's all about developing individual and crew proficiency—those types of simulators are very much allowing you to practice a set of actions or decisions. It's good for building in those kinds of skills to where they become second nature" (interview 2017). Many in the CoP argue that such games' utility emanates from their capacity to promote action before conscious thought. One instructor argued that gaming leads you to a mode of acting in which "you don't spend a lot of time thinking about [what to do]. You just know. It's intuitive. You know what 'it' is and we got that through repetitions. . . . You could say it's muscle memory for the brain" (interview 2017). Gaming is thus recognized as influencing players' affective processes and reactions.

An alternative way the CoP expresses this process is through the vernacular of altering players' neutral pathways. Discussing the example of advertising, de la Vega asked: "How do people's current values affect [whether they] want to buy something? They . . . introduce advertising or media to then change the neural pathways of their viewers in order to get them to buy what they want" (interview 2017). One instructor elaborated on this point, noting that "different areas of the brain respond to different chemical reactions, so winning is something that specifically stimulates a particular area of the brain so that it, kind of, reinforces that piece. In that particular capacity, I think that gaming could be good because you're trying to reinforce certain positive aspects of the training" (interview 2017).

This suggests that gaming is explicitly geared toward intervening in and changing affective registers of players. A designer confirmed this: "If the simulation game is convincing enough that they're relating it to reality, they explore and discover that their previous value system doesn't work as well as the value system you're trying to push them in the direction of. It can change your attitudes because of the immersive aspect of it. We tend to be prone to getting involved in the make-believe of whatever role we're playing in a competition" (interview 2017).

Wargaming is, then, a method of research, education, and training that produces subjectifying effects. As de la Vega summarized:

> [I]t's not just their fingers that we're [training]. It's their mind. It's their complete body. . . . It goes back to your training objectives: what do you want them to learn? Muscle memory, critical thinking, processing, understanding and learning and remembering processes, understanding your operational and mission variables? That is how they relate to the environment—how do their actions cause reactions in the environment? If you're creating a good scenario, you're going to anticipate those. . . . Then you crank up the complexity, and so by the end of their training iteration, when they're ready to get certified, they are really able to [engage in] good high-critical-thinking decision-making in a complex environment." (interview 2017)

As this suggests, wargames intervene at the levels of both the cognitive and affective domains. As wargames pioneers and practitioners at RAND in the mid-twentieth century concluded: "Personnel training should . . . be approached as systems training—that is to say, cohorts of human operators should be regularly and methodically subjected to the pressures of crisis conditions so as to compel the group to adapt, to modify and adjust their practices to critical stresses" (Ghamari-Tabrizi 2000, 187). This is effective because wargames allow access to "the subjective properties, e.g. the perceptions, evaluations, and choices of participants" (Richard Snyder, quoted in Banks, Groom, and Oppenheim 1968, 10). The hope was that studying participants' actions would be a step toward "the systematic formulation of propositions about the behaviour of decisionmakers under crisis, which may then throw some light on the processes by which foreign policy is made" (Banks, Groom, and Oppenheim 1968, 17).

In more contemporary forms of wargaming, the aspirations have expanded to cultivating mental and physical muscle memory, generating real experience using synthetic environments, and shortening decision-making protocols such as the OODA loop. As Caffrey explains:

> A fundamental reason why wargames "work" is that the side that makes more-effective use of them can (all other things being equal) complete OODA loops more quickly than an adversary that does not use wargaming as effectively or at all. . . . But what if you could shrink your OODA loop faster than your adversary can his, or better yet, what if you could shrink your OODA loop while your adversary's remains unchanged? Either would provide a great relative advantage—and of the type that matters. Wargaming can shrink OODA loops faster and do so without prompting an improvement in an adversary's speed. (2019, 285)

As noted in Chapter 2, the ultimate aim of this process is to short-circuit conscious elements of decision-making in order to bring about actions more quickly. To cite White again:

> The "observe, orient, decide, and act" (OODA) loop decision cycle—must be compressed in the short-term to "recognize, decide, act" (RDA). Observation and orientation as discrete actions will be a luxury that the future battlefield will not allow. Superiority will be predicated on further evolving the decision cycle to "predict, decide, and act" (PDA)—with the goal of reducing (or ultimately eliminating) the time to decide—or "predict and act" (PA)—through automation, AI, and IA. (White 2017, 23–24)

As this suggests, wargaming seeks to intervene in the temporality of warfare and the decisions that constitute its conduct. If tempo is the fourth dimension of US warfare (Der Derian 2009, xxxi), wargames can speed up the maturation of aptitudes in the use of technologies and skills: "[T]he greatest advantage comes not simply from having more advanced technology or a more effective doctrine but by maturing all elements of an MTR [military technical revolution] or RMA more quickly than your adversary" (Caffrey 2019, 287). One key means by which they do this is creating mental and physical muscle memory in players.

Compromising Player Agency

Many in the CoP are at pains to emphasize the agential character of wargaming. Perla, for example, argues that games are brought to life and directed by their players: "The game itself takes shape only when the players enter the scene. The success and value of the game revolves around the players and their decision process" (1990, 153). This suggests, players should and do have considerable agency: "Participants in wargames are not a passive audience.... They deserve and should demand an explanation of why events run counter to their expectations. They must be allowed, indeed encouraged, to be wary and skeptical" (Perla 1990, 182). In this framing, any change that takes place in players' beliefs, values, or emotions as a consequence of a wargame is a result of their considered modification of their prior position.

One designer provided a helpful reflection on this point:

If you'd like to convince a group of students of the demerits of some course of action or something like that, you could use a simulation to illustrate the point and let them discover on their own. Because with teaching . . . adults it doesn't seem to work too well to say "Okay, here is what you should believe." You need to let them experience something and discover something on their own and then let them reflect on that so that they go, "Oh wow, yeah, okay" and then themselves reach their conclusions on whether they want to change their beliefs, their values, their attitudes. (interview 2017)

Here, players are framed as the subjects of the game, critically interrogating and evaluating the subject matter, mechanics, and results. Such a narrative suggests that, through gaming, players change themselves. As Perla and McGrady explained, games can promote agency by involving "the players not only in the decision-making but also in the discussion about what are the implications and the outcomes of these decisions. This gives them an opportunity to learn from each other the same way that in a box game the players learn from what's in the box" (interview 2017).

This framing is offset, however, by the ways in which sponsors, designers, and facilitators/ adjudicators deliberately influence these processes of change. As noted above, this is sometimes framed in the language of assistance, as in Perla's suggestion that "the game's designer must build his game to *help* the player suspend their disbelief" (1990, 202; emphasis added). At other times, the intervention is more forcefully put: "The designer must, of necessity, *make* the players want to play the game" (Perla 1990, 203; emphasis added). In addition, while many in the CoP argue that players are afforded considerable freedom in games, such freedom is highly restricted and permitted only insofar as it is compatible with the sponsor's objectives. As David Williamson Shaffer and colleagues explain:

> [G]ames give players *freedom to act within the norms* of a valued community of practice—norms that are embedded in nonplayer characters. . . . To work successfully within the norms of a community, players necessarily learn to think as members of the community. . . . This is situated learning at its most profound—a transfer of ideas from one context to another that is elusive, rare, and powerful. It happened not because the student learned more information but because she learned it in the context of a new way of thinking—an epistemic frame—that let her see the world in a new way. (Shaffer et al. 2005, 109; emphasis added)

This indicates that players' apparent freedom and agency are on further inspection highly circumscribed by institutional and doctrinal principles and processes. While many in the CoP claim that wargaming teaches players *how* to think, as opposed to *what* to think, the analysis developed here has shown that their craft also comprises the latter. As a wargames designer noted, "I think that's entirely accurate that games can create experiences and really shape the attitudes and experiences of individuals" (interview 2017).

Consequently, even in apparently open-ended games, the agency exercised by players is highly mediated and directed. This is because it is a secondary concern; the satisfaction of the game's objectives is always the primary directive. In Perla's words, "[T]he game designer must be sure that the scenario allows players enough decision-making flexibility *to let the game meet its objectives. Because a game's objectives should focus on exploring the factors and reasoning that affect specific types of decisions,* scenarios should be designed to minimize artificial restrictions and allow players as much freedom of choice as possible in making those decisions" (1990, 204; emphasis added).

While it may appear that the concern here is to promote player agency through decision-making, on reflection it is clear that this agency is not an end in itself but rather promoted so that the game's objectives—in this case, mapping decision-making trajectories—might be realized. As Perla puts it, "[T]he structure of the game provides the player with a framework for understanding what decisions he must make, what factors he should consider in making those decisions, and what form the decisions should take" (1990, 199). A game with more rigid objectives—such as a tactical game dealing with surface-to-surface missiles—would afford players much less freedom. In such a game, player decisions "will be limited to those required to maneuver against, target, and destroy the opponent" (Perla 1990, 204). Most wargame designers would consider such intensely directed play to be entirely acceptable in the service of a game's objectives. Players' agency in wargaming thus extends to the limits of the game's objectives and conformity to the broader assumptions and values of the military's research, education, and training regimes.

Part of what compromises agency is the way in which wargaming deliberately targets players' unconscious, as well as conscious, registers. As noted above, Koster argues that all games are edutainment (2013, 47). Games are powerful pedagogical tools, he continues, because "conscious thought is really inefficient. If you have to think about what you're doing, you're more liable to screw up. Your reaction times are orders of magnitude slower, and odds are good you'll get in a wreck" (2013, 22). He goes on to argue that games "primarily teach us things that we can absorb into the unconscious, as opposed to things designed to be tackled by the conscious, logical mind" (2013, 76). He invokes the notion of "grokking" to describe a form of mental muscle memory generated in gameplay in which "you understand something so thoroughly that you have become one with it and even *love* it" (2013, 28; emphasis in original). He explains:

> There's a very large part of your body that works based on the *autonomic nervous system*, which is a fancy way of saying that it makes its own decisions. Some of it is stuff you can learn to bring under more conscious control, like your heart rate. Some of it is reflexes, like snatching your fingers out of the fire. And some of it is stuff you train your body to do . . . [W]e're not just talking about muscle memory, but about whole sets of decisions we make instinctively. (Koster 2013, 30)

Games, Koster posits, accelerate the grokking process because they allow repeated practice of solving a particular puzzle through iterative permutations and feedback. Because it impacts the unconscious, autonomic systems, players learn games' "underlying patterns, grok them fully, and file them away so that they can be rerun as needed" (2013, 34).

The consequence of this lodging of gaming lessons in players' autonomic systems is that reactions occur without players consciously thinking about them. As Gee candidly puts it, pedagogical gaming

> *offloads some of the cognitive burden* from the learner, placing it in smart tools that can do more than the learner is currently capable of doing by him or herself. It allows the player to begin to act, with some degree of effectiveness, before being really competent—*"performance before competence"* . . . Such distribution also allows players to internalize not only the knowledge and skills of a professional (a professional soldier in this case), but also the concomitant values ("doctrine" as the military says) that shape and explain how and why that knowledge is developed and applied in the world. (Gee n.d., 12–13; emphasis added)

Curtiss Murphy similarly concludes that games facilitate effective learning by "reducing the number of steps, abstracting the process, limiting options, and *reducing the cognitive load*" with which learners have to grapple (2012, 388; emphasis added). The language here is noteworthy: seeking to "unload" or "reduce" players' "cognitive burden" means circumventing their conscious thinking processes. Similarly, "performance before competence" translates to encouraging actors to act before fully understanding the action. By seeking to intervene at the level of players' conscious and unconscious minds in this way, gaming can be read as a process of subjectification.

Another way of putting this is that the production of "epistemic games" is built upon the epistemic frames of particular communities of practice. Epistemic games teach

> understandings, effective social practices, powerful identities, shared values, and ways of thinking of important communities of practice. To build such worlds, one has to understand how the epistemic frames of those communities are developed, sustained, and changed. Some parts of practice are more central to the creation and development of an epistemic frame than others, so analyzing the epistemic frame tells you, in effect, what might be safe to leave out in a recreation of the practice. The result is a video game that preserves the linkages between knowing and doing central to an epistemic frame—that is, an epistemic game. Such epistemic games let players participate in valued communities of practice: to develop a new epistemic

frame or to develop a better and more richly elaborated version of an already mastered epistemic frame. (Shaffer et al. 2005, 108)

What unites these analyses is the notion that gaming intervenes at the level of players' unconscious in ways that are productive of self and identity.

Such processes map onto what Patrick Crogan and Samuel Kingsley have analyzed as the "attention economy." They explain: "In the digital era the function and impact of the 'programme industries' attains a new level of influence and penetration with profound potential to transform the enabling dynamics of social, cultural and political relations, negotiations, and identity formation," which cultivates consumption through mass-produced attentional technologies (2012, 12). Under conditions of an overabundance of information, they argue, attention becomes a commodity. When such attention is acquired, it endures over time, inviting the question of the ways in which the "wetware" of the brain becomes a site of capital accumulation. In an era of cognitive capitalism—in which the human capacity for attention has been commodified and the program industries have attained unprecedented capacities to influence society, culture, politics, and identity—it is attention, not information, that is the principal currency (Crogan and Kinsley 2012).

Consequently, Crogan and Kinsley build on the call issued by Bernard Stiegler, who "announces a battle for criticality that must be fought—or, rather, re-commenced—against the mainstream adoption of digital technology's potential visible in notions like the attention economy" (Crogan and Kinsley 2012, 2). Stiegler argues that the digital area has brought about a shift from biopower to globalized psychopower, which involves "the tendency towards the displacement of 'attentional' techniques, which produce 'deep' attention, by industrially mass-produced 'attentional technologies' that are designed to generate one particular kind of attention—to consumption" (cited in Crogan and Kinsley 2012, 12). Catherine Malabou has also engaged with this question through a philosophical engagement with neuroscience, and cautions that "it is precisely because . . . the brain is not already made that we must ask what we should do with it, what we should do with the plasticity that makes us, precisely in the sense of a work, sculpture, modelling, architecture" (quoted in Crogan and Kinsley 2012, 13). The question that remains is how we might reconstitute and reform psychosocial attention in ways that resist the pharmacotic reconfigurations of psychotechnologies (Stiegler 2010, 35) as they play out in military wargaming.

Conclusion

As the above discussion suggests, in addition to wargaming global politics, the US military wargames its personnel. This chapter has shown that while many designers and practitioners emphasize the importance of player agency, it is also clear that players' choices, beliefs, and even identities are deliberately targeted as part of military wargaming. It has thus shown that in addition to intervening at the level of the cognitive, wargaming produces subjectivity by targeting players' affective domains. The chapter began by demonstrating the politics of game design and situating the uneven power relations at work between designers and players, showing that the former persuade and coerce the latter through the promotion of an Apollonian play mode and the alignment of players' goals with those of the game. Consequently, it showed that by means of cultivating synthetic experience and mental and physical muscle memory, wargames function to subjectify players as part of the games' production of hyperreality. The implication of this is that wargaming plays its players.

Having argued in this chapter and the preceding one that wargaming subjectifies people through its hyperreal productions at the levels of the cognitive and affective, the final two chapters of this book interrogate the two key drivers of these processes. Chapter 7 argues that it is the pursuit of victory conditions (a win state) that incentives the player to play, and to keep playing, a game. By harnessing—and denying the satisfaction of—this desire to win, it argues, wargaming is able to generate a perpetual-motion machine through which its subjectifying processes can take place. Chapter 8 then explores the politics of the condition of immersion generated in these processes, which place players in an unreflexive flow state.

7

For the Win

The game offers us a purpose. It says: Win. And we study the game,
we learn the rules and regulations, the strategies that will help us
win. Given the purpose, we seek the means.

—Bernie DeKoven

Introduction: Driving Pedagogical Play

Chapters 5 and 6 demonstrated that wargaming serves to subjectify players
by targeting their cognitive and affective registers. Having demonstrated
how wargaming works in this way, it remains to examine what drives these
people-producing processes. This chapter demonstrates that the imperative to win—that is, the pursuit of victory conditions—is key to this process.
As Sabin notes: "In the end . . . calculations still come down to cost-benefit
choices framed by the designer in terms of an abstract currency of victory
points" (2014, 163). While it is often argued that people seek to win because
winning is fun (Koster 2013), gaming is frequently hard work and enjoyable
for the limits and rules it imposes rather than because it is fun (Bogost 2016).

Accordingly, this chapter critically interrogates the winning imperative's
role in the production of people in military wargaming. The core argument
advanced is that while the *pursuit* of victory conditions is crucial to driving
pedagogical play, the *attainment* of such conditions is both ultimately irrelevant from the perspective of the game's objectives and unsatisfying for the
player because it fails to yield the promised resolution. This means that what
the player thinks is at stake is really meaningless. In other words, players are
encouraged to play for reasons other than those they believe govern and incentivize the game. It also means that the resolution, praise, and triumph that
the realization of victory conditions is expected to bring do not arrive; instead, the player is evaluated in ways that are opaque and is compelled toward
further gameplay as the striving for satisfaction persists. In this way, players
are incentivized to win, often committing vast amounts of time and energy to

Politics of Play. Aggie Hirst, Oxford University Press. © Oxford University Press 2024.
DOI: 10.1093/oso/9780197629192.003.0008

doing so, all the while with the payoff being denied in advance. Read in this way, wargames can be understood as perpetual-motion machines driven by the desire for, rather than the realization of, a win state.

To make this case, the chapter opens by examining the claim that fun drives the desire to win in military wargaming. From there, it turns to the place of winning and competition in US military culture in general and its wargaming regimes in particular, tracing the ways in which competition and agonism are used in and by the CoP. Having established prevailing naturalist assumptions in the CoP that view the winning imperative as a spontaneously occurring feature of human nature, the chapter argues that wargames function by producing and harnessing precisely these tendencies in players as part of their subjectifying capacity. It demonstrates how wargames use systems of reward and punishment, orchestrate profusive forms of loss and failure, and instantiate systematic iterative irresolution that at once incentivizes, precludes, and devalues winning. While the attainment of a win state is broadly immaterial to a wargame's success or failure, players are often kept in the dark about this. This becomes part of how players are subjectified through the hyperreal productions of wargaming.

What's Fun About Wargames?

> No other artistic medium defines itself around an intended effect on the user, such as "fun." (Koster 2013, 156)

It is widely claimed that people play wargames because they experience them as fun. And yet what constitutes this fun requires evaluation. Fun is neither apolitical nor removed from processes of subjectification. And, contrary to popular assumptions, fun has serious effects. As Koster puts it, "That's what games are, in the end. Teachers. Fun is just another word for learning" (2013, 46). At the heart of descriptions of fun proffered by the wargaming CoP, winning and pursuit of victory conditions feature centrally. The basic assumption is that people like playing games because they have a chance of winning, and winning is fun. While this may seem intuitively to make sense, it begs a series of questions surrounding the place and politics of fun, winning, and fun as winning. Indeed, as David Webster notes, "when my idea of relaxing after a hard day is to sit in a dark room and simulate acts of murder and violence . . . '[a]ll a bit of fun' seems to be inadequate as a means of capturing what is going on" (2014, 189).

Some in the wargaming CoP approach the fun of wargaming as being of benefit for its pedagogical applications. As discussed in Chapter 5, Machuga posited that gaming involves "taking mundane things that may not be a lot of fun to study on your own and giving it a spin . . . It's the candy-coated shell on the bitter pill of knowledge" (interview 2017). The experience of fun associated with wargaming is central to how games subjectify players. And yet the military has conventionally been cautious about the presence of fun in its teaching and training regimes. As one designer commented, "There's an attitude within the services . . . which is, if it's fun it's not of value. . . . If it's fun you can't be learning anything. You're not gaining anything out of it if you're not in pain, essentially" (interview 2017).

However wargaming has successfully demonstrated to at least some in the military that fun and learning are not mutually exclusive. Tappen and colleagues reflected: "One of the biggest advantages I see to this wargaming effort is we're starting to get people to think differently than they have previously. It's almost like we're giving people permission to have a little bit of fun at work. . . . It's been interesting to watch the skepticism at the beginning of some of the games, but as we go through the series, by the end of the game we have quite a few converts that are excited and we regularly hear insights that people have discovered from the games" (interview 2017). The fun of games comprises affective elements, including "optimal experience, an escape, a release" (Sutton-Smith 2001, 174), wish fulfillment (de Zamaróczy 2017, 168), and group bonding. A designer affirmed: "It is absolutely fun . . . It is camaraderie. You do things as a team. You are sharing an experience" (interview 2017).

The experience of fun in military wargaming, however, must not overdetermine the game's objectives. As Bartels cautioned: "It's certainly true that you can have a really engaging classroom game from which people don't learn anything. I've seen those run, where everybody walked out of the room going, 'That was great, that was fun,' and then you sit down in the next session and you start debriefing it and there's no substance there. That was an enjoyable experience and nothing else" (interview 2017). Another designer similarly warned that wargaming "can become entertainment. That's always a danger. I suppose with games there's a danger that you can become a victim of its success. . . . If you're a game designer, [it's your] responsibility to have the game communicate whatever it is you're trying to communicate. . . . Are the students really learning what you want them to learn rather than just enjoying playing the game?" (interview 2017).

This suggests—somewhat paradoxically—that fun is both key to and potentially damaging for military wargaming. As emphasized in previous chapters, the core goal in military wargaming has to be the realization of training objectives. Robinson put it this way: "The key is to make sure the . . . game is built so that it provides good training feedback, not entertainment. That's sometimes the other problem. Good training isn't always entertaining." And yet, he continued, designers seek to make games fun: "Even the most sophisticated games that they tried to build for accuracy take certain steps to make it entertaining. The way they set up your turns, the different things they keep track of" (interview 2017). Similarly, Hall explained that fun can be helpful in realizing the game's objectives by promoting buy-in and iterations: "We're not playing this game for fun, although it can be fun, and it's better if it's fun because then they will play it again" (interview 2017).

Importantly, though, the extent to which fun is a key driver of games has been contested. Ian Bogost issues a thoroughgoing challenge to this assumption, claiming that "[g]ames aren't appealing because they are fun, but because they are *limited*. Because they erect boundaries. Because we must accept their structures in order to play them . . . The *limitations* make games fun" (2016, x, emphases in original). This counter-reading frames fun not as a way of describing the pleasure associated with gaming but rather as "the aftermath of deliberately manipulating a familiar situation in a new way." Bogost explains: "We've misunderstood *fun* to mean enjoyment without effort" (2016, 57, emphasis in original); on the contrary, "fun and work, fun and exhaustion, fun and seriousness live together as intertwined threads in a common rope. The fun, it would seem, arises from the work, from the responsibility, from the discomfort and anxiety." This results, he concludes, in a "paradox of fun," in which "we think fun is enjoyment, but in practice it often feels like quite the opposite" (Bogost 2016, 66).

The fun associated with gaming is far from innocent, intertwined as it is with labor, effort, and stress. Writes Bogost: "Fun isn't a distraction or escape from the world, but an ever deeper and more committed engagement with it . . . Fun is not only the delight in success, but also the panic of uncertainty, the agony of failure" (2016, 81). It also involves accepting, rather than seeking to challenge, status quo conditions: "[W]e do not arrive at fun by expanding our circumstances to allow for less wretched alternative, but by embracing the wretchedness of the circumstances themselves. We might even go so far as to say fun comes from wretchedness. . . . Fun *is* impoverishment, blight, and squalor" (Bogost 2016, 92). Perhaps troublingly, then, the fun associated with wargaming masks a series of more labor-intensive demands that it places upon players, in particular the drive to win.

For the Win

The desire to win is frequently framed as a key driver of game play: "[I]t is the winning that counts. Every victory *represents*, that is, realizes for the victor the triumph of the good powers over the bad" (Huizinga 2016, 56; emphasis in original). Sutton-Smith echoes this claim: "The thought that 'we're number one' reigns in the heart of all players" (2001, 64). In most games, realizing a win state—which can be variously construed—signals the completion of the game's objectives and hence its end. This is because games usually contain a "satisfying 'win condition' that terminates its algorithm" (Wark 2007, 215).

A key quality of the fun—or, if Bogost is correct, the hard work we mistake for fun—generated through (the pursuit of) winning is the experience of mastery and control: "Fun is all about our brains feeling good—the release of endorphins into our system. . . . One of the releases of chemicals triggering good feelings is that moment of triumph when we learn something or master a task. . . . After all, it is important for the survival of the species that we learn. . . . Fun from games arises out of mastery" (Koster 2013, 40). This experience of mastery spans such spheres as "anxiety, self, and the world" (Sutton-Smith 2001, 135). As Chapter 8 will explore in detail, the accompanying sense of control is vital for the experience of flow in gameplay. Milahy Csikszentmihalyi posits: "A sense of control is definitely one of the most important components of the flow experience" (1975, 46).

The centrality of this winning imperative is acknowledged by many in the CoP. Downes-Martin and Pellegrino asserted: "You've got to get people who are beginning to do this addicted to winning. So you give them some easy wins up front. You can't keep doing that because they stop bothering, so you give them a couple of wins up front without telling them. That gets them addicted to winning. Now you start making them lose and they start working. They work real hard to get back to that winning." They raised the notion of the "fun meter," which shows the extent to which players are engaged in a game: "At the beginning of any game, for people to willingly engage, they have to think that we all have an equal sense of winning or losing. Otherwise why am I playing this game? If I know you're going to win . . . why am I here? So, we kind of think of every player as a needle on the fun meter and they all start pointing straight up. Equal chance of winning to the left, equal chance of losing to the right. As the game proceeds they start to move" (interview 2017). Indeed, as many interviewees affirm, winning sits at the heart of broader military values and subjectivities. Kligge similarly commented: "Within the Department of Defense we are programmed to win. People are programmed to win to varying degrees" (interview 2017). And one designer stated: "Absolutely people want to win. It's in our DNA" (interview 2017).

Some in the CoP attribute this focus on winning to a trait shared by people who are drawn to the military. De la Vega claimed: "There are a lot of A type personalities who have that human nature instinct to win and of course that's great in gaming" (interview 2017). Bateman reflected: "One of the things we see with our students, like any military, they are all Type A. It's all win, win, win" (interview 2017). In military wargaming, such Type A behavior can, one designer explained, "be useful in that it can push people really to work hard on a problem. That's something that might not always occur in something such as a seminar or just a regular planning exercise, where there's no fixed outcome and you're not really competing against anything" (interview 2017). Such personality types are quick to engage enthusiastically with wargaming, according to Hall: "The extroverted people will get into it faster, [as] they like that competitive aspect" (interview 2017).

Others in the CoP emphasize the deep engagement of other personality types in wargaming. As Downes-Martin and Pellegrino noted, "Conventional wisdom would tell you extroverts love games. But apparently there is a body of work that shows that introverts actually are drawn to gaming as well because it provides a structured environment in which to engage socially. [Gaming] draw[s] introverted kids in, getting them to engage in a learning experience" (interview 2017). This point was echoed by Hall: "There were some introverts in some of the games I ran, and you can watch them come out of their shell if you've got the right environment. Some will just stay in that shell, especially if you have someone who is extroverted, and you let them run the game. As a facilitator you have to say, 'Okay, you shut up' politely, and pull that person into the game and let them express their opinions. And then, a lot of times, that introvert will have a very huge impact on the game, [providing] some insights that the other people wouldn't have thought of" (interview 2017).

Reflecting on the integration of "nerds" in the military, one designer observed that, perhaps counterintuitively, "the geeks are actually, I would argue, more competitive. There's nothing worse than some of these computer jocks because in their whole lives they've never had anything, they were always last to get picked for the basketball team in school, and so this is their arena and they are absolutely out there" (interview 2017). This is because, Goodwin commented: "In our business, where the consequences of failure are so bad, we talk in our doctrine about seizing the initiative and a desire to win, impose your will and whatnot. So giving people a place to practice that and develop that mindset, I think, is an important thing" (interview 2017). Hall similarly noted: "The overarching imperative, in our profession, is to win. Because second place isn't good" (interview 2017). Another designer neatly surmised, "From a military standpoint, I think the desire to win is something that is strong and almost ingrained in everyone. Because, from our standpoint, if you lose you die" (interview 2017).

Such a desire, while not unique to service members, is key to military socialization. Rupert described it like this: "I think there's a certain desire to win in general with people, but the military is an organization that is taught and socialized that their job is to win. . . . If you're in basic training, you don't want to be the person who comes in last place. Yes, you're a team, you have each other's backs, but there is still this strong competition to be the best. There are a percentage of alpha males or alpha females in the military or higher, most likely; whether it's by design or not, they kind of instill that for you to be that kind of person. And even gaining rank is seen as a process of winning—'I've earned this. I've made this position' " (interview 2017).

The imperative to win, then, is intense in the military. As one instructor summarized, "I certainly know that with American officers, it's been my experience that winning is still the number one incentive to drive them to take anything seriously. And I say that completely without constraint or limitation, at least for American officers, but this is probably true especially for young officers from any army in the world that's worth its salt. If you take them out there and you make something into a competition, the American soldier will mow the lawn with more efficiency if it's a race. They are by nature as competitive as athletes." Such winning in the military is often team-based: "The desire to for your team to win is just as strong as your individual desire to win. And that's one of the reasons why if they're simple enough and adapted enough, wargames even work for the tactical level. As long as you make it about beating somebody else, they'll go at it" (interview 2017).

In-game victories can have important real-world effects for service members. Guillory reflected: "Pre the Global War on Terror . . . a lot of guys had their officer recommendation written around how well they performed at NTC [National Training Center] because that was the only chance they ever had to do anything. There wasn't a war to go fight, and so that's what they were evaluated on. . . . There were a lot of guys who were hyperfocused on 'I have to win at NTC, it doesn't really matter how much I learn while I am there. I have to win because I want to look good on my OERs [Officer Evaluation Reports] because I want to get promoted'" (interview 2017).

Too great a desire to win can derail a wargame. Huizinga cautions: "The passion to win sometimes threatens to obliterate the levity proper to a game" (2016, 47). Bernie DeKoven posits that

> there is a difference between playing to win and having to win. When you're playing to win, you're judging your behavior in terms of how it helps you achieve your goal. You've accepted the game completely—that is, you are following a certain set of rules, working within them. When you *have* to win, you're willing to break whatever rules you can if that would help you get closer to your goal. (DeKoven 2002, 139)

Examples of the latter kind of behavior were highlighted by members of the CoP. As one designer put it: "The danger is just always that you get people who are so wired to win stuff that it gets in the way of other learning objectives" (interview 2017). The result is that players seek to win by means other than those permitted in the games—means that often are at odds with the game's objectives. As Perla and McGrady commented: "Players want to win, meaning achieving your victory conditions. If you can't win [via] the victory conditions that the game has set for you, you will often see people change their objectives so that their personal victory conditions can be achieved" (interview 2017). This process of gaming the game takes advantage of designers' oversights and the game's parameters. Moreland echoed: "All games and simulations have their limitations and have loopholes that can be exploited, so the first thing that we always try to establish is a spirit of learning and training, and not gaming the game. . . . You're only cheating yourself if you cheat the game" (interview 2017).

This tendency to game the game can be read as itself a manifestation of the desire to win. "That's where the real competitive nature comes in: them trying to game the game," acknowledged Goodwin. In one recent wargame that he described, players "hacked the email systems here, which is great espionage, but it gets beyond what we're trying to accomplish here. We want you to learn about how to work as part of the National Security Council, not how to hack the other side's email system. . . . And we recognize it. We're glad that they got excited about it. . . . But, at the same time, it defeats our purpose. Although your purpose was to win, ours was for you to learn" (interview 2017). Lee elaborated: "[P]eople try to game the system. They will figure out how to make the simulation enable them to win. They find out that if you keep doing a particular entry you will overload it, so the other guy won't be able to fire his weapons. Well, that's not helping. That's not a learning event. You've just simply figured out a way to fool the computer" (interview 2017).

Such behavior is discouraged by facilitators and adjudicators, as Guillory pointed out: "You want the guys to do their best in the situation they're in, but you want them to do it in a situation that has the same constraints as the ones they will be facing on the battlefield. If they're focusing too much on the game and they're trying to manipulate the constraints that they won't have the opportunity to manipulate on the battlefield, then that completely takes away from preparing for war" (interview 2017). Moreland concluded: "It's really a matter of establishing a culture of let's let the game do for us what it was designed to do. Let's not exploit it because we're missing out on learning opportunities and not taking what it's trying to teach us" (interview 2017).

One common effect of too much of a focus on winning is the use of ethically ambiguous actions. Observed Lee: "I think there's a real desire to win, and a lot of times folks will slide into the—you might say—gray zone about right and wrong in order to achieve victory" (interview 2017). The pursuit of victory conditions can overdetermine a wargame's learning objectives and transgress established moral norms. A designer commented, "[O]ne of the problems we have in our experimentation is everybody wants to win. That's not necessarily the training point or outcome we are trying to achieve. We're trying to learn something. We're trying to teach something. We're trying to evaluate something. If everybody wants to win, including the opposing force, then I may not be able to get the training objectives completed with my training audience. So I think it's the same—you see it regardless of whether it's a simulation or a game, everybody wants to win and that can cause an issue" (interview 2017). Consequently, as Bartels affirmed, "you need to balance the desire to win with the desire to learn. If they're just trying to win, and all they care about is 'I won the game and therefore I got the A, everything is great,' versus 'I lost really badly but I learned a lot in the process'" (interview 2017). Therefore, a good wargame "combines a desire to win with a need to follow doctrine and the game objective (which could be to train)" (Caffrey quoted in Pournelle ed. 2017, 23).

As this suggests, precisely what winning looks like in a wargame is not self-evident. Dunnigan notes that there are various grades of victory, specifically "draw, marginal victory, substantial victory, decisive victory, overwhelming victory." While hobby gamers will settle for the closer calls, he continues, "[a] general wants unconditional victory" (quoted in Allen 1989, 95–96). Several interviewees made a similar point. Kligge, for example, suggested that "sometimes there is no win. Sometimes there is just not losing" (interview 2017). Rupert also stated that "winning is sometimes just surviving" (interview 2017). Casey and Martin elaborated: "Winning is great and I'm not going to deny that. It is how you define the winning. . . . It's about reward mechanisms. You can define winning as 'I completed the game.' That's one type of winning. Or winning could be 'I successfully figured out this puzzle,' or 'I successfully got a higher score than Joe'" (interview 2017).

This runs against common assumptions, often held among military training audiences, that winning involves coming in first in terms of the game's coded-in metrics. In the words of one instructor: "When we're talking about winning or losing in simulation, a lot of times with the kids out there playing games and all that, their concept of winning is killing everybody on the opposing forces. The concept of winning on the simulation that we're using is completing the mission. The mission could mean not killing anybody, just getting a piece of key terrain denying the ability for bad guys to use it. So it's not really about body count. It's about the mission itself" (interview 2017).

As this suggests, winning might be processual rather than the realization of an end state. In pedagogical wargaming, Moreland elaborated, it's important to set

an expectation up front, defining what win means. Winning might not mean winning the game. Winning might mean, "Okay, we've now established a certain level of proficiency in a given task" or "We've now formed as a team and we can effectively plan," [or] "Yeah, our plan didn't work, but by golly we really came together and we understood to talk to each other and we built the plan." So the plan itself, not whether or not it worked, was the learning outcome. So there's still always ways to get a win out of it, even if the game doesn't produce that confetti-and-banners sort of outcome that they're looking for. (interview 2017)

A designer made a similar observation: "I like to think about it more in terms of objective accomplishment than winning because in a lot of the games . . . you talk to the players at the end and everyone thinks they won. If you have seven objectives for each side to accomplish, if they've satisfied four out of the seven, they say they won" (interview 2017). Another wargames designer commented that in the military, players "are not trying to win, strictly speaking. They are trying to accomplish the task that they are given. They are given a set of tasks and . . . they are trying their hardest to accomplish [those] tasks" (interview 2017). Perla and McGrady summarized: "You always need victory conditions in a game. You just need to make sure it doesn't become dominated by the victory conditions" (interview 2017).

The realization of a wargame's training objectives is often deemed more of a win than the score achieved or victories attained. Wong asserted: "I've seen games . . . with multiple players where the focus was not on winning, but people were simply trying to carry out objectives which were not necessarily in conflict with each other but finding themselves in conflict. That people can greatly enjoy learning from that and be very immersed in something that is not necessarily set up to be a zero-sum game" (interview 2017). Indeed, a distinction can be drawn between the respective win states of hobby and military gaming. As one designer explained, "As a hobbyist, I would say win state or achieving one's own personal objectives on a tabletop type of game is hugely important because that is what gives the person the degree of fun. I don't necessarily think that win states are as important with the army simulations. . . . The win state is actually the lessons that we can gain from them" (interview 2017).

That said, whether or not it constitutes a clear "win state," players must have a target or objective for a game to function. As one wargames designer commented, "Winning isn't as important as making sure that the players are immersed in the game and doing the best they can with what they have. But they do need to have tangible goals they are trying to accomplish" (interview 2017). Moreland offered a similar comment: "The big thing is what are you considering success. Winning the game isn't always your measure for success. [You have to consider] how can you make sure your audience understands how you're measuring success and what they should be striving for" (interview 2017). The drive to compete and win is cultivated even in games that do not explicitly offer a win state. As another designer argued: "Even in exercises where there isn't an ultimate win-lose outcome, there's some kind of mechanism in the exercise that could be interpreted as winning or losing. There's an exercise that we run where you're working through a crisis and there's not really a right answer, but at the end of the exercise, two of the ten student groups are selected to present before a panel. And . . . . there's a lot of competition to be those two groups that are selected" (interview 2017). Indeed, competition sits at the heart of wargaming's incentivization of the pursuit of victory conditions.

Competition and A(nta)gonism

Among theorists of gaming, it is common to claim that competition functions as a key driver of player engagement:

> Rules alone are not always enough to get a person involved with the game. Hence, the structure of games provides motivational elements which will draw the player into play. Perhaps the simplest of these inducements in competition. The addition of a competitive element to a game usually ensures the undivided attention of a player who would otherwise not be motivated. When being "beaten" is one of the possible outcomes of an activity, the actor is pressured to attend to it more closely. (Csikszentmihalyi 1975, 41)

Koster makes a similar claim, arguing that "most games in history have been competitive head-to-head activities. It's the easiest way to constantly provide a new flow of challenges and content" (2013, 124).

   In much of the literature on games, competition is framed as simply a natural or essential dimension of human behavior. As Huizinga argues, "From the life of childhood right up to the highest achievements of civilization one of the strongest incentives to perfection, both individual and collective, is the desire to be honoured for our virtues. . . . Doing something well means doing it better than others. . . . Competition serves to give proof of superiority" (Huizinga 2016, 63). Koster echoes: "Given we're basically hierarchical and strongly tribal primates, it's not surprising that so many of the basic lessons taught by our early childhood play are about power and status. . . . Games almost always teach us tools for being the top monkey or tribe of monkeys. . . . [I]t's outright unnatural for a human being to see another human being succeeding at something and not want to compete" (Koster 2013, 52, 120). In this framing, competition is endemic to human behavior. As Huizinga puts it, "[T]he agonistic impulse . . . is innate. . . . At bottom it is always a question of winning" (Huizinga 2016, 101).

Many in the wargaming CoP take a similar position. Guillory phrased it this way: "If you're practicing decisions, you want to win. You want to beat the other guy. You want to beat the AI. You want to beat whatever it is that's out there and so the urge to win is absolutely vital because humans are animals. The 'Ha, I'm better than you' always comes through" (interview 2017). Competition, then, is a defining quality of wargames. Indeed, it is a rare matter of consensus in the wargaming CoP that pedagogical gaming requires competition of some form. According to Sabin, it is this competitive character that makes war and games similar: "[T]he key characteristic uniting war and games which sets them apart from other human activities, is their competitive and agonistic nature. . . . Both war and games pit humans against one another in a dynamic interactive contest of wits and resources, as the opposing sides struggle to prevail" (Sabin 2014, xvi). Similarly, Goodwin commented: "I think that's definitely a component of why people who game, game. Because—much like warfare—it's a competition of wills" (interview 2017).

Such competition can feature not just between players but also between other stakeholders in a wargame. A MORS Working Group discussed "the relationship of analysis (and analysts) and wargaming (wargamers) and the need for it to be competitive but not antagonistic (or dismissive)" (McGrady and Vebber quoted in Pournelle ed 2017, 33). Thus, "[f]rom its very start, gaming had drawn much of its value from the tension between opposing intellects and the competitive instincts of players" (Perla 1990, 126).

As a vital component of wargaming, competition is present even in ostensibly collaborative games. Downes-Martin and Pellegrino affirmed: "Even cooperative games have a win-loss mechanism. Take *Pandemic*, a relatively popular cooperative game. While we together aren't in competition, there is a group win or a group lose, and the gaming mechanics are such that if we fail to eradicate all the disease, we lose. So even though we're working together, it's still a competition against a circumstance. I think without a problem to solve, without a conflict to overcome, what's the point?" (interview 2017). This holds too for simulations that don't feature an explicit win condition. As Lee posited, "If you're learning how to drive the tank or how to fly the plane, you want to be improving so that your plane doesn't crash. You want to have it land better, more accurately, and so you are competing, you might say, with yourself to improve the quality of your performance and your knowledge on the system as time goes on" (interview 2017). Such competition extends beyond player dynamics to include designers, facilitators, and game sponsors. One designer recounted: "This also goes for cooperative gaming, puzzle-solving kinds of endeavors, in which you are really competing with the designer, who's trying to pose a challenge to you and you're trying to meet that challenge. So right away there's that power" (interview 2017).

So central is competition to wargaming that it plays a key part in developing the CoP: "[T]o develop the next generation of avid wargamers, the first step is both radical and simple: Let them compete. Great games make people want to tackle the challenge again and again. Through competition, they learn the principles of chance, strategy, competition, and reward. Eventually, players devise new tactics and strategies, recognize patterns, and employ new concepts. The cycle of learning and competing is intellectually addicting" (Bae 2018). This is because player "involvement and excitement produce the atmosphere of intense competition that can lead to the development of original ideas . . . [M]uch of the learning derived from playing games is based on the dynamic interaction of competing ideas and wills of players" (Perla 1990, 243, 257). As one designer argued, a game "definitely has to be competitive. It should have tangible goals within the game context for [players] to achieve" (interview 2017). Markley summarized it similarly: "There absolutely must be a competitive element, otherwise what you have is a discussion. Even at the simplest level, with the least of game mechanisms, there must be at least a competition of ideas, or there is no game" (interview 2017).

Competition need not be explicitly coded into or incentivized in a wargame because, as Moreland explained, "competition will come regardless. If you plug a bunch of folks together in a gaming environment they're going to find ways to compete, even if the game wasn't designed for that. . . . I think it's inherent in human nature that competition will emerge, but I don't think it's necessary to build it into the game if that's not the outcome you're looking for. I don't think you have to stimulate competition. I think that will come of its own" (interview 2017). Accordingly, the CoP argues, the DoD should institutionalize this kind of competition (Bae 2018).

Competition thus motivates and animates wargaming. One designer reflected: "You've got to have something that drives the game. Everybody's got to have goals. No one is really interested in games where there's just cooperation. You can have a team that cooperates versus another team but a win-win situation for everybody is inherently less challenging. Everybody wants to feel validated in some form in terms of their decision-making or prowess or something. And it's just in the nature of the people we recruit, we tend to recruit competitive people in some form or fashion. So driving a game, you have to have that competitive element" (interview 2017). Indeed, another designer suggested that competition is a necessary criterion of a game: "I think competition is inherent. I can't think of something that meets that definition of a game and doesn't have some kind of aspect of competition. If it's cooperative and all of the participants are trying to achieve a joint goal, all the players are still winning or losing together, so that means that it's a competition still. You are competing against the system, the puzzle, the game designer, the card deck, something" (interview 2017).

Even in simulators that do not contain victory conditions, competition obtains. Robinson pointed out that when someone is training "in a helicopter, there's no competing in the same way, but they'll still compete against their own and others' performance. If a pilot is behind the stick and his performance is recorded, he'll want to fly better than the other pilot. And in all cases I've seen, trainers take advantage of that competitive nature to push people to do their best even in the simulator" (interview 2017).

As we have seen, many in the CoP hold that competition is a necessary criterion of a wargame. One designer asserted: "The distinction that I make between a game and a wargame is that element of competition. If you don't have that it's not truly a wargame. . . . [A game] becomes a wargame when you have two or more sides directly competing with each other to achieve . . . goals. But they have to have that notion that there is someone else, there is another human, who is trying to thwart their goal achievement." Thus, the designer concluded, "the integration of a competition for many can be a motivator in the game to drive them to participate. For many people that is the drive, the competition that energizes them and helps them think about how to beat the game" (interview 2017).

Without competition and the pursuit of victory conditions, then, a wargame has no driving force. Lee elaborated: "If there's no competition, if there's no desire to win, if there's no opportunity to win, then the interest in the game or the simulation would fade very quickly. People would get bored with it, I think, and it would not be a tool that would be effective at all . . . I agree with the idea of the competitiveness in a gaming environment. You very much need that to drive the gaming event to be of any interest" (interview 2017). And Markley pointed out that wargaming works by "engaging people to begin to care. Competition helps drive that. The desire for success/ winning forces you to take the time to think, really react" (interview 2017).

As this implies, some in the CoP treat the imperative to win and the presence of a competitive element in games as one and the same. Guillory, for example, argued that "a game is an inherently competitive exercise that needs a winner and a loser. . . . If there's no potential for a winner or loser then it's no game, it's a simulation" (interview 2017). Others suggest that winning and competition should be considered separately. Perla and McGrady took the position that "competition is engaging for the players. Winning is the idea of defeating your opponent and coming out at the end in a victorious state. . . . Competition is trying to struggle against someone else who is trying to accomplish something while you're trying to accomplish something. Winning subverts the process aspect of gaming and turns it into an immediate calculation of every move as to whether that is part of my overall win strategy" (interview 2017).

Whichever position one takes, for this driving force to animate the wargaming, an opponent is required. As Gadamer explains, "[T]here is an ultimate sense in which you cannot have a game by yourself. In order for there to be a game, there always has to be, not necessarily literally another player, but something else with which the player plays and which automatically responds to his move with a countermove" (2004, 106). Perla echoes this sentiment, noting that "[b]ecause so much of the learning derived from playing games is based on the dynamic interaction of the competing ideas and wills of its players, the wargame player needs an opponent (even if it is only himself)" (1990, 257). Wargames require an antagonist, whether human or virtual. Most players "get more engaged mentally by the effort not just to excel but to do better than somebody else," said a designer (interview 2017).

The antagonistic relation to an opponent is thus a key driver of wargaming. Lademan explained: "You always get people excited with competition [because there's] another human being who's doing the best he can to subvert your plans and bring victory to his side. That element of competition is always very helpful in terms of spurring not only involvement but also imagination from individuals that are involved" (interview 2017). While one might object that some games—for example, those that encourage cooperative rather than competitive player behavior—appear not to feature an opponent, all wargames require this figure. As Guillory echoed: "I've had some of these discussions with folks about that cooperative gaming doesn't really have an opponent, but I scream back at them, 'Hogwash, it does! It's the AI. It's built into the system itself.' If you pull out a game of *Pandemic*, the opponent is the virus that's busy trying to take over the world that you're trying to stop. The opponent is the clock—the virus is trying to take over the planet. Now, you're collectively trying to solve the problem, you're not just trying to be the individual hero and have your peers in the game not save the world and therefore look bad, you're all trying to save the world together. But there is an opponent. It is the clock" (interview 2017).

Accordingly, a relation of antagonism is at work in wargaming. As Wark explains, games that target opponents "draw a line between a character and its enemy. They polarize a net into antagonistic fronts" (2007, 141). Perla similarly notes that wargames involve "exposure to the agonistic will of another who is operating on the basis of very different assumptions" (1990, 112). Such an a(nta)gonistic relation to the other involves a desire to master or dominate other players. Csikszentmihalyi recounts the words of a chess player: "I get a tyrannical sense of power. I feel immensely strong, as though I have the fate of another human in my grasp" (1975, 44). It remains arguable what takes precedence: the desire to win in itself, or the desire to succeed in relation to the other player(s). As one instructor reflected, "I don't know if it's actually winning the game. I think it's more of that particular individual wanting to have power over somebody else. I don't know if it has anything to do with winning. I mean, winning is a different thing. When you compete with somebody it's a battle of wits. It's a battle of your knowledge and mind. And it's also a respect for the other person that you're battling with or competing against" (interview 2017).

Perhaps most significantly, competition is vital, as another designer stated, in modeling the antagonisms at work between individuals and institutions in the global political/military arena: "Competition among the players is a tremendously useful proxy for the competition between human beings in institutions, nations, bureaucracies that you're trying to model and learn about. And so we can run a computer program, a computational model that simulates human affairs, and those can be very useful and they have a lot of advantages, but we tend to put humans into that because of their potency to simulate the human beings or the human institutions that are competing in real life." Wargames work, he reflected, by "harnessing player competitiveness, giving them objectives and victory conditions that are somewhat or completely opposed to one another, depending on what we are playing. And let them go and let human ingenuity and competitiveness take over" (interview 2017).

What this exploration of the role of competition in the generation of a desire to win ultimately suggests is that it is not the realization of winning or victory conditions that drive wargaming, but rather the pursuit of these. Consequently, I posit that wargames can be interpreted as perpetual-motion machines insofar as they at once harness and produce a desire to chase a win state that is not satisfied by its realization.

How the Desire to Win Drives Play

While the above accounts diverge in the respective roles and significance attributed to fun, winning, and competition, it is clear that a game that does not provoke the desire to succeed lacks a driving force. One designer observed: "The competitive urge and the desire to win is a great primal motivator" (interview 2017). Another designer put it this way: "If you don't believe you can win, you are probably not going to put as much effort into it" (interview 2017).

This is because, Lademan affirmed, "the desire to win is essentially the motivation that causes people to engage and to accept . . . the scenario and the forces that they're given. Competition in that sense, and the desire to win, kind of drives the training and learning experience, particularly in young officers, whose enthusiasm sometimes exceeds their understanding of the profession and what's entailed in the profession" (interview 2017). As Lee similarly reflected, "It gives you focus. It gives you desire to push yourself. It gives you desire to learn more, to expand your horizons, to use the tool to learn so that the next time you do it maybe you will win, rather than getting beat up again" (interview 2017).

Such a pursuit of victory conditions, then, is key for wargames' efficacy as a research, teaching, and training tool. Guillory explained:

> If you're not fighting to win, you're doing something wrong. Even in your staff process rehearsals, even in whatever it is you're practicing, you always want to perform at your very best. . . . The danger in dialing back that competitive drive in any kind of game goes back to this idea that . . . you train as you fight. The reason for that is that the reverse is also going to be true, you're going to fight the same way as you train. If you don't train to go all out every single time, then you're not automatically going to fall back on that when you fight. For the purpose of the participants in the game, you want that competitive drive to overwhelm as much as possible so that they

are putting their best foot forward in every single one that they do. (interview 2017)

Markley made a similar point:

> If there is not a built-in desire to win, to have some definition of success—not necessarily winning—you don't have a very good game. There's no reason to, other than a personal pride or some other sort of intrinsic motivation, to want to bother yourself with the task of that game if there's not some sense that your efforts lead to success. Also, I think you want the players to be giving you their best, not just participating. To do that there has to be some goal in mind, some place to be going to, a destination for the game that leaves you believing that your efforts have resulted in success. (interview 2017)

The kinds of victory conditions coded into a game will depend on its target audience. Specifically, clear and regular win states that generate a sense of reward are useful for lower-rank deterministic games. Rupert remarked that at "the low levels, when it's training and process, the winning is just little tokens of 'you've done well.' When you get to the higher level you just have to make sure that winning is about the proper practice that included the operations and strategy as opposed to playing the mechanics of the game to your advantage" (interview 2017). Such regular positive reinforcement is less vital, several in the CoP argued, in games aimed at higher-ranking audiences. Lademan noted:

> When you get to the higher levels the desire to win is a little less important. Certainly, these are professionals and they want to do the best they can and come out with a sense that we bested our opponents and so forth. But really at that point the games are less serving the interests of the individuals and more the demands and requirements of the institution. So it becomes important to understand that really the objective of these higher-level games is less about winning and losing and more about fulfilling the objectives of the game. . . . You're still harnessing the idea that the player wants to win, but it becomes less of an important factor, because now what you're doing is servicing the needs and the interests of the institution as opposed to that of the individual. (interview 2017)

As this suggests, games of different types will incentivize, and disincentivize, particular behaviors.

Rewards and Punishments

Whichever level is targeted, the winning imperative is cultivated through the exercise of rewards and punishments coded into the game. As Koster explains, to make a game function properly, players must be motivated through rewards: "Rewards are one of the key components of a successful game activity if there isn't a quantifiable advantage to doing something, the brain will often discard it out of hand" (2013, 120). And Moreland observed: "People aren't going to willingly play games, even if they're work-related games, if there's not something that they find stimulating and rewarding coming out of it" (interview 2017).

Such rewards are designed to make the player feel particular things. An instructor posited, "[Y]ou want the participants to obviously feel good about the fact that they are learning or they're engaged in this game. As they gain these rewards or these wins as they go through . . . It's the carrot and stick thing. You could punish them if they do things wrong too. . . . But you want it to be challenging. You want them to feel like they've accomplished something" (interview 2017).

When it comes to rewards, a distinction can be drawn between intrinsic and extrinsic forms. As Sutton-Smith explains, play is often theorized as intrinsically motivated and autotelic in character (2001, 174). An activity can be considered autotelic, "(from the Greek *auto = self* and *telos = goal, purpose*) [,] if it required formal and extensive energy output on the part of the actor, yet provided few—if any conventional rewards" (Csikszentmihalyi 1975, 10). In this sense, then, players can experience rewards from the experience of gameplay as an end in itself, serving no external purpose. At the same moment, however, gaming can be extrinsically motivated. Rewards such as money and status can be primary reinforces of behavior (Csikszentmihalyi 1975, 2). Such extrinsic rewards are more concerning than intrinsic forms:

> The fact is that the ease with which external rewards can be used conceals real dangers. When a teacher discovers that children will work for a grade, he or she may become less concerned with whether the work itself is meaningful or rewarding to students. Employers who take for granted the

wisdom of external incentives may come to believe that workers' enjoyment of the task is irrelevant. As a result, children and workers will learn, in time, that what they have to do is worthless in itself and that its only justification is the grade or paycheck they get at the end. (Csikszentmihalyi 1975, 3)

The ultimate consequence of this, Csikszentmihalyi concludes, is that "a social system learns to rely exclusively on extrinsic rewards . . . creates alienation among its members, and it places a drain on material resources which eventually may prove fatal" (1975, 4). In spite of these warnings, the wargaming CoP relies heavily on this form of reward. In Goodwin's words, "This is an organization whose members have been literally really trained to prize extrinsic reward. And definitely the game results are extrinsic" (interview 2017).

Importantly, while the experience of play is often motivated by intrinsic rewards, it is readily possible for external parties—such as designers or facilitators—to attached extrinsic rewards. While it is clear from the outside that these have been externally imposed, players frequently absorb and pursue them as though they were part of the intrinsic rewards of the game. Wargaming works, then, by smuggling in external goals that come to be experienced as autotelic. As Sutton-Smith shows, while intrinsic ends are more important to players at play, external actors can attach their desired ends without compromising the enjoyment of gameplay (2001, 88). While often not detectable to those at play, the addition of such extrinsic ends diminishes the autonomy of the game and the player (Boluk and LeMieux 2017).

Wargaming is organized, and player motivation cultivated, through more or less explicit systems of encouraging and discouraging behavior. Many among the CoP view this framing of games as accurate. Lademan, for example, posited: "In wargaming there are rewards and punishments. Within the game itself you're rewarded for a good decision perhaps, or you're punished for incompetence or because you misunderstood the reality of a circumstance and you made a decision that was out of context. . . . The control cell of a game will try to explain, you know, the adjudications, and where a mistake was made and so forth, so, you know, to the joy and the despair of the gathered participants" (interview 2017). An instructor elaborated: "The term 'carrot and stick' has been used with training and military performance since Marius put mules in the Roman army. . . . There is the reward of winning and the punishment of losing. I would say that for the average military trainee, the opportunity to win and the threat of light embarrassment with your squadmates is incentive enough to train harder. So I'd say there's nothing wrong with reward and punishment as part of the system" (interview 2017). As Pournelle similarly reflected:

> By definition there has to be some sort of a reward to create a competitive environment which is the game, but it's modified by factors of is this a non-cooperative game, semi-cooperative game, competition, zero-sum game. So I guess in the abstract, that concept is correct: it is a reward and punishment mechanism. . . . For the purpose of the work that I use gaming for, of diagnosing competitions, by definition, there's a competition going on and so there's a reward for success and a detriment to failure. Better that it be done in a game than in the real world. (interview 2017)

Others in the CoP are less comfortable with the notion that wargames function through mechanisms of reward and punishment. In the words of one designer:

> I'm reacting against the terms "reward" and "punishment." I don't see that as kind of the point in a lot of these cases. Especially games that are aimed at exploring a problem and strategic space. In those games frequently the people that you've got playing are the ones who know more about it than the people who built the game. Essentially, you're trying to create a setting for them to have a constructive kind of interchange with the problem . . . that I think there's, there's a lot less kind of focus on "Here's the specific kind of thing that we want you to learn." It's more like, "Here's the stuff that we want you to practice doing and get experience in thinking about these things." (interview 2017)

An instructor similarly reflected:

> There's more to it than rewards and punishments. We have to think of it at a more sophisticated level in that when you play the game and you test the probabilities. A master chess player tries to think through all the permutations to help him at all levels—that's the part that's more than a reward or punishment. . . . There's nothing wrong with having rewards and punishments as part of the system as long as they drive people to try to make the best decisions they can because it conditions their brain to look at the factors, consider them, and make a decision. (interview 2017)

FOR THE WIN 249

Notwithstanding these cautions, a common form of reward and punishment mechanism in wargaming is the use of points or scores. As Moreland explained, "To engage you and to keep your interest in an otherwise boring topic, but necessary topic, they'll often use points-based incentives to just try to keep the learners engaged." He went on to explain that other reward systems are often used to retain player attention and cultivate motivation: "You can use points-based systems. You can use level-based systems. . . . You can it set up where if they take an action that can definitively be said was a bad action or a wrong action, there can be some sort of negative consequence. That's essential to gameplay, particularly gameplay in the world that I work in, where decisions should have consequences. [Players need] feedback that's either positive or negative related to that decision" (interview 2017). While achieving points or a higher score motivates and affirms specific player behaviors, the withholding or retraction of points serves to punish other behaviors.

A distinction is drawn by many in the CoP between higher- and lower-level reward and punishment mechanisms. In a higher-rank environment, where you want critical thinking, wargames should not impose rigid reward and punishment mechanisms. As de le Vega argued, "If you're taking the approach of reward and punishment, all you're going to get is compliance. You're not going to inspire critical thinking. You're going to get leaders stuck on process, which is not an effective leader." Instead, "you have to give them challenges. You have to give them goals, objectives, and not just the sense of 'You have to do this' but 'What can you contribute to your organization which is going to be your legacy? What can you do for your nation? What can you do for your organization?'" (interview 2017).

On the other hand, Hall noted, "at the tactical level, in general, you want to reinforce doctrinal behavior. . . . [For example,] you react to an ambush this way, because the cumulative combat experience of the institution shows that when you counterintuitively attack into the ambush, rather than just jumping into the ditch, you perform better. . . . So, I think there's absolutely a reward-punishment. But you have to make the reward realistic, and it has to be for a certain purpose" (interview 2017).

However, others view this distinction as minimal, arguing that rewards and punishment structure all military wargaming. One designer argued:

> I tend to set up games . . . that reward the players by giving them plenty of opportunities to make decisions. The reason for that is, I'm not as worried

about what the decisions are. I really want them to make decisions because that's what they need to practice. . . . They then feel there's some degree of control over what's going on if they're the ones making decisions, so there's that reward piece there. If they're not making decisions, what I find is, it's not necessarily a punishment, but you could look at it as a punishment, in that, it's not as interesting. (interview 2017)

Some in the CoP assert that rewards should be distributed in specific ways to maximize their motivating effects. Moreland offered an example: "Teams are built around wins. So when you're in team-building phase, you want them to win. Once they've become a mature staff that is now trying to streamline their processes . . . then you want the outcomes to be a little more challenging and a little less certain" (interview 2017).

Others reflected on the power of in-game reward and the capacity of players to tolerate hardships for its sake. As one wargames designer ruminated, it remains arguable why people will tolerate so many punishments to get their rewards. One reason, he suggested, is that "they know there's . . . the hidden reward. There are hidden rewards even in the punishments. The most satisfying games are the ones where, as you lose, you go, 'Ah, I was so close! If I had just done this one thing better!' It makes you want to go back. And you can fail time and time and time again, but if you feel like you only lost by that much, then you are going to go back" (interview 2017). In this sense, failure of a particular kind—more than winning—can be rewarding for players.

Such rewards must, as this suggests, be granted under specific conditions if they are to successfully motivate further play. A veteran commented, "If you have a game that you win in every time, no matter what you do . . . it loses its luster. You need the challenge and so I think winning is necessary, but it can be overdone. You need to lose to understand what it is to actually win" (interview 2017). Consequently, as de la Vega reflected, you want games that are "challenging but not overwhelming, that motivate them to achieve their goals and gets them some sense of rigor . . . Then once they're there, in the next exercises or the next iteration, you can kick it up a notch. That's how you find in gaming, you have these escalated challenges that they go through. It comes with experience and they get this muscle memory" (interview 2017). One designer concluded: "We have to try and find that just that right spot where it is just difficult enough to produce lessons, but it doesn't defeat the start point" (interview 2017).

In this framing, as Kligge argued, "learning comes from struggle" (interview 2017). Another designer echoed : "You want to make it difficult. You're not trying to make it easy to get into this strategic flow state where everything seems like it's going well. No, you want them to struggle to a degree. . . . You're trying to calibrate it so that it's a struggle but not so much that they give up. But not so little that it seems like it's easy. Because it's not supposed to be easy. In a lot of cases you're trying to stimulate them to do the work" (interview 2017). This is important because, as de la Vega put it, "you want something that's challenging because that's what people really get excited about. It's not just winning. When the winning is arduous [is] when the winning is worth the effort. That's what makes the prize more alluring" (interview 2017). As this suggests, while the drive to win is key, and player behavior is managed through rewards and punishments, failure also plays a key role in how wargames subjectify their players.

Orchestrating Failure

As a corollary of the centrality of competition and the drive to win, one might expect that losing would be simply discouraged and experienced as social sanction, whether within or outside the game. Koster puts it this way: "Failure must have a cost" (2013, 124). The experience of losing certainly brings with it these dimensions. As one designer reflected, "Nobody likes to lose. It's really hard to lose when everybody's looking at you, when it's a more formal setting and everybody's got their uniform and their rank on" (interview 2017). And yet it is common practice to structure games in such a way that losing is possible, likely, or inevitable. Bartels explained: "The assumption is that you lose more often than you win. Even solitaire on the computer has that sense to it. If you start winning too much it stops being fun. The point is that you lose more often than not" (interview 2017). Guillory made a similar argument: "A lot of people assume that if we didn't win, the game was a failure somehow. That's not always the case. We've designed situations in the past, like 'Kobayashi Maru' from *Star Trek*, where we want people to lose so that they're going to listen to us when we tell them how to do better." He cited the example of the National Training Center in Fort Irwin, California, and explained that the training "is set up so that you get your butt kicked every time no matter how well you do. It's so rare for anybody to win when they're out there training, and they do it intentionally. Even if you win, there are still some things you could have improved. They learned really early on in the 1980s that if you win, you start tuning out the coaches. So they intentionally set it up out there so that you get your butt kicked for two weeks so that you listen to the coaches as they tell you, 'You could have done this better.' That's by design" (interview 2017).

Orchestrating loss, then, is a central dimension of how games subjectify their players. Perla and McGrady elaborated: "In any serious game where you test to succeed, as opposed to test to fail, you're really not learning very much because [you think,] 'In this particular situation I have succeeded. Yay me. I don't have to do anything.' However, if you test to fail, now you understand what conditions you fail in and what things you may need to do to mitigate that risk" (interview 2017). Wong makes a similar case, affirming that "there are some real benefits to failing. . . . When you fail, you can ask yourself what went wrong" (2016, 537).

Thus, failure can be deliberately cultivated in gaming as a means of learning. Casey and Martin pointed out that "you need loss conditions in games because . . . it keeps you going and sometimes motivates people too" (interview 2017). Squire similarly relays that "level design or time constraints can induce participant failure, using 'seductive failure states' to entice learners into making mistakes that are tied to their misconceptions about a domain." He concludes: "Making success of a failure is a key to learning through games" (2008, 22).

In this sense, in some forms of gaming, losing is not losing and winning is not winning. Moreland elucidated: "You set expectations so that the participants know this is an experiment. Failure isn't a loss. It's one avenue we needed to explore and see what happened. . . . That's the hardest thing, . . . establishing the idea that failure is an outcome that we can learn from in experiments . . . [in] a community that's used to winning, and that associates success with winning" (interview 2017). Goodwin succinctly summarized this idea: "For me it's a win-win. Even when you lose you learn something and that's a form of winning" (interview 2017). Pournelle similarly noted that "failure can be a very powerful tool. . . . Failure can be very instructive. But in that situation, you also want the players to come to the determination that they failed. You don't want the referee to come down and say, 'You failed.' You want the players to recognize this themselves and then come to an analysis of why. That's far more instructive" (interview 2017).

One way that the experience of irresolution is orchestrated is to stop the game before a win/loss conclusion arises. Goodwin gave an example:

One of the things that a mentor of mine told me early on [was to] finish the game before there's a result where the students clearly know which side won, so there's one or two decisions that were left to be made and the answer hangs in the balance. That way when the students leave the classroom they still talk about the game. When they're in the coffee shop or in the hallways or at the water cooler, they can say, "If we had just gotten another turn, I had this thing to do to you," and the other guy [can say], "Well, I had this thing," and so they continue the game outside of the organized way and it allows for more conversation. I think that goes to the nature of needing to win, needing to prove that you came out on top. And it allows the game to continue well beyond the life cycle, whereas if somebody clearly got to the victory conditions, the side that loses will stop talking about it. (interview 2017)

And yet, this orchestration of losing risks player disengagement. As Moreland observed, military "simulations for decades now have been designed for you to lose. You go into a wargame knowing that the conditions are going to be such that the war is going to be unwinnable . . . [However,] they've started to realize in recent years maybe that's not effective because if you go into the game with the attitude that they're going to continue to pile it on me until I am defeated, a lot of times you don't try in the first place. So there's got to be that tantalizing opportunity to win" (interview 2017). In this sense, winning must at least appear possible in order for players to buy in, and this is true for all opposing forces in a wargame. As Pournelle noted, in addition to the Blue team, "Red has to be able to win. And for the purpose of my work, if red can't win it's not a wargame. It's a pageant" (interview 2017). What this shows is that the *apparent* terms of success and failure in a game, as perceived by players, are often not the actual terms of evaluation.

Importantly, however, just as the drive to win is a key motivator of gaming, so too is the experience of (orchestrated) failure. This is because, as Jesper Juul argues, the desire to overcome failure keeps players playing. This amounts, he posits, to a "paradox of failure":

It is safe to say that humans have a fundamental desire to succeed and feel competent, but game players have chosen an activity in which they are almost certain to fail and feel incompetent, at least some of the time. . . . However, while games uniquely induce such feelings of being inadequate, they also motivate us to play more in order to escape the same inadequacy, and the feeling of escaping failure (often by improving our skills) is central to the enjoyment of games. (Juul 2013, 2–7)

Just as the achievement of a victory or win state brings not the end of gameplay but rather its continuation, so too does a loss or failure state. As DeKoven explains, "If we lose, we want to continue playing until we've won. If we win, we play over and over again until we've finally, ultimately, lost" (2002, 152).

This involves, as Kevin McSorley argues, a continued affective investment on the part of players that hope remains that their failure can be overcome. Such "complex emotional gambles" and the management of disappointment and failure, he continues, engender a "particular configuring of the user [that] is itself highly resonant with a wider reconfiguring of political subjectivity that has occurred across numerous other domains in recent decades—the political constitution of the resilient subject" (2020, 41). Aligned with the broader "*dispositif* of resilience," he concludes, wargames players can be understood as resilient survivors, driven toward continual emotional and practical engagement disciplined by the threat of failure (2020, 47). As will be explored further in Chapter 8, this compulsion quiets reflexivity in favor of action: "While permanent anticipatory arousal and inevitable failure may make the player feel continuously enlivened and indeed deeply frustrated at times, this vitality and anger is predominantly directed towards a delimited form of self-improvement rather than towards structural critique of the gameworld" (2020, 47).

Systemic Iterative Irresolution

At the heart of games, Sutton-Smith argues, is thus an egocentric motivation driven by personal victory (2001, 64). Importantly, this means that for games to function properly, players must play to win. That is, they must commit to the game and try in earnest to deduce and realize the victory conditions. Rubel explains, "It is a fundamental, if tacit, assumption of war gaming that players will make the best decisions they can. They need not be the right decisions—after all, somebody has to lose—but they must not be capricious or negligent. Players are expected to try to win, or at least to carry out doctrine in a faithful way. When they do not, as a result of alienation, inattention, or malice, the game's results are contaminated." If, for example, players react to a controller's decision with disillusionment or cynicism, they may " 'mentally disengage' from the game and make very different decisions than if they were properly immersed and motivated." Under such circumstances, "the game results cannot be accepted" (Rubel 2006, 115–116). This point is vital because it shows that the results of a game depend for their veracity on players working hard to win in the terms set by the game.

As Chapter 3 showed, many theorists of play note the self-perpetuating quality of the intense commitment and focus of a game. Gadamer argues that this application of effort involves a "tendency to repetition that emerges in the player and in the constant self-renewal of play" (2004, 105). This is because, as Laura Ermi and Frans Mäyrä put it, the "suspense, anxiety, and physical arousal elicited by playing are interpreted as positive feelings because players anticipate a resolution and a closure such as winning the game or completing the task" (2007, 39). Wark describes this intense pursuit of victory conditions as "a single, endless, furious striving, a pointless, destabilizing pursuit of that unreal instant when triumph can bring rest" (2007, 116). And yet the notion that the realization of a win state brings resolution is illusory. It is, then, the *pursuit*, as opposed to the *attainment*, of victory conditions that is the key driver of games. The win itself does not bring with it the promised resolution but instead simply resets the processes.

On the one hand, a win state—in contradistinction to the pursuit of this state—is ultimately irrelevant to the game's success or failure. "In analytic games, the winning of it has no relation," noted a designer. "There's no interest in who won in an analytic game. It's about . . . what the impetus was for the players to make the decisions they did" (interview 2017). Similarly, in teaching or training games, "part of the education thing here is not the result," Downes-Marin and Pellegrino argued. "It's how innovatively did you play? I would penalize someone for winning by just boringly following doctrine unless the person could point out why that was the best ahead of time. I would credit someone who lost but did so with some very interesting innovations. . . . We've learned something from that, as has that person" (interview 2017). As Goodwin put it, "The important thing is the proper lessons drawn. Not whether you win or lose. Now, in the real world, winning and losing is absolutely critical, but in gaming the more important thing is are you drawing the proper conclusions and lessons from the experience? . . . In the classroom, half the people are going to be losers, so you've got to make it so that winning isn't the goal. But it certainly provides a level of motivation to the students" (interview 2017). Winning as an end state is thus broadly irrelevant, yet players must apply effort and focus for its sake.

On the other hand, the attainment of a win state does not bring with it the resolution it promises. DeKoven claims: "Winning isn't enough. It doesn't provide us with a clear sense of completion. It doesn't work to end the game the way we want to end it—satisfied, accomplished, fulfilled" (2002, 152). Huizinga makes a similar point, noting that "at bottom it is always a question of winning—though we know well enough that this form of 'winning' can bring no gain" (2016, 101). This is because, as Nisbett explains, while "you're encouraged to continually project your excitement forwards and imagine you're about to get to something really interesting . . . there's a constant denial of resolution which keeps you obsessively projecting forward" (quoted in Buse 1996, 176). Instead of bringing rest, calm, or resolution, the attainment of a win state serves only to reset the game system. Nietzsche argues that the play impulse is self-renewing—the child throws away their toys only to start again (Spariosu 1989, 75). The player is thus compelled endlessly onward both by the denial of the win state and, ultimately, by the win state's unsatisfactory character.

It is this endless compulsion that engages and retains player engagement, making wargaming a powerful tool of player subjectification. As Ermi and Mäyrä explain, "It is the aesthetic of repetition that characterizes pleasures of gameplaying" (2007, 39). Wark elaborates:

> As a gamer you have no sense of worth and no faith in salvation other than through your own efforts. But those efforts are fraught, and you are soon lost in the maze of the game. The gamer achieves worth through victories of character; but that character invariable faces defeat in turn. The only thing worse than being defeated is being undefeated. For then there is nothing against which to secure the worth of the game other than to find another game. One game leads to the next. (2007, 038)

In this sense, games can be read as perpetual-motion machines readily amenable to subjectifying players by harnessing and directing the play compulsion. As Wark notes, this process works by replacing quality with quantity in the form of scores and progressions: "Any qualitative difference between levels is just the effect of an underlying quantity. A higher level is essentially more than a lower level. And so there's nowhere to go but to more, and more, until the gamer . . . is left with nothing" (2007, 038).

At the same moment, wargames function to produce and reproduce the win compulsion through the simultaneous promise and denial of resolution through victory conditions. One wargames designer commented: "Predominantly it would be that the folks entering the military have some competitive spirit. But there's some of that ingrained as well through the training. As I said before, if you lose, you or someone else dies" (interview 2017). And Moreland elaborated: "It's a personality trait that's encouraged, for sure. I mean when your profession is the profession of arms, and—without sounding too Hollywood—it might be part of your day-to-day business to kill someone, you're going to want to instill a competitive spirit" (interview 2017). Another designer concurred: "You have this idea kind of ingrained into people. There is a victory, or a set of victory conditions, and your job is to achieve those conditions" (interview 2017).

The desire to win is, then, self-consciously cultivated as part of the wargaming enterprise even as it is evident to all but the player that the win state might be denied by the game's designer and compel simply a restart of the game if realized. A wargaming instructor explained, "The will to win—the desire to win, it's called—is a training element" (interview 2017). Unaware that it is the drive and not the end state that matters, players must continue to apply themselves in earnest to pursuing an ultimately irrelevant win state. This Sisyphean enterprise "inscribes the game-space within the subject itself" (Wark 2007, 96). Read in this way, the subjectifying processes of the game operate through a joyless instantiation of Nietzsche's repetition compulsion: "The other, negative name for the eternal return is the Freudian 'compulsion to repeat,' and its source can be traced back, paradoxically, beyond the pleasure principle, to the death wish—the secret wish of every 'commander' to 'obey'" (Spariosu 1989, 87).

Conclusion

This chapter has shown that wargames work as perpetual-motion machines by cultivating and harnessing the drive to win. They do this by at once incentivizing, devaluing, and withholding a win state that itself is both ultimately unsatisfying and productive of further player effort for that very reason. Such a process is productive of subjectivity. As Nicolas de Zamaróczy observes, by establishing specific win conditions, "games *foster* an attitude of unremitting conflict" (de Zamaróczy 2016, 165; emphasis added). Simon

Parkin similarly observes that games "are competitive, *driving* players to strive for domination" (2015, 44; emphasis added). Against naturalist assumptions prevalent in the CoP, this chapter has shown that wargames produce competition in players and operationalize this as a key driver of gameplay. In other words, wargames harness and direct the play impulse for specific objectives coded into and administered by the game while at the same moment producing in players these tendencies as it subjectifies them.

Through this cultivated winning imperative, players are both object and engine of wargaming. In the words of a designer: "We're really asking players mentally to do two things at once, and it's a challenging and intellectually intense activity. We're asking them to pursue a role of some kind, a simulation, and to help drive the model by pursuing the victory conditions within the rules of the game. And that's difficult. And absorbing and fun, hopefully" (interview 2017). In the end, however, this simultaneously crucial and irrelevant win is only part of what drives play. As Csikszentmihalyi explains, the "achievement of a goal is important to mark one's performance, but is not in itself satisfying. What keeps one going is the experience of acting outside the parameters of worry and boredom: the experience of flow" (1975, 38). It is to the politics of the states of flow and immersion that Chapter 8 now turns.

8

The Politics of Immersion

What we're doing is, we're using gaming to indoctrinate through the power of immersive experience.

—Wargames designer, interview 2017

Introduction: Where Do We Go When We Play?

This chapter explores the politics of the condition of immersion generated in wargames, which places players in a pleasurable desubjectified state.[1] Building on Chapter 6's exploration of the role of affect in gaming's edutainment goals, this chapter shows that the different states of immersion generated in different game types—across manual, digital, research, teaching, and training—serve to apprehend players in a state of rapt engagement. Having demonstrated in Chapter 7 the ways in which wargames cultivate and capitalize upon the drive to win, making players both object and engine of the game, this final chapter explores a second key element of how they subjectify players: generating reflexes through a non-reflective state of immersion. The core claim made is that because it suppresses or circumvents their self-reflective capacities, immersion plays a key role in wargaming's subjectification of its players.

The chapter begins by conceptualizing immersion and the related—but different—notion of flow, drawing in detail on the work of psychologist Mihaly Csikszentmihalyi, who coined the latter term in the 1970s. Having examined this non-reflective state, the chapter shows that while flow, like play, is often framed as being autotelic in character—that is, an end in itself—Csikszentmihalyi notes that it is readily possible to attach extrinsic rewards or goals. It is precisely this, the chapter argues, that occurs in military wargaming. Having established these conceptual points, the chapter then turns

---

[1] I borrow the question that starts this chapter, "Where do we go when we play?," from Prof. Debbie Lisle, who posed it at a panel titled "Becoming War" at ISA 2019 in Toronto, Canada.

Politics of Play. Aggie Hirst, Oxford University Press. © Oxford University Press 2024.
DOI: 10.1093/oso/9780197629192.003.0009

to the wargaming CoP's accounts of the power of immersion in their activities. It shows that many argue that immersion is vital for efficacious wargaming because it generates and prolongs player focus, confers game validity, and improves the extent to which the game's lessons are internalized and experienced as "real."

The chapter examines the variation in immersive experience that occurs across manual and digital gaming, showing a divergence of opinion among the CoP as to the correlation between total-immersion digital technologies and the depth, duration, and quality of immersion achieved. While some suggest that high-tech gadgetry improves immersion, others believe that simple and even analog games can be just as deeply immersive, or even more so. From there the chapter discusses the possibility that an excess of immersion can derail a wargame from its intended pedagogical purpose.

Having established these debates in the CoP, the chapter turns finally to the question of how, and with what effects, immersion functions as a tool of player subjectification. It begins by showing how a state of immersion can be cultivated—namely, through the use of narrative, through the (apparent) exercise of choice, and by encouraging the player to refer to their in-game persona in the first person. This process of player apprehension can be viewed, as Csikszentmihalyi argues, as one of "suspending" players between the experiential poles of anxiety and boredom. Moreover, the chapter shows that this process involves a series of de- and re-subjectifying interventions: the fusing of action and awareness, the removal of self-reflective mediation, cultivating consensus, and binding the player to rule systems. The ultimate consequence of this is that immersive play desubjectifies players by circumventing the self-conscious and self-reflective capacities. At the same moment, immersive gaming resubjectifies players by instilling in them reflex actions. Drawing on John Protevi's distinction between ownership and agency, the chapter concludes that immersive training locates ownership of action in players while suspending agency through the cultivation of new reflexes.

The Focus of Flow and the Spell of Immersion

In the current ludic century, we have cultivated a "flow culture" that flourishes through games (Bolter 2019, 105). Theorists of play and games have dedicated a good deal of energy to trying to describe and analyze the pleasurable state of absorption associated with gameplay. When focused on a game, players are drawn into another world. In this play world, they take on the identities and goals of their role or character as though they were their own. This experience belongs, Huizinga argues, to the realm of affect and emotion. In such an experience, the player is enthralled in the game's spell: "The words we use to denote elements of play belong for the most part to aesthetics, terms with which we try to describe the effects of beauty: tension, poise, balance, contrast, variation, solution, resolution, etc. Play casts a spell over us; it is 'enchanting,' 'captivating.' It is invested with the noblest qualities we are capable of perceiving in things: rhythm and harmony" (2016, 10).

One common problem associated with the study of this experience is that the key terms used to describe it—"immersion" and "flow"—are conflated in much of the literature. As Braxton Soderman notes, rather than treating them as synonymous, it is important to understand the relationship between them. Flow, he argues, is best understood as one—but not the only—form of immersion. Specifically, he continues, flow is best understood as challenge-based immersion. The key difference between the concepts, he explains, is that immersion is "unreflective," while flow "does not erase thinking, but it does inhibit thoughts about anything *outside* and activity while concentrating our thoughts on the activity itself" (Soderman 2021, 12, 147–148, emphasis in original).

This distinction is useful because it illustrates how games can be deeply stimulating and engaging while also involving a loss of self-consciousnesses and reflexivity. Flow connotes a powerful directed engagement, while immersion entails an enthralled loss of critical awareness. Both involve a state of deep absorption and a diminishing of the world external to the activity at hand, but the former is decidedly active and the latter more passive. Maintaining this conceptual difference, the following sections explore the related states of flow and immersion.

Coining the notion of flow in the 1970s, Csikszentmihalyi argued that by staving off both boredom and anxiety, a person in flow is entirely focused on the activity at hand. In his interviews with people who experience flow in various pursuits across the arts, sports, religious worship, and gameplay, he established a remarkably similar description of "a peculiar state of experience . . . that is not accessible in 'everyday life.' In each case, intrinsic rewards appeared to overshadow extrinsic ones as the main incentives for pursuing the activity" (Csikszentmihalyi 1975, 35). Csikszentmihalyi examined "why people are so highly motivated by their experiences of personal enjoyment," and through the course of his research discovered that "the 'peak experience' of chess players, rock climbers, rock dancers, and surgeons . . . were basically similar," a state he called "flow" (Sutton-Smith 2001, 184). He described this as a "dynamic state—the holistic sensation that people feel when they act with total involvement" (Csikszentmihalyi 1975, 36).

While none of these activities guarantees the pleasurable experience of flow, they offer its possibility. So great is the appeal of flow that "people are sometimes willing to forsake a comfortable life for its sake." Importantly, it is not the end result of the enterprise that generates this pleasure but rather "the doing is the thing. . . . What keeps one going is the experience of acting outside the parameters of worry and boredom: the experience of flow" (Csikszentmihalyi 1975, 37–38). Flow thus involves finding an optimal state between boredom and anxiety that entirely captivates the actor, generating a powerful and enduring focus.

Flow is frequently linked to play and games. Indeed, Soderman argues that flow is most easily reached through play (Soderman 2021, 3) and Csikszentmihalyi explicitly identifies gameplay as a key site of flow: "Games are obvious flow activities, and play is the flow experience *par excellence*" (Csikszentmihalyi 1975, 36–37). As this suggests, flow is viewed as a form of peak enjoyment generated by challenge. In Soderman's words, it is typically associated with "mastery, optimal experiences, expert performance, intense absorption, fun, and a positive state of enjoyment" (Soderman 2021, 223). As one of Csikszentmihalyi's interviewees elaborated: "The game is a struggle, and the concentration is like breathing—you never think of it. The roof could fall in and, if it missed you, you would be unaware of it" (Csikszentmihalyi 1975, 39). Flow can be understood, then, as a "complex form of sustained engagement—one that is distinct from both pleasure and immediate gratification" (Soderman 2021, 3). It has the capacity not only to bring focus but also to prolong attention and engagement.

Sutton-Smith helpfully draws out several other key features of Csikszentmihalyi's conceptualization of flow. It involves, he shows, the merging of participants' action and awareness, the centering or narrowing of their attention on a limited field, and a loss of self-consciousness as they are absorbed into the activity (Sutton-Smith 2001, 185). In this merging of action and awareness, a person "has no dualistic perspective: he is aware of his actions but not of the awareness itself." Indeed, this is a necessary criterion of flow: "[F]or flow to be maintained, one cannot reflect on the act of awareness itself" (Csikszentmihalyi 1975, 38). The flow state, Csikszentmihalyi argues, is often framed as autotelic, or engaged in for its own sake. As he puts it, an "autotelic experience is one of complete involvement of the actor with his activity. The activity presents constant challenge. There is no time to get bored or worry about what may or may not happen. A person in such a situation can make full use of whatever skills are required and receives clear feedback to his actions; hence, he belongs to a rational cause-and-effect system, in which what he does has realistic and predicable consequences" (Csikszentmihalyi 1975, 36).

And yet, while many flow activities are autotelic in character, it is readily possible to attach extrinsic rewards to them: "[O]ne may experience flow in any activity, even in some activities that seem least designed to give enjoyment—on the battlefront, on a factory assembly line, or in a concentration camp" (Csikszentmihalyi 1975, 36). As discussed in Chapter 6, flow describes the experience of being absorbed in an autotelic activity, one performed for its own intrinsic rewards (Csikszentmihalyi 1975, 10). According to Fink, attaching such external goals undermines play as such: "Play has only internal purpose, unrelated to anything external to itself. Whenever we play 'for the sake of' physical fitness, military training, or health, play has become perverted and has become merely a means to an end" (quoted in Ehrmann 1971, 21). Incentives like monetary or practical gain involve an "extrinsic contamination" belying an "ulterior motive" (Hackett 2014, 124). While this may discount wargaming from being considered as play in the strict sense, it makes it clear that the power of flow can be harnessed for external ends.

The notion of immersion, in contrast to flow, involves not a powerful directedness of action but rather a deep state of unselfconsciousness and temporal slip. John Dovey and Helen Kennedy write: "Immersion is clearly offered as a fundamental aspect of gameplay experience and pleasure, yet it also features as potentially the most problematic element within that experience" (Dovey and Kennedy 2006, 9). The spell of immersion can be understood as the experience of being transported to, and enclosed within, a gameworld. In this immersed state, the player's attention is wholly focused on the game environment. In B. Joseph Pine and James H. Gilmore's framing, this involves "the sensation of being surrounded by a completely other reality . . . that take over all of our attention, our whole perceptual apparatus" (quoted in Ermi and Mäyrä 2007, 40). Games are thus often characterized by their "immersive hold on the attention of rapt and near-motionless players" (Giddings 2016, 8), creating a "narcotic" effect (Frasca 2004, 87). Importantly, this experience of immersion is pleasurable because it involves a relief from contradictory demands and the pressures of everyday life. It is often linked to the idea that gameplay generates a "magic circle" in which "special meanings accrue and cluster around objects and behaviors. In effect, a new reality is created, defined by the rules of the game and inhabited by its players" (Salen and Zimmerman 2003, 96). Such intensive gameplay, as Dovey and Kennedy note, is often associated with "a loss of a sense of time, place or self" (Dovey and Kennedy 2006, 8).

As this suggests, immersion can be experienced as transcendental in several senses. It involves the suspension of ordinary patterns of linear time— in Simon Parkin's terms, "chronoslip" (2015, 20). As compared with other media, like television and movies, he explains, we have far greater consumption limits when it comes to games:

> [Games] do not temporarily suppress our free will. Rather they demand
> it. We step into a game world and emerge, hours later, with little sense of
> where the time has gone. Sometimes the immersion is so complete that our
> bodies' physical signals do not penetrate the unreality: we forget to eat, to
> shift position in our chair. We neglect to keep warm, to pee. Time becomes
> yoked, not to the ticking of the clock, but to the pattern of our interactions,
> the pleasing rhythms of cause and effect. . . . [V]ideo games are not mere
> time-wasters. . . . Rather, they are time-killers: they destroy time. (Parkin
> 2015, 20–21)

In such an experience, as Ermi and Mäyrä put it, "one often loses one's sense of time and gains powerful gratification" (2007, 38). This relieves us of the relentless futurity of everyday life; as Fink explains, immersed "play is characterized by calm, timeless 'presence' and autonomous, self-sufficient meaning—play resembles an oasis of happiness." Such an experience makes possible "human timelessness in time . . . one full moment that is, so to speak, a glimpse of eternity" (quoted in Ehrmann 1971, 21). As one of Csikszentmihalyi's interviewees put it: "Although I am not aware of specific things, I have a general feeling of wellbeing, and that I am in complete control of my world" (Csikszentmihalyi 1975, 45). And Huizinga wrote: "Frivolity and ecstasy are the twin poles between which play moves" (2016, 21). Sutton-Smith similarly notes that players' "ecstasy may lie in the performance of unique ludic acts" (2001, 64).

Importantly for the account of deconstructive play set out in this book, the states of flow and immersion generated in games are broken when the self-consciousness of the player returns. If the participant notices a flaw or reflects on something within or outside the game, the flow is broken and the spell of immersion is lost. When this happens, Csikszentmihalyi claims, "the self reappears to negotiate between the conflicting definitions of what needs to be done, and the flow is interrupted" (1975, 47). He elaborates:

> When awareness becomes split, so that one perceives the activity from "outside," flow is interrupted. Therefore, flow is difficult to maintain for any length of time without at least momentary interruptions. Typically, a person can maintain a merged awareness with his or her actions for only short periods, which are broken by interludes when he adopts an outside perspective. These interruptions occur when questions flash through the actor's mind: "Am I doing well?" "What am I doing here?" "Should I be doing this?" When one is in a flow episode (*in ludus* as opposed to *inter ludes*), these questions simply do not come to mind. (Csikszentmihalyi 1975, 38)

Such an experience is one of rupture and loss: "'[O]rdinary life' may reassert its rights either by an impact from without, which interrupts the game, or by an offence against the rules, or else from within, by a collapse of the play spirit, a sobering, a disenchantment" (Huizinga 2016, 21). Key to efficacious gaming, then, is the cultivation and maintaining of a self-forgetting state of immersion.

Equally importantly, this chapter shows that states of flow and immersion are productive of subjectivity. While some argue that "the game experience leaves us changed" (Webster 2014, 191), I submit that gaming both subverts particular reflective dimensions of subjectivity and cultivates new reflexes in their stead. Before exploring the implications of this from the perspective of player subjectification, the following section presents the CoP's views of the types and importance of immersion for military wargaming.

Immersive Wargaming

Within the mainstream commercial games sector, immersion is almost uniformly viewed as key to the successful functioning of a game. As Berger affirms, "Most games strive to achieve what is called, colloquially, immersion. This means that the game world—or virtual space—is so interesting and so detailed that players forget they are playing a game" (2008, 47). The CoP broadly—though not universally—agrees that immersion is vital for successful military wargaming.[2] This is because immersion is key to generating and retaining player buy-in. As Tappen and colleagues put it: "Immersion is absolutely crucial. . . . Having a strong sense of immersion helps them understand the importance of what they're doing and getting that buy-in of involvement that I think will last after the exercise as well" (interview 2017). Lademan elaborated: "One of the things you can do with a wargame [is] you can certainly begin to immerse people into a problem and make them interested in taking ownership of a problem such that it becomes theirs, and they begin to develop not only an intellectual but perhaps even an emotional interest in this particular problem and seeing it to its conclusion" (interview 2017). Moreland had a similar perspective: "Immersion is important because that's what keeps them engaged" (interview 2017).

The state of immersion generated in wargaming involves a deep engagement with the game. Downes-Martin and Pellegrino explained: "It's almost like a focus issue, in terms of how you get the player to willingly direct all of their focus, their attention, to the problem at hand even though it's a dumb abstract game with black-and-white stems" (interview 2017). This deepened state of engagement is vital for the wargame to successfully impart its lessons. One wargames designer commented: "I think games can be very successful in creating an immersive state. It is very important from a pedagogical perspective. . . . For the soldiers coming in, if the environment isn't representative and at the level of commercial [games], then they're going to walk away" (interview 2017).

Immersion thus involves players identifying with, and internalizing elements of, the game. One designer provided an example: "We get them into character because the more in character they are, the better they are going to negotiate. . . . The more immersed the students get within their rules, the better the game that comes out of it. . . . The more you accept that 'I am Russian and this is what I want to do as a Russian team,' the better the game plays" (interview 2017). Markley made a similar observation: "Effective gaming, which involves the student be[ing] immersed in a role, forces the student to think and reflect on a subject or subject matter in a way that perhaps may not

---

[2] Having set out the conceptual differences between flow and immersion above, I refer to immersion in the remainder of this chapter as this term was used by interviewees to capture both players' active engagement and their deep absorption in games.

necessarily come to pass in a seminar-style discussion . . . because there's a stake involved in putting into action your thinking" (interview 2017).

Immersion nullifies the distance between the real world and the gameworld. As an instructor asserted: "Hopefully that immersion helps them mentally associate the decisions and the processes they have made in the course of that game with the way that their mind would then apply their thoughts to that scenario in real life or a scenario like it. . . . One of the ways I might define immersion is when your mind integrates the lessons of the game into the way you would respond to that situation in the rest of your life" (interview 2017). A player is immersed in a wargame, then, when the mind treats the game lessons as pertinent to the real world. Explained a wargames designer: "Immersion is very important in a command post exercise environment. . . . [You want] those people [to] feel like there's a real battle going on, it's very important. Ideally you've got casualty reports coming in, and it says that people moving to the rear and ambulances and stretchers and somebody's unit has collapsed and the enemy is moving through a gap in your line. Boy, if you think that it's real, then it really forces you to sit back, think critically, stay calm" (interview 2017).

Immersion involves the player's adoption of elements of the game, often linked to characters or teams. A designer posited that immersion takes place not when a "player sees something that looks realistic, but [when] the player has fully taken on the role of the character they are in the game, . . . [when] I accept the context within which I'm making decisions and I've immersed myself in that context in my head. Not by seeing it on the screen but by sort of internalizing that decision-making process . . . It's more than decision-making. It's more than 'I've got to make this decision, I've got to make that decision.' It's about me, the thought process that goes into accomplishing my goal" (interview 2017). Another designer asserted: "The immersion to me is, are they actually feeling that what they're doing is reflective of the kind of things they'd be doing if they were doing that outside the wargame in real life? We tend to think of immersion as putting them into something that looks just exactly like real life. Whereas I look at it as it's real life in a sense that the choices they have are real" (interview 2017).

Key to this is playing the game earnestly. In line with the importance of playing to win, as discussed in Chapter 7, playing within an immersed state is important for the game's process and results. Indeed, many in the CoP claim that players need to be immersed for games to be valid. Wong was of the opinion that in a "game where you have more qualitative outcomes, where you have more geopolitical, social [and] political decision-making, if it's not immersed, I don't think your game is valid" (interview 2017). A designer also explained that "the immersive state is necessary if you want to make decisions. If you're not immersed in whatever the scenario is you're creating, then it's too easy to apply a different set of values . . . , to overanalyze or underanalyze it, to misapply what it is you're going at. . . . At that point it's an analytic problem. It's not a gaming problem. You're not looking at what are the factors that affect his decision, you're looking at what are the mechanics of the system and how do they come together. So, I think that the need for immersion is critical" (interview 2017).

Playing in a state of immersion can, then, be read as connoting not just that the players are taking the game seriously but that they are taking into themselves the elements of the game. "In our current culture with gamers," said de la Vega, "when they play a videogame they get so pulled into the game that they are training at it like reality. We try to achieve the same thing with our simulations. We have to reinforce that suspension of disbelief and treat this as reality. Don't treat it as just a trivial game. . . . You're only going to get a learning experience if you're getting the right feedback. . . . If they're not taking their training seriously, you're not going to get the learning outcomes you want" (interview 2017). In this reading, immersion is key for the game to yield valid or valuable results. This means, as Bartels described: "I need to sustain immersion because if I don't, I worry that I can't generalize my findings to the right calculations. If you're not taking it seriously, and you're not engaged in the decision-making process, how well are you replicating the actual process that's going on in the real world?" (interview 2017).

Total Immersion Technologies

There is a variety of opinions within the CoP about the necessity of advanced technology in the production of a state of immersion. Some in the CoP argue that technologies that engage players' senses provide the most immersive experience. Hall argued: "At the lower levels . . . immersion can be defined in a technical sense. Do you have the game environment . . . to give them the fidelity and the graphics and the sounds and the noises? . . . So that's immersion in one sense, that's the tactical level. The controls and switches and everything in that simulator should exactly replicate the interior of the tank, the cockpit, the helicopter or the aircraft" (interview 2017). Lee added: "It's valuable that you do generate and create an immersive state to have good training. You want that person to feel like they are walking the street, that they are kicking in the door and going into the building" (interview 2017).

Many in the CoP suggest that advanced technologies can be especially important for generating immersion in the context of wargames training. Guillory reflected: "For something like a flight simulator, a tank simulator, you want a certain level of immersion because you want them to make their decisions as close to the real world as you can get them. You want to feel like you're in the cockpit when you're doing the flight simulator" (interview 2017). Similarly, Lee asserted: "When you really do good immersive virtual gaming-type environments, especially as we introduce 3D or put people into simulators that have a sense of movement, potentially providing some smells and stuff like that, I have seen folks get literally motion-sick. Really, they're just sitting still, but the inputs to their brain are such that they get the sensation of movement and it's thrown them out of whack" (interview 2017)

Such virtual tools are also useful, several in the CoP argue, for group-level computer-assisted command post exercises (CPXs). As Lee explained, CPXs are

> predicated on a soldier and staff officer using their actual tools to send commands which then are grabbed by the simulation, input into the sim, and generated output that is then returned to the players on their battlefield systems. So they are essentially immersed in a fight. All they see is what's happening electronically coming into them. You see a lot of the competitiveness that comes out in that. By immersing them in that people get angry when their attack is faltering, when they lose resources, when things don't go correctly. And there is a lot of emotion that manifests itself, especially when you begin to have multiday events and fatigue begins to play a role with that. (interview 2017)

One advantage of such technology is that you can prolong the training experience and make alterations to extend the immersive experience. "The learning management system has to be able to take into account if we're seeing a plateau and then generate stimulus through the simulation environment," offered a designer. "And I think you might agree that when you win the game at the end of whatever you're playing, the game might not be as interesting to you anymore. At least in video gaming. So you have to be able to create stimulus and change the training." He gave the following example: "During the scenario the instructor could view into the room with cameras. He could hear with microphones and we could see a visual representation of where the soldier was. So when they got too comfortable in the simulation, we added sniper fire. And it was very realistic when you have folks coming back from recent deployments diving on the floor and almost shitting themselves. It got them back into the training circle" (interview 2017).

Several in the CoP noted the immersive potential of virtual and augmented reality (VR/AR) systems. One advantage of these virtual technologies, as McGrady and Vebber note, is that they "completely immerse the player in the environment, and allow players to manipulate and interact with digital objects." VR is especially useful for training, in their opinion: "For games that place a premium on players making decisions about the environment they are in—squad combat simulations, for example—VR may be a preferred technology" (McGrady and Vebber 2017, 38). Lee had a similar perspective: "A virtual simulation or a virtual gaming environment . . . where you can begin putting 3D goggles on and that sort of thing, can be hugely powerful for getting at that soldier-level experience. It's not as easy to get the leader into those circumstances, because generally the leader is trying to think at the organizational level, not at the individual level. So it's harder to get the immersive effect for your NCOs and officers" (interview 2017).

Advanced technologies can generate immersion through multisensory stimulation. As a designer explained, "Electronic games can make dynamics very vivid. That can be immersive because of what you see and hear, and how this very fast-moving visual or multisensory world reacts to what you do and decide. That can be very immersive. Any manual simulation is going to have a hard time providing that" (interview 2017). However he went on to reflect this is just one form of immersion. While multisensory stimulation can indeed draw players into the action, "my bias is I see that as a more superficial kind of immersion," because

as soon as I have a computer code involved in delivering the simulation, I've imposed a barrier between the player and the model. While I'm immersed—perhaps because when I run around, the scenery changes and it reminds me of actually running around in a field—I don't necessarily know why what just happened, happened. . . . When the soldier is shot it is realistic, but the soldier probably doesn't know why he was just shot. So that might be immersive in the sense that "Oh wow, I was just shot." But how much have I learned? . . . However, if I learn the rules to a manual game, to operate the model, I know exactly why I just lost. To me that's a deeper immersion because it's a deeper opportunity to understand the complexities involved. (interview 2017)

As this suggests, some in the CoP argue that manual games can generate a more profound experience of immersion.

The Power of Analog Immersion

There are many in the CoP who assert that virtual technologies are not a vital component of immersive wargaming. Such a view is shared by some in the commercial games industry: While "[i]t is often taken for granted that a bigger screen and a better quality of audio equal greater immersion . . . [these are] by no means the only or even the most significant factor[s]" (Ermi and Mäyrä 2007, 40–41). Instead, players' emotional investment can serve just as well. As Wong put it, "Training doesn't actually have to be all that realistic to be effective. I think as long as people buy into the tools and systems, the things they using are sort of extraneous, if the players are actually role-playing in an emotionally involved way" (interview 2017). A designer elaborated: "there tends to be this notion that the higher [the resolution of] visualization I present the players with, the more immersive the game is going to be. I feel the opposite. Realistic visualizations become distractions and players lose sight of the objectives" (interview 2017).

In part this is because, as Casey and Martin explained, technology isn't "something that will cover up bad design decisions. You can't say, 'Well, I'm going to use virtual reality so it looks just like reality' and then try to hope that that teaches people" (interview 2017). A designer echoed this perspective: "There are kind of superficial elements to immersion which help it along, and optics is one of them. But at the core, the dynamics of the model have to be satisfying and [they should demonstrate] fidelity to whatever conception I already have of the topic of the system being represented" (interview 2017).

It is quite possible, then, for players to be deeply immersed in an analog game. As Perla and McGrady noted, "It depends on engaging the players' imaginations . . . If it's a good game, you can engage people's imaginations and their minds. It's the whole package—your mind, your imagination, your emotions. and your intellect" (interview 2017). Another designer commented: "If a person believes, as a player, that they are actually the fleet commander of the Athenian fleet during the Peloponnesian War, it helps that there is better graphics on the game board, and it helps that there is graphics on the cards to help a person visualize. But the longer that they are playing, that broad helmet and the linen armor start to feel real" (interview 2017).

Factors other than multisensory stimulation affect the degree of immersion generated in a game. Casey and Martin asked, "How do you immerse them, and how does that actually affect what they're going to get out of that, whether it is entertainment or education or whatever the game is for? You can get people that get totally sucked into some really ugly games. But if the story and the gameplay is compelling enough, they will still feel immersed in it. They will still feel it" (interview 2017). Pournelle made a similar observation: "[I]mmersion doesn't have to be like videogame-level immersion. In fact, you can get greater levels of immersion with a hex board table than in many other approaches because, just as a good novel reaches directly into the brain and the reader assembles the imagery around themselves, a good game will do the same. It doesn't necessarily have to have all the mechanics of virtual reality. You can get to that level because it's about what's going on in part of your brain. . . . I think you can get as good as if not better flow or imagination in that environment without doing virtual reality or another technique" (interview 2017). Indeed, a comparable level of immersion can be generated using analog artifacts. As Markley explained, often "visualizations are necessary to be successful—the common one is a map . . . that represents the realities of some level of abstraction. [Failure to provide a map] detracts from the ability to become immersed" (interview 2017).

According to many in the CoP, while multisensory high-tech immersion is most efficacious in the context of training, analog immersion of this kind is especially possible in higher-level, less deterministic games. Lademan noted: "A game that's tactical or grand-tactical in its objectives and in its form, I think, requires a greater degree of immersion than a game that's run at an operational or certainly the strategic or grand-strategic level." This is because in tactical games "you want things to be present and immediate to the player—pieces and forces and the consequences of your actions—just like they would be in a tactical circumstance. Immediate to the consciousness of the player and demanding kind of an immediate response" (interview 2017). Another designer pointed out, "As you move up the decision tree, so you get further up into the operational/strategic [sphere], the immersion comes from feeling that the actual decisions that they're making are reasonable and realistic in the context of the game" (interview 2017). Similarly,

Guillory observed that "you want the flight simulator to have as high-level visual fidelity as you can possibly get because you're practicing recognizing the giant electrical tower and not run into it. I don't think that's anywhere remotely necessary when you are talking about a strategic-level game" (interview 2017). Hall summarized: "As you go up in the senior levels . . . you can get immersive in a low-technology sense, which . . . is you get immersed into it because you are given the role of what's not typically you" (interview 2017).

One implication of this is that the type of immersion that is most appropriate depends on who will be playing. As Downes-Martin and Pellegrino revealed, you can have the "same environment [but a] different level of immersion. The immersion has to take into account the people. If the person is already skilled you can rely on his or her imagination to fill in the gaps, to fill in the seams, to flesh out the environment. [A less experienced player] would look and see a cartoon image of the terrain, [while a more experienced player] was seeing, in his mind, the real terrain" (interview 2017). A designer elaborated on this point: "If you're attempting to get junior officers or NCOs so that they can function on a battle space under high degrees of stress, then you need to have to a great extent that immersion. Even if it's a safe environment, there needs to be some aspect of that immersion because you have to recreate the kinds of problems in the type of environment to make it useful for them in terms of actually focusing on the decision" (interview 2017).

At the higher-ranked levels, games can generate immersion only if they're consistent with players' existing knowledge and sense of plausibility. As one designer characterized it:

If I'm ordering Panzer divisions around on the East[ern] Front in 1941 and the Panzer divisions can fly, I'm not going to be immersed. I need to see how the ends, ways and means, the victory conditions and the rules of the game, I need to see how they relate to history and interact in ways that first remind me of interactions I've read about or seen in history or imagined, and then go a little bit further in showing me more about these interactions and not just what happened but plausibly what could have happened and didn't and why. . . . . Now I'm getting immersed because I feel like I can experiment with this miniature model of some grand endeavor or highly stressful situation or something else that I actually can't in real life experiment with. When I play this game I can experiment with the representation of it that has sufficient fidelity in my mind that I buy it. And now I become transported and I feel like I really am playing out that historical role and so that aspect of it is to me what is most deeply immersive, that I feel like I am refighting the Vietnam War, that I am intercepting Luftwaffe bombers heading for London or whatever. So there's an imaginative aspect to it, but what triggers and sustains that imaginative leap most importantly is the quality of that model, that representation. I am operating and executing it, but it is showing me how these motions work, how these interactions work. (interview 2017).

The implication here is that wargames of various types generate different kinds of immersion. Some in the CoP argue, in this vein, that we should refer to immersions, in the plural. For example, one designer suggested that we can identify three broad types of immersion: "The first one is just the sheer adventure and excitement of it. This is where a lot of the computer game designers have to go, and it's really about excitement. It's kind of a Hollywood immersiveness. That's probably the lowest level of immersiveness and it's quite honestly pandering. That's sheer adrenaline rush and excitement." The second type of immersion is "the role-playing aspect—the decisions a player makes [which] correspond with the decisions a player would make in a real-world situation." Finally, there is "problem-solving in general. Whether it's a math equation, whether it's a chess problem, it's inherently difficult, so you're drawn into it and you're obsessed by it. That's an abstract level of immersion in terms of problem-solving. It's doing something difficult" (interview 2017).

Such forms of immersion appeal to different types of gamers, he explained: "The first is the one that gets people through the door, especially if they are young. But as a professional, I'm far more interested in the latter two." While the "cheap thrills" of the first type "are fine," it is the third type that is most powerful: "Your third immersiveness, even though your game isn't very realistic and you're not having that role-playing aspect . . . it's the problem that drives you in. That's what makes the immersive experience and that's why you play" (interview 2017). Hall made much the same point, suggesting that some games are "not technically immersive but role-play immersive. I think it's important that whatever game you're using immerses the player either technically or cognitively, so that they buy into the game" (interview 2017).

Immersion of one form or another, then, is vital for efficacious wargaming. Just as with the drive to win, however, an excess of immersion can interfere with a game's objectives and ultimately derail it. It is possible, as one instructor noted, for the multisensory stimulation of advanced technologies to distract a player rather than to encourage focus. When "playing simulations on laptops you do get immersed, but you also get distracted." When using HoloLens technologies, trainees focus on "trying to look at different angles as you're going through the terrain. And I've seen that even though you can actually see a tree they're so immersed in what they've seen in the 3D simulated things that they will bump into the tree" (interview 2017).

Such distraction can also occur in analog games, as Moreland acknowledged: "A big part of it is building teams and stimulating human interactions. I have to be careful that they don't get so immersed in the game that they don't forget about each other. I have to manage the tendency to overimmerse in the game." He continued, "As recently as ten years ago we would have probably struggled to keep an audience engaged and to suspend their disbelief to have them embrace the training outcome. Now it's just the opposite. They'll get so sucked into the game that they forget why they're playing it in the first place." In light of this, "immersion is something that has to be managed. I'd say now, if anything, it's not how do we get more immersion. It's how do we manage the level of immersion we can already create in a way that achieves the effects we're hoping to achieve" (interview 2017).

In spite of these pitfalls, there is broad consensus on the importance of immersion for effective wargaming. Key to this are the often-heard phrases "Don't fight the scenario" and "Don't break the spell." As Downes-Martin and Pellegrino explained, "[T]here are certain things we know, like Peter [Perla's] 'golden circle': [don't] break the narrative or you break the activity. The classic example for us from a data collection perspective is the survey. If during play you've got them to get into the problem and . . . suddenly it's like 'stop the clock—take a survey.' So we do talk about trying not to interrupt, that you're in the moment, you're in there and you've got them bought into the problem and then you don't want to do something which pulls them out of the circle" (interview 2017). The following section turns to the question of how a state of immersion is produced and sustained in wargames.

Cultivating Immersion

There are many design techniques used to generate a state of immersion in games. Indeed, as Nacke and Lindley argue, if precise algorithms to cultivate immersion could be established, they would become industry standard (cited in Soderman 2021, 118–119). Berger describes the techniques that can be used, including "referencing the real world, familiarity and reuse, using signifiers, and maintaining geometric and logical consistency." This involves coercing the player into thinking of the game as real, restricting their sphere of action until they come to identify with the space, deploying narrative to invest the players in characters or mission objectives, and ensuring the consistent application of rules (Berger 2008, 47–54). A designer offered further details: "Immersion comes from a number of things. Competition can help, but realism and the ability to influence things and have reactions that seem to have some fidelity to whatever the subject matter is and time span . . . are all factors that could go into immersion" (interview 2017).

Generating a state of immersion can begin prior to the start of gameplay. As Tappen and colleagues explained, "One of the things that they do with our wargames here is they'll write up a scenario and then they'll talk a little bit about how matrix wargames work. And this will be handed out to each of the participants prior to the game so that they have some homework to do. I think that helps to serve that immersion purpose into the role that they're going to play" (interview 2017). It can also be beneficial to use technologies and software packages already familiar to players. One instructor recounted: "Back in 2006 when we first started doing this, the Marines were like, 'We don't want the Xbox-type handout. We want to use the key[boards] because you can do more with it.' These guys now are saying, 'No, we need the Xbox because we're spending too much time getting distracted doing the W key or the F key or the D key.' With the decision toolkit they're going to have Xbox hand controls so they're not distracted, so they can get more immersed" (interview 2017).

The rule system too has an effect on the degree of immersion generated. If it is too complex, players will struggle to become immersed. As Hall warned, you should avoid "a lot of lengthy rules and you have to have a facilitator who is knowledgeable enough and really energetic and passionate enough to get the group going . . . When you have a bunch of senior or very intelligent people that you want to get into playing the game, you don't want a lot of complicated rules because people's eyes will glaze over and you will lose them" (interview 2017).

A sense of realism is important for immersion in games that use equipment designed to emulate a real-world equivalent. As one designer noted, "If we did not represent the size, the weight, and the button functionality for the military equipment that they were using, it detracts from the training and gives the soldiers the feeling that this isn't right, so they don't get immersed into it" (interview 2017). With analog objects too, realism and consistency are necessary to avoid breaking the spell of immersion. The designer continued: "We do multinational training at the Fires Center of Excellence, and it was a room with a rug on the floor and there were some clothes in the drawers. Some of our multinational participants saw the rug on the floor, which appeared a little bit like a prayer rug, and some of the clothes which were hanging out of the drawer was women's lingerie. So that distracted immediately from the environment as he walked in there. So you have to take into account some of those cultural aspects if you do multinational training" (interview 2017).

Also important in the generation of immersive gameplay is the experience of having a degree of freedom over choices and actions. Wong explained: "The more you actually let [players] determine things like . . . negotiating who plays the roles and having freedom of action and not constraining them in ways that they feel are artificial, I think gets you that buy-in and gets you that flow" (interview 2017). While this freedom is always constrained by the game's rules and objectives, the players should not experience this directly. An instructor commented:

An immersive game . . . generally tends to be something in which the walls and boundaries are not obvious. You are not constantly bumping up against them. The less you realize that what you are in or the less it actively impedes your ability to interact with the game, less of those walls or rules whatever . . . The less the structure of the game interferes with natural operation of someone in the way that the game designers either intended or wanted to allow for towards whether, in our case, a specific educational goal or, whether it's a commercial environment for the sake of having fun, oftentimes the solution itself, escapism is the goal and in that case, I think then the more immersive the game is. (interview 2017)

Several interviewees emphasized the importance of narrative and storytelling for generating immersion. One veteran remarked: "For me, it's about a story. . . . It can be related to magic or the future, technology, aliens, or whatever, but if it's a relatable story, or characters that can really drive it, then you really fall into a whole different universe. Really the only thing that will break the immersion is a touch of reality, [someone] walking in the door—'Ah, and we're back'—[that] kind of thing" (interview 2017). David Crouse, a former Marine Corps staff sergeant, similarly reflected: "For me immersion in games generally comes with a rich, engrossing story where I'm using my

278 POLITICS OF PLAY

brain to put myself in that world, like when you're a kid and you play pretend" (interview 2017). This is true for both digital and manual games, and across tactical and strategic registers. As Goodwin put it, the key issue "ultimately in either is quality of the story. Students are willing to accept a certain level of unrealism. Otherwise there wouldn't be a need to game it. Ultimately, can they buy the storyline, and are they willing to make the adjustments and sacrifices?" (interview 2017).

Suspending Players

Reflecting Csikszentmihalyi's notion that a flow state charts a course of stimulation between anxiety and boredom, many in the CoP argue that immersion involves "suspending" players between particular poles. One framing of such suspension is between the poles of realism and speed. As Pournelle explained, "You want the players to be suspended in a state of flow between two competing poles of realism and speed. You don't want a game in which people are defying the laws of physics because then players will say, 'This is a bunch of nonsense, why am I here?' That's the realism side. But on the other hand, if it takes you so long to adjudicate the decisions people make, they just check out while they're waiting for the results to come in" (interview 2017).

A second and oft-invoked framing is suspending the player between tension or anxiety and boredom or disengagement. Perla and McGrady pointed out that "you want a sufficient amount of tension to propel the player forward but not so much tension as to produce anxiety and or unhappiness in the player, a feeling of annoyance. You need to make it easy enough for the player to manage it but just hard enough to get the player a significant challenge to overcome so that they feel good about themselves" (interview 2017). And Casey and Martin acknowledged that "you do need to keep people engaged so there is kind of a balance between boredom and engagement" (interview 2017).

The reason for this, as Downes-Martin and Pellegrino elaborated, is that

games have to be able to dynamically change to adapt to the skill set of the player because a game that is too hard you frustrate and pitch out. A game that's too easy you get bored and pitched out. So flow is where a game continually keeps you in that zone where as my skill increases the game gets more complicated to balance that. So, that in a sense is incredibly important for just that reason in terms of keeping players from being frustrated. I can stress them to the point of frustration . . . Stress is good. So much stress they kick out is bad. And they can't be bored because they then pick up the newspaper and they disengage. So that's the flow part. (interview 2017)

Goodwin had a similar perspective: "The game has to figure out how to keep the challenge going. How do you keep a level of excitement in the game? . . . The player ought to see some path towards victory, otherwise they'll lose interest and stop. If it's too easy they lose interest, and if they can't win they lose interest. So how do you build the environment or frame the environment so that there's still decisions to be made, there's still rewards to be had, there's still a reason to continue to immerse yourself in that situation?" (interview 2017).

Reflecting on this point, Guillory posed a similar question: "If the ability of the participant is matched with the difficulty of the game—that's kind of your textbook definition of the state of flow there. But . . . if the game is too easy for the skill level of the participant, then they get bored. And if it's too hard for the skill level of the participant, then they get too frustrated or anxious and quit. So the question is, how do we match the difficulty of that game to their skill level? The first step in all of that is how do I measure the skill level of the participant coming in? That's been our main challenge" (interview 2017). He suggested that there has been more success at this with individual gaming as opposed to group immersion. "On the individual level, I think the theorists have answered that long, long ago. Like with *Tetris*, the better you get at it, the faster the game goes until it overwhelms you. The game itself has an algorithm that matches based on your performance how fast it is going to be. We can do that with a rifle marksmanship trainer. If you show ability with the stationary and nearby targets, we start moving them around and moving them faster—that's algorithm-driven and easy" (interview 2017). However, he continued, "how do you average across [a] group what those skill levels are and how you should train for them? That's the tough nut of flow that nobody has ever cracked. . . . It gets tougher with a process-based game where I am training processes, not decisions. What do I do once I have a whole group of people involved?" (interview 2017). Having established how an immersive state is generated, the following section explores the experience of immersion from the perspective of players.

Inside Immersion

One key sign of immersion is when players refer to their in-game role or character in the first person. As Wong noted, you "want to see people using the first person when they talk about their side" (interview 2017). Bartels said much the same thing: "When I'm watching one of my games run, I'm very conscious of [whether] people refer to themselves [as in] the position of the secretary, [or] are they embracing that first-person shift that indicates to me that they've assumed the role?" (interview 2017). The use of "I" in this way indicates that the player has taken on the game's goals and themes as though they were their own. "Immersion comes about because you can see yourself in the role," observed Markley (interview 2017). Another designer noted this as well: as players "take on those roles, they get incredibly immersed . . . As they take on those roles and they become more and more part of that role . . . that is where people get consumed by it" (interview 2017).

This involvement is profound and results in a depletion of consciousness of the immediate surroundings. Downes-Martin and Pellegrino commented that immersion "involves becoming so absorbed with the logic of the game that you don't actually see or stay aware of stuff going on around you. When you go to sleep that night, you close your eyes and you see the board" (interview 2017). In the words of a designer, "You sort of get almost mesmerized. It's the whole thing where . . . you're so into something that you lose track of time. To me that's one of the hallmarks of being in that flow moment, where you the most yourself in the game" (interview 2017). Sometimes this bleeds over into the analog world. As another designer relayed, "I have actually had people dress up. There's a fun element . . . [and] it comes back to that competition piece. When someone dresses up it . . . allows them to almost take on a persona. It might be as simple as giving them a World War II helmet and telling them they're Patton. Then you will see them puff out their chest and they're getting immersed" (interview 2017).

This involves a streamlining of focus, the filtering out of extraneous details, and a resultant distancing from real-life worries. Gaming "allows people a very easy way to transition their brain from focusing on twenty different things to 'This is my single focus,'" asserted a designer. "'This is what I'm working on and I don't have to think about the ten bills that I don't know how I'm going to pay because I'm working on a VA loan or I don't have to think about [that] my wife that left me while I was on tour. I can just focus on getting this guy from point A to point B and beating the level" (interview

2017). Machuga added, "It's almost like it's working a different part of my brain and allowing me to kind of go into a comatose state while playing. I don't know what that is but there's a relaxing piece of it. I'm not exactly sure how it works but it does" (interview 2017). And Crouse noted, "If the game is . . . created immersively, and attention to detail is there, then there's a pretty good likelihood that I can lose myself in the game" (interview 2017).

Immersion involves a sense of "fusion with the world" (Csikszentmihalyi 1975, 42, quoting Malow). Csikszentmihalyi describes this as "the merging of action and awareness." He continues: "[F]or flow to be maintained, one cannot reflect on the act of awareness itself. When awareness becomes split, so that one perceives the activity from 'outside,' flow is interrupted" (Csikszentmihalyi 1975, 38). Under these conditions, "action and reaction have become so well practiced as to be automatic. The person is too involved with the experience to reflect on it" (Csikszentmihalyi 1975, 46–47). In Nietzsche's terms, this is experienced as a childlike "blissful self-forgetfulness" (quoted in Sutton-Smith 2001, 113).

In such an immersed state, "action follows upon action according to an internal logic that seems to need no conscious intervention by the actor. He experiences it as a unified flowing from one moment to the next, in which he is in control of his actions, and in which there is little distinction between self and environment, between stimulus and response, or between past, present, and future" (Csikszentmihalyi 1975, 36). Importantly, "in flow, one does not stop to evaluate the feedback; action and reaction have become so well practiced as to be automatic. The person is too involved with the experience to reflect on it" (Csikszentmihalyi 1975, 46). This suggests, according to David Webster, "a qualitative opposition between thinking and being" (2014, 190).

In Ermi and Mäyrä's framing, this amounts to a "psychological experience of non-mediation" (2007, 40). Csikszentmihalyi writes, "Activities which allow flow to occur (activities such as games, rituals, or art) . . . usually do not require any negotiation. Since they are based on freely accepted rules, the player does not need to use a self to get along in the activity. As long as all the participants follow the same rules, there is no need to negotiate roles. The participants need no self to bargain with about what should or should not be done" (1975, 42–43). In other words, in a state of immersion, explicit negotiation with other players and self-consciousness mediation with the game are suspended.

What remains is a complete focus on the game and its goals. As Lori J. Ducharme and Gary Alan Fine put it, "[A]ttention must be given completely and exclusively to those elements constituting play" in order that the player be transported fully into the game world such that "the game framework occupies players' awareness completely; at the same time, irrelevant matters are disattended, such that players effortlessly become unaware of the world beyond the frame" (1994, 94–96). Csikszentmihalyi's account supports this reading: "What is usually lost in flow is not the awareness of one's body or of one's functions, but only the self *construct,* the intermediary which one learns to interpose between stimulus and response" (Csikszentmihalyi 1975, 43). As Monica Vilhauer writes, the player "attends whole-heartedly to the tasks required of him . . . The game requires the players' full involvement" (Vilhauer 2014, 77).

In a state of immersion, then, a person engages with the world around them in a different way to everyday life: "[T]he flow experience differs from awareness in everyday reality because it contains ordered rules which make action and the evaluation of action automatic and hence unproblematic. When contradictory actions are made possible (for instance, when cheating is introduced into a game), the self reappears to negotiate between the conflicting definitions of what needs to be done, and the flow is interrupted" (Csikszentmihalyi 1975, 47). Ducharme and Fine similarly note that because players are both "lodged in" and "exposed to" the game's framework, they "are obliged to maintain the 'ceremonial order' governing the encounter" (1994, 96). Reflecting Baudrillard's critique of the age of simulation, Wark writes that in the "total game . . . 'one cannot go into exile in a unified world'" (Wark 2007, 182, quoting Dubord). This is because a wargame is "a social system with no deviance" (Csikszentmihalyi 1975, 43).

Such conformity is experienced by players as pleasurable. Caillois points out that a player is free to act only "within the limits set by the rules." This accounts in part for the pleasure the game excites (Caillois 2001, 8). This signals a "masochistic element" that is often not acknowledged (Hackett 2014, 124). As Diane Ackerman puts it, play instructs: "Give up your will, all who travel here." She continues: "Giving up my will, self, uniqueness—happily, with a saint's devotion—has its own special appeal" (Ackerman 2000, 23).

Murray similarly observes that games require that players "behave according to negotiated rules," which involves limiting attention and action to "what counts in the game." Something about this limiting of the "exploratory delights of play," then continues, makes games enjoyable for players (Murray 2007, 13). Games, then, rather than players, are the "arbiters of rules." Games serve to "comfort us as their worlds abide by certain rules and order" (Parkin

2015, 78). In Gadamer's words, the player "enjoys a freedom of decision which at the same time is endangered and irrevocably limited" (Gadamer 2004, 106).

The Politics of Immersion

Perhaps because of the power of flow and immersion as techniques of engaging players, and the pleasure associated with them, their politics are rarely explored. While in games studies and beyond, scholars have examined the pernicious effects of (excessive) immersion, or disputed the depth of flow's immersive power, few have developed explicitly political critiques. However, a handful of prescient recent texts—most notably that of Braxton Soderman—have begun to buck this trend. Soderman notes that the "experience of flow often seems natural, benign, and innocuous," appearing to offer a "serene, calming, and beautiful experience" (2021, 31). Steven Kotler goes further, asserting that flow "appears to be the only practical answer to the question: What is the meaning of life? Flow is what makes life worth living" (quoted in Soderman 2021, 236). However, Soderman argues, this reading neglects to engage with the history, ideology, and politics of flow and immersion (2021, 31). Jay David Bolter echoes this, urging that we should interrogate the politics of flow (2019, 163).

Both Soderman and Bolter point to the political context in which Csikszentmihalyi conceptualized flow:

> It was a response to Marxism, an attempt to create a Western democratic solution to alienation. . . . Flow offered an alternative to Marxist modes of social change. Unlike Marx, who argued that alienation would be solved only by collective revolution . . . Csikszentmihalyi imagined that flow experiences could reimmerse people in their own lives without the need for revolution, removing alienation by allowing them to experience the absorbing effects of play. (Soderman 2021, 5)

Against a Soviet/Marxist collectivism, Soderman continues, Csikszentmihalyi's "politics of enjoyment" sought to empower people "to find playfulness, satisfaction, and flow in their own lives. The hope was that this would then spark a social movement to redesign all aspects of life to produce flow and thus cure alienation" (Soderman 2021, 211). As this suggests,

Csikszentmihalyi's was a distinctly individualist paradigm: "Flow was a therapy for the individual who found herself in a society without universally agreed values: each individual had to find her own path toward fulfilment" (Bolter 2019, 167). However, Soderman argues, that approach has proven readily co-optable by capital, functioning as a mode of "palliative medicine for treating the symptoms of alienation without curing its causes" (Soderman 2021, 22).

Acknowledging this historical context is important because it opens a pathway to engaging with the politics of immersion. Soderman provides a detailed tracing of these political implications, showing how immersion and flow are set to work to sustain engagement, boost consumption, and retain users both within and beyond the gaming world. In his words: "Games, play, and flow experiences inscribe a focused attention, meaning that they align with the attention economy that seeks to extend media consumption." He elaborates:

> The absorbing and enjoyable properties of flow align with capitalism and its mobilization of enjoyment to sustain consumption . . . [reflecting] capitalism's dynamic adjustment of our desires to the rhythms of its streams of consumption . . . [Games] are designed to capture our attention while keeping us playing and paying. (Soderman 2021, 136)

He notes also the ways flow is connected to the wellness and fitness industries in ways that motivate people "to increase their productivity, ignoring their exhaustion," and shows how it is offered as a "coping mechanism for the status quo" that offers salve for "instability, uncertainty, risk, overwork, and psychological maladies such as anxiety and depression." The central problem these applications share, he suggests, is that "the popular rise of flow does not couple this feeling with a metasocial critique: flow is the end of social change, not the beginning" (Soderman 2021, 212–214). This is because flow shuts down, rather than encourages, reflection and questioning: "Flow quiets doubt, the hallmark of the critical attitude. It does not exercise and grow this form of questioning because it threatens the immersive experience of flow itself" (Soderman 2021, 154). Instead, it promotes a problematic ideology of the endless growth of the individual in line with capitalist imperatives, ultimately "promising salvation through a long life of managing exhaustion" (Soderman 2021, 236). As this suggests, the flowing subject too has a politics that requires interrogation.

Desubjectification: Suspending the Reflective Subject

This leads back to the question of player agency and its associated paradoxes, explored in Chapter 4. Soderman critically analyzes the figure of the flowing subject: "Flowing subjects are not simply game players experiencing the psychological state of flow; they are being positioned as media consumers in a way that promotes flow's ideologies" (2021, 6). He is interested in exploring the politics at work in forms of subjectivity cultivated by flow and immersion. Looking again at the historical and political context in which flow theory developed, Soderman contrasts its conceptualization of the subject with that of its contemporaries. Against poststructuralist, Marxist, and linguistic theories that emphasize the ways in which the subject is produced and incomplete, he shows, flow theory insisted upon a unitary and self-possessed subject as the locus of emancipation:

> Critical theorists in the last half of the twentieth century analyzed the death of the author, decentered and fragmented subjects, in order to raise awareness about the absence of full agency and intentionality. Meanwhile, flow theory advocated for a subject fully capable of agency and actionable intentions. . . . [F]low theory posited a subject [who] could attain fullness, harmony and unity . . . as the precondition for social liberation. (Soderman 2021, 54)

As a result of this, the critical possibilities associated with problematizing subjectivity were missed by flow theory, which chose instead to promise an always illusory completeness and wholeness. The cost of this promise was that the flowing subject became "the ideological subject that capitalism uses to sustain consumption, increase productivity, grow the individual at the expense of the social, and subdue critical consciousness" (Soderman 2021, 213).

One key drawback of this is the suspension of critical and reflective thinking. In flow, the "why" of one's actions is removed, leading to a danger of that thought being shut down in favor of "pure automaticity" (Soderman 2021, 154, 213–215). This risks a situation in which "the player is subsumed into the procedural rhetoric of the game" (Bolter 2019, 103). All of this points to the question: Where is the I when I play? Where does the player go when in play? On the one hand, as Renata Gomes argues, players experience a feeling of agency when they are able to do things in a game: "[A] player will have, immersed in a game world, a greater feeling of *presence*—and, as a consequence, greater agency potential—the more a virtual body is capable of executing, or not, certain tasks required for participation in the virtual world." This "kinesthetic acting," she explains, "gives agency to the player, turning her into agent of both story and enunciation" (Gomes 2007, 55–57).

Conversely, as Julian Stallabrass argues, "the immersive pull of ever-more realistic games leaves a rapidly dwindling space for critical reflection" (cited in Giddings 2018, 769). This loss of reflective engagements is the result of the "'loss of ego,' 'self-forgetfulness,' 'loss of self-consciousness,' and even 'transcendence of individuality'" (Csikszentmihalyi 1975, 42, quoting Maslow) associated with flow. In Gadamer's words: "The ease of play—which naturally does not mean that there is any real absence of effort but refers phenomenologically only to the absence of strain—is experienced subjectively as relaxation. The structure of play absorbs the player into itself, and thus frees him from the burden of taking the initiative, which constitutes the actual strain of existence" (Gadamer 2004, 105). Accordingly, as Dean Lockwood and Anthony Richards note, critics argue that immersion "robs the player of conscious awareness and critical distance" (Lockwood and Richards 2008, 177).

As this last claim suggests, many theorists of play and games argue that players' reflective capacities are suspended in the state of immersion. The suggestion here is that when in play, players' capacity to critically think about and decide upon courses of action is circumscribed by the game's processes and objectives. As Csikszentmihalyi succinctly puts it, when in flow "the person is too involved with the experience to reflect on it" (Csikszentmihalyi 1975, 46). The subject's reflective abilities are suspended in play. As Gadamer explains, "In playing, all those purposive relations that determine active and caring existence have not simply disappeared, but are curiously suspended" (Gadamer 2004, 102). Elsewhere he states: "[T]he concept of the game becomes important, for absorption into the game is an ecstatic self-forgetting that is experienced not as a loss of self-possession, but as the free buoyancy of an elevation above oneself" (Gadamer 2008, 55).

Huizinga makes a similar point: "The player can abandon himself body and soul to the game, and the consciousness of its being 'merely' a game can be thrust into the background" (Huizinga 2016, 21). Fink also describes this process of player subsumption: "The player hides his real self behind his role and is submerged in it. He lives in his role with a singular intensity. . . . The player can recall himself from his role; while playing, man retains a knowledge of his double existence, however greatly reduced this knowledge may be. Man exists in two spheres simultaneously, not for lack of concentration or out of forgetfulness, but because this double personality is essential to play" (quoted in Ehrmann 1971, 23).

Such an experience involves a loss of one's sense of self. One of Csikszentmihalyi's interviewees described it this way: "You yourself are in an ecstatic state to such a point that you feel as though you almost don't exist. I've experienced this time and time again. My hand seems devoid of myself, and I have nothing to do with what is happening. I just sit there watching it in a state of awe and wonderment. And it just flows out by itself" (Csikszentmihalyi 1975, 44). Gadamer makes a similar claim: "Play fulfils its purpose only if the player loses himself in play" (Gadamer 2004, 103). As Csikszentmihalyi summarizes: "Because the flow activity has clear and non-contradictory rules, people who perform in it can temporarily forget their identity and its problems" (Csikszentmihalyi 1975, 48).

Instead of experiencing the gam as oneself, then, in a state of immersion the player takes on roles or characteristics of another. In such play "the disguised or masked individual 'plays' another part, another being. He *is* another being" (Huizinga 2016, 13; emphasis in original). Such an experience "absorb[s] the players intensely and utterly" (Huizinga 2016, 13). The result is that the player "can utterly abandon himself body and soul to the game, and the consciousness of its being 'merely' a game can be thrust into the background" (Huizinga 2016, 21). Rob Fullop reflects that, "when you play a game repeatedly, "the graphics become invisible. It's all impulses. It's not the part of your brain that processes plot, character, story. If you watch a movie, you become the hero—Gilgamesh, Indiana Jones, James Bond, whomever. The kid says, I want to be that. In a game, Mario isn't a hero. I don't want to be him; he's me. Mario is a cursor" (quoted in Frasca 2001, 168).

What this means, as Gadamer put it, is that "[t]he structure of play absorbs the player into itself, and this takes from him the burden of initiative" (quoted in Hans 1981, 7). This suggests that immersion and critical reflection are fundamentally at odds with each other. Gadamer uses the example of a theatrical performance: "[T]o investigate the origin of the plot on which it is based is to move out of the real experience of a piece of literature, and likewise it is to move out of the real experience of the play if the spectator reflects about the conception behind a performance or about the proficiency of the actors" (Gadamer 2004, 116). The implication is that to interrupt gameplay by reflecting on the game's narrative or trajectory is to break the spell of immersion.

There are good reasons to be concerned about this loss of self in gameplay. As Gadamer cautions: "[T]he game itself is a risk for the player. One can play only with serious possibilities. Obviously this means that one may become so engrossed in them that they outplay one, as it were, and prevail one. . . . [P]lay does not have its being in the player's consciousness or attitude, but on the contrary play draws him into its dominion and fills him with its spirit. The player experiences the game as a reality that surpasses him" (Gadamer 2004, 106–109). This is because "play is less of a thing a person does and more of a thing done to him" (Vilhauer 2014, 77). In other words, "the player gives herself over to the game" (Feezell 2014, 26). In leisure gaming, at least, this involves a free decision to offer up the self to this loss of self-consciousness, a "temporary captivity" in which the player "freely choose[s] to suspend his freedom" (Hackett 2014, 124). In institutional gaming, of course, this voluntarism is often absent.

Hackett suggests that gaming ultimately leads the player to a state of non-being. Building on Freudian theory, he argues that we find in play a "daemonic force," a "death instinct" understood as an urge to return to "the state of non-being" (Hackett 2014, 125). Others have described this loss of self as the adoption of an animal state. Massumi argues that humans "permit themselves to abandon themselves to play. In play, the human enters a zone of indiscernibility with the animal" (Massumi 2014, 8). Paolo Freire suggests that what distinguishes humans from other animals is that the former, unlike the latter, are able to conceptualize and alter the world they inhabit. "[H]umankind, as beings of the praxis, differ from animals, which are beings of pure activity. Animals do not consider the world; they are immersed in it" (Freire 2000, 125). What unites these accounts is the figure of a will to nothingness through which the player's critical engagement with their actions is powerfully suspended in a process of desubjectification.

(Re)Subjectification: Producing Reflexes in the Subject

Critics of this line of analysis argue that such a framing is reductive and overstates the degree to which games master players. Lockwood and Richards, for example, object to the idea that games are nothing more than a rendering of instructions and decrees because "such statements recuperate games for a respecified vision of old-style [Althusserian] interpellation, jazzed up in the terminology of new media" (2008, 177). Indeed, it is certainly important to avoid a framing that implies players are dupes living under a veil of false consciousness. And yet, optimistic accounts that celebrate the game as freeplay and affirm players' capacity to exercise agency through decision-making underestimate the extent to which games (re)subjectify players. As Murray argues, in such environments "we do not merely 'suspend' a critical faculty; we also exercise a creative faculty. We do not suspend disbelief so much as we actively *create belief*" (Murray 1997, 110). We do this by enacting "emotionally authentic experiences that we know are not 'real'" (Murray 1997, 125). While the game falls outside of ordinary "reality," the realness of its emotional effects is deeply felt and contributes to new forms of acting and reacting long after the gameplay has ended.

Importantly, beyond conscious thoughts and beliefs, gaming can cultivate reflex actions in players, understood as actions that are taken before or beyond a conscious decision. Games involve a process of "being seized" and the cultivation of "reflex action" through which play enraptures and teaches players (Huizinga 2016, 17). This suggests that in addition to processes of desubjectification, through which the self-consciousness of the subject is suspended, games at the same moment resubjectify players through the cultivation of reflex actions that are enacted without conscious thought.

Because they allow for multiple iterations, games can embed rote training aims through the cultivation of mental and physical muscle memory and new reflex actions. As one instructor described it, in many training environments "there is a desired outcome that is 'the preferred outcome.'" A designer affirmed that games training is designed, through exposure and repetition, for players to learn to "do the right thing" (interview 2017). Dan Evans expands on this: "[T]he process of becoming a trained soldier and finally acquiring the prereflexive practical sense of the institution (doxa) requires the continual repetition of new ways of moving and holding oneself until . . . the synthesis of knowledge and action come to pervade the soldier's very flesh until that which was formerly external and alien becomes prereflexive" (Evans 2020, 49). As one instructor put it: "What you're trying to do is stimulate learning which is changing the neural pathways. What's being changed is inside the student's mind and so anything having to do with changing the neural pathways in your training audience is learning" (interview 2017). Another instructor likewise noted: "Some games and learning have been used to help people kind of rewire the brain" (interview 2017).

John Protevi has explored the role of precognitive reflexes in infantry combat, noting the ways in which the military has sought historically to overcome proto-empathetic sensibilities on the part of warfighters that disincline them toward lethal engagement. In order to answer the question of who does the killing when precognitive reflexes are activated, he argues that we must "distinguish agency and ownership of bodily actions. Ownership is the sense that my body is doing the action, while agency is the sense that I am in control of the action, that the action is willed. Both are aspects of subjectivity, though they may well be a matter of prereflective self-awareness rather than full-fledged objectifying self-consciousness" (Protevi 2008, 407–408). Protevi describes the "reflexes, rages, and panics" experienced by service members as a "de-subjectified state" (2008, 407), and draws our attention to the "emergent assemblages that skip subjectivity and directly conjoin larger groups and the somatic. To follow this line of thought, let us accept that in addition to nonsubjective body control by reflexes, we can treat basic emotions as modular 'affect programs' . . . that run the body's hardware in the absence of conscious control" (Protevi 2008, 408). He concludes that "in some cases, the military unit and nonsubjective reflexes and basic emotions are intertwined in such a way as to bypass the soldiers' subjectivity qua controlled intentional action" (Protevi 2008, 408).

Of course, not all wargaming is aimed at lethal skills of the kind discussed by Protevi. But his analysis does point to the ways in which, in addition to suspending players' critical faculties, games have the capacity to cultivate precognitive reflex behaviors. As Protevi puts it: "[W[hether it is a simulation or an embodied intersubjectivity, there is a fundamental linkage of affect, body image, and bodily integrity in the experience of proto-empathic identification" (Protevi 2008, 407). One feature of such processes is "the player's necessary development of various, delimited forms of resilient subjectivity through continual exposure to contingency and inevitable failure" (McSorley 2020, 38). The ultimate consequence of this, Protevi concludes, is that "modern military training . . . reconfigures reflex action" (Protevi 2008, 410).

As well as being disruptive to existing modes of subjectivity, wargames are productive of new ones in ways we have only begun to grasp. This implies that processes of desubjectification—in which reflective thought is suspended—is itself productive of new forms of (only partially agential) subjectivity in the form of reflex actions. In other words, at the same moment that self-conscious thinking is diminished, intuitive reflexes are cultivated. To that extent, while the CoP is at pains to emphasize that wargaming focuses on decision-making, at least some forms of military gaming cultivate reflex actions that in fact circumvent decision-making altogether. Again, although this is in an area we are just beginning to understand, it has serious implications for the experience of moral injury by (ex-)warfighters for whom reflexes engage them in action before their conscious selves have had the opportunity to catch up (MacLeish 2019; Subotic and Steele 2018).

The profundity of this de- and resubjectification is shown in its continuation after service, and often against the wishes of trainees. (Ex-)warfighters frequently describe an inability to "switch off" (Higate 2013, 116). This is experienced as "a constant state of bodily activation" (MacLeish 2013, 118) in which soldiers' "bodies as much as their minds . . . refused to calm down" (MacLeish 2013, 123–124), and a debilitating result is the feeling of being "pinned between involuntary sensory impacts and involuntary institutional compulsions" (MacLeish 2013, 56). As Protevi also cautions, a crucial problem with training that "reconfigures reflex action lies in going beyond what the restored subjectivity of many soldiers can withstand" (Protevi 2008, 411).

Deconstructing Immersion

In light of these political and subjectificatory issues, in the remainder of this chapter I argue that we should interrupt and deconstruct immersion. Soderman poses the problem well: "What is the relationship between flow, play, and thinking? Does privileging the continuous flow of action and removing interruptions erase moments of reflection and critical distance?" He answers this question by positing that flow and reflexive thinking sit in tension with each other because games "truncate the power of critical distance" by replacing "self-consciousness with continuous action" (Soderman 2021, 138–139). Flow thus quiets questioning and doubt, encouraging players to "do" rather than reflect (Soderman 2021, 140–141).

It would seem reasonable, then, to seek to break this state of unreflexive immersion by punctuating it with critical thinking and questions. If flow and immersion direct action and suspend reflection, a deconstructive mode of engagement would seek to interrupt these smooth flows of attention by turning them into objects of critical reflection. Soderman draws a distinction between forms of critical reflection that he terms "critical instances," which are compatible with, and hence quickly recuperable by, ideologies of consumption and obedience, and those that he calls "critical distance," which have the capacity to offer more significant forms of critique or resistance (Soderman 2021, 152). Through their management of our critical capacities, he explains, our attempts to evaluate games can be managed and contained by the games themselves, providing a sense that our curiosity has been fulfilled when in fact we have simply been looped back into the status quo. In short, "[w]e are not witnessing the loss of critical distance in contemporary culture, but rather its proliferation, absorption, and commodification" (Soderman 2021, 143). To rectify this, he concludes, we must seek more substantive critical thinking.[3] He points to the asking of questions that would serve to reorient the subject and jar them out of the woozy state of immersion cultivated in the game: "Why am I doing *this* instead of something else? What determines and conditions my actions? What external forces or dominant cultural norms drive people to pursue this activity? . . . What ideologies influence the game that I am playing? What are its political meanings? Why am I playing it? Should I be playing it? Why am I pursuing flow instead of something else?" (Soderman 2021, 154).

Soderman argues that in order to move away from the "miniaturization of critique" and the reduction of critical consciousness of the flow era, we must reclaim more challenging forms of critical distance and questioning. He refers to the Enlightenment's cultivation of a critical attitude that would use reason to "uncover hidden truths, to expose forms of ideology and falsity within individual consciousness, and to take a step back from inherited viewpoints in order to become aware of determining forces that influence human behavior" (Soderman 2021, 152). Citing Fredric Jameson, he argues that the rise of postmodernism heralded the end of modernity's slogans of opposition, subversion, and critique, and paved the way for ineffective forms of postmodern ironism and avant-garde experimentation readily co-optable by capitalism. Thus "popular culture and high art intermingled and mass consumer culture absorbed and internalized critical distance" (Soderman 2021, 143–144)

A key culprit responsible for this state of affairs, in Soderman's estimation, is play itself, because there is a tension between play and critical thought: "[W]e tend to think of play as an interlude in an otherwise serious life[;] . . . proponents of flow and play desire to extend the occasion

---

[3] This form of critical thinking is not the same as that discussed in Chapter 2; when the language of critical thinking appears in wargames manuals, it means problem-solving or calculative thinking that promotes rather than problematizes the game's directives, and which occurs within the model's parameters and goals.

and duration of these experiences until they become central to life. This vision runs counter to the idea that people should cultivate a *critical attitude* towards life" (Soderman 2021, 140). What is suggested here is that play and playfulness have become a key part of the culture of flow that suspends critical thinking and enraptures the subject.

Part of the reason he makes this case is that he counterposes play with reason, making an Apollonian case for order, clarity, and the resolution of ambiguity: "[C]ritical thinking weighs alternatives in order to resolve a problem, while play seeks alternatives and messes around with them. If play adds ambiguity to the world in order to mess around with its possibilities, critical thinking subtracts ambiguity from the world, resolving it as one resolves an image to make it clearer" (Soderman 2021, 149). His wager is that such a reordering is necessary because play is not the solution to the problem but rather part of it, part of our current reality, offering no purchase in changing it. In his words, "[W]hile the playful attitude seeks distance from the world, this stepping back is not necessarily enacted to critique reality, but rather to engage us more within it. . . . It transforms how we see or perform an activity . . . but ultimately leaves it intact" (Soderman 2021, 163).

It is here that I part company with Soderman. I do so for three main reasons. First, his account of "critical distance" is problematic insofar as it emphasizes the need to step away from, or out of, the content at hand in order to evaluate it. He states: "The word *critical* signifies the crucial or decisive distance that one needs in order to remove oneself from the immediate influence of the experience. . . . Distance aids criticism, allowing the time and space for interpretation to unfold and consider an experience from multiple perspectives. . . . Thus, the term *critical distance* implies that one attains crucial distance from an activity or situation in order to reflect on and articulate an experience" (Soderman 2021, 139).

It is of course possible to step out of a game in the sense that it can be switched off or put away. But Soderman's account seems to imply that critique is possible only after or outside of a game. Through deconstructive play, in contrast, one can switch between immersion and reflexivity while still in a gameworld. Soderman seems to acknowledge this when he discusses the possibility of "critical flow where the player becomes involved within more expansive forms of critique" (Soderman 2021, 172), but this seems to sit in tension with his claim that reflexivity requires both spatial and temporal distance from gameplay.

The notion of stepping outside becomes more problematic still when we consider the difficulty of identifying the boundaries of the flow culture within which we are situated. Just as there is no "outside" to our metaphysical, ontopolitical, or linguistic systems, so too has a vantage point outside of capitalism and its associated forms of popular culture become radically problematic, often serving rhetorical rather than truly emancipatory purposes. While we can step outside of a game, any reflexive thinking we might do necessarily happens within our political and social context, rather than far away from it. As Baudrillard shows, the hyperrealities of the era of simulation have no "real" reality hidden behind them.

Instead of seeking an "outside" from which to cultivate critique, I wager it is possible to critique immersion from a position of immanence by using a deconstructive mode of engagement. While this is not to discourage radical and subversive game design as salient political sites, it is to suggest that these do not occur outside of the hegemonic dynamics they critique. This is not to give up on seeking change, but rather to acknowledge that strategies for change must be devised from within. A strategy for subversion that proceeds from its location within has a better chance than one that seeks temporal distance in modernist reason or cognitive distance in critique from outside.

Second, Soderman argues—somewhat paradoxically—that the solutions to the problems of playful capitalism and flow culture are to be found within games themselves. At the same moment that he seeks to step outside of hegemonic power relations and popular culture to develop critiques of them, he posits solutions to the problems he identifies precisely from within them. Throughout the book, Soderman provides examples of games that encourage players to engage critically with the subject matter, in some cases regarding the flow and play modes they experience and in other cases to communicate a political message. While these are interesting in their own right, in providing this analysis and critiquing as always already co-optable a playful engagement with games, Soderman's critique is limited to seeking solutions from within games and their design. To that extent, he limits sites of resistance to hegemonic power relations to the openings written into games by their designers. Against this, I wager it is better to reconfigure our (inevitable) insideness to games and flow culture in order to cultivate critique from within through playing with games, whether or not designers allow for it, rather than relying on games that permit subversion.

Finally, and most importantly, Soderman reproduces the binary of reason (serious) versus play (unserious) that was traced through the Western philosophical tradition earlier in this book. This is much more than a conceptual or semantic point. Just as flow and play have a politics to be unearthed, so too does reason. As explored in Chapters 3 and 4, the malediction of play in Western philosophy corresponds to a series of broader power relations. The domestication and banishment of play are linked to the reification of a particular form of philosophy reserved for specific privileged groups and the devaluation of practices associated with subjugated social groups. Play's (auto) deconstructive tendency thus challenges the supremacy of reason, exposing the politics and power relations at work in the devaluation of knowledge and being which cannot be apprehended in rational terms. Rather than being satisfied with the conventional binary of reason as serious and play as frivolous, I submit that the binary should be deconstructed.

Derrida argues that a demonstrative challenge proceeds in two steps. First, it must "overturn the hierarchy at a given moment. To overlook this phase of overturning is to forget the conflictual and subordinating structure of opposition." In this first move, then, the devalued end of the binary is placed at the valued end, and vice versa. The second step subverts the binary more fully by generating new concepts that challenge those at work in it: "[W]e must also mark the interval between inversion, which brings low what was high, and the interruptive emergence of a new 'concept,' a concept that can no longer be, and could never be, included in the previous regime." Derrida's strategy of deconstruction is intended "to avoid both simply neutralizing the binary oppositions of metaphysics and simply residing within the closed field of these oppositions, thereby confirming it" (Derrida 1998b, 38–39).

To operationalize this with the binary of reason (serious) versus play (unserious), first reason (serious) and play (unserious) should be inverted. I have shown through this book the myriad ways in which play is serious business while challenging the conceits and universalisms of reason. Second, to subvert the binary, I have conceptualized the notion of deconstructive play as a seriously unserious mode of critical thinking that conforms neither to reason as usually understood nor to play as normally conceptualized. Instead it combines elements of both, occupying reason and using it differently but tracing its playful productions, limits, and contradictions.

Far better than reproducing the conventional reason/play binary, I argue, is to attempt an occupation of reason to push at its limits and critically evaluate our circumstances. Such a deconstructive play of reason is emphatically not an ironic endeavor but rather an earnest enterprise that takes ongoing critical work of precisely the kind Soderman refers to when he articulates

the "hope of critical theory to emancipate humans from dominant and op-
pressive norms" (Soderman 2021, 141). Deconstruction is "the act of taking
a position, in the very work it does with regard to the political-institutional
structures that constitute and govern our practices, our competences, and
our performances" (Derrida, quoted in Elam 1994, 90).

Conclusion

This chapter has explored the concepts of flow and immersion, their uses in
US military wargaming, and the politics at work within them. Having established the key conceptual differences between the directed attention of
flow and the loss of self-consciousness of immersion, the chapter addressed
the question of how, and with what effects, the latter functions as a tool
of player subjectification. It showed how a state of immersion can be cultivated through the use of narrative, the exercise of choice, and player use
of the first person. The ultimate consequence of this is that immersive play
desubjectifies players by circumventing the self-conscious and self-reflective
capacities.

At the same moment, immersive gaming resubjectifies players by instilling
in them reflex actions. Drawing on John Protevi's distinction between ownership and agency, the chapter demonstrated that immersive training locates
ownership of action in players while suspending agency through the cultivation of new reflexes. Finally, it concluded by building upon the critique of flow
offered by Braxton Soderman in order to demonstrate how a deconstructive mode of critical thinking avoids the pitfalls of attempting to step outside flow culture to develop critique while at the same time seeking solutions
within games produced from precisely within this culture. A deconstructive mode also avoids the reproduction of the reason (serious) versus play
(unserious) binary that leads him to leave the politics of reason unexplored
and its emancipatory potential simply assumed. Accordingly, it showed how
a deconstructive engagement with immersion can introduce ruptures in
wargaming's production of people.

Conclusion

This book has developed the first in-depth analysis in the field of IR of the twenty-first-century US military wargaming renaissance. Presenting original interview testimony gathered with wargaming pioneers and practitioners, it has shown how wargames are productive not only of realities but also—by intervening in players' cognitive and affective registers—of people. Seeking to expose the politics at work in wargames, and between their designers, sponsors, facilitators, and players, it has developed a mode of critical analysis called "deconstructive play" and put this to work critically examining the power relations that influence both how players think and also their values, beliefs, and identities. It has demonstrated how, in an epoch of ludic militarism that extends far beyond military institutions to permeate our cultural and recreational worlds, wargaming works to produce subjectivities. It has argued that play—as distinct from gameplay—can open cracks in the closed systems of wargames, thereby pushing against the smooth running of their hyperreal productions in the age of simulation.

To do this, the first two chapters presented a conceptualization and contextualization of US military wargaming over the first decade of the renaissance. Chapter 1 charted a course through the definitional and conceptual quagmire that persists among the wargaming community and those who study it, clarifying the relationship between wargames, simulations, and exercises; diverging views on the respective merits of digital and manual gaming; variations between process and product gaming; and the overlaps and divergences between research, educational, and training wargames. Chapter 2 traced a largely elided history of wargaming in the academic discipline of IR and set out the origins of the current wargaming renaissance that began in 2014. It showed that the reinvigoration of wargames called for by then Secretary of Defense Chuck Hagel and Deputy Secretary Bob Work brought together the commercial gaming sector in a bid to game the human dimension, specifically critical thinking, managing complexity, and improving decision-making, and set out the methodological divide between those who view wargaming as an art and those for whom it is a science.

Politics of Play. Aggie Hirst, Oxford University Press. © Oxford University Press 2024.
DOI: 10.1093/oso/9780197629192.003.0010

From there, the book took a deep dive into theories and philosophies of play. It did so because if we are to understand wargaming and interrupt its production of reality and people, we must explore the politics and possibilities of play. Establishing a genealogy of play from the Presocratics to the modern phenomenologists, Chapter 3 traced a dialectical struggle of two discursive play modes—the Apollonian and the Dionysian—through the Western philosophical tradition. Building upon Nietzsche's reintroduction of the Dionysian, and moving beyond it by cultivating a deconstructive player subject, Chapter 4 set out a new third mode of play—deconstructive play—grounded in the thought of Jacques Derrida. It argued that deconstructive play can be mobilized to introduce cracks in the closed system of any given game, exposing and contesting its hidden assumptions, politics, and power relations.

Having established this philosophical inheritance and offered this retheorization of play, the book sought to operationalize this deconstructive mode of thinking by critically analyzing how wargaming works to produce people. Chapter 5 argued that wargaming subjectifies players by intervening in their cognitive realms, generating buy-in and engagement, playing iteratively, employing critical thinking, and promoting retention. It then returned to the work of Der Derian and Baudrillard to examine how wargames produce realities, both in terms of effecting specific changes in the geopolitical landscapes and contributing to the broader production of hyperreality in the age of simulation. From there, Chapter 6 showed how wargames produce people by engaging the affective realm, including values, motivations, and identities. To do so, it examined the relationships between designers, sponsors, facilitators, and players, drawing out a series of hierarchies and power relations that are usually ignored. It argued that by promoting Apollonian play, forcing player decisions, and generating synthetic experience, gaming impacts upon players in ways that are productive of subjectivity. By seeking to intervene at the levels of their choices, beliefs, and even identities, it argued that players are deliberately targeted as part of military wargaming. To that degree, following Gadamer's argument, wargaming plays its players.

The final two chapters of the book drew out two key drivers of military wargaming, playing to win and the state of immersion, developing a deconstructive reading of each. Chapter 7 argued that the imperative to win—that is, the pursuit of victory conditions—is cultivated through systems of reward and punishment, profusive forms of loss and failure, and systematic iterative irresolution that at once incentivizes, precludes, and devalues winning. Finally, Chapter 8 demonstrated that immersion functions as a tool of player subjectification through the use of narrative, through the (apparent) exercise of choice, and by encouraging the player to refer to their in-game persona in the first person. It concluded that immersive play desubjectifies players by circumventing their self-conscious and self-reflective capacities, while at same moment resubjectifying players by instilling in them reflex actions. Accordingly, the final two chapters show how the winning imperative and immersion work to promote wargames' production of people.

In developing this argument, this book has sought to intervene in academic debates in IR and associated fields by shifting the focus from leisure to military gaming and introducing the study of play; to open up new critical debates among wargames professionals by interrogating the power relations and politics at work in their craft; and to invite global gaming communities to explore the critical properties of deconstructive play as a tool by means of which gameplay and gamespace might become more reflexive.

An Academic Field of Wargaming

At the time of writing, the US military wargaming renaissance has been under way for a decade. During this period, demand for professional wargaming across the military has increased, both in the US and elsewhere. In NATO, the Audacious Wargaming project was launched in 2022, bringing together more than two hundred participants from twenty member states with a view to creating an alliance-wide capability that "includes state-of-the-art wargaming practices and enables collaborative capabilities in industry partners to ensure the Alliance can defend against any adversary—now and in the future" (NATO Allied Command Transformation 2022). As tensions mount in Europe surrounding NATO expansion in response to Russia's invasion of Ukraine, wargaming could play a vital role in examining the consequences of Scandinavian nations joining the alliance. The Indian military has recently signed a contract for a new AI-enabled wargame center (IMR Reporter 2022), while China is transforming the training of the People's Liberation Army by seeking to "learn warfare from the laboratory" using wargaming (Kania and McCaslin 2021). In Australia, analysts are calling for a possible Chinese invasion of Taiwan to be more extensively wargamed (Schultz 2023), for the purposes of both deterrence and preparedness. Existing wargaming

conducted at the Center for Strategic and International Studies suggests that
such a conflict would involve huge costs for the US, Japan, and Taiwan, with
Australia likely being drawn in as well (Hannaford 2023).

In light of these developments, the CoP is currently concerned with how
to avoid a dip in the sine wave of popularity characteristic of US military
wargaming since the mid-twentieth century. In order to do this, several issue
areas have been identified. Advocates have argued that wargaming should
be applied to emergent security issues in novel ways. Some in the CoP have
identified the cyber domain as a key area of wargaming expansion. Benjamin
Schechter writes: "Cyber security is hard, but cyber wargaming can
help. . . . [C]yber wargames provide a unique vehicle for cyber experts and
non-experts to work together towards resolving common problems" (2020).
Others have argued that wargaming is well placed to explore the emergent
issue of artificial intelligence. For example, Paul K. Davis and Paul Bracken
have set out how AI might be usefully employed in wargaming scenarios
involving weapons of mass destruction, including as "decision aids" that
could, for example, compute possible enemy reactions to a move (2022).
Similarly, Danielle C. Tarraf and colleagues outline that experimental wargaming can show how AI-enabled vehicles with situational awareness perform in company-level engagements (Tarraf et al. 2020).

In order to meet these new demands, and if the CoP wishes to more
conclusively demonstrate the added value of military gaming in general,
further academic research will be key across a number of areas. While anecdotal evidence of wargaming efficacy as a research, teaching, and training
tool is plentiful, this claim has yet to be rigorously academically scrutinized
and demonstrated. Scholarly research on wargaming can be divided into at
least two approaches. The first approach concerns the study of wargaming
as an academic method to be utilized by scholars and practitioners to create
knowledge. Such knowledge might be within the academy in a discipline like
IR, psychology, or economics, or it might be within a military or business
institution for the purposes of combat readiness or corporate competition.

While many such institutions already rely on wargaming, unlike other research methods like interviews, case studies, or regression analysis, a body of
literature that sets out best practices and provides criteria by which good and
bad versions might be judged does not yet exist. If a researcher wants, for example, to know how to conduct good participant observations in the course
of a research project, they can take courses and read scholarly publications
to learn how to do it effectively. Similar expertise and guidance must be

generated if wargaming is to become a comparably credible academic method. A handful of scholars have, in recent years, begun to do precisely this. Key here are Ellie Bartels' exploration of the philosophies of science for research gaming (Bartels 2020), David Banks' typology of wargaming's "methodological machineries" (Banks 2022), and Lin-Greenberg and colleagues' tracing of how game validity might be conferred (Lin-Greenberg, Pauly, and Schneider 2022). If wargaming is to become a broadly accepted, rigorous method of inquiry, much more work will be necessary to build on these first steps.

It is worth bearing in mind as this work gets under way, however, that methods too come with a politics. As Claudia Aradau and Jef Huysmans have argued (2014), methods and methodological claims can often serve as disciplinary mechanisms that privilege some forms of scholarly inquiry and writing over others. This is most obviously in positivism's broad dismissal of postpositivist and critical approaches across IR and in other social science fields. As a field of wargaming develops, this caution must be borne in mind so that scholarship and practice can be made more rigorous and reliable but methodological variety and praxiological contestation remain.

The second approach to the academic exploration of wargaming is to treat it as an object of study. Research in this area does not seek to make wargaming more methodologically rigorous but rather treats it as a phenomenon to be empirically documented and critically analyzed. This could involve studies of gaming in particular parts of the world, along the lines of specific security issues, or in various institutional settings and sectors. It might involve exploring the ethics of wargaming from both historical and contemporary perspectives, considering not just how to integrate ethics into wargaming but the ethics of wargaming itself (Allen and Baker 2022). It could trace the place of gender, colonialism, and other forms of hierarchical power relations at work in wargaming and examine the effects of these on foreign and security policy, as well as on those who play wargames.

For my part, I seek to cultivate a critical community of wargames researchers employing reflexivist approaches to continue to interrogate the politics of play and games. While advocates in both the military and commercial sectors espouse the freedom and agency of their medium, this book has shown that wargames conform to the logic of the hyperreal model, in which the dialectical play of meaning is replaced by a totalized system. Games produce outcomes and conclusions that are delimited in advance by the assumptions and power relations coded in by designers and executed by facilitators. This is not to say that the results of wargames are known in advance, but rather that the range of possible outcomes and insights is circumscribed by the rules and norms of those who create and run those games.

If a wargame exploring nuclear deterrence, for example, is developed in accordance with realist assumptions—including that the state and/or combatants are the only actors that need to be modeled, that states act in the pursuit of self-interest alone, that the international system is one of anarchy and self-help, and so on—then the rules, incentives, and outcomes of the game will serve to pre-produce these assumptions. Far from value-neutral and apolitical, then, games are a "utopia of rules" (Graeber 2015) that contribute to producing and maintaining the world around us. An academic literature that takes seriously the political character of wargames does not yet exist. Accordingly, as the practice of wargaming continues to proliferate, the scholarly community must get to work producing it.

A further key consideration is how to move beyond advocacy and engage people who are not already convinced of wargaming's utility or importance. While most wargames practitioners and proponents are fans of gaming, both professionally and recreationally, liking games is not the only reason to study them. A good number of people, myself among them, are not habitual or natural gamers. While some take to games intuitively and easily, others are left cold. Games are, however—and in part for this very reason—fascinating. One need not enjoy playing games to conduct research on them. Indeed, there may be advantages to examining games from a perspective other than that of advocate. Opening the field of study to those who are not already committed gamers would only strengthen the research produced, in my view. Among its other goals, this book seeks to show why games are important and interesting, beyond any particular individual's like or dislike of them.

This opens up the question of why it is that some people enjoy games, while others are ambivalent and still others resistant or avoidant. Wong has long argued for the integration of psychologists into the games research community in order to address the question of whether and how wargaming works from the perspective of learning and innovation (Wong and Heath 2021). Research conducted in this field might be able to shed light on why some take to gaming more than others. If Bogost's analysis discussed in Chapter 7 is correct, one answer to this is that people enjoy games not because they are fun but because of the pleasures of limits. In his account, constraints and limits create possibility spaces through which players can inject their ideas and interventions into a game. As he puts it, the "pleasure of limits arises no matter how easy or hard, no matter how automatic or arduous the process is of discovering something new about the system contained by its magic circle" (Bogost 2016, 172).

This argument appears to suggest that the pleasure of games relies on a degree of trust or acceptance on the part of the player. It implies that pleasure will be granted if players embrace, and explore within, the parameters of a game. What this argument lacks, however, is an imperative to critically evaluate the game, its objectives, directives, and assumptions. There is, then, a certain obedience or submission that must take place on the part of the player for the game to generate pleasure for the player. Perhaps it is the case that those of a more suspicious disposition find it harder to enact this initial acceptance, retaining a discomfort with the process of taking on the game's roles and missions that prevents them from doing so. While I can imagine that overcoming this resistance might be an objective of military gamers, I am interested in the politics of this resistance and think it might be of value as part of the deconstructive play mode set out in this book.

As part of this, the question of how players play also requires further scholarly attention. Players play differently depending on where, when, and with whom, they are playing. While, as Chapter 8 explored, gameplay can generate a sleepy and disconnected experience of immersion, it is also the case that players—to differing degrees—remain alert to the circumstances within which they play. A military officer might, for example, play a given game differently if they are playing with friends and family rather than in the course of their job. Military players might play a game differently depending on the urgency and realism of a situation—for example, if a given game was being played while a war was under way rather than in peacetime. Players who have firsthand experience of combat might play differently than those for whom war is an easy hypothetical. When considering these questions, we must continue to pose the question "Where do we go when we play?," but we must also refine it to examine which of our multiple selves plays in a given instance.

A further important area of research is that of the role of diversity in gaming. It is clear that the US military wargaming community is overwhelmingly white and male; accordingly, it is important to work to improve representation of other groups. This is true both for the obvious normative reasons and because a concentration of people with broadly similar views and assumptions tends to bias a game in specific ways. Including a wider range of people from different gender, class, religious, ethnic, and linguistic (to mention just a few) backgrounds is likely to introduce a greater range of ideas, options, and pathways. It will, however, be important not to fall into the trap of crude essentialisms by assuming, for example, that having one or more Indian people in the room will give a clear sense of how India might behave in a given game, or having more women in a game will lead to more peaceable outcomes. While increasing the numbers of currently underrepresented groups is important, generalizing assumptions about who they are and how they will play must be avoided.

A further area of study relating to diversity surrounds the issue of whether and how the different security concerns of marginalized groups—for example, LGBT+ people—are factored into games and the strategies and operational plans that emerge from them. Reflecting the erasures that occur in traditional approaches to security studies that focus on the level of the state, it will be important to explore, and promote, the integration of human security concerns into games to explore how specific groups might be affected in a given crisis or conflict. It is also vital that efforts to improve diversity do not become an alibi through which military violence is legitimized – whether within or outside of gaming. Adding minority groups to flawed security or foreign policy platforms or military interventions can do nothing to mitigate the latters' ill-effects, as critiques of "pinkwashing" and "purplewashing" have established.

Across these varied research topics, the establishment of an academic (sub)field of wargaming will be vital in building a community of world-leading scholars and producing reliable and useful knowledge about the rigorous application of wargaming to pressing global issues.

Deconstructing Deconstructive Play

In keeping with the deconstructive mode of thinking advocated in this book, it is important to push at the limits of the argument offered here in order to expose its assumptions and lay the groundwork for further analysis and critique. As Derrida explains, deconstruction can be understood as a "principle of interminable analysis: an axiom of interminability, perhaps" (1998a, 33). Because the work of deconstruction is never finished, but rather continues disrupting any and all theories and claims, it is vital to expose one's own arguments to it as much as those offered by others. Far from a fruitless unpicking or destruction that leads nowhere, such movements are generative and productive of new insights and arguments, as demonstrated in Chapter 4. Deconstruction is not destruction; rather, it involves building, disassembling, and rebuilding, creating things anew all the while. And, of course, this is precisely how academic debate works; to scrutinize and expose the assumptions and oversights of a treatise or text is not to obliterate it but rather to build upon it.

As Terry Eagleton has argued, and as I have discussed elsewhere (Hirst 2015) while on the one hand deconstruction appears to be an "extraordinary modest proposal: a sort of patient, probing reformism of the text," on the other hand this framing ignores the other fact of deconstruction which is its hair-raising *radicalism*—the nerve and daring with which it knocks the stuffing out of every smug concept and leaves the well-groomed text shamefully dishevelled. It ignores, in short, the *madness* and violence of deconstruction, its scandalous urge to think the unthinkable, the flamboyance with which it poses itself on the very brink of meaning and dances there, pounding away at the crumbling cliff edge beneath its feet and prepared to fall with it into the sea of unlimited semiosis or schizophrenia. (Eagleton 1981, 134, emphases in original)

Deconstruction can allow us to glimpse the dynamic, if paradoxical, play of constitutive concepts and thereby problematize the hegemonic discourses and forces on which they rely. But by first inverting, then subverting, the reason/play binary, I advocate a mode of deconstructive thinking that functions—on an ongoing basis—as play.

So, what deconstructive critiques might be made of the mode of play proffered in this book? First, we might return to Soderman's argument that, far from a site of critique or challenge to the status quo, play has always already been recuperated and put to work in the service of capital and governance. As he puts it: "[P]layfulness *is* the dominant reality, and what we need is a critique of playfulness, not its uncritical embrace. . . . [A certain] playful mindset [is] a key attribute that drives and sustains ludic capitalism. . . . [P]olitics needs to shape and channel play and flow to offer an alternative world beyond the precarity of ludic capitalism" (Soderman 2021, 24, emphasis in original).

In response to this, I would argue that while it is always possible for play—especially if understood, as discussed in Chapter 4, as gameplay—to be captured and put to work in the service of a particular aim or project, if we decouple play from games, it can function precisely as a mode of critique and politicization of the kind Soderman advocates. Disentangled from current conflations with gameplay, play understood as the dynamic movements of thought, meaning, and subjectivity can be a powerful tool in the disruption of the enclosures of games. This book calls, therefore, for a form of "playification" to counter the widespread gamification that is aligned with conventional modes of ordering and governance, and suggests we should shift our subject position from being gamers to being players who play *with* games.

A second auto-deconstructive reflection concerns the question of resistance. I have argued that deconstructive play can be read as a site or mode of resistance to the passive acceptance of a game's goals, politics, and assumptions. But this leaves unposed the question of existing forms of resistance at work in wargaming and broader gaming worlds. By no means do I intend to claim that deconstructive play is the only possible way to critically engage with, and problematize, games. Insofar as games are cultural artifacts and non-linear communication devices, there exists a wide range of repurposing and subversive practices.

I have written elsewhere about the uses to which veterans put games in promotion of community-building, therapeutic relief, and suicide prevention, which serve to expose the limitations of official reintegration and mental health programs (Hirst 2021). As noted in the Introduction, the veterans' gaming organization Stack Up was founded in 2015 by Stephen Machuga, a former Army infantry/intelligence officer who claims that videogames saved his life (Machuga 2015). Experiencing debilitating mental health issues that left him unable to leave his house after his return from Iraq, Steve explains that gaming helped him manage "the anxiety that living in a combat zone for a year built up" (Machuga 2015). Run by a core team of ex-military and civilian staff, Stack Up has sponsored 346 community events across its twenty-nine chapters in the contiguous United States, in addition to those in Canada, Australia, New Zealand, Japan, South Korea, and Scotland, and provided support to 35,944 service members and veterans on and after deployment through gaming and gaming culture. By countering the instrumentalizing elements of official transition programs, this project of mutual assistance amounts to a powerful form of everyday resistance. Unsettling critical-scholarly assumptions about what resistance looks like and where it takes place, these practices show that it is possible to resist the embodied alienations of militarism from within (Hirst 2021). They also shows that resistance can and does take place beyond a deconstructive mode of thinking.

A third deconstructive challenge relates to the question of how a play mode that punctuates immersion with reflexivity might work. On the one hand, it might be asked whether such a process creates sufficient space for substantive critical reflection. If one simply takes a few seconds to think about what one is doing in a game, and why, this may lead only to a moment of awareness after which the game proceeds as it would have done anyway. On the other hand, it is possible that interrupting immersive play to think actively and critically about the game's power relations, incentivizations, and assumptions will lead to gameplay being lost altogether. If the game is interrupted entirely, this might mean the player is no longer playing, so there is nothing to critically deconstruct.

One solution to this might be to leave deconstructive critique until after the end of a game, augmenting and integrating further critical layers into the after-action review or hotwash. While this might be a useful step in its own right, I wager that while the precise balance between immersed gameplay and playful deconstructive reflection cannot perhaps be prescribed in advance, experimenting with these experiential modes during gameplay is compatible both with an enjoyable immersive experience and with self-conscious and deliberate actions grounded in critical thinking. While one might well interrupt gameplay in doing so, one may remain within deconstructive play as such a process takes place.

A fourth question is that of for whom deconstructive play is useful. While it might make good sense to encourage recreational gamers to think more reflexively about the politics and power relations at work in their games, and to play with their games, military gaming cannot incorporate such exploratory forms of play. As Losh notes, "[G]ames developed by the US military actively discourage transgressive play for obvious reasons. The chain of command depends on submitting to orders from those in authority without questioning those commands. For example, a player in *America's Army* who experiments by shooting his commanding officer in the first few seconds of the game forecloses any future opportunities for learning, because he immediately finds himself in the brig" (2005, 5). Here I would say that while players in the military may not, especially in the most product-oriented and deterministic games, be able to actively play transgressively while training, this does not prevent them from thinking critically about a game's design or execution during and after the training event. While they may be obliged to play "uncritically" in the course of their duties, this does not prevent them from reflecting deconstructively upon the games they play. Deconstructive play is, I would suggest, useful to military personnel whether within or outside of their official capacities, as well as to leisure gamers.

In addition, I would argue that deconstructive play can be made use of in IR classrooms in which games are used. The starting point for many IR instructors appears to be a problem engaging students in course material, especially when it comes to theory. Richard Arnold states that "one of the challenges of teaching American undergraduates 'Introduction to International Relations' is finding a way to make the topic and themes seem relevant to students" (2015, 162). Some go further, arguing that educators "battle against an ever-growing number of students with increasingly short attention spans who often expect education to be entertaining above all else" (Baranowski and Weir 2015, 391). Accordingly, it has been argued that games "simplify the world and focus on certain relational and structural issues while downplaying others—making them perfect for simpler introductory courses, where the aim is to familiarize students with the basics of international relations as quickly as possible" (Romano 2014, n.p.).

I disagree with this framing and account of how games might be useful. As I have set out elsewhere, I am wholly convinced that students have both a good deal of experience of global politics in their everyday lives before they study it at university and a perfectly adequate attention span with which to explore it if they are encouraged to do so (Hirst et al. 2023). I believe also that the best use to which games could be put is not as a novel way to impart conventional theory but rather as political artifacts to be deconstructed. For example, while it is often suggested that *Risk* might be useful for teaching realism, a more reflexive form of gameplay could enable a critique of the game's imperial logics and teach postcolonial and decolonial theory. When properly supported in becoming critical and reflexive thinkers, students can find their confidence and interest in the subject matter growing immensely.

A fifth issue relates to my claim that it matters more how, as opposed to what, we play, specifically the possibility that it overlooks the ways in which game design can itself encourage players toward critique and reflexivity. As discussed in Chapter 8, Soderman looks to designers to produce games that encourage players to engage critically with the subject matter, in some cases regarding the flow and play modes they experience and in others to communicate a political message. In doing so, he proposed that different forms of games—rather than play—hold the key to addressing the enclosure of games in capital and profit. I wager, in contrast, that we need not wait for designers to change their approach; rather, we can engage deconstructively with any and all games, regardless of whether or not a designer has encouraged us to play reflexively. However, while I maintain that such reflexivity does not depend on facilitation by designers, the proliferation of critical forms of design can only be a good thing. As Flanagan points out:

> I have not played many wargames in which players literally stop conflict by having a moving aesthetic experience that changes their worldview. I have not played a wargame in which the public acts as a real player in the game, and surprises the powers-that-be with an effective pacifist move. Our models for wargames need to continue to evolve using unusual, creative solutions to problem solving. (Flanagan 2016, 705)

The problem is that games—like any text—carry within them the assumptions and categories of their designers. If a game is designed with realist assumptions—such as that the state is the key actor (and hence the only one that need be represented), that states are motivated by self-interest alone, that the international system is akin to a Hobbesian state of nature, and so on—and these are taken as given, the solutions you will get to the problems examined will be circumscribed in advance by these assumptions. To that extent, wargamers' critiques of the impossibility of generating new knowledge in modeling and simulation—because you get out simply what is coded in— actually applies to wargames themselves. Consequently, changing the theoretical and conceptual assumptions sutured into wargames by their designers will be key to moving beyond the constraints of realist assumptions that have been widely, and convincingly, critiqued since the 1980s (Ashley 1984; Cohn 1987; Tickner 1988).

If the argument proffered in this book is correct and wargames produce subjectivity, this raises the question of what, through our gameplay, we are turning ourselves into. It is often assumed that games are purposeless and effectless—after all, "it's only a game." From our vantage point in the era of simulation, so powerfully elucidated by Baudrillard, games are now more than ever serious business in their production of both hyperreality and people. It is my wager that play can conjure relational movements of the kind banished by closed systems of simulation. It is my hope that by means of a deconstructive play mode, we can glimpse something of the ways our games produce our realities and ourselves. In doing so, it is perhaps possible to reintroduce the difference, tension, and contradiction necessary for something other than the reproduction of the same.

References

Aarseth, E. 2007. "I Fought the Law: Transgressive Play and The Implied Player." Paper delivered at DiGRA Conference, University of Tokyo.

Ackerman, D. 2000. *Deep Play*. New York: Vintage Books.

Aistrope, T. 2019. "Popular Culture, the Body and World Politics." *European Journal of International Relations* 26(1): 163–186.

Allen, J. and D.-P. Baker. 2022. "Can the Robots Save the City? Ethics, Urban Warfare, and Autonomous Weapons." In *The Ethics of Urban Warfare*, edited by D. Stanar and K. Tonn, 172–186. Leiden: Brill Nijhoff.

Allen, T. B. 1989. *War Games: The Secret World of the Creators, Players, and Policy Makers Rehearsing World War III Today*. New York: Berkley Books.

Anderson, N. 2003. "The Ethical Possibilities of the Subject as Play: In Nietzsche and Derrida." *Journal of Nietzsche Studies* 26: 79–90.

Anderson, N. 2006. "Free-Play? Fair-Play! Defending Derrida." *Social Semiotics* 16(3): 407–420.

Antley, J. 2016. "Struggling with Deep Play: Utilizing Twilight Struggle for Historical Inquiry." In *Zones of Control: Perspectives on Wargaming*, edited by P. Harrigan and M. G. Kirschenbaum, 463–470. Cambridge: MIT Press.

Appleget, J., F. Cameron, R. E. Burks, and J. Kline. 2016. "Wargaming at the Naval Postgraduate School." *Journal of Cyber Security and Information Systems* 4: 18–23.

Aradau, C. and J. Huysmans. 2014. "Critical Methods in International Relations: The Politics of Techniques, Devices and Acts." *European Journal of International Relations* 20(3): 596–619.

Army War College. 2015. *Strategic Wargaming Series Handbook*. Contributions by J. Brashear et al. Edited by J. Markley. Carlisle: Army War College.

Arnold, R. 2013. "Where's the Diplomacy in Diplomacy? Using a Classic Board Game in 'Introduction to International Relations.'" *PS: Political Science and Politics* 48(1): 162–166.

Asal, V. 2005. "Playing Games with International Relations." *International Studies Perspectives* 6(3): 359–373.

Asal, V. and J. Kratoville. 2013. "Constructing International Relations Simulations: Examining the Pedagogy of IR Simulations Through a Constructivist Learning Theory Lens." *Journal of Political Science Education* 9(2): 132–143.

Ash, J. 2010. "Architectures of Affect: Anticipating and Manipulating the Event in Processes of Videogame Design and Testing." *Environment and Planning D* 28(4): 653–671.

Ash, J. 2013. "Technologies of Captivation: Videogames and the Attunement of Affect." *Body and Society* 19(1): 27–51.

Ashley, R. K. 1983. "The Eye of Power: The Politics of World Modeling." *International Organization* 37(3): 495–535.

Ashley, R. K. 1984. "The Poverty of Neorealism." *International Organization* 38(2): 225–286.

Augier, M. and S. F. X. Barrett. 2021. "General Anthony Zinni (Ret.) on Wargaming Iraq, Millennium Challenge, and Competition." *CIMSEC*, October 18. https://cimsec.org/general-anthony-zinni-ret-on-wargaming-iraq-millennium-challenge-and-competition/.

Axelos, K. 1971. "Planetary Interlude." In *Game, Play, Literature*, edited by J. Ehrmann, 6–18. Boston: Beacon Press.

Aycock, A. 1993. "Derrida/Fort-Da: Deconstructing Play." *Postmodern Culture* 3(2): n.p.

Bae, S. 2018. "Just Let Them Compete: Raising the Next Generation of Wargamers." *War on the Rocks*, October 9. https://warontherocks.com/2018/10/just-let-them-compete-raising-the-next-generation-of-wargamers/.

Banks, D. 2022. "Begin at the Beginning: The Methodological Machinery of Wargaming and its Epistemological Implications." Under review with *International Studies Review*.

Banks, M. H., A. J. R. Groom, and A. N. Oppenheim. 1968. "Gaming and Simulation in International Relations." *Political Studies* XVI(1): 1–17.

Baranowski, M. K. and K. A. Weir. 2015. "Political Simulations: What We Know, What We Think We Know, and What We Still Need to Know." *Journal of Political Science Education* 11(4): 391–403.

Barbrook, R. 2014. *Class Wargames: Ludic Subversion Against Spectacular Capitalism*. Wivenhoe: Minor Compositions.

Bartels, E. M. 2016. "Inhabited Models and Irregular Warfare Games: An Approach to Educational and Analytical Gaming at the US Department of Defense." In *Zones of Control: Perspectives on Wargaming*, edited by P. Harrigan and M. G. Kirschenbaum, 503–512. Cambridge: MIT Press.

Bartels, E. M. 2017. "Adding Shots on Target: Wargaming Beyond the Game." *War on the Rocks*, October 9. https://warontherocks.com/2017/10/adding-shots-on-target-wargaming-beyond-the-game/.

Bartels, E. M. 2018. "Building a Pipeline of Wargaming Talent: A Two-Track Solution." *War on the Rocks*, November 14. https://warontherocks.com/2018/11/building-a-pipeline-of-wargaming-talent-a-two-track-solution/.

Bartels, E. M. 2020. "Building Better Games for National Security Policy Analysis: Towards a Social Scientific Approach." PhD dissertation, RAND Pardee Graduate School.

Barthes, R. 1985. *The Rustle of Language*. Translated by R. Howard. New York: Hill and Wang.

Barzashka, I. 2019. "Wargaming: How to Turn Vogue into Science." *Bulletin of the Atomic Scientists*, March 15. https://thebulletin.org/2019/03/wargaming-how-to-turn-vogue-into-science/.

Baudrillard, J. 1983. *Simulations*. Translated by P. Foss, P. Patton, and P. Beitchman. New York: Semiotext(e).

Behler, E. 1991. *Confrontations: Derrida/Heidegger/Nietzsche*. Stanford: Stanford University Press.

Berents, H. and B. Keogh. 2018. "Virtuous, Virtual, but Not Visceral: (Dis)Embodied Viewing in Military-Themed Videogames." *Critical Studies on Security* 6(3): 366–369.

Berger, P. 2008. "There and Back Again: Reuse, Signifiers and Consistency in Created Game Spaces." In *Computer Games as a Sociocultural Phenomenon: Games Without Frontiers, War Without Tears*, edited by A. Jahn-Sudmann and R. Stockmann, 47–55. Basingstoke: Palgrave Macmillan.

Bessner, D. 2014. "Weimar Social Science in Cold War America: The Case of the Political-Military Game." German Historical Institute Washington Bulletin, Supplements Bd. 10: 91–109.

Bestard, J. J. 2016. "Air Force Research Laboratory Innovation: Pushing the Envelope in Analytical Wargaming." CSIAC Journal of Cyber Security and Information Systems 4(3): 12–17.

Bitan, S. 2012. "Winnicott and Derrida: Development of Logic-of-Play." International Journal of Psychoanalysis 93(1): 29–51.

Bogost, I. 2008. Unit Operations: An Approach to Videogame Criticism. Cambridge: MIT Press.

Bogost, I. 2010. Persuasive Games: The Expressive Power of Videogames. Cambridge: MIT Press.

Bogost, I. 2016. Play Anything: The Pleasure of Limits, the Uses of Boredom, and the Secret of Games. New York: Basic Books.

Bogue, R. 1994. "Foucault, Deleuze, and the Playful Fold of the Self." In The Play of the Self, edited by R. Bogue and M. Spariosu, 1–22. Albany: State University of New York Press.

Bolter, J. D. 2019. The Digital Plenitude: The Decline of Elite Culture and the Rise of Digital Media. Cambridge: MIT Press.

Boluk, S. and P. LeMieux. 2017. Metagaming: Playing, Competing, Spectating, Cheating, Trading, Making, and Breaking Videogames. Minneapolis: University of Minnesota Press.

Botz-Bornstein, T. 2013. "Speech, Writing, and Play in Gadamer and Derrida." Cosmos and History: The Journal of Natural and Social Philosophy 9(1): 249–264.

Bousquet, A. 2015. "A Short History of Wargames." In Simulation, Exercise, Operations, edited by R. Mackey, 13–19. Falmouth: Urbanomic.

Bousquet, A., J. Grove, and N. Shah. 2020. "Becoming War: Towards a Martial Empiricism." Security Dialogue 51(2–3): 99–118.

Boyd, A. J. and M. Kimball. 2017. "The Future Operating Environment and the Third Offset." In Closer than You Think: The Implications of the Third Offset Strategy for the U.S. Army, edited by S. R. White Jr., 3–14. Carlisle Barracks: US Army War College Press.

Brown, M. L. 2017. "Never Alone: (Re)Coding the Comic Holotrope of Survivance." Transmotion 3(1): 22–44.

Brynen, R. 2015. "Role-Play Games and Simulations in International Relations: An Overview." Revista española de desarrollo y cooperación 35: 15–26.

Brynen, R. 2016. "Gaming the Nonkinetic." In Zones of Control: Perspectives on Wargaming, edited by P. Harrigan and M. G. Kirschenbaum, 485–502. Cambridge: MIT Press.

Bucholtz, A. 2023. "History Is Political: Games Are Propaganda." Conflicts of Interest 7. https://sdhist.com/history-is-political-games-are-propaganda/.

Burke, S. and A. H. Cameron. 2022. "Wargaming Climate Change: Who Plays for the Red Team?" War on the Rocks, November 9. https://warontherocks.com/2022/11/wargaming-climate-change-who-plays-for-the-red-team/.

Burns, S. 2015. War Gamers Handbook: A Guide for Professional War Gamers. Technical Report, Naval War College.

Burwick, F. 1990. "The Plagiarism of Play: The Unacknowledged Source of Gadamer's Ontological Argument in 'Truth and Method.'" Pacific Coast Philology 25(1–2): 60–68.

Buse, P. 1996. "Nintendo and Telos: Will You Ever Reach the End?" Cultural Critique 34 (Autumn): 163–184.

Caffrey, M. B. 2019. *On Wargaming: How Wargames Have Shaped History and How They May Shape the Future*. Newport: Naval War College Press.

Caillois, R. 2001. *Man, Play and Games*. Translated by M. Barash. Urbana: University of Illinois Press.

Caldwell, L. and T. Lenoir. 2016. "Wargaming Futures: Naturalizing the New American Way of War." In *Zones of Control: Perspectives on Wargaming*, edited by P. Harrigan and M. G. Kirschenbaum, 253–280. Cambridge: MIT Press.

Carter, S. 2023. "U.S. 'Concerned' as South Africa to Hold War Games with Russia, China on Ukraine Invasion Anniversary." *CBS News*, January 23. https://www.cbsnews.com/news/ukraine-news-russia-war-south-africa-china-military-exercise-us-concerned/.

Caso, F. and C. Hamilton, eds. 2015. *Popular Culture and World Politics: Theories, Methods, Pedagogies*. Bristol: E-International Relations Publishing.

Césaire, A. 2000. *Discourse on Colonialism*. Translated by Joan Pinkham. New York: Monthly Review Press.

Chess, S. and A. Shaw. 2015. "A Conspiracy of Fishes, or, How We Learned to Stop Worrying About #GamerGate and Embrace Hegemonic Masculinity." *Journal of Broadcasting & Electronic Media* 59(1): 208–220.

Christiansson, M. 2018. "Defense Planning Beyond Rationalism: The Third Offset Strategy as a Case of Metagovernance." *Defence Studies* 18(3): 262–278.

Ciută, F. 2016. "Call of Duty: Playing Video Games with IR." *Millennium: Journal of International Studies* 44(2): 197–215.

Cohen, R. A. 1983. "The Privilege of Reason and Play: Derrida and Levinas." *Tijdschrift voor Filosofie* 45(2): 242–255.

Cohn, C. 1987. "Sex and Death in the Rational World of Defense Intellectuals." *Signs* 12(4): 687–718.

Coker, C. 2013. *Warrior Geeks: How the 21st-Century Technology Is Changing the Way We Fight and Think About War*. London: C. Hurst.

Colder Carras, M., A. Kalbarczyk, K. Wells, J. Banks, R. Kowert, C. Gillespie, and C. Latkin. 2018a. "Connection, Meaning, and Distraction: A Qualitative Study of Video Game Play and Mental Health Recovery in Veterans Treated for Mental and/or Behavioral Health Problems." *Social Science and Medicine* 216: 124–132.

Colder Carras, M., A. J. Van Rooij, D. Spruijt-Metz, J. Kvedar, M. D. Griffiths, Y. Carabas, and A. Labrique. 2018b. "Commercial Video Games as Therapy: A New Research Agenda to Unlock the Potential of a Global Pastime." *Frontiers in Psychiatry* 8: 1–7.

Compton, J. 2018. "Working Group I: Wargaming and Analysis." In *MORS Wargaming III Special Meeting October 2017*, edited by P. Pournelle and H. Deaton, 24–27. Alexandria: MORS.

Condis, M. 2018. *Gaming Masculinity: Trolls, Fake Geeks, and the Gendered Battle for Online Culture*. Iowa City: University of Iowa Press.

Consalvo, M. 2009. "There Is No Magic Circle." *Games and Culture* 4(4): 408–417.

Coplin, W. D. 1966. "Inter-Nation Simulation and Contemporary Theories of International Relations." *American Political Science Review* 60(3): 562–578.

Costikyan, G. 2013. *Uncertainty in Games*. Cambridge: MIT Press.

Cremin, C. 2016. *Exploring Videogames with Deleuze and Guattari: Towards an Affective Theory of Form*. London: Routledge.

Crogan, P. 2011. *Gameplay Mode: War, Simulation, and Technoculture*. Minneapolis: University of Minnesota Press.

Crogan, P. and H. Kennedy. 2009. "Technologies Between Games and Culture." *Games and Culture* 4(2): 107–114.

Crogan, P. and S. Kinsley. 2012. "Paying Attention: Towards a Critique of the Attention Economy." *Culture Machine* 13: 1–29.

Csikszentmihalyi, M. 1975. *Beyond Boredom and Anxiety*. San Francisco: Jossey-Bass.

Curry, J. 2016. "The History of Wargaming Project." In *Zones of Control: Perspectives on Wargaming*, edited by P. Harrigan and M. G. Kirschenbaum, 33–42. Cambridge: MIT Press.

Daniel, J. F. and P. Musgrave. 2017. "Synthetic Experiences: How Popular Culture Matters for Images of International Relations." *International Studies Quarterly* 61(3): 503–516.

Davies, C. 2022. "US and South Korea Launch War Games for First Time in 4 Years." *Financial Times*, August 22. https://www.ft.com/content/da8e143e-f8f8-495d-9096-6da7621fd32c.

Davis, T. K. 2017. "Paul Davis's Personal Observations." In *MORS Wargaming Special Meeting October 2016*, edited by P. Pournelle, 13–16. Alexandria: MORS.

Davis, P. K. and P. Bracken. 2022. "Artificial Intelligence for Wargaming and Modeling." *Journal of Defense Modeling and Simulation*, online. https://doi.org/10.1177/154851 29211073126.

De Castell, S. and J. Jenson, eds. 2007. *Worlds in Play: International Perspectives on Digital Games Research*. New York: Peter Lang.

Deaton H. L. and S. M. Stetson. 2018. "Wargaming Workshop Overview and Summary of Events." In *MORS Wargaming III Special Meeting October 2017*, edited by P. Pournelle and H. Deaton, 13–20. Alexandria: MORS.

DeKoven, B. 2002. *The Well-Played Game: A Playful Path to Wholeness*. San Jose: Writers Club Press.

de Mul, J. 2005. "The Game of Life: Narrative and Ludic Identity Formation in Computer Games." In *Handbook of Computer Games Studies*, edited by J. Raessens and J. Goldstein, 251–266. Cambridge: MIT Press.

Der Derian, J. 1990a. "The (S)pace of International Relations: Simulation, Surveillance, and Speed." *International Studies Quarterly* 34(3): 295–310.

Der Derian, J. 1990b. "The Simulation Syndrome: From War Games to Game Wars." *Social Text* 24: 187–192.

Der Derian, J. 1997. "The Virtualization of Violence and the Disappearance of War." *Cultural Values* 1(2): 205–218.

Der Derian, J. 2000. "Virtuous War/Virtual Theory." *International Affairs* 76(4): 771–788.

Der Derian, J. 2003. "War as Game." *Brown Journal of World Affairs* 10(1): 37–48.

Der Derian, J. 2009. *Virtuous War: Mapping the Military-Industrial-Media-Entertainment Network*. New York: Routledge.

Derrida, J. 1982. *Margins of Philosophy*. Translated by A. Bass. Brighton: Harvester Press.

Derrida, J. 1985. *The Ear of the Other: Otobiography, Transference, Translation: Texts and Discussions with Jacques Derrida*. Edited by C. McDonald. New York: Schocken Books.

Derrida, J. 1997. *Of Grammatology*. Translated by G. C. Spivak. Baltimore: Johns Hopkins University Press.

Derrida, J. 1998a. *Resistances of Psychoanalysis*. Translated by P. Kamuf, P.-A. Braultt, and M. Naas. Stanford: Stanford University Press.

Derrida, J. 1998b. *Positions*. Translated by A. Bass. Chicago: University of Chicago Press.

Derrida, J. 2004. *Dissemination*. Translated by B. Johnson. London: Continuum.

Derrida, J. 2009. *Writing and Difference*. Translated by A. Bass. London: Routledge.

de Zamaróczy, N. 2017. "Are We What We Play? Global Politics in Historical Strategy Computer Games." *International Studies Perspectives* 18(2): 155–174.

Diamond, L. 2004. "What Went Wrong in Iraq." *Foreign Affairs* 83(5): 34–56.

Dillon, M. 2003. "Intelligence Incarnate: Martial Corporeality in the Digital Age." *Body and Society* 9(4): 123–147.

Dittmer, J. 2010. *Popular Culture, Geopolitics, and Identity*. Lanham: Rowman & Littlefield.

Dixon, B. 2014. "Gadamer and the Game of Dialectic in Plato's *Gorgias*." In *The Philosophy of Play*, edited by E. Ryall, W. Russell, and M. MacLean, 64–74. London: Routledge.

Dovey, J. and H. W. Kennedy. 2006. *Game Cultures: Computer Games as New Media*. Maidenhead: Open University Press.

Ducharme, L. and G. A. Fine. 1994. "No Escaping Obligation." In *The Play of the Self*, edited by R. Bogue and M. Spariosu, 89–111. Albany: State University of New York Press.

Dudziak, M. L. 2013. *War Time: An Idea, Its History, Its Consequences*. New York: Oxford University Press.

Duncan, M. C., G. E. Chick, and D. A. Aycock, eds. 1998. *Diversions and Divergences in Fields of Play*. Greenwich: Ablex.

Dunnigan, J. F. 2000. *Wargames Handbook: How to Play and Design Commercial and Professional Wargames*. San Jose: Writers Club Press.

Dunnigan, J. F. 2016. "Foreword: The Paper Time Machine Goes Electric." In *Zones of Control: Perspectives on Wargaming*, edited by P. Harrigan and M. G. Kirschenbaum, xxxiii–xxxviii. Cambridge: MIT Press.

Dursun, Y. 2007. "The Onto-Theological Origin of Play: Heraclitus and Plato." *Lingua Ac Communitas* 17: 69–78.

Dyer-Witheford, N. and G. De Peuter. 2009. *Games of Empire: Global Capitalism and Video Games*. Minneapolis: University of Minnesota Press.

Eagleton, T. 1981. *Walter Benjamin, or, Towards a Revolutionary Criticism*. London: Verso.

Echeruo, M. 1994. "Redefining the Ludic: Mimesis, Expression, and the Festival Mode." In *The Play of the Self*, edited by R. Bogue and M. Spariosu, 137–156. Albany: State University of New York Press.

Edery, D. and E. Mollick. 2009. *Changing the Game: How Video Games Are Transforming the Future of Business*. Upper Saddle River: FT Press.

Egan, D. 2014. "Playing Well: Wittgenstein's Language-Games and the Ethics of Discourse." In *The Philosophy of Play*, edited by E. Ryall, W. Russell, and M. MacLean, 54–63. London: Routledge.

Ehrmann, J. (ed.). 1971. *Game, Play, Literature*. Boston: Beacon Press.

Ehrmann J. 1971. "Homo Ludens Revisited." In *Game, Play, Literature*, edited by J. Ehrmann, 31–57. Boston: Beacon Press.

Elam, D. 1994. *Feminism and Deconstruction: Ms. En Abyme*. London: Routledge.

Eliason, W. T. 2017. "An Interview with Robert O. Work." *Joint Force Quarterly* 84(1): 6–11.

Ellman, J., S. Cohen, A. Hunter, K. Johnson, R. McCormick, and G. Sanders. 2017. *Defense Acquisition Trends, 2016: The End of the Contracting Drawdown*. CSIS Report. Lanham: Rowman and Littlefield.

Ellman, J., L. Samp, and G. Coll. 2017. *Assessing the Third Offset Strategy*. Washington: CSIS.

Emery, J. R. 2021. "Moral Choices Without Moral Language: 1950s Political-Military Wargaming at the RAND Corporation." *Texas National Security Review* 4(4): 11–31.

Ermi, L. and F. Mäyrä. 2007. "Fundamental Components of the Gameplay Experience: Analyzing Immersion." In *Worlds in Play: International Perspectives on Digital Games Research*, edited by S. De Castell and J. Jenson, 37–54. New York: Peter Lang.

Evans, D. 2020. "Basic Training." In *Making War on Bodies: Militarisation, Aesthetics and Embodiment in International Politics*, edited by C. Baker, 31–53. Edinburgh: Edinburgh University Press.

Fallows, J. 2004. "Blind into Baghdad." *The Atlantic*, January–February. https://www.thea tlantic.com/magazine/archive/2004/01/blind-into-baghdad/302860/.

Feezell, R. 2014. "A Pluralist Conception of Play." In *The Philosophy of Play*, edited by E. Ryall, W. Russell, and M. MacLean, 11–31. London: Routledge.

Ferguson, C. J. 2008. "The School Shooting/Violent Video Game Link: Causal Relationship or Moral Panic?" *Journal of Investigative Psychology and Offender Profiling* 5(1–2): 25–37.

Fink, E. 1971. "The Oasis of Happiness: Toward an ontology of play." In *Game, Play, Literature*, edited by E. Fink, 19–30. Boston: Beacon Press.

Flanagan, M. 2013. *Critical Play: Radical Game Design*. Cambridge: MIT Press.

Flanagan, M. 2016. "Practicing a New Wargame." In *Zones of Control: Perspectives on Wargaming*, edited by P. Harrigan and M. G. Kirschenbaum, 703–708. Cambridge: MIT Press.

Flint, K. 2014. "What's Play Got to Do with the Information Age?" In *The Philosophy of Play*, edited by E. Ryall, W. Russell, and M. MacLean, 152–163. London: Routledge.

Foley, J. A. 2016. "*Combat Commander*: Time to Throw Your Plan Away." In *Zones of Control: Perspectives on Wargaming*, edited by P. Harrigan and M. G. Kirschenbaum, 121–132. Cambridge: MIT Press.

Franklin, S. 2009. "We Need Radical Gameplay, Not Just Radical Graphics: Towards a Contemporary Minor Practice in Computer Gaming." *Symplokē* 17(1–2): 163–180.

Frasca, G. 2001. "Rethinking Agency and Immersion: Video Games as a Means of Consciousness-Raising." *Digital Creativity* 12(3): 167–174.

Frasca, G. 2004. "Videogames of the Oppressed: Critical Thinking, Education, Tolerance, and Other Critical Issues." In *First Person: New Media as Story, Performance, and Game*, edited by N. Wardrip-Fruin and P. Harrigan, 85–94. Cambridge: MIT Press.

Freeman, E. 1972. "Objectivity as 'Intersubjective Agreement.'" *The Monist* 57(2): 168–175.

Freire, P. 2000. *Pedagogy of the Oppressed*. Translated by M. B. Ramos. New York: Continuum.

Gadamer, H.-G. 2004. *Truth and Method*. Second revised edition. Translated by J. Weinsheimer and D. G. Marsh. London: Continuum.

Gadamer, H.-G. 2008. *Philosophical Hermeneutics*. Translated by D. E. Linge. Berkeley: University of California Press.

Galloway, A. R. 2006. *Gaming: Essays on Algorithmic Culture*. Minneapolis: University of Minnesota Press.

Gani, J. K. 2017. "The Erasure of Race: Cosmopolitanism and the Illusion of Kantian Hospitality." *Millennium: Journal of International Studies* 45(3): 425–446.

Garite, M. 2003. "The Ideology of Interactivity (or Video Games and Taylorization of Leisure)." Paper delivered at DiGRA International Conference, University of Utrecht.

Gee, J. P. n.d. "Why Are Video Games Good for Learning?" Unpublished paper.

Gekker, A. 2018. "Let's Not Play: Interpassivity as Resistance in 'Let's Play' Videos." *Journal of Gaming and Virtual Worlds* 10(3): 219–242.

Ghamari-Tabrizi, S. 2000. "Simulating the Unthinkable: Gaming Future War in the 1950s and 1960s." *Social Studies of Science* 30(2): 163–223.

Ghamari-Tabrizi, S. 2016. "Wargames as Writing Systems." In *Zones of Control: Perspectives on Wargaming*, edited by P. Harrigan and M. G. Kirschenbaum, 331–354. Cambridge: MIT Press.

Giddings, S. 2009. "Events and Collusions: A Glossary for the Microethnography of Video Game Play." *Games and Culture* 4(2): 144–157.

Giddings, S. 2016. *Gameworlds: Virtual Media and Children's Everyday Play*. New York: Bloomsbury Academic.

Giddings, S. 2018. "Accursed Play: The Economic Imaginary of Early Game Studies." *Games and Culture* 13(7): 765–783.

Gill, S. 2009. "The Powerful Play Goes On: Friedrich Schiller to Jacques Derrida on Play." Unpublished paper. https://sam-gill.com/PDF/schiller.wpd.pdf.

Gold, M. 2004. "Serious Play: Derrida and Whitman in the Theory Classroom." *Symplokē* 12(1–2): 216–231.

Golumbia, D. 2009. "Games Without Play." *New Literary History* 40(1): 179–204.

Gomes, R. 2007. "The Design of Narrative as an Immersive Simulation." In *Worlds in Play: International Perspectives on Digital Games Research*, edited by S. De Castell and J. Jenson, 55–62. New York: Peter Lang.

Goodfellow, T. 2016. "A New Kind of History: The Culture of Wargame Scenario Design Communities." In *Zones of Control: Perspectives on Wargaming*, edited by P. Harrigan and M. G. Kirschenbaum, 149–156. Cambridge: MIT Press.

Gorak, M. 2016. "Introduction." *CSIAC Journal of Cyber Security and Information Systems* 4(3): 4–7.

Graeber, D. 2015. *The Utopia of Rules: On Technology, Stupidity, and the Secret Joys of Bureaucracy*. Brooklyn: Melville House.

Grayson, K., M. Davies, and S. Philpott. 2009. "Pop Goes IR? Researching the Popular Culture—World Politics Continuum." *Politics* 29(3): 155–163.

Griffin, P. 2013. "Deconstruction as 'Anti-Method.'" In *Critical Approaches to Security: An Introduction to Theories and Methods*, edited by L. J. Shepherd, 208–222. Abingdon: Routledge.

Guetzkow, H. and L. Jensen. 1966. "Research Activities on Simulated International Processes." *Background* 9(4): 261–274.

Guillaume, X. 2011. "The International as an Everyday Practice." *International Political Sociology* 5(4): 446.

Hackett, T. 2014. "Passion Play: Play, Free Will, and the Sublime." In *The Philosophy of Play*, edited by E. Ryall, W. Russell, and M. MacLean, 120–129. London: Routledge.

Hagel, C. 2014a. "The Defense Innovation Initiative." Department of Defense Memorandum. November 15.

Hagel, C. 2014b. "Keynote Speech." Reagan National Defense Forum, Ronald Reagan Presidential Library, Simi Valley, CA, November 15.

Hammond, P. and H. Pötzsch H. 2020. "Introduction: Studying War and Games." In *War Games: Memory, Militarism and the Subject of Play*, edited by P. Hammond and H. Pötzsch, 1–14. New York: Bloomsbury Academic.

Hanley, J. 2018. "Validity and Utility of Pseudo-Experimentation Using Wargames and Combat/Campaign Simulation." In *MORS Wargaming III Special Meeting October 2017*, edited by P. Pournelle and H. Deaton, 54–69. Alexandria: MORS.

Hannaford, P. 2023. "The US and Its Allies Could Defeat a Chinese Invasion of Taiwan but Only at a 'High Cost,' a War-Game Simulation Has Found." *Sky News Australia*, January 10. https://www.skynews.com.au/australia-news/the-us-and-its-allies-could-def

eat-a-chinese-invasion-of-taiwan-but-only-at-a-high-cost-a-wargame-simulation-has-found/news-story/c71ddd3ab04c8f52d4c81acd07243070.

Hans, J. S. 1981. *The Play of the World*. Amherst: University of Massachusetts Press.

Hans, J. S. 2009. "The End(s) of Play in Contemporary Culture." *Philosophy Today* 53(4): 356–376.

Harker, C. 2005. "Playing and Affective Time-Spaces." *Children's Geographies* 3(1): 47–62.

Harrigan, P. and M. G. Kirschenbaum. 2016. "Editors' Introduction." In *Zones of Control: Perspectives on Wargaming*, edited by P. Harrigan and M. G. Kirschenbaum, xv–xxx. Cambridge: MIT Press.

Hayden, C. 2016. "The Procedural Rhetorics of *Mass Effect*: Video Games as Argumentation in International Relations." *International Studies Perspectives* 18(2): 175–193.

Hayles, N. K. 2004. "Refiguring the Posthuman." *Comparative Literature Studies* 41(3): 311–316.

Heidegger, M. 1996. *The Principle of Reason*. Translated by R. Lilly. Bloomington: Indiana University Press.

Henderson, E. A. 2014. *Hidden in Plain Sight: Racism in International Relations Theory*. Abingdon: Routledge.

Henricks, T. S. 2015. *Play and the Human Condition*. Urbana: University of Illinois Press.

Higate, P. 2013. "'Switching On' for Cash: The Private Militarised Security Contractor as Geo-Corporeal Actor." In *War and the Body: Militarisation, Practice and Experience*, edited by K. McSorley, 106–127. London: Routledge.

Hirst, A. 2013. *Leo Strauss and the Invasion of Iraq: Encountering the Abyss*. London: Routledge.

Hirst, A. 2015. "Derrida and Political Resistance: The Radical Potential of Deconstruction." *Globalizations* 12(1): 6–24.

Hirst, A. 2019. "Play in(g) International Theory." *Review of International Studies* 45(5): 891–914.

Hirst, A. 2021. "'Videogames Saved My Life': Everyday Resistance and Ludic Recovery Among US Military Veterans." *International Political Sociology* 15(4): 482–503.

Hirst, A., D. de Merich, J. Hoover, and R. Roccu. 2023. *Global Politics: Myths and Mysteries*. New York: Oxford University Press.

Hoffman, M. 1991. "Restructuring, Reconstruction, Reinscription, Rearticulation: Four Voices in Critical International Theory." *Millennium: Journal of International Studies* 20(2): 169–185.

Homan, C. 2014. "'Whoever Cannot Give, Also Receives Nothing': Nietzche's Playful Spectator." In *The Philosophy of Play*, edited by E. Ryall, W. Russell, and M. MacLean, 98–108. London: Routledge.

Hopsicker, P. and C. Carlson. 2014. "To Play or to Parent? An Analysis of the Adult-Child Interaction in Make-Believe Play." In *The Philosophy of Play*, edited by E. Ryall, W. Russell, and M. MacLean, 175–184. London: Routledge.

Horn, L., O. Rubin, and L. Schouenborg. 2016. "Undead Pedagogy: How a Zombie Simulation Can Contribute to Teaching International Relations." *International Studies Perspectives* 17(2): 187–201.

Howell A. 2018. "Forget 'militarization': Race, Disability and the 'Martial Politics' of the Police and of the University." *International Feminist Journal of Politics* 20(2): 117–136.

Huizinga, J. 2016. *Homo Ludens: A Study of the Play-Element in Culture*. Kettering: Angelico Press.

Huntemann, N. and M. T. Payne, eds. 2010. *Joystick Soldiers: The Politics of Play in Military Video Games*. New York: Routledge.

IMR Reporter. 2022. "Army Signs Contract for Developing AI-Powered Wargame Centre." *Indian Military Review*, May 21. https://imrmedia.in/army-signs-contract-for-develop ing-ai-powered-wargame-centre/.

Jacobs, T. 2014. "Thinking Racist Thoughts? The Problem Might Be Your Video Game Avatar." *Pacific Standard*, March 20. https://psmag.com/social-justice/acting-racist-problem-might-avatar-77109.

Jahn-Sudmann, A. and R. Stockmann, eds. 2008. *Computer Games as a Sociocultural Phenomenon: Games Without Frontiers, War without Tears*. Basingstoke: Palgrave Macmillan.

Jarvis, L. and N. Robinson. 2021. "War, Time, and Military Videogames: Heterogeneities and Critical Potential." *Critical Military Studies* 7(2): 192–211.

Jennings, S. 2019. "A Meta-Synthesis of Agency in Game Studies: Trends, Troubles, Trajectories." *Game* 8: 85–106.

Jensen, B., S. Cuomo, and C. Whyte. 2018. "Wargaming with Athena: How to Make Militaries Smarter, Faster, and More Efficient with Artificial Intelligence." *War on the Rocks*, June 5. https://warontherocks.com/2018/06/wargaming-with-athena-how-to-make-militaries-smarter-faster-and-more-efficient-with-artificial-intelligence/.

Joint Publication 5.0. 2017. "Joint Planning." Joint Chiefs of Staff, Washington, DC, June 16.

Jones, J. 2016. "Play On: Supporting Decision-Makers by Sustaining Wargaming." *War on the Rocks*, April 15. https://warontherocks.com/2016/04/play-on-supporting-decis ion-makers-by-sustaining-wargaming/.

Jovanovic, B. 2023. "Gamer Demographics: Facts and Stats About the Most Popular Hobby in the World." *DataProt*. https://dataprot.net/statistics/gamer-demographics/.

Juul, J. 2003. "The Game, the Player, the World: Looking for a Heart of Gameness." In *Level Up: Digital Games Research Conference Proceedings*, edited by M. Copier and J. Raessens, 30–45. Utrecht: University of Utrecht.

Juul, J. 2013. *The Art of Failure: An Essay on the Pain of Playing Video Games*. Cambridge: MIT Press.

Kaempf, S. 2019. "'A Relationship of Mutual Exploitation': The Evolving Ties Between the Pentagon, Hollywood, and the Commercial Gaming Sector." *Social Identities* 25(4): 542–558.

Kania, E. B. and I. B. McCaslin. 2021. *Learning Warfare from the Laboratory: China's Progression in Wargaming and Opposing Force Training*. Washington DC: Institute for the Study of War.

Kaplan, F. 2003. "War-Gamed: Why the Army Shouldn't Be So Surprised by Saddam's Moves." *Slate*, March 28. https://slate.com/news-and-politics/2003/03/the-officer-who-predicted-saddam-s-moves.html.

Kaufman, E. 2019. "Fact Check: Are Violent Video Games Connected to Mass Shootings?" *CNN Politics*, August 5. https://www.cnn.com/2019/08/05/politics/violent-video-game-shooting-fact-check/index.html.

Koerner, B. 2002. "How Do the Pentagon's 'War Games' Work?" *Slate*, September 17. https://slate.com/news-and-politics/2002/09/how-do-the-pentagon-s-war-games-work.html.

Koster, R. 2013. *A Theory of Fun for Game Design*. Second edition. Sebastopol: O'Reilly.

Küchler, T. 1994. *Postmodern Gaming: Heidegger, Duchamp, Derrida*. New York: P. Lang.

Kumar, R. 2022. "India-US Yudh Abhyas: Why China Is Rattled by the Joint Military Exercise." *ABP Live News*, December 22. https://news.abplive.com/india-at-2047/india-us-yudh-abhyas-2022-why-china-is-rattled-as-new-delhi-hosts-joint-military-exercise-auli-uttarakhand-near-lac-1569137.

Lacey, J. 2016. "Wargaming in the Classroom: An Odyssey." *War on the Rocks*, April 19. https://warontherocks.com/2016/04/wargaming-in-the-classroom-an-odyssey/.

Lacey, J. 2019. "How Does the Next Great Power Conflict Play Out? Lessons from a Wargame." *War on the Rocks*, April 22. https://warontherocks.com/2019/04/how-does-the-next-great-power-conflict-play-out-lessons-from-a-wargame/.

Laing, C. M. 2012. "In Play, at Play." *Journal of Applied Hermeneutics*: 1–10.

Lammes, S. and S. de Smale. 2018. "Hybridity, Reflexivity and Mapping: A Collaborative Ethnography of Postcolonial Gameplay." *Open Library of Humanities* 4(1): 1–31.

Lee, C. and P. Strong. 2016. "Women in War." *WiW Group News Letter* 17. https://paxsims.files.wordpress.com/2016/12/wiw-newsletter-17-final.pdf.

Lee, M. and Z. C. Shirkey. 2017. "Going Beyond the Existing Consensus: The Use of Games in International Relations Education." *PS: Political Science and Politics* 50(2): 571–575.

Lenoir, T. 2000. "All but War Is Simulation: The Military-Entertainment Complex." *Configurations* 8: 289–335.

Leonard, D. 2009. "Young, Black (and Brown) and Don't Give a Fuck: Virtual Gangstas in the Era of State Violence." *Cultural Studies ↔ Critical Methodologies* 9(2): 248–272.

Levis, A. H. and R. J. Elder. 2016. "Model-Driven Military Wargame Designs and Evaluation." In *Zones of Control: Perspectives on Wargaming*, edited by P. Harrigan and M. G. Kirschenbaum, 471–482. Cambridge: MIT Press.

Lin-Greenberg, E. 2019. "Game of Drones: What Experimental Wargames Reveal About Drones and Escalation." *War on the Rocks*, January 10. https://warontherocks.com/2019/01/game-of-drones-what-experimental-wargames-reveal-about-drones-and-escalation/.

Lin-Greenberg, E., R. B. C. Pauly, and J. G. Schneider. 2022. "Wargaming for International Relations Research." *European Journal of International Relations* 28(1): 83–109.

Lockwood, D. and T. Richards. 2008. "Presence-Play: The Hauntology of the Computer Game." In *Computer Games as a Sociocultural Phenomenon: Games Without Frontiers, War Without Tears*, edited by A. Jahn-Sudmann and R. Stockmann, 175–185. Basingstoke: Palgrave Macmillan.

Longley-Brown, G. 2019. *Successful Professional Wargames: A Practitioner's Handbook*. History of Wargaming Project.

Losh, E. 2005. "In Country with Tactical Iraqi: Trust, Identity, and Language Learning in a Military Video Game." Paper delivered at International Conference on the Digital Arts and Culture.

Losh, E. 2016. "Playing Defense: Gender, Just War, and Game Design." In *Zones of Control: Perspectives on Wargaming*, edited by P. Harrigan and M. G. Kirschenbaum, 355–370. Cambridge: MIT Press.

Lovelace, D. C., ed. 2016. *Terrorism: Documents of International and Local Control*. New York: Oxford University Press.

Lovelace, D. C. 2017. "Foreword." In *Closer than You Think: The Implications of the Third Offset Strategy for the U.S. Army*, edited by S. R. White Jr., ix–x. Carlisle: Strategic Studies Institute and U.S. Army War College Press.

Lowood, H. 2016. "War Engines: Wargames as Systems from the Tabletop to the Computer." In *Zones of Control: Perspectives on Wargaming*, edited by P. Harrigan and M. G. Kirschenbaum, 83–106. Cambridge: MIT Press.

Lugones, M. 1987. "Playfulness, 'World'-Travelling, and Loving Perception." *Hypatia* 2(2): 3–19.

Machuga, S. 2015. "The Story and Launch of Stack Up." *Stack Up*, October 31. https://www.stackup.org/post/the-story-and-launch-of-stack-up.

MacLeish, K. 2013. *Making War at Fort Hood: Life and Uncertainty in a Military Community*. Princeton: Princeton University Press.

MacLeish, K. 2019. "On 'Moral Injury': Psychic Fringes and War Violence." *History of the Human Sciences* 31(2): 128–146.

MacLeish, K. 2020. "Churn: Mobilization–Demobilization and the Fungibility of American Military Life." *Security Dialogue* 51(2–3): 194–210.

Mälksoo, M. 2012. "The Challenge of Liminality for International Relations Theory." *Review of International Studies* 38(2): 481–494.

Markey, P. M., J. D. Ivory, E. B. Slotter, M. B. Oliver, and O. Maglalang. 2020. "He Does Not Look Like Video Games Made Him Do It: Racial Stereotypes and School Shootings." *Psychology of Popular Media* 9(4): 493–498.

Martinage, R. 2014. "Toward a New Offset Strategy: Exploiting US Long-Term Advantages to Restore US Global Power Projection Capability." *Center for Strategic and Budgetary Assessment*, October 27. https://csbaonline.org/research/publications/toward-a-new-offset-strategy-exploiting-u-s-long-term-advantages-to-restore.

Massanari, A. 2017. "#Gamergate and the Fappening: How Reddit's Algorithm, Governance, and Culture Support Toxic Technocultures." *New Media and Society* 19(3): 329–346.

Massumi, B. 2014. *What Animals Teach Us About Politics*. Durham: Duke University Press.

McArdle, J., T. Kehr, and G. Colabatistto. 2020. "Pandemics and the Future of Military Training." *War on the Rocks*, March 26. https://warontherocks.com/2020/03/pandemics-and-the-future-of-military-training/.

McBrien, T. 2022. "Little Wars, Big Dreams: H. G. Wells' Failed Pacifist Project." *Yale Journal of International Affairs*, April 29. https://www.yalejournal.org/publications/little-wars-big-dreams-hg-wells-failed-pacifist-project.

McGonigal, J. 2012. *Reality Is Broken: Why Games Make Us Better and How They Can Change the World; Includes Practical Advice for Gamers*. London: Vintage.

McGrady, E. and P. Vebber. 2017. "Working Group 2: Communications and Implementation in Games." In *MORS Wargaming Special Meeting October 2016*, edited by P. Pournelle, 30–53. Alexandria MORS.

McSorley, K. 2020. "Playing in the End Times: Wargames, Resilience, and the Art of Failure." In *War Games: Memory, Militarism and the Subject of Play*, edited by P. Hammond and H. Pötzsch, 37–52. New York: Bloomsbury Academic.

Mead, C. 2013. *War Play: Video Games and the Future of Armed Conflict*. Boston: Eamon Dolan/Houghton Mifflin Harcourt.

Mehta, A. 2016. "Defense Department Budget: $18B Over FYDP for Third Offset." *Defense News*, February 9. https://www.defensenews.com/2016/02/09/defense-department-budget-18b-over-fydp-for-third-offset/.

Michelfelder, D. P. and R. E. Palmer, eds. 1989. *Dialogue and Deconstruction: The Gadamer-Derrida Encounter*. Albany: State University of New York Press.

Mitic, I. 2022. "Video Game Industry Revenue Set for Another Record-Breaking Year." *Fortunly*, March 2. https://fortunly.com/articles/video-game-industry-revenue/.

Modelski, G. 1970. "Simulations, 'Realities,' and International Relations Theory." *Simulation & Gaming* 1(2): 111–134.

Morgan, T. D. 1991. "Wargames: Training for War." *Army History* 19 (Summer): 32–35.

Mortensen, T. E. 2018. "Anger, Fear, and Games: The Long Event of #GamerGate." *Games and Culture* 13(8): 787–806.

Mukherjee, S. 2017. *Videogames and Post-Colonialism: Empire Plays Back.* Cambridge: Palgrave Macmillian.

Muriel, D. and G. Crawford. 2020. "Video Games and Agency in Contemporary Society." *Games and Culture* 15(2): 138–157.

Murphy, C. 2012. "Why Games Work and the Science of Learning." Paper delivered at MODSIM World Conference and Expo.

Murray, J. H. 1997. *Hamlet on the Holodeck: The Future of Narrative in Cyberspace.* New York: Free Press.

Murray, J. H. 2007. "Games as Joint Attentional Scenes." In *Worlds in Play: International Perspectives on Digital Games Research*, edited by S. De Castell and J. Jenson, 11–20. New York: Peter Lang.

Murray, S. 2016. "Upending Militarized Masculinity in *Spec Ops: The Line*." In *Zones of Control: Perspectives on Wargaming*, edited by P. Harrigan and M. G. Kirschenbaum, 319–328. Cambridge: MIT Press.

Nagel, M. 1998. "Play in Culture and the Jargon of Primordiality: A Critique of Homo Ludens." In *Diversions and Divergences in Fields of Play*, edited by M. C. Duncan, G. E. Chick, and D. A. Aycock, 19–30. Greenwich: Ablex.

Nagel, M. 2002. *Masking the Abject: A Genealogy of Play.* Lanham: Lexington Books.

Nakamura, T. 2016. "The Fundamental Gap Between Tabletop Simulation Games and the 'Truth.'" In *Zones of Control: Perspectives on Wargaming*, edited by P. Harrigan and M. G. Kirschenbaum, 43–48. Cambridge: MIT Press.

NATO Allied Command Transformation. 2022. "Wargaming Initiative for NATO." October 19. https://www.act.nato.int/article/wargaming-initiative-for-nato-2022/.

Naval War College. 2015. *War Gamers' Handbook: A Guide for Professional War Gamers.* Contributions by D. Della Volpe, R. Babb, N. Miller, and G. Muir. Edited by S. Burns. Newport Naval War College.

Neale, D. 2018. "Potential Contributions of the Study of Psychology to Wargaming." In *MORS Wargaming III Special Meeting October 2017*, edited by P. Pournelle and H. Deaton, 21–23. Alexandria MORS.

Neumann, I. B. and O. Waever. 2005. *The Future of International Relations: Masters in the Making?* London: Routledge.

Newzoo. 2019. "Global Games Market Report." June 19.

Newzoo. 2022. "Global Games Market Report 2023." June 26.

Nietzsche, F. W. 1962. *Philosophy in the Tragic Age of the Greeks.* Washington: Regnery.

Nietzsche, F. W. 1968. *The Will to Power.* Translated by W. Kaufmann and R. J. Hollingdale. New York: Vintage Books.

Nietzsche, F. W. 2007. *Twilight of the Idols: With The Antichrist and Ecce Homo.* Translated by A. M. Ludovici and R. Furness. Ware: Wordsworth.

Nordin, A. H. M. and D. Öberg. 2015. "Targeting the Ontology of War: From Clausewitz to Baudrillard." *Millennium* 43(2): 392–410.

North, R. C. 1963. "International Relations: Putting the Pieces Together." *Background* 7(3): 119–130.

Norwood, P. and B. Jensen. 2016. "Wargaming the Third Offset Strategy." *Joint Force Quarterly* 83(4): 34–39.

Öberg, D. 2020. "Exercising War: How Tactical and Operational Modelling Shape and Reify Military Practice." *Security Dialogue* 51(2–3): 137–154.

Ochmanek, D. 2014. "The Role of Maritime and Air Power in DoD's Third Offset Strategy." Presentation to the Committee on Armed Services Subcommittee on Seapower and Projection Forces, US House of Representatives.

Oriard, M. 1991. *Sporting with the Gods: The Rhetoric of Play and Game in American Culture*. Cambridge: Cambridge University Press.

Parkin, S. 2015. *Death by Video Game: Tales of Obsession from the Virtual Frontline*. London: Serpent's Tail.

Patel, T. N. 2019. "The Connection Between Violent Video Games, Racial Bias and School Shootings." *ABC News*, September 17. https://abcnews.go.com/Health/connection-violent-video-games-racial-bias-school-shootings/story?id=65640371.

Pauly, R. 2018. "Would U.S. Leaders Push the Button? Wargames and the Sources of Nuclear Restraint." *International Security* 43(2): 151–192.

Peer, P. 2022. "How Word Games Became War Games in the Taiwan Strait." *The National Interest*, September 1. https://nationalinterest.org/feature/how-word-games-became-war-games-taiwan-strait-204571.

Pellerin, C. 2016. "Deputy Secretary: Third Offset Strategy Bolsters American's Military Deterrence." *DoD News*, October 31. https://www.defense.gov/News/News-Stories/Article/Article/991434/deputy-secretary-third-offset-strategy-bolsters-americas-military-deterrence/.

Perla, P. P. 1990. *The Art of Wargaming: A Guide for Professionals and Hobbyists*. Annapolis: Naval Institute Press.

Perla, P. P. 2016. "Operations Research, Systems Analysis, and Wargaming: Riding the Cycle of Research." In *Zones of Control: Perspectives on Wargaming*, edited by P. Harrigan and M. G. Kirschenbaum, 159–182. Cambridge: MIT Press.

Perla, P. P. 2017. "Synthesis Working Group." In *MORS Wargaming Special Meeting October 2016*, Final Report, edited by P. Pournelle, 82–93. Alexandria: MORS.

Perla, P. P. 2018. "Thoughts on Wargame Validity." In *MORS Wargaming III Special Meeting October 2017*, edited by P. Pournelle and H. Deaton, 74–78. Alexandria: MORS.

Perla, P. P. 2022. "Wargaming and the Cycle of Research and Learning." *Scandinavian Journal of Military Studies*, 5(1): 197–208.

Perla, P. P. and E. McGrady. 2011. "Why Wargaming Works." *Naval War College Review* 64(3): 111–130.

Peterson, J. 2016. "A Game Out of All Proportions: How a Hobby Miniaturized War." In *Zones of Control: Perspectives on Wargaming*, edited by P. Harrigan and M. G. Kirschenbaum, 3–32. Cambridge: MIT Press.

Pettyjohn, S. and D. Shlapak. 2016. "Gaming the System: Obstacles to Reinvigorating Defense Wargaming." *War on the Rocks*, February 18. https://warontherocks.com/2016/02/gaming-the-system-obstacles-to-reinvigorating-defense-wargaming/.

Pournelle, P., ed. 2017. *MORS Wargaming Special Meeting October 2016*. Alexandria: MORS.

Pournelle, P. and H. Deaton. 2018. *MORS Wargaming III Special Meeting October 2017*. Alexandria: MORS.

Protevi, J. 2008. "Affect, Agency and Responsibility: The Act of Killing in the Age of Cyborgs." *Phenomenology and the Cognitive Sciences* 7(3): 405–413.

Reddie, A. W., B. L. Goldblum, K. Lakkaraju, J. Reinhardt, M. Nacht, and L. Epifanovkaya. 2018. "Next-Generation Wargames: Technology Enables New Research Designs, and More Data." *Science* 362(6421): 1362–1364.

Rizzo, A., J. Difede, B. O. Rothbaum, G. Reger, J. Spitalnick, J. Cukor, and R. McLay. 2010. "Development and Early Evaluation of the Virtual Iraq/Afghanistan Exposure Therapy System for Combat-Related PTSD." *Annals of the New York Academy of Sciences* 1208: 114–125.

Robinson, M. S. 2018. "Ensuring the Validity and Utility of Wargames." In *MORS Wargaming III Special Meeting October 2017*, edited by P. Pournelle and H. Deaton, 79–80. Alexandria: MORS.

Robinson, N. 2015. "Have You Won the War on Terror? Military Videogames and the State of American Exceptionalism." *Millennium: Journal of International Studies* 43(2): 450–470.

Robinson, N. 2016. "Militarism and Opposition in the Living Room: The Case of Military Videogames." *Critical Studies on Security* 4(3): 255–275.

Robinson, N. 2019. "Military Videogames: More than a Game." *RUSI Journal* 164(4): 10–21.

Roman, P. A. and D. Brown. 2008. "Games—Just How Serious Are They?" Paper delivered at Interservice/Industry Training, Simulation, and Education Conference (I/ITSEC).

Romano, D. 2014. "Teaching International Relations Through Popular Games, Culture and Simulations (Part 1)." *PAX Sims*, September 7. https://paxsims.wordpress.com/2014/09/07/teaching-international-relations-through-popular-games-culture-and-simulations-part-1/.

Rubel, R. C. 2006. "The Epistemology of War Gaming." *Naval War College Review* 59(2): 108–128.

Ruberg, B. 2019. *Video Games Have Always Been Queer*. New York: New York University Press.

Ryall, E., W. Russell, and M. MacLean. 2014. "Introduction." In *The Philosophy of Play*, edited by E. Ryall, W. Russell, and M. MacLean, 1–10. London: Routledge.

Sabin, P. 2014. *Simulating War: Studying Conflict Through Simulation Games*. London: Bloomsbury Academic.

Sabin, P. 2016. "Wargames as an Academic Instrument." In *Zones of Control: Perspectives on Wargaming*, edited by P. Harrigan and M. G. Kirschenbaum, 421–438. Cambridge: MIT Press.

Salen, K. and E. Zimmerman. 2003. *Rules of Play: Game Design Fundamentals*. Cambridge: MIT Press.

Salter, M. B. 2011a. "Gaming World Politics: Meaning of Play and World Structure." *International Political Sociology* 5(4): 453–456.

Salter, M. B. 2011b. "The Geographical Imaginations of Video Games: Diplomacy, Civilization, America's Army and Grand Theft Auto IV." *Geopolitics* 16(2): 359–388.

Samuel, H. 2022. "Britain to Join France in Largest War Games Since the Cold War." *The Telegraph*, November 16. https://www.telegraph.co.uk/world-news/2022/11/16/britain-join-france-largest-war-games-since-cold-war/.

Sawyer, D. 2015. "Playing Seriously with Bad Faith: A Derridean Intersection." *Sartre Studies International* 21(1): 34–52.

Schechter, B. 2020. "Wargaming Cyber Security." *War on the Rocks*, September 4. https://warontherocks.com/2020/09/wargaming-cyber-security/.

Scholder, A. and E. Zimmerman, eds. 2003. *Re:Play: Game Design + Game Culture*. New York: Lang.

Schuety, C. and L. Will. 2018. "An Air Force 'Way of Swarm': Using Wargaming and Artificial Intelligence to Train Drones." *War on the Rocks*, September 21. https://warontherocks.com/2018/09/an-air-force-way-of-swarm-using-wargaming-and-artificial-intelligence-to-train-drones/.

Schultz, M. 2023. "Wargaming Will Be a Key to Strengthening Deterrence in the Indo-Pacific." *The Strategist*, March 7. https://www.aspistrategist.org.au/wargaming-will-be-a-key-to-strengthening-deterrence-in-the-indo-pacific/.

Schulzke, M. 2017. "Military Videogames and the Future of Ideological Warfare." *British Journal of Politics and International Relations* 19(3): 609–626.

Seo, Y. and J. Griffiths. 2019. "US, South Korea Cancel Major War Games 'to Support Diplomatic Efforts.'" *CNN*, March 3. https://edition.cnn.com/2019/03/03/asia/south-korea-north-korea-us-war-games-intl/index.html.

Shaffer, D. W., K. [D.] Squire, R. Halverson, and J. P. Gee. 2005. "Video Games and the Future of Learning." *Phi Delta Kappan* 87(2): 105–111.

Shanker, T. 2007. "New Strategy Vindicates Ex-Army Chief Shinseki." *New York Times*, January 12. https://www.nytimes.com/2007/01/12/washington/12shinseki.html.

Shepherd, L. J. 2013a. *Gender, Violence and Popular Culture: Telling Stories.* Abingdon: Routledge.

Shepherd, L. J., ed. 2013b. *Critical Approaches to Security: An Introduction to Theories and Methods.* Abingdon: Routledge.

Shepherd, L. J. and C. Hamilton, eds. 2016. *Understanding Popular Culture and World Politics in the Digital Age.* London: Routledge.

Sicart, M. 2014. *Play Matters.* Cambridge: MIT Press.

Sicart, M. 2016. "We the Soldiers: Player Complicity and Ethical Gameplay in *Call of Duty: Modern Warfare*." In *Zones of Control: Perspectives on Wargaming*, edited by P. Harrigan and M. G. Kirschenbaum, 309–318. Cambridge: MIT Press.

Simón, L. 2016. "The 'Third' US Offset Strategy and Europe's 'Anti-Access' Challenge." *Journal of Strategic Studies* 39(3): 417–445.

Simpson, A. W. and B. Kaussler. 2009. "IR Teaching Reloaded: Using Films and Simulations in the Teaching of International Relations." *International Studies Perspectives* 10(4) 2009: 413–427.

Smith, R. 2010. "The Long History of Gaming in Military Training." *Simulation and Gaming* 41(1): 6–19.

Soderman, B. 2021. *Against Flow: Video Games and the Flowing Subject.* Cambridge: MIT Press.

Spariosu, M. 1989. *Dionysus Reborn: Play and the Aesthetic Dimension in Modern Philosophical and Scientific Discourse.* Ithaca: Cornell University Press.

Spariosu, M. 1991. *God of Many Names: Play, Poetry, and Power in Hellenic Thought from Homer to Aristotle.* Durham: Duke University Press.

Sparrow, R., R. Harrison, J. Oakley, and B. Keogh. 2018. "Playing for Fun, Training for War: Can Popular Claims About Recreational Video Gaming and Military Simulations Be Reconciled?" *Games and Culture* 13(2): 174–192.

Squire, K. D. 2008. "Video Game–Based Learning: An Emerging Paradigm for Instruction." *Performance Improvement Quarterly* 21(2): 7–36.

Stahl, R. 2010. *Militainment, Inc: War, Media, and Popular Culture.* New York: Routledge.

Statista. n.d. "Percentage of Adults in the United States Who Ever Play Video Games in the United States from 2020 to 2022." https://www.statista.com/statistics/499703/share-consumers-ever-play-video-games-by-age-usa/#:~:text=According%20to%20a%20survey%20conducted,on%20at%20least%20one%20platform.

Stiegler, B. 2010. *Taking Care of Youth and the Generations.* Stanford: Stanford University Press.

Strother, R. 2006. "Post-Saddam Iraq: The War Game." *National Security Archive*, November 4. https://nsarchive2.gwu.edu/NSAEBB/NSAEBB207/index.htm.

Subotic, J. and B. J. Steele. 2018. "Moral Injury in International Relations." *Journal of Global Security Studies* 3(4): 387–401.

Susi, T., M. Johannesson, and P. Backlund. 2007. *Serious Games—An Overview*. Technical Report, HS-IKI-TR-07-001. University of Skövde.

Sutton-Smith, B. 2001. *The Ambiguity of Play*. Cambridge: Harvard University Press.

Tanenbaum, K. and .T. J. Tanenbaum. 2010. "Agency as Commitment to Meaning: Communicative Competence in Games." *Digital Creativity* 21(1): 11–17.

Tarraf, D. C., J. M. Gilmore, D. S. Barnett, S. Boston, D. R. Frelinger, D. Gonzales, A. C. Hou, and N. P. Whitehead. 2020. *An Experiment in Tactical Wargaming with Platforms Enabled by Artificial Intelligence*. Santa Monica: RAND. https://www.rand.org/pubs/research_reports/RRA423-1.html.

Tickner, J. A. 1988. "Hans Morgenthau's Principles of Political Realism: A Feminist Reformulation." *Millennium: Journal of International Studies* 17(3): 429–440.

Timpson, T. 2013. "Little Wars: How HG Wells Created Hobby War Gaming." *BBC News*, August 3. https://www.bbc.com/news/magazine-22777029.

TRADOC. 2015. *The Applied Critical Thinking Handbook*. January. https://irp.fas.org/doddir/army/critthink.pdf.

Train, B. and V. Ruhnke. 2016. "Chess, Go, and Vietnam: Gaming Modern Insurgency." In *Zones of Control: Perspectives on Wargaming*, edited by P. Harrigan and M. G. Kirschenbaum, 513–530. Cambridge: MIT Press.

Tulloch, R. 2014. "The Construction of Play: Rules, Restrictions, and the Repressive Hypothesis." *Games and Culture* 9(5): 335–350.

Turkle, S. 1995. *Life on the Screen: Identity in the Age of the Internet*. New York: Simon and Schuster.

Turnitsa, C. 2016. "Adjudication in Wargaming for Discovery." *CSIAC Journal of Cyber Security and Information Systems* 4(3): 28–35.

United States Joint Force Command. 2007. *Millennium Challenge 02 Documents*. September 28. http://web.archive.org/web/20070928005405/http://www.jfcom.mil/about/experiments/mc02.htm.

Van Puyvelde, D. 2018. "Qualitative Research Interviews and the Study of National Security Intelligence." *International Studies Perspectives* 19(4): 375–391.

Vasey, C. 2016. "The Amateur Designer: For Fun and Profit." In *Zones of Control: Perspectives on Wargaming*, edited by P. Harrigan and M. G. Kirschenbaum, 455–461. Cambridge: MIT Press.

Vaughan-Williams, N. 2005. "International Relations and the 'Problem of History.'" *Millennium: Journal of International Studies* 34(1): 115–136.

Verba, S. 1964. "Simulation, Reality, and Theory in International Relations." *World Politics* 16(3): 490–519.

Vilhauer, M. 2014. "Gadamer and the Game of Understanding: Dialogue-Play and Opening to the Other." In *The Philosophy of Play*, edited by E. Ryall, W. Russell, and M. MacLean, 75–86. London: Routledge.

Wallman, J. 2016. "Cultural Wargaming." In *Zones of Control: Perspectives on Wargaming*, edited by P. Harrigan and M. G. Kirschenbaum, 545–551. Cambridge: MIT Press.

Walton, T. A. 2016. "Securing the Third Offset Strategy: Priorities for the Next Secretary of Defense." *Joint Force Quarterly* 82(3): 6–15.

Wardrip-Fruin, N., P. Harrigan, and M. Crumpton. 2004. *First Person: New Media as Story, Performance, and Game*. Cambridge: MIT Press.

Wark, M. 2007. *Gamer Theory*. Cambridge: Harvard University Press.

Webster, D. 2014. "Game Over: Calling Time on Kidult Accounts of Masculinity." In *The Philosophy of Play*, edited by E. Ryall, W. Russell, and M. MacLean, 185–195. London: Routledge.

Weinstein, D. and M. A. Weinstein. 1990. "Deconstruction as Symbolic Play: Simmel/Derrida." *Diogenes* 38(150): 119–141.

Weldes, J. 1999. "Going Cultural: Star Trek, State Action, and Popular Culture." *Millennium: Journal of International Studies* 28(1): 117–134.

Weldes, J. 2003. "Popular Culture, Science Fiction, and World Politics." In *To Seek Out New Worlds*, edited by J. Weldes, 1–27. New York: Palgrave Macmillan.

Wells, H. G. 2004. *Little Wars*. Whitefish: Kessinger.

White, S. R., Jr. 2017a. "The Urgency of the Third Offset." In *Closer than You Think: The Implications of the Third Offset Strategy for the U.S. Army*, edited by S. R. White Jr., 15–27. Carlisle: Strategic Studies Institute and U.S. Army War College Press.

White, S. R., Jr. 2017b. "Summary." In *Closer than You Think: The Implications of the Third Offset Strategy for the U.S. Army*, edited by S. R. White Jr., xi–xx. Carlisle Barracks: US Army War College Press.

Wilson, R. R. 1986. "Play, Transgression and Carnival: Bakhtin and Derrida on 'Scriptor Ludens.'" *Mosaic: An Interdisciplinary Critical Journal* 19(1): 73–89.

Wojtowicz, N. 2022. *Wargaming Experiences: Soldiers, Scientists and Civilians*. n.p.

Wojtowitz, N. 2023. *Wargaming Experiences: Discussions*. n.p.

Wong, Y. H. 2016. "Irregular Warfare: The *Kobayashi Maru* of the Wargaming World." In *Zones of Control: Perspectives on Wargaming*, edited by P. Harrigan and M. G. Kirschenbaum, 531–538. Cambridge: MIT Press.

Wong, Y. H. and G. Heath. 2021. "Is the Department of Defense Making Enough Progress in Wargaming?" *War on the Rocks*, February 17. https://warontherocks.com/2021/02/is-the-department-of-defense-making-enough-progress-in-wargaming/.

Work, R. 2015a. "The Third US Offset Strategy and Its Implications for Partners and Allies." Speech delivered at the Willard Hotel, January 28. https://www.defense.gov/News/Speeches/Speech/Article/606641/the-third-us-offset-strategy-and-its-implicati ons-for-partners-and-allies/.

Work, R. 2015b. "Third Offset Strategy." Speech delivered at the Reagan Defense Forum, November 7. https://www.defense.gov/News/Speeches/Speech/Article/628246/rea gan-defense-forum-the-third-offset-strategy/.

Work, R. 2015c. "Wargaming and Innovation." Department of Defense Memorandum, February 9. https://paxsims.files.wordpress.com/2015/04/osd-memowargaming-innovationdepsecdefworkfeb15.pdf.

Work, R. and P. Selva. 2015. "Revitalizing Wargaming Is Necessary to Be Prepared for Future Wars." *War on the Rocks*, December 8. https://warontherocks.com/2015/12/revitalizing-wargaming-is-necessary-to-be-prepared-for-future-wars/.

Zimmerman, E. 2013. *Manifesto for a Ludic Century*. https://jakoblacour.com/wp-content/uploads/2013/10/Manifesto_for_a_Ludic_Century.pdf.

Zyda, M. 2022. "Weapons of Mass Distraction: The America's Army Game at 20." *Computer* 55: 112–122.

Index

For the benefit of digital users, indexed terms that span two pages (e.g., 52–53) may, on occasion, appear on only one of those pages.